Italy captain Giuseppe Meazza (below, left) shakes hands with Hungary captain Gyorgy Sarosi, at the start of the 1938 FIFA World Cup final in Paris.

# DK

LONDON, NEW YORK, MUNICH,
MELBOURNE, AND DELHI

**Senior Designer** Guy Harvey
**Managing Editor** Catherine Saunders
**Editors** Jo Casey, Julia March and Victoria Taylor
**U.S. Editor** Maragaret Parrish
**Design Assistant** Rhys Thomas
**Art Director** Lisa Lanzarini
**Publishing Manager** Simon Beecroft
**Category Publisher** Alex Allan
**Production Controller** Nick Seston
**Production Editor** Marc Staples

Acknowledgments
The publisher would like to thank Steve Ellis for high res work,
Martin Copeland, Will Jones, and Rob Nunn
for picture research, Lindsay Kent for the index, Louise Hughes for
legal advice, Medi-Mation for Body illustration on pages 34–35 and
Dr. Robert Marshall for medical expertise.

First published in the United States in 2008
This revised and extended edition published in 2010
by DK Publishing
375 Hudson Street
New York, New York 10014

10 11 12 13 14 10 9 8 7 6 5 4 3 2
176230 – 02/10

© 2010 DK Publishing

ISBN: 978-0-7566-6318-6

Reproduced by Media Development and Printing Ltd., UK
Printed and bound in China by Hung Hing.

Discover more at
**www.dk.com**

*Italy celebrates its 5–3 penalty
shootout victory over France in the
2006 World Cup final.*

# soccer

# THE ULTIMATE GUIDE

**Written by** Martin Cloake, Glenn Dakin,
Mark Hillsdon, Adam Powley,
Aidan Radnedge, and Catherine Saunders

# CONTENTS

*Brazilian player Zito celebrates scoring the second goal for Brazil during the 1962 World Cup final in Santiago, Chile. Brazil beat Czechoslovakia 3–1.*

A group of children play soccer barefoot, overlooking Rio de Janeiro, Brazil.

# THE BEAUTIFUL GAME

"FOOTBALL IS ONE OF THE WORLD'S BEST MEANS OF COMMUNICATION. IT IS IMPARTIAL, APOLITICAL, AND UNIVERSAL. FOOTBALL UNITES PEOPLE AROUND THE WORLD EVERY DAY. YOUNG OR OLD, PLAYERS OR FANS, RICH OR POOR, THE GAME MAKES EVERYONE EQUAL, STIRS THE IMAGINATION, MAKES PEOPLE HAPPY AND MAKES THEM SAD."

FRANZ BECKENBAUER, GERMAN WORLD CUP WINNING PLAYER AND COACH

Football, soccer, fussball, futebol, futbol, voetball—whatever you call it, it's the same beautiful game. For many of us it is quite simply the greatest game on Earth. Its popularity has spread across the globe to every tiny island and remote wilderness. The love of the game brings people together—whether it is to play it, watch it, or just endlessly debate the referees' decisions! Rich and poor, boys and girls, young and old, everyone and anyone can play the game. Best of all, you don't need any fancy equipment. All you need is a ball...

**IMPORTANT NOTE**

This guide to the beautiful game has it all—from the history of the game to the anatomy of a player, the greatest teams to the most famous players, the most prestigious competitions to the die-hard fans. However, soccer is an ever-changing game: every effort has been made to verify all facts and statistics, but they may be subject to change or revision at any future time.

## FIFA

World soccerl is governed by FIFA (Fédération Internationale de Football Association). Founded in 1904, FIFA looks after the organization and development of the game around the world and also oversees the World Cup, including the allocation of its hosts. FIFA's headquarters are in Zürich, Switzerland, and its current president is Joseph "Sepp" Blatter. Today, FIFA has more than 200 member countries.

# ORIGINS OF SOCCER

"SOMEONE SAID 'FOOTBALL IS MORE IMPORTANT THAN LIFE AND DEATH TO YOU' AND I SAID 'LISTEN, IT'S MORE IMPORTANT THAN THAT.'" BILL SHANKLY, FORMER MANAGER OF LIVERPOOL FC

No one can say precisely when, how, or even why the game of soccer developed. Games resembling soccer can be traced back as far as the ancient Chinese, Greek, and Roman civilizations. However, the rules of these games differed widely—from the number of players, to the handling of the ball, and the size of the goal. A standard set of rules was needed and eventually the English took on the job. In 1863, the English Football Association was formed and it published the "Laws of the Game." This meant that every team could play by the same rules, creating the foundation for the way soccer is played today, all over the world.

## CUJU

The first game believed to have involved players kicking a ball was an ancient Chinese game called cuju. Popular in the 2nd century BCE, the object of cuju was to kick a leather ball through a hole in a piece of silk held up by two 30ft (10m) poles.

## DID YOU KNOW?

*More countries are members of FIFA than of the United Nations (an organization that aims to promote international cooperation).*

## KEMARI

The Japanese sport of kemari developed from the Chinese game cuju. It was first played in about 600 CE but has been revived in modern times. The object of kemari is to keep the ball in the air. The game is unique because all the players must work together, so there are no winners or losers.

## MEDIEVAL SOCCER

In the Middle Ages soccer games were popular throughout Europe. However, they were often little more than mass brawls between neighboring towns or villages. By the 16th century, soccer was also being played in English "public" schools (schools that charge for tuition). Although this helped the game to develop, each school had its own set of rules, which made it very difficult for them to play each other.

*By 1881, some teams had begun to wear coordinated uniforms.*

## DEVELOPING GAME

By the end of the 19th century, soccer was growing rapidly in popularity. Once again, it was the British who helped to spread the game around the world, first to continental Europe and then on to South America, North America, Africa, Asia, and Australasia.

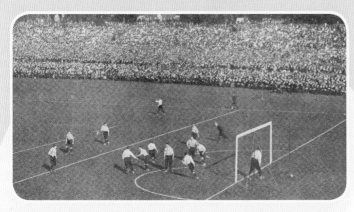

At first players were just talented amateurs, but in 1885 they became professionals and, therefore, could be paid. Organized leagues and cup competitions were formed and games attracted huge crowds. In 1901, more than 110,000 fans watched Tottenham Hotspur and Sheffield United in the English FA Cup final.

# THE MODERN ERA

### "THE ONLY THING THAT HAS NEVER CHANGED IN THE HISTORY OF THE GAME IS THE SHAPE OF THE BALL."

DENIS LAW, FORMER SCOTLAND STRIKER

Throughout the 20th century the game of soccer continued to develop across the world. As its popularity grew, rules were standardized, clubs were formed, and professional leagues sprouted up in all corners of the globe. Now, in the 21st century the game of soccer is bigger, brighter, and better than ever.

Above, West Bromwich Albion players enjoy a training session—a brisk walk in their suits! In 1901, the English FA set the maximum wage for a player at a lowly £4 (about $20) a week.

### 1880s

In the 1880s teams began to wear coordinated uniforms for the first time. They were usually long shorts with knee-length socks and knitted jerseys.

### 1900s

After 1901, players were allowed to show their knees so shorts became shorter. Striped shirts with collars also became fashionable.

### 1930s

During the 1930s, shorts became even shorter and also baggier. There was more variation in uniform style.

### 1950s

During the 1950s, soccer fashions really began to take off. Lightweight shirt fabrics were introduced and gear design became more colorful and daring.

### 1960s

By the 1960s cleats as well as uniforms were much more lightweight. Surprisingly, during the 1960s plain uniforms were fashionable, since they showed up better under the floodlights.

### 1970s

During the 1970s, teams began to assert their individuality with distinctive uniform. They also began to realize the marketing potential of uniform sponsorship and replica shirts.

## THE BALL

The first balls were inflated pigs' bladders or skins stuffed with straw or sawdust. In the 19th and early 20th centuries, soccer balls were made of animal bladders wrapped in leather. They often lost their shape during a game and became very heavy in wet conditions. Modern balls are lighter and are usually made of leather or plastic with a special waterproof coating. Balls must be 27–28 in (68–70 cm) in circumference and weigh 14–16 oz (410–450 g).

## CLEATS

Early players nailed studs into their heavy leather work boots and the first soccer shoes were heavy, ankle-high leather boots. Lighter, shorter shoes, made of a mixture of leather and synthetic materials were first introduced in the 1960s. Today's cleats use the latest technology: They are light, and sleek, with plastic cleats.

### 1980s

*During the 1980s, uniform fabrics became even more lightweight but for many the decade was defined by the players' hairstyles. Curly perms and the "mullet" (below) were the height of fashion.*

### 1990s

*The 1990s saw a trend for bright colors and crazy patterns. Thankfully, this fad had passed by the end of the decade.*

### 1970s

*In the 1970s, players began wearing numbers on their shorts. Although with shorts this tiny, it is a wonder they found space...*

## DREAM TEAM

It's not just the game that has developed over the years, the players and uniforms have changed, too—from the long shorts and perfectly groomed moustaches of the 19th century to the long hair and tight shorts of the 1970s and the high-tech, ever-changing gear of the 21st century. Check out this all-time fantasy eleven of professional soccer through the ages.

### 2000s

*In the 21st century, replica soccer uniforms and sponsorship deals are even bigger business. Most teams have at least three uniforms that they change every season.*

### 2000s

*Even in the 21st century, players still make some serious fashion mistakes. Cameroon's body-hugging one-piece uniform in 2004 earned the team a fine and a points deduction from FIFA.*

# PLAYING THE GAME

### "YOU HAVE TO WORK HARD TO BE A SUCCESS BUT YOU ALSO HAVE TO ENJOY IT AND THINK OF FOOTBALL AS YOUR HOBBY."
ENGLISH PLAYER DAVID BENTLEY

There are many obvious reasons why soccer is the world's most popular sport, but one of the best things about the game is that anyone can play it. It doesn't matter how young or old you are, where you live or how skillful you are—the game of soccer is for you. Soccer doesn't have to be 11-a-side, last 90 minutes, or even played on grass—leave that to the professionals—all you really need is a ball. From beach soccer to street soccer, five-a-side to freestyle, there is a version of the game to suit everyone.

## BEACH SOCCER

Beach soccer is popular in hot, soccer-loving countries such as Brazil, Argentina, Spain, and Italy. In 1992, a set of beach soccer rules was introduced to make the game suitable for international competitions. Teams are 5-a-side, substitutions are unlimited, shoes must not be worn, and there is no offside rule. Games are characterized by lots of goals and matches cannot end in a draw. The first annual Beach Soccer World Cup took place in 1995 and was won by host Brazil, which has dominated the competition ever since.

## STREET SOCCER

If there's no grass or no beach nearby, the street can make a great soccer field. Rules can be adapted to suit any number of players and abilities, and the field of play is any mutually agreed upon area. And, of course, sweaters make great goalposts! The first Street Football World Festival took place in Germany in 2006 during the FIFA World Cup Finals. It featured 24 street soccer teams from around the world and was won by a team from the Netherlands.

*Children play soccer in the street in Bloemfontein, South Africa.*

## PARALYMPIC SOCCER

Soccer can be adapted for people with most kinds of disabilities. Wheelchair and amputee soccer is widespread, while versions for the visually impaired and those with cerebral palsy are official paralympic sports. Deaf soccer is also played around the world, although many partially deaf players such as Rodney Marsh (QPR, Manchester City, Fulham, and England) have enjoyed successful professional careers.

*Visually impaired players from Brazil and China in the 2008 Paralympic Games in Beijing, China.*

*Brazil's Sidney (left) and Portugal's Bilro in action during the Beach Soccer World Cup in 2008. Brazil won the tournament.*

## INDOOR/FUTSAL

Indoor soccer is popular all over the world and is usually 6-a-side (US and Spain) or 5-a-side (UK). The game is fast and high-scoring and walls are used instead of touchlines. FIFA's official form of 5-a-side is known as "futsal". Invented in Uruguay in the 1930s, it uses a special small, heavy ball, and showcases skill and speed. A futsal World Cup is held every four years.

*Players from Uruguay and Libya fight for the ball in a 2008 World Cup qualifying match. Brazil eventually won the competition.*

## GRASSROOTS

Organized junior teams and local leagues are a great way to start learning how to play soccer. It is also where the next generation of professional soccer can be found. But remember, grassroots soccer is not just for kids—there are teams and leagues out there for people of every size, shape, age, gender, and ability.

*Girls and boys playing soccer in Los Angeles in a game supported by the American Youth Soccer Association.*

*Freestyle soccer world champion Sean Garnier of France in action.*

## DID YOU KNOW?

*Soccer video games are among the most popular in the world, but there is also another way that armchair fans can live out their dreams—fantasy soccer. Players assume the role of a soccer manager and pick an imaginary team of real-life players. Points are scored (and deducted) as a result of those players' actual performances. Fantasy soccer leagues are usually organized informally or by media outlets such as newspapers, magazines, or websites.*

## FREESTYLE

You don't need any other players for freestyle soccer. Freestylers use any part of their body, aside from their hands, to perform tricks and skills. This form of soccer began as an urban street art but looks set to become a sport in its own right.

# A WOMAN'S GAME

## "THE FUTURE OF FOOTBALL IS FEMININE."

FIFA PRESIDENT SEPP BLATTER

Today, there are more than 26 million female players in the world and it is women who have led soccer's long-awaited advances in the US and China. Although the first women's professional league collapsed in the US in 2003, it was only a temporary setback (see p.169). Semiprofessional domestic leagues have sprung up all over the world, and international tournaments such as the Women's World Cup have become compelling fixtures in the soccer calendar.

No one, man or woman, has scored more international goals than Mia Hamm, with 158.

## DICK, KERR'S LADIES

The first-ever women's international was played in 1920 between France and a team of factory workers from Lancashire, England, who had defeated male players at the Dick, Kerr and Co.'s base in Preston. Dick, Kerr's Ladies became a touring sensation and played soccer to raise money for injured World War I soldiers. The team played on until 1965 as Preston Ladies, despite many obstacles, such as the English FA banning women from using official fields between 1921 and 1971.

## MIA HAMM

US star player Mia Hamm is more famous than most of her male counterparts. She spearheaded US victories in the 1991 and 1999 Women's World Cup finals and is her country's top scorer. Now retired, Hamm and her strike partner Michelle Akers were the only women included in Pelé's 2004 list of the 125 greatest living players.

China striker Sun Wen has had to settle for several second-place finishes behind US players—in the 1999 World Cup, and a series of end-of-year prize-givings. However, her goal-scoring and passing abilities finally received top billing when FIFA named her the Woman Player of the Century in 2002, although she still had to share the title with American Michelle Akers.

Karren Brady (left) proved the sceptics wrong by making a success of Birmingham City when she took over as managing director in 1992, at the age of 23. She left the club in 2009, after helping to pave the way for other women to work in all areas of soccer.

WOMEN'S DREAM TEAM?   1. Bente Nordby (Norway) 2. Kerstin Stegemann (Germany) 3. Sandra Minnert (Germany) 4. Hege Riise (Norway) 5. Carla Werden Overbeck (US) 6. Steffi Jones (Germany) 7. Kristine Lilly (US) 8. Michelle Akers (US) 9. Mia Hamm (US) 10. Sun Wen (China) 11. Julie Foudy (US)

## INKA GRINGS

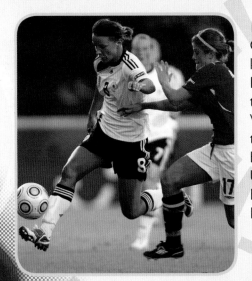

Opponents of Germany's women's team know that if Birgit Prinz doesn't score, then Inka Grings (left) probably will. Grings was top scorer when Germany won the UEFA Women's Championship in 2005. She then took four years out of international action before reuniting with Prinz to take the 2009 UEFA Women's Championship. Grings and Prinz each scored twice in a 6–2 victory over England in the final.

Like her predecessor Hanna Ljungberg, Sweden captain and leading scorer, Victoria Svensson (above) can claim to be one of the finest female players in the world, while playing for one of its unluckiest national teams. Sweden's last trophy was the first UEFA Women's Championship in 1984. Svensson and Ljungberg were both on the losing side in the 2003 Women's World Cup final.

Although England's women are still striving for their big international breakthrough, they have one of the world's most recognized female players—star striker Rachel Yankey. Her goals in 2007 helped Arsenal Ladies to the UEFA Women's Cup, two years after she and international teammate Rachel Unitt won the American W-League with the New Jersey Wildcats.

*Women were banned from playing soccer in Brazil until 1975.*

## ONE TO WATCH

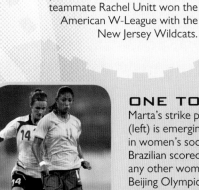

Marta's strike partner Cristiane (left) is emerging as serious talent in women's soccer. The dynamic Brazilian scored more goals than any other woman at the 2008 Beijing Olympics, although her country was beaten by the US in the final, yet again. At club level, Cristiane has showcased her skills in Germany, Sweden, and the US, as well as her homeland.

## DID YOU KNOW?

*Dutch amateur club FC de Rakt swapped traditional shorts for skirts in September 2008. The KNVB (Dutch Football Association) tried to punish Rakt for breaching soccer's dress code, which states that players must wear shorts. However, players revealed that they were in fact wearing shorts underneath their skirts, so the KNVB had to admit defeat.*

## MARTA

Brazilian midfielder Marta Vieira da Silva had her cleats imprinted in cement outside Rio's Maracanã Stadium after Brazil beat the US in the 2007 Pan American Games. FIFA Women's Player of the Year in 2006, 2007 and 2008, Marta plays her club soccer for Los Angeles Sol in the US.

# PLAYING BY THE RULES

**"MY JOB IS NOT TO CHANGE THE GAME BUT MAKE IT WORK TO EVERYONE'S SATISFACTION."**

FORMER REFEREE PIERLUIGI COLLINA

Soccer is a simple game. It is based on 17 laws first agreed to in 1863 that have been revised and updated to fit in with the modern game. The rules are the same whether you are playing in your local park or in the World Cup Finals. A game lasts for 90 minutes and is contested by two teams, each with 11 players. One player on each team must be a goalkeeper and the winners are the team who score the most goals. Check out the glossary on pp.202–203 for extra information.

*Italian Pierluigi Collina was widely considered to be the best referee in the world until he retired from the game in 2005.*

## GAME OFFICIALS

A referee ensures that the rules of the game are followed. He or she is supported by two assistants, one on each touchline. Assistant referees carry a flag to signal infringements such as offside or a foul. Being a game official is a tough job and requires skills such as physical fitness (game officials must keep up with play at all times), good eyesight, and the ability to make split-second decisions while under pressure.

## CARDS

Free kicks are awarded for minor fouls and infringements, but for persistent or serious breaches of the rules, referees will show a yellow card. Two yellow cards in a game result in a red card and the player must leave the field for the rest of the game. A serious foul will result in an immediate red card.

## FOULS

When one of the laws of soccer is broken, it is generally known as a "foul." The most common types of foul are tackles in which the player (deliberately or accidentally) trips or makes contact with the opposition player rather than the ball. Other common fouls are handball, obstruction, and dangerous play.

LA Galaxy's Kyle Martino (right) fouls DC United's Fred and earns a red card. If a foul occurs inside the penalty area, a penalty kick will be awarded.

The assistant referee flags to signal that a player is offside.

## OFFSIDE

The attacking player is in an offside position if he is closer to the goal line than the ball and the second-to-last opponent. (The last opponent is usually the goalkeeper.) However, offside is judged from the moment the ball is played, not when it is received and it is only an offence if the player gains an advantage, is interfering with play or affecting his opponent.

## KEY

1 Goal line
2 Goal
3 Six-yard box
4 Penalty spot
5 Eighteen-yard box

6 Center spot
7 Center circle
8 Halfway line
9 Corner arc
10 Touchline

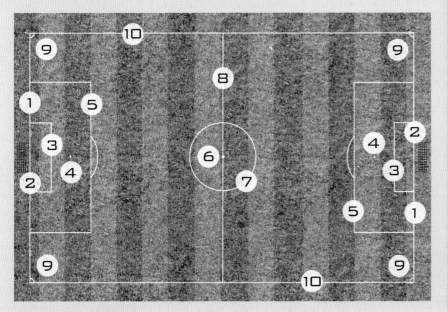

## THE FIELD

Above is an illustration of a typical soccer field with the key areas marked. According to the Laws of the Game, not all fields have to be the same size. They must be rectangular, and between 100 and 130 yards (90 and 120 meters) long and between 50 and 100 yards (45 and 90 meters) wide. One part of the field must always be the same size—the goal. It must be 8 feet by 8 feet (2.44 meters high and 7.32 meters wide).

## THE LAWS OF THE GAME
Here are some key laws of soccer.

### THE REFEREE
The referee's decision is always final. He or she can only reverse a decision (usually on the advice of the assistant referee) immediately after the incident, if play has not been restarted.

### THE PERIOD OF PLAY
A 90-minute game is divided into two equal halves of 45 minutes, with a halftime interval of not more than 15 minutes. Extra time is added on to each half to make up for stoppages such as substitutions and injuries.

### IN AND OUT OF PLAY
A ball is only out of play if the whole of the ball has crossed the touchline or goal line, whether it is on the ground or in the air. It is in play if it rebounds off a goal post, crossbar, corner flag, or even the referee, as long as it lands on the field of play.

### SCORING
A goal is scored when the whole of the ball crosses the goal line, between the goalposts and underneath the crossbar, as long as none of the Laws of the Game have been infringed. The winning team is the one that scores the most goals. If the score is equal at the end of the game, it is known as a "draw."

### PENALTIES
Infringements on the attacking team in the penalty area usually result in a penalty kick—a one-on-one shot with the goalkeeper. The ball is placed on the penalty spot and the penalty taker steps forward. The goalkeeper faces the kicker but must remain on the goal line. All other players must stand outside the penalty area, behind the penalty spot. As soon as the penalty is taken the ball is in play but the penalty taker cannot strike the ball again until it has touched another player.

### SUBSTITUTIONS
Before a game begins, each team can name a number of substitute players (the number varies between competitions). Of these named substitutes a fixed number (usually three) can be brought on during the course of the game, if the referee consents.

# IN THE CLUB

Although the players are the ones who grab the glory, the headlines and the big salaries, a soccer club is about more than just the team. The club is a business and many people work behind the scenes to ensure that it is profitable off the field as well as successful on the field. From the people who sell the game day tickets to the people who negotiate big-money sponsorship deals, everyone plays a part in the club's success. Take a look at this pyramid, which shows how the average club is structured and who does what.

## CENTER STAGE

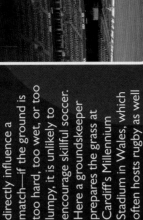

It takes a lot of hard work to maintain a world class soccer field. The condition of the field can directly influence a match—if the ground is too hard, too wet, or too lumpy, it is unlikely to encourage skillful soccer. Here a groundskeeper prepares the grass at Cardiff's Millennium Stadium in Wales, which often hosts rugby as well as soccer games.

## STRUCTURE

Not all clubs are run in exactly the same way. Some are privately owned, while others have shareholders and a Board of Directors. Some clubs have a Director of Soccer and head coach instead of a manager. However, this illustration should give you some idea of just how many different people are involved in the smooth running of a soccer club.

### THE TEAM

The team is picked from a squad of players. Squad size varies from about 20–30 (there are no set rules) and this system provides cover for injured players.

### YOUTH TEAM

Most clubs want to find and keep young soccer talent so many have academies, development programs, and under-18 teams.

### RESERVES

Every player in the squad needs to be game ready. Reserve team games give players who are not in the first 11 a chance to play and also help injured players to regain their sharpness.

### ASSISTANT MANAGER

The assistant manager works closely with the manager and the team. If a manager is fired, the assistant may take temporary charge of the team.

### MANAGER

A manager or head coach is in charge of the first team. He controls training, picks the team, and sets the tactics. At some clubs, he also scouts for new players and handles transfer negotiations.

### OTHER COACHES

The reserve and youth teams also have dedicated coaches. They will liaise with the manager and discuss which players may be ready to move into the first team.

### UNIFORM MANAGER

Most teams have two or three different uniforms and it is this manager's job to ensure that every member of the squad has a complete set of gear for every game.

### PRESS OFFICER

The press officer has the vital job of liaising with the media—TV, newspapers, and magazines—to ensure that facts about the club are reported correctly.

### GROUNDS CREW

A team of expert groundskeepers ensure that the field is in peak condition at all times, from the depths of winter to the height of summer.

### HEALTH AND FITNESS

Many different people look after the health and fitness of the players, from team doctors and physical therapists to fitness and skills coaches.

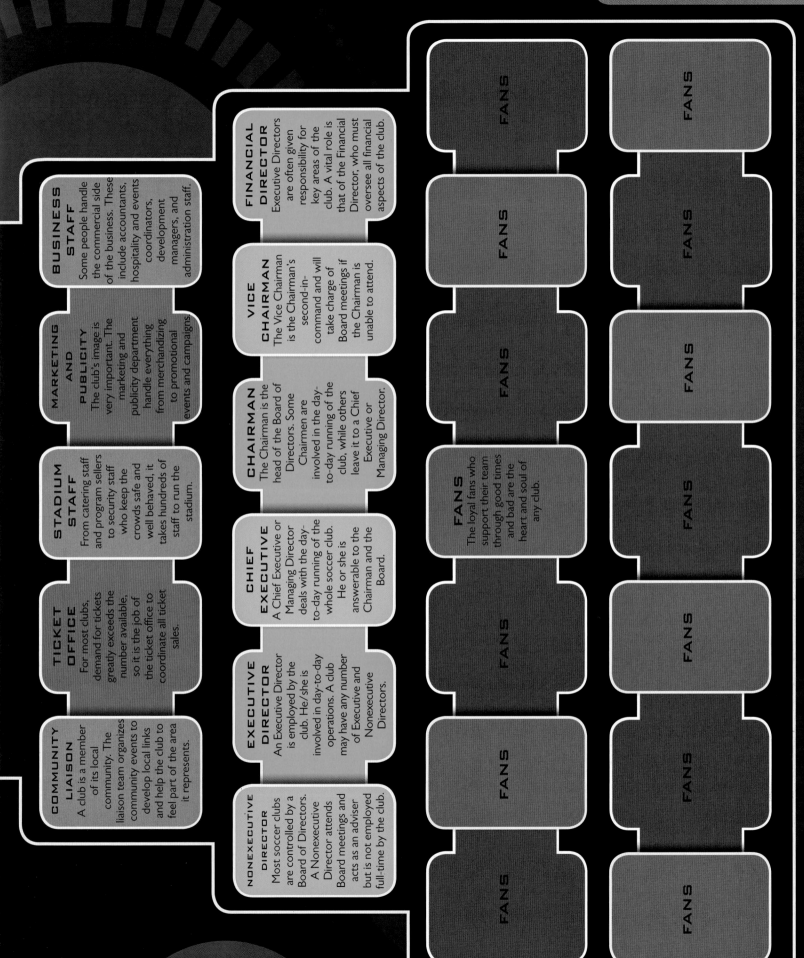

### BUSINESS STAFF
Some people handle the commercial side of the business. These include accountants, hospitality and events coordinators, development managers, and administration staff.

### MARKETING AND PUBLICITY
The club's image is very important. The marketing and publicity department handle everything from merchandizing to promotional events and campaigns.

### STADIUM STAFF
From catering staff and program sellers to security staff who keep the crowds safe and well behaved, it takes hundreds of staff to run the stadium.

### TICKET OFFICE
For most clubs, demand for tickets greatly exceeds the number available, so it is the job of the ticket office to coordinate all ticket sales.

### COMMUNITY LIAISON
A club is a member of its local community. The liaison team organizes community events to develop local links and help the club to feel part of the area it represents.

### FINANCIAL DIRECTOR
Executive Directors are often given responsibility for key areas of the club. A vital role is that of the Financial Director, who must oversee all financial aspects of the club.

### VICE CHAIRMAN
The Vice Chairman is the Chairman's second-in-command and will take charge of Board meetings if the Chairman is unable to attend.

### CHAIRMAN
The Chairman is the head of the Board of Directors. Some Chairmen are involved in the day-to-day running of the club, while others leave it to a Chief Executive or Managing Director.

### CHIEF EXECUTIVE
A Chief Executive or Managing Director deals with the day-to-day running of the whole soccer club. He or she is answerable to the Chairman and the Board.

### EXECUTIVE DIRECTOR
An Executive Director is employed by the club. He/she is involved in day-to-day operations. A club may have any number of Executive and Nonexecutive Directors.

### NONEXECUTIVE DIRECTOR
Most soccer clubs are controlled by a Board of Directors. A Nonexecutive Director attends Board meetings and acts as an adviser but is not employed full-time by the club.

### FANS
The loyal fans who support their team through good times and bad are the heart and soul of any club.

FANS
FANS
FANS
FANS
FANS
FANS
FANS
FANS
FANS
FANS
FANS
FANS
FANS

## RICH OWNERS

Some clubs are owned by shareholders, others by families or small groups of people, but in recent years many billionaires have begun to see soccer as a worthwhile investment. When Russian billionaire Roman Abramovich (above) bought UK's Chelsea in 2003 it gave the club unrivaled spending power and success soon followed.

## MERCHANDISE

Fans love to show their support for their favorite team by wearing badges, replica shirts, scarves, etc. and it is a great source of revenue for clubs. Most soccer teams have a club store selling a range of official merchandise, from pens to pillowcases and shirts to shower caps.

# BIG BUSINESS

"THE MONEY COMING INTO THE GAME IS INCREDIBLE. BUT... IT COMES IN AND GOES STRAIGHT OUT AWAY."

LORD ALAN SUGAR, FORMER FOOTBALL CHAIRMAN

Over the last few decades, worldwide television coverage, lucrative sponsorship deals, increased merchandising, and product endorsements have poured more and more money into the global game. Today, the top professionals are highly paid and highly trained superstars, earning massive salaries for their talents, both on and off the field. Take a look at some of the ways in which the game of soccer has become seriously big business.

## TECHNOLOGY

Modern technology has also brought more financial opportunities to the game. Television rights to games bring in huge revenues, while TV sports packages and single-club TV channels are a must-have for fans. Cell phone and internet updates and downloads are just the latest ways of making money.

## SPONSORSHIP

Corporate sponsorship brings in lots of money for soccer clubs. From shirt sponsors, to gear and shoe manufacturers—every aspect has a big-money deal behind it. Leagues, cup competitions, and even soccer grounds can attract lucrative sponsors from a range of businesses.

*FC Dallas plays its home games at Pizza Hut Park (below). Other MLS teams also have sponsored grounds, including LA Galaxy (Home Depot Center) and Chicago Fire (Toyota Park).*

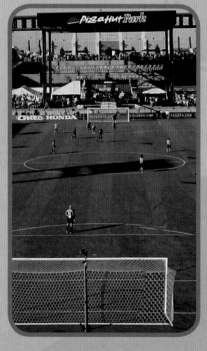

*Barcelona is one club that bucks the trend of corporate sponsorship. Although it has uniform deals, its shirts bear the UNICEF (United Nations Children's Fund) logo. The club also donates $1.9 million per year to UNICEF.*

## SUPER AGENTS

Most soccer players employ agents to look after their interests. An agent negotiates transfers, endorsements, and any other contracts on the player's behalf. Although some people dislike the power of agents in the modern game, they are strictly regulated, and, like the Bosman rule, are designed to give players more rights over their own careers.

*Wayne Rooney's agent, Paul Stretford (above, left) talks to Manchester United chief executive David Gill.*

## DID YOU KNOW?

*In 1995, European soccer changed forever when Belgian player Jean-Marc Bosman won a court case that allowed him to transfer to the club of his own choice at the end of his contract. Known as the "Bosman Rule" it means that any player from the European Union is a free agent at the end of his contract and can now choose which EU club he moves to.*

## TRANSFERS

When players move between clubs it is known as a "transfer." The most skilled and admired players can command huge transfer fees, but only a select few clubs can afford to pay them, such as Real Madrid, Barcelona, and Chelsea. English club Manchester City became the world's richest club in 2008, when it was bought by Sheikh Mansour bin Zayed Al Nahyan's Abu Dhabi United Group. The new owners gave manager Mark Hughes (below, right) a huge transfer budget and he splurged on the likes of Robinho, Carlos Tevez, Roque Santa Cruz, and Kolo Toure (below, left).

*Defender Kolo Toure moved from Arsenal to Manchester City in July 2009 for a fee of $22 million.*

# TEAM TALK

*"THERE ARE TWO CERTAINTIES IN LIFE. PEOPLE DIE, AND FOOTBALL MANAGERS GET THE SACK."*

EOIN HAND, REPUBLIC OF IRELAND MANAGER 1980–1985

The day-to-day running of a soccer team is hard work. Keeping a talented squad of individuals fit, healthy, happy, playing well, and working together is a tough job. Players might get injured or they might lose their form for a few games; they might have a better offer from another club or they might not fit in with the style or direction in which the manager wishes to take the club. In the modern game expectations are high, but the rewards are even higher.

## TEAM BOSS

The manager (or sometimes the Head Coach) takes charge of training, picks the team, and decides the tactics. It is a high-pressure role and too many bad results can cost a manager his job. Dutch manager Guus Hiddink's (above) impressive CV includes PSV Eindhoven, Valencia, Netherlands, Real Madrid, Republic of Korea, Australia, Chelsea, and Russia, while Manchester United's Sir Alex Ferguson is a rarity in soccer management—he has been in the same job for more than 20 years.

*FC Barcelona lines up before a Champions League match with Dinamo Kiev at Camp Nou in 2009.*

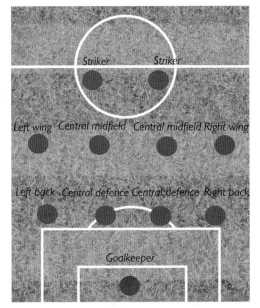

*Striker*    *Striker*

*Left wing*   *Central midfield*   *Central midfield*   *Right wing*

*Left back*   *Central defence*   *Central defence*   *Right back*

*Goalkeeper*

**4–4–2** This illustration shows a traditional 4–4–2 formation: four defenders, four midfielders, and two strikers. There is a flexibility within this formation since midfielders can play deep to provide defensive cover or even sit just behind the strikers in an attacking 4–4–2 formation.

## TACTICS

Tactics and formations vary depending on the abilities of the players in the squad, the nature of the opposition, and the manager's preferred style of play. They can even be changed during the course of a match to protect a lead or provide more attacking options. There are many different styles of play and variations within them, but here are three common formations.

**4–5–1** This formation involves four defenders, a five-man midfield, and a lone striker and is primarily used when a team wants to keep possession of the ball and prevent the other team from scoring. It is particularly useful in games when away goals count and the home team needs to stop the visitors from scoring.

**4–3–3** This attacking formation involves four defenders, three midfielders, and three strikers. The emphasis is on attack with this style of play so it is only really used against weaker opposition or when chasing a goal during a match.

## THE CAPTAIN

The manager chooses one player to be the leader on the field. Known as the captain or "skipper," this player is usually one of the oldest or longest-serving members of the team, such as Italy's Fabio Cannavaro (above). He has no official authority but wearing the captain's armband for club or country is a great honor. Captains must also participate in the pregame coin toss that decides who plays at which end.

## THE FIRST ELEVEN

Players train hard every day in the hope of making it into the team and when they are on the field, it is their job to carry the hopes and expectations of the manager, the Board, and the fans.

### TRAINING

Players such as Germany's Michael Ballack (right) and Miroslav Klose (far right) train to stay fit and also to practice skills and tactics. Training methods can vary between clubs, between managers, and between individuals.

# BEING A SOCCER PLAYER

### "I LOVE LITTLE KIDS LOOKING UP TO ME, YOUNG PLAYERS LOOKING UP TO ME, RESPECTING ME." DAVID BECKHAM

*Rafael van der Vaart and the Dutch team in training before a 2009 friendly game against Tunisia.*

Many people dream of being a professional player, but it's a tough job. Players often dedicate their lives to their chosen sport from a young age and it takes the right blend of talent, hard work, and self-discipline to succeed. Life as a professional player is first and foremost about preparing for every game, both physically and mentally. However, with only one game in an average week, players are left with a lot of spare time. Here are some of the ways in which a player might spend his days.

## GAME PREPARATION

Most teams train every morning, working on general fitness. Soccer can also involve a lot of traveling to away fixtures. Depending on the distance, time zone, or climate, the team may arrive one or two days before the game in order to prepare fully.

Managers often devise specific tactics and formations for each game in order to exploit the opposition's weaknesses and play to his team's strengths.

## GAME DAY

Most players have their own pregame preparations to make sure they are ready for the challenge ahead. They usually arrive at the ground a couple of hours before kick off and then have a light group warm-up.

David Beckham poses with children from local schools at London's David Beckham Academy in 2007. That day, 120 children were taking part in the Academy's free school day visiting program.

## ROLE MODELS

Players can use their high public profiles in different ways. Many are offered lucrative product endorsements, while others diversify outside soccer into areas such as music, movies, politics, and business.

Ronaldinho's on-field talents make him a popular choice for advertisements, such as this one for Pepsi (above).

The Ivory Coast's Didier Drogba uses his soccer fame to highlight important issues in Africa. He was appointed a United Nations Development Program Goodwill Ambassador in 2007 (above).

## GIVING BACK

Players can earn very high salaries, and many players use their wealth and influence to benefit humanitarian or charitable causes. Former French international Lilian Thuram has set up a foundation aiming to combat racism, both in soccer and in wider culture; while England's David Beckham has founded children's soccer schools in London and Los Angeles. They are known as David Beckham Academies and more sites are already planned in Brazil and Asia.

In addition to cheering their team on during games, some fans even attend training sessions. Here, Italy's Fabio Grosso (right) signs autographs after a 2009 training session.

## DID YOU KNOW?

Players usually retire from the game in their mid to late thirties. After that, many stay involved in the game, becoming managers, agents, or television pundits. Others find whole new careers, such as France's Eric Cantona and Wales' Vinnie Jones who became movie stars.

## FANS

Fans are the 12th person in a soccer team. Their support can turn a game round and their investment in tickets, replica shirts, and merchandise can help to finance the team. Many players attend fan events to show their appreciation.

## PUNCHING

The only kind of punch that is allowed in a soccer game is a punch by the goalkeeper to the ball, in the penalty area. In high-pressure situations, the goalkeeper may not be able to catch the ball cleanly so he must punch it away. It is important to get height and distance on a punch so that the goal threat is cleared. A poor punch can rebound off a player and end up in the back of the net!

*Czech Republic and Chelsea goalkeeper Petr Cech punches clear of Spain and Liverpool's Fernando Torres in an English Premier League game.*

# GOALKEEPING

### "IF YOU'RE A GOALKEEPER, IT DOESN'T MATTER WHAT YOU SAVE THE BALL WITH— IF YOU KEEP IT OUT, IT'S NOT A GOAL."

FORMER REPUBLIC OF IRELAND AND LIVERPOOL DEFENDER MARK LAWRENSON

In some ways goalkeepers are the odd-ones-out of the soccer team. For a start, they wear a different uniform (to distinguish them from the rest of the team) and are the only players permitted to handle the ball in open play. Moreover, they are often all that stands in the way of a certain goal—a great save and the goalkeeper is the hero, a clumsy fumble and he is the villain!

## DIVING SAVE

Goalkeepers need quick reactions, agility, and the courage to put themselves in dangerous situations. If the ball comes at them from a low angle, the goalkeeper must make a diving save, as Brazil keeper Júlio César demonstrates (right).

*Height and agility are also key assets for goalkeepers. At 6ft 5in (1.96m) tall, Petr Cech has these qualities in abundance.*

## REACTIONS

Goalkeepers must always be alert and ready to react to goal threats. Sometimes they have to improvise, as Netherlands keeper Edwin Van der Sar demonstrates with a brave point-blank stop against Russia striker Roman Pavlyuchenko during the Euro 2008 quarterfinal.

## DID YOU KNOW?

*There have been many spectacular saves, but probably none more inventive than former Colombian goalkeeper René Higuita's famous "scorpion kick." It occurred during a friendly match between Colombia and England at Wembley in 2003. Instead of catching an England cross, Higuita performed this acrobatic kick (right).*

# DISTRIBUTING THE BALL

In addition to being the last line of defense, a goalkeeper can also be the launch pad for an attack. Above, Russia goalkeeper Igor Akinfeev takes a goal kick, aiming to put pressure on the opposition's defense. Goalkeepers must be able to distribute the ball effectively and accurately with their hands and their feet.

## UNDERARM THROW

Italy goalkeeper Gianluigi Buffon (above) demonstrates the underarm throw, which is perfect for moving the ball a short distance.

## OVERARM THROW

Spain goalkeeper Iker Casillas (above) uses an overarm throw to launch a quick counterattack. This technique requires accuracy, strength, and power.

### CATCHING

When catching the ball, it is important to take it firmly and cleanly. Here, US goalkeeper Kasey Keller (left) clutches the ball safely to his body in a friendly game against Germany in 2006.

## INDIVIDUAL STYLE

Goalkeepers are famous for their individuality and eccentricities, but probably none more so than former Mexico goalkeeper Jorge Campos, (left). Despite his short stature (5 ft 8 in/1.73 m) Campos was extremely agile and played for his country in 130 matches. He was famous for his eye-catching gear, which he designed himself and his occasional fondness for playing as a striker, all of which helped to make him a cult figure with fans around the world.

Ricardo saves a penalty from England's Frank Lampard during Portugal's penalty shootout victory in the 2006 World Cup quarterfinals.

# PENALTIES

For most goalkeepers, penalties are the ultimate test. This one-on-one situation favors the attacker and gives the goalkeeper very little chance of glory. Even if he correctly guesses which way the attacker will shoot, a well struck penalty is virtually impossible to save. However, some goalkeepers have a reputation for saving penalties, such as former Portugal keeper Ricardo (right).

## TACKLING

A tackle is the most direct way of winning the ball back from the opposition and breaking down an attack. Tackles must be from the side or the front, never from behind, and timing is vital to win the ball cleanly and safely.

Per Mertesacker of Germany (far right) tackles Norway's Thorstein Helstad in a friendly match in 2009.

# IN DEFENSE

*"STRIKERS WIN YOU GAMES, BUT DEFENDERS WIN YOU CHAMPIONSHIPS."*

FORMER ENGLAND MIDFIELDER AND VETERAN CLUB MANAGER, JOHN GREGORY

Although strikers and midfielders often steal all the glory, the defense is the backbone of the team. Defenders must be strong, aware, skillful, and cool under pressure. However, it is important for every player to know how to defend, since during a game any player could find himself needing to make a goal-saving tackle or goal line clearance.

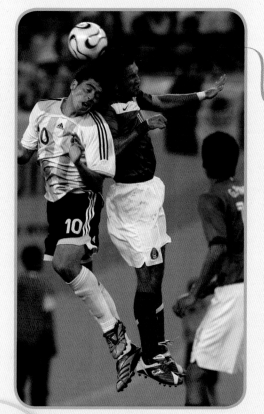

Argentina won the match 2–1 thanks to goals from Hernán Crespo and Maxi Rodríguez.

## HEADING

Defenders need to have a strong physical presence, particularly in the air. Here, Mexico's José Fonseca (right) rises above Argentina's Juan Roman Riquelme (left) to head the ball during the 2006 World Cup Finals. An effective defensive header should travel as far and as high as possible.

## TEAM DEFENDING

Organization is an important part of good defending. Whether it is trapping the attacker offside, marking for a corner, or covering for each other, defenders must work together. Above, Ronaldinho of Brazil prepares to take a free kick from just outside the area, but he must get past England's defensive wall.

## WINNING THE BALL

Sometimes a defender doesn't even have to make a tackle to win the ball—by reading the game or marking tightly he can intercept a pass or cheekily steal the ball right off an attacker's toes! Pace and skill can also help the defender to stay one step ahead of the attacking player.

Italy's Fabio Cannavaro (right) beats France's Franck Ribéry (left) to the ball in the 2006 World Cup final.

Fabio Cannavaro lifted the World Cup in 2006 as Italian captain. He was also named World and European Footballer of the Year in 2006.

## STRENGTH

Strength and determination are key parts of a defender's game. Winning headers, making tackles, and passing under pressure all require strength as well as skill and good technique. Above, Brazil defender Daniel Alves (right) uses his strength to shield the ball from Egypt's Ahmed Hassan in a 2009 FIFA Confederations Cup match.

# MIDFIELD MASTERS

**"THE MIDFIELD IS THE MOST CRUCIAL AREA OF THE GAME, THE ONE WHERE MATCHES ARE WON OR LOST."**

FORMER ENGLAND AND MANCHESTER CITY MANAGER SVEN-GÖRAN ERIKSSON

The midfield is the engine of the team. Midfielders provide a vital link between defense and attack, tracking back and making tackles to win the ball and then driving forward with vision and awareness. Some midfielders embody all these attributes, while others have more specialized roles. A "holding" midfielder plays a defensive game, while an attacking midfielder may play just behind the strikers. It is the job of a winger to make runs on the outside of the field, beating defenders and supplying accurate crosses.

## PACE AND POWER
Attacking midfielders like Spain's Cesc Fàbregas (above, left) need pace to outrun defenders, strength to hold off challenges, and the skills to supply accurate passes.

## TACKLING
The midfield is a key area of the field and winning the ball in this area can quickly turn defense into attack. This means that tackling is often a vital part of a midfielder's role. Here, Chelsea midfielder Michael Essien (right) stretches beyond Liverpool's Emiliano Insua (far right) to win the ball.

*Argentina defensive midfielder Javier Mascherano is admired for his passing and tackling skills.*

## PASSING
Passing and distribution are also important skills for a midfielder. Whether it is having the vision to play a cross-field pass and set up an attack or calmly passing the ball out of defense, a midfielder needs to blend creativity with coolness under pressure.

## DID YOU KNOW?
*Many midfielders claim that they work the hardest out of everyone in the team and they certainly cover the greatest distance. In fact, a top level midfielder covers more than 6 miles (10 km) per game.*

## WING PLAY

Wingers use the far sides of the field to make attacking runs, beat defenders, and supply accurate crosses to the strikers. They need speed, strength, and versatility plus excellent dribbling and passing skills. Real Madrid and Portugal's Cristiano Ronaldo (right) is one of the finest— and most expensive—wingers in the world.

*A prolific goalscorer, Ronaldo is a skilled header of the ball and often takes free kicks.*

*Ronaldo is versatile and can play on the right or left wing.*

*Ronaldo is also famous for his stepovers and tricks that bamboozle defenders.*

## GOALSCORING

Midfielders, especially attacking ones, must also be able to score goals. After a penetrating forward run or fast-paced attack a midfielder can often find himself in a goal-scoring position. Above, France midfielder Franck Ribéry confidently rounds the stranded Spain goalkeeper Iker Casillas to score a goal.

## GOAL HUNGRY

The best strikers have a natural instinct for goals. They are always looking to get into goal-scoring positions and to create chances. Not all strikers and forward players have the same role—some play deep and link play with the midfield, while others play farther forward, looking to poach close-range goals at the slightest opportunity.

# ON THE ATTACK

**"SOMETIMES IN FOOTBALL YOU HAVE TO SCORE GOALS."**

FRANCE AND BARCELONA STRIKER
THIERRY HENRY

The object of the game of soccer is to score goals, so it is often the all-out attacking players, such as strikers, who grab the headlines and the glory. Strikers need quick reactions, accurate shooting technique, and an eye for goal in order to turn chances into goals. However, good attacking play requires more than just the ability to score goals—awareness, positional play, passing, and determination are also key attributes.

*France striker Karim Benzema is a promising young striker and heir apparent to the great Thierry Henry.*

## HEADING

Attacking players also need to be skilled in the air. A good attacking header should be aimed downward, toward goal or into the path of a teammate. Right, Ivory Coast and Chelsea striker Didier Drogba (left) aims for the goal with a header against Liverpool.

## PENALTIES

A penalty is a high-pressure situation so nerves can play a huge part. Most players choose their spot before they strike the ball and hope that the goalkeeper dives the wrong way. Above, Spain striker David Villa takes an unsuccessful penalty in a FIFA Confederations Cup match in 2009.

## SWERVE

Being able to strike the ball in different directions takes great skill. Above, England striker Wayne Rooney turns his body and strikes across the ball to produce a fierce swerve shot. This kind of shot is very difficult for goalkeepers to save.

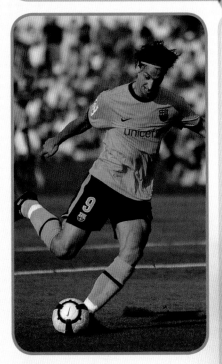

## DID YOU KNOW?

*Pelé never played at England's Wembley Stadium. So when filming an ad there long after he had retired, he couldn't resist the opportunity of scoring a "goal" on the famous Wembley turf.*

## SPECTACULAR GOALS

Scoring a goal is great, but scoring a spectacular goal is even better! Powerful shots from a distance, strikes conjured from the most impossible angles, or impressive solo skill all make fantastic goals. Below, Roma and Italy's Francesco Totti attempts an acrobatic overhead shot with his back to goal.

*An overhead kick requires great balance, good technique—and a lot of confidence!*

## PASSING

Whether it is an attacking pass or a shot on goal, timing and accuracy are vital. A pass must be accurately delivered to reach the intended teammate and perfectly timed to reach the target while he is in an onside position. Above, Barcelona striker Zlatan Ibrahimovic launches a long-range attacking pass.

# BODY MATTERS

### "FOR A PROFESSIONAL SPORTSMAN, BEING INJURED IS LIKE LIVING IN A STRANGER'S BODY."

FORMER FRANCE MIDFIELDER ROBERT PIRÈS

A player's body is the tool of his trade so he must look after it. This means working hard in training, eating the right foods, and living a healthy lifestyle. Professional players won't get far without natural talent, but agility, speed, strength, and power are also must-haves for modern players. Take a look inside the body of a super-fit player and see how it works, then check out some common soccer injuries. WARNING: SENSITIVE READERS MAY WANT TO SKIP THIS PAGE!

## WARM-UP

Players train regularly during the soccer season. They must not only practice their soccer skills, but also work on their strength and stamina. At the beginning of every training session and before a game, players prepare their muscles and increase their heart rate with special warm-up and stretching exercises. Warm-ups prepare the body for more strenuous activity and can help to prevent injury. When the game or training session is over, players "warm down" to allow their bodies to recover gradually.

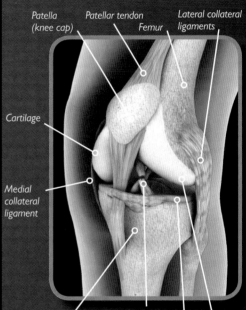

Patella (knee cap) · Patellar tendon · Femur · Lateral collateral ligaments · Cartilage · Medial collateral ligament · Tibia · Anterior and posterior cruciate ligaments · Meniscus · Cartilage

## THE PHYSICAL THERAPIST treats injuries

during a game. He or she is only allowed on the field if the referee gives permission. The physical therapist also helps players recover from long-term injuries using treatments such as massage and specially developed exercise programs.

## KNEE

Sharp turns when all the weight is borne by the knee can damage the meniscus (known as cartilage damage), while turns, awkward landings, and over extending can damage the cruciate and medial ligaments.

## FAKING IT

Players might suffer hard or dangerous tackles during a game, but sometimes the reaction can be worse than the foul! What FIFA diplomatically calls "simulation" is the kind of play acting that belongs on a movie screen, not a soccer field. Theatrical dives while clutching a supposedly injured body part are designed to fool the referee into penalizing the opposition. Unfortunately, it sometimes works...

## FOOT

From sprained ankles to broken toes, damaged tendons or severe bruising, the foot and ankle area of the body can take a lot of punishment during a soccer game. A particularly common injury is the broken metatarsal (right). The five metatarsals are the long bones which attach the toe bones (phalanxes) to the bones near the ankle (collectively known as the tarsals). The metatarsals are usually broken by impact, e.g., a mis-timed tackle or bad landing.

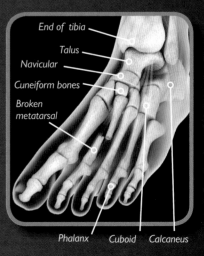

End of tibia · Talus · Navicular · Cuneiform bones · Broken metatarsal · Phalanx · Cuboid · Calcaneus

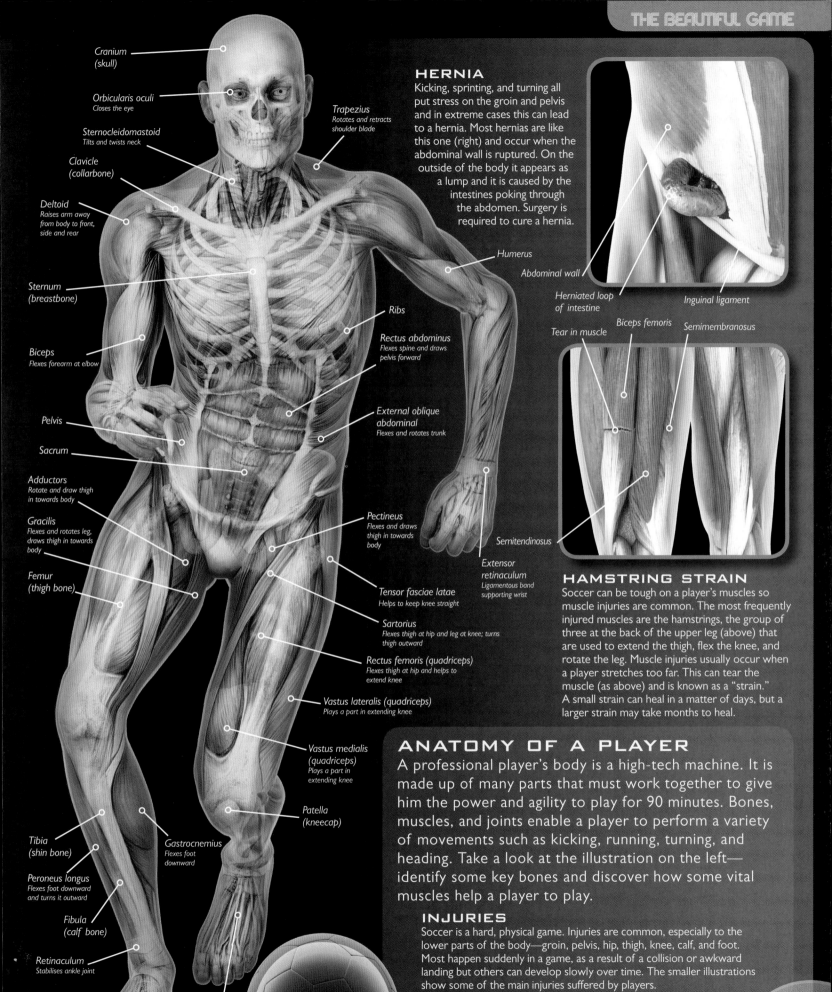

Cranium
(skull)

Orbicularis oculi
Closes the eye

Sternocleidomastoid
Tilts and twists neck

Clavicle
(collarbone)

Deltoid
Raises arm away
from body to front,
side and rear

Sternum
(breastbone)

Biceps
Flexes forearm at elbow

Pelvis

Sacrum

Adductors
Rotate and draw thigh
in towards body

Gracilis
Flexes and rotates leg,
draws thigh in towards
body

Femur
(thigh bone)

Tibia
(shin bone)

Peroneus longus
Flexes foot downward
and turns it outward

Fibula
(calf bone)

Retinaculum
Stabilises ankle joint

Trapezius
Rotates and retracts
shoulder blade

Humerus

Ribs

Rectus abdominus
Flexes spine and draws
pelvis forward

External oblique
abdominal
Flexes and rotates trunk

Pectineus
Flexes and draws
thigh in towards
body

Tensor fasciae latae
Helps to keep knee straight

Sartorius
Flexes thigh at hip and leg at knee; turns
thigh outward

Rectus femoris (quadriceps)
Flexes thigh at hip and helps to
extend knee

Vastus lateralis (quadriceps)
Plays a part in extending knee

Vastus medialis
(quadriceps)
Plays a part in
extending knee

Patella
(kneecap)

Gastrocnemius
Flexes foot
downward

Extensor
retinaculum
Ligamentous band
supporting wrist

Semitendinosus

Tendons of foot

## HERNIA

Kicking, sprinting, and turning all put stress on the groin and pelvis and in extreme cases this can lead to a hernia. Most hernias are like this one (right) and occur when the abdominal wall is ruptured. On the outside of the body it appears as a lump and it is caused by the intestines poking through the abdomen. Surgery is required to cure a hernia.

Abdominal wall

Herniated loop
of intestine

Inguinal ligament

Tear in muscle

Biceps femoris

Semimembranosus

## HAMSTRING STRAIN

Soccer can be tough on a player's muscles so muscle injuries are common. The most frequently injured muscles are the hamstrings, the group of three at the back of the upper leg (above) that are used to extend the thigh, flex the knee, and rotate the leg. Muscle injuries usually occur when a player stretches too far. This can tear the muscle (as above) and is known as a "strain." A small strain can heal in a matter of days, but a larger strain may take months to heal.

## ANATOMY OF A PLAYER

A professional player's body is a high-tech machine. It is made up of many parts that must work together to give him the power and agility to play for 90 minutes. Bones, muscles, and joints enable a player to perform a variety of movements such as kicking, running, turning, and heading. Take a look at the illustration on the left—identify some key bones and discover how some vital muscles help a player to play.

### INJURIES

Soccer is a hard, physical game. Injuries are common, especially to the lower parts of the body—groin, pelvis, hip, thigh, knee, calf, and foot. Most happen suddenly in a game, as a result of a collision or awkward landing but others can develop slowly over time. The smaller illustrations show some of the main injuries suffered by players.

# EUROPE

ICELAND

Formed in 1954, the Union of European Football Associations (UEFA) now has 53 members. It is the most powerful of the world soccer confederations and has 13 World Cup Finals places. Former Soviet countries Georgia, Armenia, Kazakhstan, and Azerbaijan are members of UEFA and so is Israel, although they are not technically part of Europe.

**"AT A TIME WHEN EUROPE IS SEEKING TO DEFINE ITSELF, NOTHING CONTRIBUTES MORE TO THIS QUEST THAN ITS LOVE FOR OUR SPORT."** UEFA PRESIDENT MICHEL PLATINI

Over the years, intensely competitive leagues such as Serie A in Italy, the Premier League in England, La Liga in Spain, and the Bundesliga in Germany have produced many world-class players. This has made Europe a powerhouse of international soccer, with many strong national teams, even from comparatively small nations such as Portugal, Greece, and Slovenia. Today, the money and prestige of European league soccer attracts the world's greatest stars to the continent.

NORTHERN IRELAND

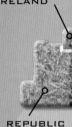

REPUBLIC OF IRELAND

## FANATICS

European fans are increasingly using soccer as a way of celebrating—and sometimes spoofing—their national stereotypes. While patriotic Norwegians, Swedes, and Danes dress as Vikings, many English fans favor the medieval knight look, while proud Scottish fans like to dig out their family tartan!

PORTUGAL

SPAIN

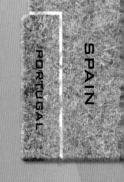

## THE ORANJE

Any city that has hosted a major soccer tournament will remember the visiting Dutch fans. Famous for their crazy orange outfits, these loyal fans often make sure that their team has the brightest and loudest support, both on and off the field.

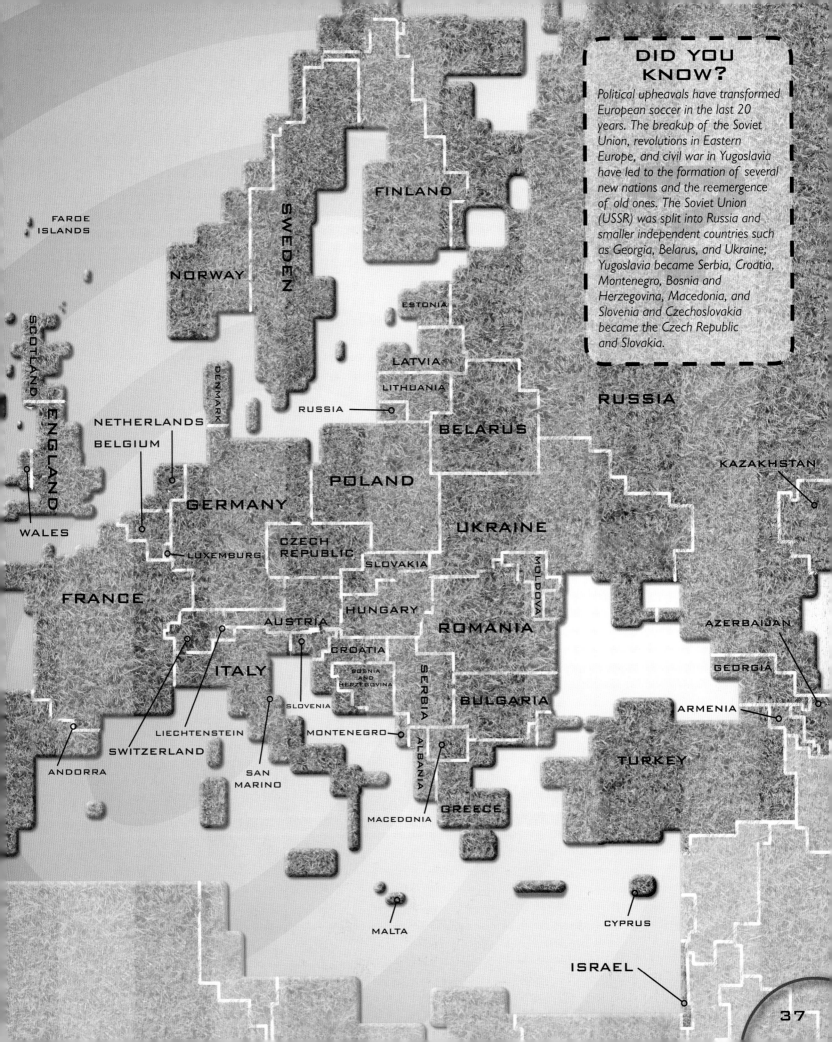

FAROE ISLANDS

FINLAND

SWEDEN

NORWAY

SCOTLAND

ENGLAND

WALES

NETHERLANDS

BELGIUM

GERMANY

LUXEMBURG

FRANCE

ANDORRA

SWITZERLAND

LIECHTENSTEIN

ITALY

SAN MARINO

DENMARK

ESTONIA

LATVIA

LITHUANIA

RUSSIA

BELARUS

RUSSIA

POLAND

CZECH REPUBLIC

SLOVAKIA

AUSTRIA

HUNGARY

CROATIA

SLOVENIA

BOSNIA AND HERZEGOVINA

MONTENEGRO

SERBIA

ALBANIA

MACEDONIA

UKRAINE

MOLDOVA

ROMANIA

BULGARIA

GREECE

KAZAKHSTAN

AZERBAIJAN

GEORGIA

ARMENIA

TURKEY

CYPRUS

MALTA

ISRAEL

# ENGLAND

*"GOD BLESS WHOEVER INVENTED FOOTBALL. IT WAS THE ENGLISH, I THINK. AND WHAT A FANTASTIC IDEA IT WAS."* ITALIAN STRIKER PAOLO ROSSI

The FA was formed in 1863 and England traditionally plays in white shirts and navy shorts. However, the current uniform is all-white and England famously won the 1966 World Cup final in a change uniform of red shirts and white shorts.

Credited as the founders of modern soccer, England is the oldest international team in the world, alongside Scotland. These two countries played the first-ever official international match in 1872. England did not play outside the British Isles until 1908 and did not enter the World Cup until 1950. Despite perennially high hopes, the team has only won one major tournament—the 1966 World Cup, in England.

## MOMENT OF GLORY

England's finest soccer playing hour came on July 30th, 1966, at Wembley Stadium. As 98,000 fans cheered the team on, it scored a famous victory in the World Cup final against West Germany. England won a thrilling game 4–2 after overtime. Some people believe that Hurst's second goal (England's third) did not fully cross the goal line, but USSR linesman Tofik Bakhramov ruled that it did.

Striker Geoff Hurst scored three goals, and remains the only player to have scored a hat trick in a World Cup final. England's other goal was scored by Martin Peters.

*England captain Bobby Moore proudly holds up the Jules Rimet trophy.*

Former England striker Gary Lineker is the only English player to top the scoring charts at a World Cup Finals. His six goals at Mexico '86 included a hat trick against Poland.

Michael Owen (right) was 18 when he scored a wonder goal against Argentina in the 1998 World Cup Finals. He ran from the center circle, through the Argentinian defense, and shot into the top corner. England still lost the second round game 4–3 on penalties.

| ENGLAND DREAM TEAM? | 1. Gordon Banks 2. Alf Ramsey 3. Ray Wilson 4. Glenn Hoddle 5. Bobby Moore 6. Billy Wright 7. Stanley Matthews 8. Bobby Charlton 9. Gary Lineker 10. Jimmy Greaves 11. Tom Finney |
|---|---|

# ENGLAND HOTSHOT

Wayne Rooney is one of English soccer's most exciting talents. The versatile and hard-working striker can play from deep in midfield or on either wing. He has great balance and a powerful shot, and his immense strength leaves opposing defenders trailing in his wake. Despite a fiery temper that saw him sent off in the 2006 World Cup quarterfinal against Portugal, Rooney has matured into a vital player for England.

*Wayne Rooney in action during England's 2010 World Cup qualifying game against Ukraine.*

## FACT FILE: ENGLAND

### NICKNAME
The Three Lions

**TOP GOAL SCORERS**
1. Bobby Charlton 49 (1958–1970)
2. Gary Lineker 48 (1984–1992)
3. Jimmy Greaves 44 (1959–1967)
4. Michael Owen 40 (1998–present)
5. Tom Finney 30 (1946–1958)
= Nat Lofthouse 30 (1950–1958)
= Alan Shearer 30 (1992–2000)

**MOST APPEARANCES**
1. Peter Shilton 125 (1970–1990)
2. David Beckham 115 (1996–present)
3. Bobby Moore 108 (1962–1973)
4. Bobby Charlton 106 (1958–1970)
5. Billy Wright 105 (1946–1959)

**TROPHIES/HONORS**
**FIFA WORLD CUP**
1966 England 4 West Germany 2 (aet)

## GOLDEN BOY

David Beckham is one of the most recognizable players in world soccer. A skillful and inspirational midfielder on the field, and a committed ambassador for the game off it, Beckham has played for Manchester United, Real Madrid, LA Galaxy, and AC Milan. He captained his country for six years and is second only to legendary goalkeeper Peter Shilton in the list of England's most-capped players.

## DID YOU KNOW?

The legendary Sir Stanley Matthews (see p. 171) achieved a series of "firsts"—he was the first Football Writers' Association Footballer of the Year (in 1948), the first European Footballer of the Year (in 1956), and the first player to be knighted (in 1965).

## MIDFIELD MEN

Chelsea's Frank Lampard (left) and Liverpool's Steven Gerrard (right) are both prolific goal scorers for club and country. Lampard is renowned for his elusive bursts into the penalty box, while Gerrard has phenomenal shooting power in his right foot. They are two of the current England team's key players and linchpins of an extremely promising midfield.

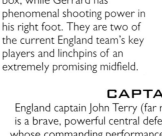

## CAPTAIN

England captain John Terry (far right) is a brave, powerful central defender whose commanding performances on the field have led to him being made captain of his club, Chelsea, as well as his country. Terry's powerful presence and heading ability also make him a goal-scoring threat.

# FRANCE

Famed for skill, flair, and entertainment, French soccer has always placed more emphasis on attack rather than the physical and tactical style favored by other European nations. Yet for all the undoubted talent of its players, France did not lift an international trophy until the 1984 European Championship. However, since then the national team has won the World Cup, and the European Championship for a second time, providing a strong challenge to Brazil's domination of the modern game.

The Fédération Française de Football was founded in 1919. French fans sing "Allez les Bleus," meaning "Go, Blues," although the uniform combines all three colors from the country's tricolor flag.

## MICHEL PLATINI

Arguably France's greatest player ever, midfielder Michel Platini was European Footballer of the Year for three consecutive years—1983, 1984, and 1985. A club player with Nancy, St. Étienne, and Juventus, he was France's top scorer for many years and managed the national side between 1988 and 1992. He was elected President of UEFA in 2007.

After narrowly failing to reach the World Cup final in 1982, the great French team of the 1980s finally won the trophy it deserved two years later, on home soil. Star players Platini, Jean Tigana, and Alain Giresse helped to secure a 2–0 victory over Spain in the European Championship final in Paris. The goals came from Platini himself (his ninth of the tournament) and Bruno Bellone.

The son of Polish immigrants, Raymond Kopaszewski, or "Kopa" for short (left), was one of the finest players of the postwar era. He was named by Pelé as one of the 125 greatest living players in a list compiled by FIFA in 2004.

## JUST FONTAINE

Striker Just Fontaine's place in soccer history is assured by his remarkable performance during the 1958 World Cup Finals in Sweden. His 13-goal total is still a tournament record for the most scored by a player at a single World Cup. France reached the semifinals but were defeated 5–2 by the eventual winners Brazil.

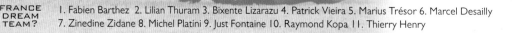

FRANCE DREAM TEAM? 1. Fabien Barthez 2. Lilian Thuram 3. Bixente Lizarazu 4. Patrick Vieira 5. Marius Trésor 6. Marcel Desailly 7. Zinedine Zidane 8. Michel Platini 9. Just Fontaine 10. Raymond Kopa 11. Thierry Henry

## ZINEDINE ZIDANE

is widely acknowledged as one of the greatest players in the history of the game. As an attacking midfielder, his range of passing, ball control, and powerful shooting made him the most influential player in the French World Cup and European Championship winning teams.

*Thierry Henry's pace is complemented by his ability to change position and confuse defenders.*

## THIERRY HENRY

Few attackers have been more feared by defenders in the last 10 years than Thierry Henry. Blessed with blistering pace, exceptional skill, and masterful movement both on and off the ball, Henry's grace and elegance disguises an almost clinical ability to punish opponents. From precise passing to spectacular finishing, Henry has it all.

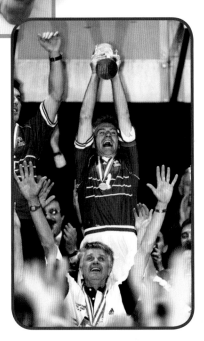

## FRANCE '98

France's finest sporting hour came on a warm evening in Paris on July 12, 1998. Sixty years after the country had last hosted the World Cup, France made the most of home advantage. Led by captain Didier Deschamps and cheered on by a passionate crowd at the Stade de France, France beat Brazil 3–0 to win the trophy for the first time.

## FACT FILE: FRANCE
### NICKNAME
Les Bleus (The Blues)

### TOP GOAL SCORERS
1. Thierry Henry 51 (1997–present)
2. Michel Platini 41 (1976–1987)
3. David Trézéguet 34 (1998–2008)
4. Zinedine Zidane 31 (1994–2006)
5. Just Fontaine 30 (1953–1960)
   = Jean-Pierre Papin 30 (1986–1995)

### MOST APPEARANCES
1. Lilian Thuram 142 (1994–2008)
2. Thierry Henry 117 (1997–present)
3. Marcel Desailly 116 (1993–2004)
4. Zinedine Zidane 108 (1994–2006)
5. Patrick Vieira 107 (1997–present)

### TROPHIES/HONORS
**FIFA WORLD CUP**
1998 France 3 Brazil 0

**UEFA EUROPEAN CHAMPIONSHIP**
2000 France 2 Italy 1 (aet)
1984 France 2 Spain 0

**OLYMPIC GOLD MEDAL**
1984 France 2 Brazil 0

**FIFA CONFEDERATIONS CUP**
2003 France 1 Cameroon 0
2001 France 1 Japan 0

## DID YOU KNOW?

*Superstitious World Cup-winning defender Laurent Blanc kissed the bald head of goalkeeper Fabien Barthez before every match because he believed it brought good luck.*

# ITALY

The Federazione Italiana Giuoco Calcio was formed in 1898. Italy's light-blue uniform is the inspiration for its famous nickname, "Azzurri."

> "YOU KNOW, THERE WILL ALWAYS BE A LITTLE BIT OF ITALY IN THIS TROPHY."
>
> SILVIO GAZZANIGA, MILANESE SCULPTOR OF THE CURRENT WORLD CUP

One of the world's great soccer nations, Italy's success is matched only by the passion of its fans. With four World Cups, Italy is the second most successful soccer nation after Brazil. Although built on a solid defensive style, the "Azzurri" have nevertheless featured some of soccer's most exciting creative talents, from Giuseppe Meazza and Sandro Mazzola to Roberto Baggio and Alessandro del Piero. Containing opponents and then hitting them with swift, skillful counterattacks are the hallmarks of Italian play.

## SPAIN '82

The 1982 World Cup final is regarded as the second best of all time, after Brazil '70. Inspired by the great Paolo Rossi and legendary goalkeeper Dino Zoff, an entertaining Italian team beat West Germany 3–1 in a game it totally dominated.

Italy's team coach Vittorio Pozzo is carried high by his squad after winning the 1934 World Cup against Czechoslovakia—the first time the Italians won the trophy. Four years later, Pozzo's team successfully defended the trophy, after winning Gold at the 1936 Olympics. Between December 1934 and 1939, Pozzo's Italy did not lose a single game.

**LUIGI "GIGI" RIVA** is Italy's all-time leading goal scorer, with 35 goals in 42 matches between 1965 to 1974. Gigi was quick and intelligent, with lightning fast reactions and great ability in the air. His powerful shot earned him the nickname "Rombo di Tuono"—or "Sound of Thunder." Here, Gigi is scoring Italy's opening goal against Yugoslavia in the 1968 European Championships final replay.

| ITALY DREAM TEAM? | 1. Dino Zoff 2. Fabio Cannavaro 3. Giacinto Facchetti 4. Gaetano Scirea 5. Franco Baresi 6. Paolo Maldini 7. Roberto Baggio 8. Gianni Rivera 9. Paolo Rossi 10. Giuseppe Meazza 11. Luigi Riva |
| --- | --- |

Roberto Baggio, or "Il Divin Codino" (The Divine Ponytail), on the way to scoring a memorable goal against Czechoslovakia in the 1990 World Cup.

## PAOLO ROSSI

Paolo Rossi's six goals helped Italy win the 1982 World Cup. He also won the Golden Boot for top scorer and Golden Ball for best player in the tournament and was named 1982 World and European Footballer of the Year.

## 2006 TRIUMPH

Italy beat France to win its fourth World Cup in 2006. It was the first all-European final since Italy last won the tournament in 1982. After extra time the score was 1–1, so for only the second time ever, the final was decided on penalties. The Italians won 5–3.

*Ecstatic captain Fabio Cannavaro holds up the 2006 World Cup.*

Gianluigi Buffon is the world's most expensive goalkeeper, and he seems worth every penny. He conceded just twice in open play—an own goal and a penalty—at the 2006 World Cup Finals.

### FACT FILE: ITALY
**NICKNAME**
Azzurri (Blues)

**TOP GOAL SCORERS**
1. Luigi Riva 35 (1965–1974)
2. Giuseppe Meazza 33 (1930–1939)
3. Silvio Piola 30 (1935–1952)
4. Roberto Baggio 27 (1988–2004)
= Alessandro Del Piero 27 (1995–present)

**MOST APPEARANCES**
1. Fabio Cannavaro 130 (1997–present)
2. Paolo Maldini 126 (1988–2002)
3. Dino Zoff 112 (1968–1983)
4. Gianluigi Buffon 99 (1997–present)
5. Giacinto Facchetti 94 (1963–1977)

**TROPHIES/HONORS**
**FIFA WORLD CUP**
1934 Italy 2 Czechoslovakia 1 (aet)
1938 Italy 4 Hungary 2
1982 Italy 3 West Germany 1
2006 Italy 1 France 1 (Italy won 5–3 in a
                      penalty shootout)

**UEFA EUROPEAN CHAMPIONSHIP**
1968 Italy 1 Yugoslavia 1 (aet)
Replay: Italy 2 Yugoslavia 0

**OLYMPIC GOLD MEDAL**
1936 Italy 1 Norway 0 (aet)

## DANIELE DE ROSSI

The 2006 World Cup Finals did not start well for midfielder Daniele De Rossi—he was sent off in the first round against US. But coach Marcelo Lippi had faith in De Rossi and he returned to the side for the final. With his battling box-to-box energy and strikes from distance, De Rossi looks set to be the hub of the national side for years to come. He even rivals Francesco Totti, another hero of 2006, in the affections of AS Roma fans.

### DID YOU KNOW?

The top scorer in the 1990 World Cup was Italian player Salvatore "Totò" Schillaci with six goals. Although Schillaci only played 16 times for his country, many Italian fans still refer to the 1990 World Cup as "Notti Magiche di Totò Schillaci" (magical nights of Totò Schillaci).

# GERMANY

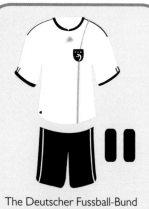

The Deutscher Fussball-Bund (soccer association) was founded in 1900. The national team's primary uniform is white shirts and black shorts, which were the colors of the 19th century Prussian state flag.

Germany is arguably the most consistent soccer nation in the world. While the national team—playing as either Germany or West Germany—may not have won the World Cup as many times as Brazil or Italy, the team has reached no less than 13 major competition finals and won a total of six tournaments. Teamwork, organization, and skill are the trademarks of "Die Nationalelf," combined with a never-say-die attitude that means no German side ever concedes defeat until the final whistle.

## GREATEST MOMENTS

Perhaps Germany's finest achievement came in the 1954 World Cup Finals. The team was beaten 8–3 in one of the earlier group games by the mighty Hungary. But, amazingly, Germany overcame the same opponents 3–2 with a fantastic comeback in the final. This unlikely victory was known as the "Miracle of Berne," after the Swiss city in which the final was played.

Germany's record goal scorer is Gerd Müller. Nicknamed "Der Bomber," he scored an amazing 68 goals in just 62 international appearances.

## "DER KAISER"

A brilliant leader known as "Der Kaiser" (the Emperor), Franz Beckenbauer also had the ability to switch defense into attack via his role as sweeper. He captained the 1974 team to World Cup victory on home soil and in 1990 became only the second man to win the trophy as a player and coach when West Germany triumphed in Italy.

Germany's World Cup triumph of 1990 was not the greatest of games, but the narrow 1–0 win over Argentina enabled West Germany to gain revenge for its defeat by the South Americans four years earlier. Victory was secured with a late penalty scored by Andreas Brehme, pictured left holding the trophy aloft.

## LOTHAR MATTHÄUS

was the modern successor to Beckenbauer. A determined, outspoken man off the field, he was just as forthright on it, driving his side to success in the 1990 World Cup. He holds the record for German international appearances with 142 caps won over a 20-year period. Matthäus was able to play as a defender or midfielder but spent most of the later stages of his career as a sweeper.

GERMANY DREAM TEAM? 1. Sepp Maier 2. Karl-Heinz Schnellinger 3. Paul Breitner 4. Wolfgang Overath 5. Lothar Matthäus 6. Franz Beckenbauer 7. Günter Netzer 8. Fritz Walter 9. Gerd Müller 10. Helmut Rahn 11. Uwe Seeler

Current Germany captain Michael Ballack is a dynamic and powerful midfielder with an eye for goal scoring and excellent heading ability. As a young player he was nicknamed "Little Kaiser," because of his similarities to the great Franz Beckenbauer.

## LAHM

Philipp Lahm is one of the world's most highly rated fullbacks. He is comfortable on both the right and the left and also offers plenty going forward. He opened the scoring at the 2006 World Cup Finals and scored a last-minute solo winner in the Euro 2008 semifinal.

Midfielder Bastian Schweinsteiger is Germany's lucky charm, since they never lose when he gets on the scoresheet. He and striker Lukas Podolski sparkled in the hosts' 2006 World Cup third-place finish.

### DID YOU KNOW?

*In the 1974 World Cup final, eventual winner West Germany was 1–0 down before it had even touched the ball! Its Dutch opponents kept the ball for two minutes from kickoff and scored a penalty.*

## FACT FILE: GERMANY
### NICKNAME
Die Nationalelf (The National Eleven)

### TOP GOAL SCORERS
1. Gerd Müller 68 (1966–1974)
2. Miroslav Klose 48 (2000–present)
3. Jürgen Klinsmann 47 (1987–1998)
= Rudi Völler 47 (1982–1994)
4. Karl-Heinz Rummenigge 45 (1976–1986)

### MOST APPEARANCES
1. Lothar Matthäus 150 (1980–2000)
2. Jürgen Klinsmann 108 (1987–1998)
3. Jürgen Kohler 105 (1986–1998)
4. Franz Beckenbauer 103 (1965–1977)
5. Thomas Hässler 101 (1988–2000)

### TROPHIES/HONORS
#### FIFA WORLD CUP
1990 West Germany 1 Argentina 0
1974 West Germany 2 Netherlands 1
1954 West Germany 3 Hungary 2

#### UEFA EUROPEAN CHAMPIONSHIP
1996 Germany 2 Czech Republic 1 (aet)
1980 West Germany 2 Belgium 1
1972 West Germany 3 USSR 0

#### OLYMPIC GAMES
1976 East Germany 3 Poland 1

### EAST GERMANY
Between 1946 and 1991 Germany was split into two nations and East Germany was overshadowed by its more successful neighbor, West Germany. When Germany became a single nation again, East German players such as Ulf Kirsten and Thomas Doll played for the new, unified team. East German-born Matthias Sammer was named European Footballer of the Year in 1996.

East Germany triumphed at the 1976 Olympics in Montreal. The 3–1 victory over Poland was a great moment in East German history, with goals from Hartmut Shade, Martin Hoffman, and Reinhard Häfner.

# NETHERLANDS

### "WE ARE THE BRAZILIANS OF EUROPE."

KEES RIJVERS, DUTCH INTERNATIONAL
1946–1960 AND MANAGER 1981–1984

The Netherlands is the greatest national team never to have won the World Cup. Despite a succession of supremely gifted players, its only major triumph has been the 1988 European Championship. Exciting, talented, and inventive it undoubtedly is, but too often disagreements between the players or an inability to rise to the occasion have let the talented "Oranje" down.

The Koninklijke Nederlandse Voetbalbond was formed in 1889. The Dutch are famous for their striking orange gear. In fact, few national teams and uniforms seem so well-matched as the exuberant Dutch and what has been described as "brilliant orange."

## MOMENT OF GLORY

When captain Ruud Gullit received the European Championship trophy in 1988, victory was made even sweeter because it came on the home soil of the team's great rivals West Germany, whom it knocked out en route to the final. In the final, Gullit scored a header and Marco van Basten a volley in a convincing victory over the Soviet Union.

## JOHAN CRUYFF

For many the greatest player of all time, Cruyff had superb technical ability. He was quick, a great passer of the ball, a fine goal scorer, and could read the game expertly. He won major honors with all his clubs, Ajax, Barcelona, and Feyenoord, and was European Footballer of the Year three times.

Gifted midfielder Arie Haan (above, right) was a member of the 1970s Dutch team and a key exponent of the famous "Total Soccer" style. During the 1978 World Cup Finals, he scored his most famous goal—a stunning 40-yard strike against Italy in the second group stage.

In 2003 the KNVB named Cruyff Dutch soccer's outstanding player of the last 50 years.

## SUPER STRIKER

Marco van Basten is regarded as one of the best strikers of all time. He scored 277 goals for Ajax, AC Milan, and the Dutch national team, including a spectacular volley in the Euro '88 final. Van Basten was European Footballer of the Year in 1988, 1989, and 1992, and World Player of the Year in 1992. As coach he led the Dutch to the second round of the 2006 World Cup and the quarterfinals of the Euro 2008 before stepping down.

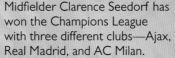

Midfielder Clarence Seedorf has won the Champions League with three different clubs—Ajax, Real Madrid, and AC Milan.

### FACT FILE: NETHERLANDS
#### NICKNAMES
Oranje, Clockwork Orange,
Orange Crush, The Orangemen

#### TOP GOAL SCORERS
1. Patrick Kluivert 40 (1994–2004)
2. Dennis Bergkamp 37 (1990–2000)
3. Faas Wilkes 35 (1946–1961)
4. Johan Cruyff 33 (1966–1977)
= Abe Lenstra 33 (1940–1959)

#### MOST APPEARANCES
1. Edwin van der Sar 130 (1995–2008)
2. Frank de Boer 112 (1990–2004)
3. Phillip Cocu 101 (1996–2006)
4. Giovanni van Bronckhorst 94 (1996–present)
5. Clarence Seedorf 87 (1994–present)

#### TROPHIES/HONORS
**UEFA EUROPEAN CHAMPIONSHIP**
1988 Netherlands 2 USSR 0

Dennis Bergkamp's fine ball control and excellent first touch, combined with quick thinking and vision, made him one of the world's top players. He was nicknamed "The Iceman" because of his calmness and he made a habit of scoring great goals, often from outside the penalty area.

### DID YOU KNOW?

*In the 1970s, the Dutch invented "Total Soccer." Under this system, every player could play in every position, giving the team a fluid formation that opponents found very difficult to play against. Although this system was great to watch, it only worked if a team had 11 super-talented players, and many coaches also felt that it gave the players too much responsibility on the field.*

### KLAAS-JAN HUNTELAAR

Klaas by name, class by nature, Klaas-Jan Huntelaar is the latest in a long line of elegant, yet deadly Dutch strikers. He made his name breaking scoring records at Heerenveen and later won big-money transfers to Ajax, Amsterdam, Real Madrid, and AC Milan. With Ruud van Nistelrooy now retired from the national team, Huntelaar is the undisputed Dutch spearhead up-front.

Wesley Sneijder is the insightful schemer at the heart of the current Dutch team's best moves. He scored two of the best goals of Euro 2008 (against Italy and France) before being named in the team of the tournament. Along with Rafael van der Vaart, Sneijder provided much of the creativity as the Dutch coasted their way through the 2010 World Cup qualifiers.

**NETHERLANDS DREAM TEAM?** 1. Edwin van der Sar 2. Wim Suurbier 3. Ruud Krol 4. Johan Neeskens 5. Ronald Koeman 6. Wim van Hanegem 7. Johan Cruyff 8. Ruud Gullit 9. Marco van Basten 10. Dennis Bergkamp 11. Johnny Rep

# SPAIN

**"REPUTATIONS DO NOT WIN MATCHES AND TROPHIES, ONLY GOALS CAN DO THAT."** REAL MADRID, ARGENTINA AND SPAIN LEGEND ALFREDO DI STÉFANO

For so many years, Spain was the great enigma of world soccer. For a country that had produced so many outstanding players, and with a population so passionate about the game, the national side had famously under-performed. But the summer of 2008 brought long overdue vindication, as Spain triumphed at the European Championships with style. It was the team's first trophy since winning the same tournament 44 years earlier.

The Real Federación Española de Fútbol was formed in 1913. The Spanish team typically plays in deep red shirts and dark blue shorts; its away uniform is either white or gold.

## VICTORIOUS HOSTS

When Spain hosted and won the European Championship in 1964, it seemed to promise a dazzling new era for the national team. Goals from Pereda and Marcelino earned Spain a 2–1 win over the USSR in the final and wild celebrations at Real Madrid's Bernabéu stadium. However, just two years later, Spain crashed out of the World Cup Finals at the group stage.

1960 European Footballer of the Year, Luis Suárez played in the 1964 final despite injury. The inspirational midfielder set up both goals.

## EMILIO BUTRAGUEÑO

Emilio Butragueño was a prolific scorer for his club Real Madrid. For the national team he scored 26 goals in 69 appearances, including four in a 5–1 thrashing of Denmark at the 1986 World Cup. He was nicknamed "El Buitre" (the Vulture) for his deadly ability to snap up chances.

*The Spanish national team celebrates in ecstatic fashion after the Euro 2008 final.*

*Butragueño in action against Northern Ireland at the 1986 World Cup Finals.*

## OVERDUE SUCCESS

It was a long time coming, but when Spain finally broke its big tournament jinx, the team did it as the runaway winner of Euro 2008. Coached by veteran Luis Aragonés and captained by goalkeeper Iker Casillas, it dazzled with both efficiency and quick-passing panache. It even enjoyed a first competitive win in 88 years over old European rival Italy.

SPAIN DREAM TEAM? 1. Ricardo Zamora 2. Marquitos 3. José Antonio Camacho 4. Luis Suárez 5. Miguel Ángel Nadal 6. Fernando Hierro 7. Amancio Amaro 8. Alfredo Di Stéfano 9. Emilio Butragueño 10. Raúl 11. Francisco Gento

## RAÚL

Raúl González Blanco is Spain's top scorer. He scored 44 goals in 102 appearances and earned a reputation as one of the best European strikers of the last 10 years. With Real Madrid his honors include three Champions League titles.

*Torres in action in the 2009 FIFA Confederations Cup.*

## FACT FILE: SPAIN

### NICKNAMES
La Furia Roja (The Red Fury),
La Selección (The Selection)

### TOP GOAL SCORERS
1. Raúl 44 (1996–2006)
2. David Villa 33 (2005–present)
3. Fernando Hierro 29 (1989–2002)
4. Fernando Morientes 27 (1998–2007)
5. Emilio Butragueño 26 (1984–1992)

### MOST APPEARANCES
1. Andoni Zubizaretta 126 (1985–1998)
2. Raúl 102 (1996–2006)
3. Iker Casillas 99 (2000–present)
4. Fernando Hierro 89 (1989–2002)
5. José Antonio Camacho 81 (1975–1988)

### TROPHIES/HONORS

#### UEFA EUROPEAN CHAMPIONSHIP
2008 Spain 1 Germany 0
1964 Spain 2 USSR 1

#### OLYMPIC GOLD MEDAL
1992 Poland 2 Spain 3

*Torres possesses pace, balance, and an abundance of skill.*

## DID YOU KNOW?

*Foreign players were banned from playing in the Spanish league from 1963 to 1973. It was felt that the high number of non-Spanish players was affecting the development of homegrown players and thereby having a negative impact on the national team. The ban was lifted when Barcelona signed the talented Dutchman Johan Cruyff.*

## SUPER STRIKER

Fernando Torres is the latest hero of Spanish soccer. After a rapid rise at his boyhood favorites Atlético Madrid, he moved to Liverpool in 2007 for a transfer fee of $43 million. The striker, nicknamed "El Niño" (the Kid), confirmed his superstar status with the winning goal against Germany in the final of Euro 2008.

Spanish hopes for future success rest on the shoulders of young players like Cesc Fàbregas (far right). The outstanding midfielder broke into the national team at the age of 18 in 2006, three years after he had won the Golden Shoe for top goal scorer and Golden Ball for best player at the FIFA U-17 World Championships.

# RUSSIA

*"ANDREY ARSHAVIN IS A PLAYER WHO MAKES QUICK DECISIONS AND WHO CAN CREATE DANGER."* RUSSIA MANAGER GUUS HIDDINK

Russia enjoyed some success as the USSR (see below) but has failed to make an impression at the World Cup in recent years, despite a rich soccer heritage and some prestigious domestic clubs. At Euro 2008 Russia was a definite contender but twice came up against the unstoppable Spain.

Russia's traditional red shirts have been replaced by maroon ones, with gold socks for 2010. Their second uniform is white.

## FACT FILE: Russia

### TOP GOAL SCORERS*
1. Vladimir Beschastnykh 26 (1992–2003)
2. Valeriy Karpin 17 (1992–2003)
3. Andrey Arshavin 16 (2002–present)
4. Roman Pavlyuchenko 15 (2003–present)
= Dmitriy Sychev 15 (2002–present)
= Aleksandr Kerzhakov 15 (2002–present)

### MOST APPEARANCES*
1. Viktor Onopko 109 (1992–2004)
2. Valery Karpin 72 (1992–2003)
3. Vladimir Beschastnykh 71 (1992–2003)
4. Sergei Semak 64 (1997–present)
5. Dmitriy Alenichev 55 (1996–2005)
= Yuriy Nikiforov 55 (1992–2002
= Aleksei Smertin 55 (1998–2006)

### TROPHIES/HONORS
(Competing as the USSR)
**UEFA EUROPEAN CHAMPIONSHIP**
1960 USSR 2 Yugoslavia 1 (aet)
(Competing as Russia)
none

* Does not include goals or appearances for the USSR

## USSR
Until 1992 Russia was part of the USSR (Union of Soviet Socialist Republics). When the Soviet Union broke up into separate countries including Russia, Ukraine, and Belarus, the USSR's records were officially attributed to Russia by FIFA.

USSR beat Yugoslavia 2–1 (aet) in the first ever European Championship final in Paris in 1960.

Arshavin was also made Russia captain in June 2009.

## LEV YASHIN
A superb goalkeeper who spent his whole career at Dinamo Moscow, Lev Yashin is the only keeper ever to win European Footballer of the Year (1963). Nicknamed "Black Spider" because of his all black uniform, it's claimed that he saved over 150 penalties during his career.

Despite playing 47 games in defense, Vasili Rats (above) will always be remembered for a superb goal against France at the 1986 World Cup Finals. His thumping shot from over 35 yards beat the French goalkeeper, Joel Bats.

## ARSHAVIN
Andrey Arshavin is one of Russian soccer's big stars. A creative and dynamic striker, who can also play in midfield, he was voted Russian Footballer of the Year in 2006. After a brilliant Euro 2008, he attracted the attention of Europe's big clubs and finally signed for Arsenal in 2009.

RUSSIA DREAM TEAM? 1. Lev Yashin 2. Mikhail Ogonkov 3. Albert Shesternyov 4. Sergei Ignashevich 5. Viktor Onopko 6. Valery Karpin 7. Dmitri Sychev 8. Valery Voronin 9. Vladimir Beschastnykh 10. Andrey Arshavin 11. Andrey Kanchelskis

# CROATIA

*"WEMBLEY WAS A SPECIAL STORY, A GLORIOUS NIGHT AT A WORLD-FAMOUS STADIUM."*

SLAVEN BILIC ON CROATIA'S 3–2
WIN OVER ENGLAND IN 2007

Croatia's uniform is very distinctive. The home shirt's famous red-and-white checkered pattern is based on the national flag. Croatia's second uniform is a more sober blue.

Croatia was the first team of the ex-Yugoslavia countries to make headlines, with third place at France '98. Despite a 3–2 victory at Wembley to deny England a place at Euro 2008, and a quarterfinal place at that tournament, Croatia failed to qualify for the 2010 World Cup Finals.

## FACT FILE: CROATIA

### NICKNAME
Vatreni (The Fiery Ones)

### TOP GOAL SCORERS
1. Davor Šuker 45 (1990–2002)
2. Darijo Srna 17 (2002–present)
3. Goran Vlaovi 16 (1992–2002)
= Eduardo da Silva 16 (2004–present)
5. Niko Kovac 15 (1996–2008)

### MOST APPEARANCES
1. Dario Simic 100 (1996–2008)
2. Robert Kovac 84 (1999–present)
3. Niko Kovac 83 (1996–2008)
4. Robert Jarni 81 (1990–2002)
5. Stipe Pletikosa 79 (1999–present)

### TROPHIES/HONORS
none

*Slaven Bilic believes that only Kaká is better than Modric.*

## DAVOR SUKER

A stylish and prolific striker, Davor Šuker (above, center) won the Golden Boot at the 1998 World Cup Finals after scoring six goals in seven games. Still the leading Croatian goal scorer of all time with 45 goals, he's also the only Croatian to be named on FIFA's list of the 125 best players of all time.

## MODRIC

Croatia's playmaker, Luka Modric, is a clever player who can conjure up defense-splitting passes with either foot. He is also prepared to do what it takes, whether playing in central midfield or out on the wing. In short, he is a manager's dream and a big favorite at Tottenham, which he joined in 2008.

### DID YOU KNOW?

*During a match between Croatia and Australia at the 2006 World Cup Finals, defender Josip Simunic was shown three yellow cards over the course of the match by referee Graham Poll, but he never actually sent him off!*

No-nonsense defender Slaven Bilic (above, right) was a key player in Croatia's World Cup adventure in 1998. He spent most of his career at Hadjuk Split, followed by a few seasons in England, with West Ham United and Everton. Bilic went on to manage the national side and is considered one of the best young coaches in world soccer.

Brazilian-born striker Eduardo Da Silva adds flair to the Croatian team. He joined Dinamo Zagreb as a 17-year-old and his 73 goals in just over 100 games soon had the soccer world sitting up and taking notice. Arsenal signed Eduardo in 2007, before an horrific broken leg in 2008 kept him out of the game for a year.

CROATIA DREAM TEAM? 1. Vladimir Beara 2. Dario Šimic 3. Robert Jarni 4. Zvonimir Boban 5. Igor Štimac 6. Slaven Bilic 7. Dario Srna 8. Robert Prosinecki 9. Stjepan Bobek 10. Davor Šuker 11. Luka Modric

# SERBIA

**"WE HAVE WRITTEN A NEW PAGE IN SERBIA'S SOCCER HISTORY."**

SERBIA COACH RADOMIR ANTIC ON
QUALIFYING FOR SOUTH AFRICA 2010

In 2006 Serbia adopted a new uniform of red shirts, blue shorts, and white socks, with an all white second choice uniform.

Although local rival Croatia enjoyed earlier success after the breakup of the former Yugoslavia, it is Serbia that now looks to be leading the way. It topped a difficult qualifying group ahead of favorites France to reach the 2010 World Cup Finals in South Africa.

## FACT FILE: SERBIA

### NICKNAMES
Beli Orlovi (White Eagles), Plavi (Blues)

### TOP GOAL SCORERS
1. Savo Milosevic 37 (1994–2008)
2. Predrag Mijatovic 28 (1989–2003)
3. Dejan Savicevic 19 (1986–2003)
4. Mateja Kezman 17 (2000–2006)
5. Dragan Stojkovic 15 (1983–2001)

### MOST APPEARANCES
1. Savo Milosevic 102 (1994–2008)
2. Dejan Stankovic 85 (1998–present)
3. Dragan Stojkovic 84 (1983–2001)
4. Predrag Mijatovic 73 (1989–2003)
5. Slavisa Jokanovic 64 (1991–2002)
= Sinisa Mihajlovic 64 (1991–2003)

### TROPHIES/HONORS
none

## YUGOSLAVIA

When Yugoslavia broke up in the 1990s, the old national soccer team formed the basis for the new Serbian squad. Confusingly, they called themselves the Federal Republic of Yugoslavia at both the 1998 World Cup and Euro 2000. In 2006, a united Serbia and Montenegro team entered the World Cup, but the two countries went their separate ways, paving the way for a team called simply "Serbia" for the first time.

Dragan Stojkovic (above) was a key player for Yugoslavia during the1980s and 90s. The legendary forward also played club soccer for Red Star Belgrade, Marseille, and Nagoya Grampus Eight, which he later managed.

*Stankovic is Serbia's creator-in-chief.*

Savo Milošević is a double record holder for Serbia, with 102 appearances and 37 goals. At Euro 2000, his five goals for Yugoslavia saw him finish joint lead scorer with Holland's Patrick Kluivert. He spent time playing in England, Italy, and Spain, and scored more than 200 career goals.

## DEJAN STANKOVIC

The national side's captain pulls the strings in midfield, whether it's marshaling the team from the center or providing an attacking option out on the wing. Stankovic plays his club soccer in Italy, and having notched up well over 100 games for Lazio, he's now heading for the 200 mark at Inter.

*Stankovic has a wicked shot.*

Tall, strong, and great in the air, Nemanja Vidic (right) is a rock at the heart of Serbia's defense. He was part of the back four that set a record by conceding just one goal during the whole 2006 World Cup qualifying campaign. Four years later he once again played a key role.

SERBIA DREAM TEAM? 1. Dragan Pantelic 2. Mladen Krstajic 3. Zoran Mirkovic 4. Nemanja Vidic 5. Siniša Mihajlovic 6. Dejan Stankovic 7. Ilija Petkovic 8. Dragan Stojkovic 9. Savo Milosevic 10. Pedja Mijatovic 11. Dragan Džajic

# PORTUGAL

"IF WE HAVE TO PLAY UGLY TO REACH THE OBJECTIVE, WE WILL PLAY UGLY."

FORMER MANAGER LUIZ FELIPE SCOLARI
BEFORE THE 2006 WORLD CUP FINALS

Portugal's uniform has gradually gotten brighter in the last few years, moving from maroon and green to a more vivid red and green. Its change uniform is a simple white.

With a passionate soccer culture and a history of gifted players and great club sides, Portugal has all the ingredients for international success. Yet for all its promise, the team has not yet realized its potential. It came close at Euro 2004, but lost the final to Greece.

## FACT FILE: PORTUGAL

**NICKNAME**
Seleção das Quinas (Team of the Five)

**TOP GOAL SCORERS**
1. Pauleta 47 (1997–2006)
2. Eusébio 41 (1961–1973)
3. Luís Figo 32 (1991–2006)
4. Nuno Gomes 29 (1996–present)
5. Rui Costa 26 (1993–2004)

**MOST APPEARANCES**
1. Luís Figo 127 (1991–2006)
2. Fernando Couto 110 (1990–2004)
3. Rui Costa 94 (1993–2004)
4. Pauleta 88 (1997–2006)
5. João Vieira Pinto 81 (1991–2002)

**TROPHIES/HONORS**
none

*In 2009 Ronaldo transferred from Manchester United to Real Madrid.*

## EUSÉBIO
Nicknamed the Black Panther, Eusébio (above, left) scored an incredible 41 goals in just 64 games for Portugal. He was voted European Footballer of the Year in 1965 and won an astonishing number of trophies, including 11 league titles and two European Cups, during 15 years with Portuguese giants Benfica.

Portugal's all time top scorer, Pauleta (above) is a player who had the striker's knack of being in the right place at the right time. He's also the only player from the Azores to have represented Portugal.

## RONALDO
Portuguese captain and midfield playmaker, Cristiano Ronaldo is a soccer superstar and was named World Player of the Year in 2008. Lightning quick, he can play on either wing and baffle defenders with endless step overs. He also has a ferocious shot and is great in the air.

### DID YOU KNOW?
*Portugal and England have a lot of soccer history. Portugal was third at the 1966 World Cup after losing to England in the semifinals. Its record defeat was 10–0 against England in 1945, but Portugal knocked England out of Euro 2004 and the 2006 World Cup, both on penalties.*

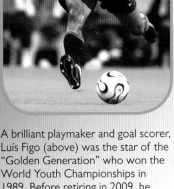

A brilliant playmaker and goal scorer, Luís Figo (above) was the star of the "Golden Generation" who won the World Youth Championships in 1989. Before retiring in 2009, he played club soccer for Sporting Lisbon, Barcelona, Real Madrid, and Inter Milan.

PORTUGAL DREAM TEAM? 1. Vítor Baía 2. João Pinto 3. Rui Jorge 4. Ricardo Carvalho 5. Fernando Couto 6. Rui Costa 7. Luís Figo 8. Cristiano Ronaldo 9. Eusébio 10. Nuno Gomes 11. Pauleta

# GREECE

*"THE GREEKS HAVE MADE FOOTBALL HISTORY. IT'S A SENSATION!"*

GREECE COACH OTTO REHHAGEL
AFTER WINNING EURO 2004

Although a type of soccer was played in Ancient Greece as long ago as 200 BC, Greece had to wait until 2004 for its first trophy. Despite being rank outsider in that year's European Championship, it pulled off one of the greatest shocks in world soccer when it edged out hosts Portugal 1–0 in the final.

The Hellenic Football Federation was founded in 1926. Greece traditionally played in a blue uniform, but since the Euro 2004 triumph, Greece has played in all-white, with blue used as a change uniform.

Nikos Anastopoulos, or "Moustakias" (Moustachioed One) is Greece's all-time highest scorer. Good in the air as well as with his feet, he tormented defenses in the Greek national league throughout the 1970s and 80s, finally notching up well over 200 career goals.

## DID YOU KNOW?

*In 2006, Greece took on Australia in a friendly game at the famous Melbourne Cricket Ground and 95,000 people turned up to see the Socceroos win 1–0.*

Greece's player with the most appearances, at 120, Theo Zagorakis (left) was an inspiration during Euro 2004. This tough tackling midfielder's no-nonsense style of play earned him the title Player of the Tournament. Unbelievably, he only scored three times for his country, and it took him over 100 games before he hit the first one!

## EURO 2004

A solid, practical, and defensive approach brought Greece an unlikely victory in 2004. Angelos Christeas headed the only goal of the game after 57 minutes. The Greeks then soaked up wave after wave of Portuguese pressure, but hung on to lift the trophy for the first time.

*Before Euro 2004, Greece had not won a game at an international tournament!*

German coach Otto Rehhagel (above) took over the Greek team in 2001. Often criticized for playing "boring" soccer, Rehhagel was voted "Greek of the Year" after Euro 2004, the first foreigner ever to win the award!

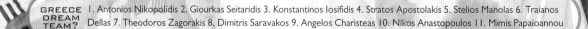

GREECE DREAM TEAM? 1. Antonios Nikopolidis 2. Giourkas Seitaridis 3. Konstantinos Iosifidis 4. Stratos Apostolakis 5. Stelios Manolas 6. Traianos Dellas 7. Theodoros Zagorakis 8. Dimitris Saravakos 9. Angelos Christeas 10. Nikos Anastopoulos 11. Mimis Papaioannou

# UKRAINE

*"REACHING THE QUARTER-FINALS AT OUR FIRST ATTEMPT IS VERY SPECIAL AND A UNIQUE ACHIEVEMENT FOR UKRAINE."*

FORMER NATIONAL BOSS OLEG BLOKHIN AT THE 2006 WORLD CUP FINALS

The Football Federation of Ukraine was formed in 1991 and joined FIFA in 1992. The team's colors reflects the yellow and blue of the national flag.

The modern Ukraine team only came into being in 1991 (see p. 37), but the national team has established itself as a major force in European soccer. In its first-ever World Cup in 2006, it reached the quarterfinals before losing to the eventual winner, Italy.

Oleg Blokhin's 112 appearances for the old Soviet Union will always remain a record, as will his 42 goals. Pictured left (middle), he was voted Ukrainian Footballer of the Year an incredible 9 times, and also managed the national team for four years in the 2000s.

Ukraine's shot stopper with the most appearances, Oleksandr Shovkovskiy (right) has played more games for his country than all Ukraine's other keepers added together! He's a penalty taker's worst nightmare too, and once saved three in a game playing for Dinamo Kiev against Shakhtar Donetsk.

## REBROV

The other half of a deadly striking partnership with Shevchenko, Serhiy Rebrov (above) scored 15 goals for his country, including a stunning 35 yard scorcher against Saudi Arabia at the 2006 World Cup. He was voted Ukrainian Footballer of the Year twice and is the Ukrainian Premier League's all-time top scorer. In 2009 Rebrov retired from the game to focus on coaching.

## FACT FILE: UKRAINE

### NICKNAME
Zhovto-Blakytni (The Yellow-Blues)

**TOP GOAL SCORERS**
1. Andriy Shevchenko 43 (1995–present)
2. Serhiy Rebrov 15 (1992–2006)
3. Serhiy Nazarenko 11 (2003–2007)
4. Andriy Vorobei 9 (2000–2008)
= Andriy Husin 9 (1993–2006)

**MOST APPEARANCES**
1. Andriy Shevchenko 94 (1995–present)
2. Anatoliy Tymoschuk 92 (2000–present)
3. Oleksandr Shovkovskiy 86 (1994–present)
4. Serhiy Rebrov 75 (1992–2006)
5. Andriy Husin 71 (1993–2006)

**TROPHIES/HONORS**
none

## SHEVCHENKO

Quite simply a goal-scoring legend, Ukraine's captain and star striker, Andriy Shevchenko keeps opposition goalkeepers very busy. He's officially the fourth most prolific player in European soccer, having scored 61 goals in club competitions such as the Champions League.

*During his eight years at AC Milan, Shevchenko scored a staggering 175 goals.*

## DID YOU KNOW?

*Since the Ukrainian national league was started in 1992, soccer ace Dinamo Kiev has won it an astonishing 13 times.*

UKRAINE DREAM TEAM? 1. Oleksandr Shovkovskiy 2. Vladimir Bessonov 3. Andriy Nesmachniy 4. Anatoliy Tymoschuk 5. Vladyslav Vashchuk 6. Oleg Luzhny 7. Oleksiy Mykhaylychenko 8. Volodymyr Muntyan 9. Andriy Shevchenko 10. Oleg Blokhin 11. Anatoly Demyanenko

# TURKEY

Not long ago Turkey was one of the minnows of European soccer, but today it is a team to be reckoned with in world soccer. In 2002 the team surprised everyone by reaching the semifinals of the World Cup, and at Euro 2008 only a last minute Germany goal prevented Turkey from making it all the way to the final.

One of the world's most reliable goalkeepers, Rüstü Reçber (left) has had more appearances for Turkey than any other player. He retired after Euro 2008 but the team missed him so much the manager convinced him to reconsider.

An elegant attacking player, Tuncay Sanli (above, right) is the current team's midfield motivator. A passionate player, who wears the captain's arm band with pride, Tuncay is a true team player and once played in goal, after keeper Volkan Demirel was sent off.

Hakan Sükür is also the proud scorer of the fastest goal in World Cup history, having found the net in just 10.8 seconds against Republic of Korea at the 2002 finals. The powerful forward scored more than 380 career goals and is his country's top scorer.

**TURKEY DREAM TEAM?** 1. Rüstü Reçber 2. Fatih Akyel 3. Abdullah Ercan 4. Bülent Korkmaz 5. Alpay Özalan 6. Tugay Kerimoglu 7. Tuncay Sanlı 8. Emre Belözoglu 9. Hakan Sükür 10. Lefter Küçükandonyadis 11. Metin Oktay

# SCOTLAND

Despite being a nation of just five million people, Scotland has enjoyed some epic international campaigns. Although the team has never won a trophy, it is one of the oldest and best supported national sides and has produced some truly world-class players.

In the 1978 World Cup Finals, Archie Gemmill skipped through the Dutch defense to score one of the greatest-ever World Cup goals (pictured left). Sadly, Scotland had already lost to Peru and did not make it past the competition's first round.

Scotland can have hope for the future thanks to promising players such as Sunderland's Craig Gordon, Manchester United's Darren Fletcher (above, right), and Birmingham's James McFadden. Two 1–0 victories over France in the qualifiers for Euro 2008 show that Scotland can get results in big matches.

Kenny Dalglish (left) was one of the world's finest players during the 1970s and early 1980s. A skillful and creative forward, he was known as "King Kenny" by the Tartan Army—the name given to Scotland's passionate and devoted fans—and is arguably the greatest player Scotland has ever produced. Dalglish is also an icon at Liverpool where he has been both a player and manager.

**SCOTLAND DREAM TEAM?** 1. Jim Leighton 2. Danny McGrain 3. Tommy Boyd 4. Alan Hansen 5. Alex McLeish 6. Graeme Souness 7. Kenny Dalglish 8. Archie Gemmill 9. Denis Law 10. Ally McCoist 11. Gordon Strachan

# SLOVENIA

Since joining UEFA in 1992, Slovenia has been quick to assert itself as a team to watch. The team qualified for both Euro 2000 and the 2002 World Cup Finals. Seven years, later it overcame a strong and much-favored Russia team in a two-legged playoff to reach the 2010 World Cup Finals in South Africa.

Milenko Acimovic (left) is a skillful midfield playmaker. He once scored with an incredible shot from the halfway line in a game against Ukraine that saw Slovenia qualify for Euro 2000.

**FACT FILE**
**TOP GOAL SCORER**
Zlatko Zahovic 35 (1992–2004)
**MOST APPEARANCES**
Zlatko Zahovic 80 (1992–2004)

**TROPHIES/HONORS**
none

# LATVIA

Latvia gained independence from Russia in 1991 and so began a new era for the national soccer team. The team made it through to the finals of Euro 2004 after winning a playoff against Turkey, and in 2009 pushed Greece hard for a place in the World Cup Finals, but ultimately missed out and had to settle for third place in its group.

A commanding midfielder, who has spent most of his career with Latvian side Skonto FC, Vitalijs Astafjevs (left) looks set to overtake Estonia's Martin Reim and break the record for the most international appearances by a European.

**FACT FILE**
**TOP GOAL SCORER**
Maris Verpakovskis 26 (1999–present)
**MOST APPEARANCES**
Vitalijs Astafjevs 157 (1992–present)

**TROPHIES/HONORS**
none

**FACT FILE**
**TOP GOAL SCORER**
Sven Rydell 49 (1923–1932)
**MOST APPEARANCES**
Thomas Ravelli 143 (1981–1997)

**TROPHIES/HONORS**
OLYMPIC GOLD MEDAL
1948 Sweden 3 Yugoslavia 1

# SWEDEN

The story of Swedish soccer is one of only moderate success. The team reached the World Cup final when it played host in 1958, and was the losing semifinalist in 1994. On both occasions, the victor was Brazil.

In 1958 Sweden made it through to the final of the World Cup (left). It was 1–0 up after four minutes against Brazil, but then a young player named Pelé took control of the game, and Brazil won 5–2.

Henrik Larsson (above) was the mainstay of the Swedish side for more than ten years. A clinical finisher, Larsson could play up front or in midfield.

Despite once suffering an international goal drought that lasted two years, Zlatan Ibrahimovic (right, middle) averages about a goal every three games for Sweden. Barcelona made the tall, powerful striker the second most expensive player in history when it gave Inter Milan a check for just over $100 million Euros in 2009.

SWEDEN DREAM TEAM? 1. Thomas Ravelli 2. Roland Nilsson 3. Bengt Gustavsson 4. Niels Liedholm 5. Patrik Andersson 6. Bjorn Nordqvist 7. Frederik Ljungberg 8. Henrik Larsson 9. Gunnar Nordahl 10. Zlatan Ibrahimovic 11. Sven Rydell

57

# REPUBLIC OF IRELAND

Although Gaelic games such as Gaelic football and hurling are hugely popular in the Republic of Ireland, soccer is the country's most popular team sport. A period of success began in the late 1980s with stars such as Niall Quinn, Ray Houghton, and Roy Keane taking them to the World Cup quarterfinals in Italia '90. In recent years, a talented Irish squad has enjoyed mixed fortunes, including a heartbreaking 2010 World Cup playoff defeat to France.

### ROBBIE KEANE

Striker Robbie Keane made his debut at 17 and is now his country's captain as well as top goal scorer. A goal poacher for club sides including Tottenham Hotspur and Leeds United, Keane is also the tenth highest scorer in the history of the Premier League.

As well as making more appearances than any other player, Steve Staunton (left) has also captained and managed the national side. He is the only player to have played in all of the country's 13 matches at World Cup Finals.

No Irish fan will ever forget Ray Houghton's (right) looping shot against Italy at USA '94. The ball just dipped in under the bar to give the Irish a famous 1–0 win and help them move into the second round.

REPUBLIC OF IRELAND DREAM TEAM? 1. Shay Given 2. Gary Kelly 3. Steve Staunton 4. Roy Keane 5. Paul McGrath 6. David O'Leary 7. Ray Houghton 8. Johnny Giles 9. Niall Quinn 10. Robbie Keane 11. Liam Brady.

# POLAND

So far, Poland has not quite lived up to its promise. The country's golden era came between the World Cups of 1974 and 1982, when it finished third, twice. That side also won medals at the Olympics but incredibly, until 2008, Poland has never qualified for a European Championships.

In recent years Jerzy Dudek (left) has been one of Poland's most consistent players. His three penalty saves for Liverpool against Milan led to a famous victory in the 2005 Champions League final.

Jan Tomaszewski (right) was labeled "The man who stopped England'" after a man of the match performance in 1974 denied England a place at the World Cup Finals.

Lukasz Fabianski (left) was twice voted Polish Goalkeeper of the Season while at Legia Warsaw and is regarded as the best of a number of young Polish goalkeepers currently coming through the ranks in Poland.

A key part of the successful Polish side of the 1970s, Grzegorz Lato's (right) seven goals at the 1974 World Cup won him the Golden Boot award. His instinct for goal scoring and direct style of play saw the right winger score 45 goals in 95 games for his country.

POLAND DREAM TEAM? 1. Jan Tomaszewski 2. Antoni Szymanowski 3. Michał Żewłakow 4. Jacek Krzynówek 5. Władysław Żmuda 6. Jacek Bąk 7. Grzegorz Lato 8. Kazimierz Deyna 9. Ernest Pol 10. Włodzimierz Lubanski 11. Zbigniew Boniek

# BULGARIA

Bulgaria's finest hour came in the 1994 World Cup Finals in the US. It beat the holders Germany 2–1 in the quarterfinal before losing by the same score to Italy in the semifinal.

A speedy left winger with a fiery temper, Hristo Stoichkov (far left) could unleash shots from anywhere, and is regarded as one of Bulgaria's all-time greats.

Manchester United forward Dimitar Berbatov (above) has already bagged 48 goals for his country, making him Bulgaria's leading scorer.

## FACT FILE

**TOP GOAL SCORER**
Dimitar Berbatov 48 (1999–present)

**MOST APPEARANCES**
Borislav Mikhailov 102 (1983–1998)

**TROPHIES/HONORS**
none

# ESTONIA

Estonia is trailing behind its Baltic neighbors Latvia and Lithuania, which have both made more of an impact on world soccer. However, Estonia did come close to qualifying for the 2006 World Cup Finals after five group wins, including an encouraging 2–1 victory over rival Latvia.

With a phenomenal 157 appearances, Martin Reim (left) is one of the most prolific European players ever, although Latvia's Vitalijs Astafjevs looks set to overtake him. The Estonian defender played his first match for his country in 1992 and finally hung up his cleats 17 years later, in 2009.

## FACT FILE

**TOP GOAL SCORER**
Andres Oper 35 (1995–present)

**MOST APPEARANCES**
Martin Reim 157 (1992–2009)

**TROPHIES/HONORS**
none

# HUNGARY

Modern soccer owes much to the great Hungarian team of the 1950s. "The Magnificent Magyars" pioneered a fast and skillful style, with imaginative passing and movement. However, in recent times Hungary has struggled to make an impact on the international stage.

Ferenc Puskás (right) is widely regarded as one of the world's best-ever players. He scored 84 goals in just six years for Hungary, before changing nationality and appearing for Spain. Puskás was part of a team that twice thrashed England and also scored an incredible 27 goals in just five games on the way to the 1954 World Cup Final. Unfortunately, Hungary was defeated 3–2 by West Germany in the final.

Puskás averaged nearly a goal a game across a 23 year career.

After 63 games, and 18 goals, Zoltan Gera (above, center) called a time out on his international career. A gifted playmaker with great vision, Gera has played club soccer for both West Bromwich Albion and Fulham in England.

## FACT FILE

**TOP GOAL SCORER**
Ferenc Puskás 84 (1945–1956)

**MOST APPEARANCES**
József Bozsik 101 (1947–1962)

**TROPHIES/HONORS**
**OLYMPIC GOLD MEDAL**
1968 Hungary 4 Bulgaria 1
1964 Hungary 2 Czechoslovakia 1
1952 Hungary 2 Yugoslavia 0

**HUNGARY DREAM TEAM?** 1. Gyula Grosics 2. Jeno Buzánszky 3. Mihály Lantos 4. József Bozsik 5. László Bálint 6. József Zakarias 7. Zoltán Czibor 8. Flórián Albert 9. Nándor Hidegkuti 10. Ferenc Puskás 11. Sándor Kocsis

## BOSNIA-HERZEGOVINA

Another team that appeared after the breakup of Yugoslavia, Bosnia-Herzegovina played its first competitive games in the qualifying campaign for Euro 2004. After several fantastic performances in its 2010 World Cup qualifying group, including wins over Belgium and Estonia, it lost a two-legged playoff to Portugal and missed out on the Finals.

Prolific marksman Edin Džeko (left) scored 9 goals in Bosnia's unsuccessful bid to reach South Africa 2010. His 26 goals for German club Wolfsburg in the 2008-09 season helped it to its first-ever German league title and also saw Džeko crowned Bundesliga Player of the Year.

### FACT FILE
**TOP GOAL SCORER**
Elvir Bolic 24 (1996–2006)
**MOST APPEARANCES**
Elvir Bolic 55 (1996–2006)

**TROPHIES/HONORS**
none

## BELARUS

Formed after the breakup of the old Soviet Union, Belarus is still looking for a major international breakthrough. The signs are encouraging, with the team having beat the Netherlands twice and had a 1–0 victory over Scotland in 2009.

An attacking midfielder who has played for Arsenal, Barcelona, and Stuttgart, Aliaksandr Hleb (left) is the national team captain. He has played more than 50 games for the side.

### FACT FILE
**TOP GOAL SCORER**
Maksim Romaschenko 20 (2000-present)
**MOST APPEARANCES**
Sergei Gurenko 80 (1994–2006)
= Aliaksandr Kulchiy 80 (1996–present)

**TROPHIES/HONORS**
none

### FACT FILE
**TOP GOAL SCORER**
Gheorghe Hagi 35 (1983–2000)
**MOST APPEARANCES**
Dorinel Munteanu 134 (1991–2007)

**TROPHIES/HONORS**
none

## ROMANIA

The Romania team of the 1990s was the best so far and made the quarterfinals of USA '94 and Euro 2000. That team revolved around Gheorghe Hagi, a strong, skillful playmaker. Since then, Romanian soccer has produced a few stars, such as Adrian Mutu, but the team hasn't reached the heights of the 1990s team.

Reliable defender and now national captain, Christian Chivu (above) has played for three of Europe's' greatest club teams—Ajax, Roma, and Inter Milan.

Dorinel Munteanu (far right) was a versatile player who could play anywhere in the midfield or in defense. He played in two World Cups and two European Championships.

Romania's "Footballer of the Century" was Gheorghe Hagi (far right), star of the famous '90s side. He was a brilliant passer, hard to knock off the ball, and had a tremendous shot. His 35 goals in 125 games remains a national record.

**ROMANIA DREAM TEAM?** 1. Bogdan Stelea 2. Dan Petrescu 3. Christian Chivu 4. Dorinel Munteanu 5. Miodrag Belodedici 6. Gheorghe Popescu 7. Florin Raducioiu 8. Gheorghe Hagi 9. Iuliu Bodola 10. Adrian Mutu 11. Marius Lacatus

# SWITZERLAND

Switzerland reached the quarterfinals of the World Cup in 1934 and 1938, but has enjoyed little success since then. The team was knocked out of the 2006 Finals tournament despite not conceding a single goal and crashed out of Euro 2008 in front of its own fans. However, it did qualify for South Africa 2010 with relative ease.

Jakob "Köbi" Kuhn played 63 times for the Swiss in the 1960s, and became coach of the national side in 2001. Despite having little experience as a manager, he guided Switzerland through qualification for the finals of three major tournaments.

Stéphane Chapuisat (above, right) enjoyed a long international career, making 103 appearances for the Swiss and scoring 21 goals. He spent most of the 1990s playing club soccer for Borussia Dortmund.

Twice named Swiss Footballer of the Year, Switzerland's leading international goal scorer Alexander Frei missed most of Euro 2008 finals after sustaining an injury in the opening game, but he bounced back to score five goals in Switzerland's successful run to South Africa 2010.

## FACT FILE

**TOP GOAL SCORER**
Alexander Frei 40 (2001–present)

**MOST APPEARANCES**
Heinz Hermann 117 (1978–1991)

**TROPHIES/HONORS**
none

**SWITZERLAND DREAM TEAM?** 1. Erwin Ballabio 2. Marc Hottiger 3. Ludovic Magnin 4. Kobi Kühn 5. Alain Geiger 6. Johann Vogel 7. Tranquillo Barnetta 8. Heinz Hermann 9. Alexander Frei 10. Stéphane Chapuisat 11. Ciriaco Sforza

Top goal scorer, Eidur Gudjohnsen (above) has played for Chelsea and Barcelona.

# ICELAND

Iceland's greatest victory was a 2–0 win over Italy in a 2002 friendly match. Its biggest win was 9–0 over the Faroe Islands.

## FACT FILE

**TOP GOAL SCORER**
Eidur Gudjohnsen 24 (1996–present)

**MOST APPEARANCES**
Rúnar Kristinsson 104 (1987–2004)

# CYPRUS

Despite being one of the underdogs of European football, Cyprus has beaten the Republic of Ireland and Slovakia.

All-time leading scorer Michalis Konstantinou (far right) has played most of his club soccer in Greece for top sides Panathinaikos and Olympiacos.

## FACT FILE

**TOP GOAL SCORER**
Michalis Konstantinou 29 (1998–present)

**MOST APPEARANCES**
Ioannis Okkas 96 (1997–present)

# ANDORRA

Andorra is the lowest ranked team in Europe, but has only been playing competitive soccer for just over a decade.

Andorra striker Xavi Andorra (right) on the ball during a 2010 World Cup qualifier against England.

## FACT FILE

**TOP GOAL SCORER**
Ildefons Lima 7 (1997–present)

**MOST APPEARANCES**
Óscar Sonejee 83 (1997–present)

## DID YOU KNOW?

During a game between Iceland and Estonia in 1996, Eidur Gudjohnsen came on as substitute for his father, Arnór. It was the first time that a father and son had ever played in the same international game.

Andorra has only scored more than one goal in a competitive international once. The opposition in a World Cup qualifier in 2000 were Cyprus, which went on to win the game 3–2.

# BELGIUM

The Belgian national team's best performance was as runner-up in the 1980 European Championship, when it lost 2–1 to West Germany in the final. A golden era had begun and the country went on to qualify for six successive World Cups.

Belgium faced Germany in the 1980 European Championship final (left.) It took a goal two minutes from time to finally end their challenge.

Italian-born Enzo Scifo (above) was the architect and playmaker of Belgium's most successful ever team. He played club soccer for eight different clubs in Belgium, Italy, and France.

**FACT FILE**

**TOP GOAL SCORER**
Paul Van Himst 30 (1960–1974)
Bernard Voorhoof 30 (1928–1940)
**MOST APPEARANCES**
Jan Ceulemans 96 (1977–1991)

**TROPHIES/HONORS**
**OLYMPIC GOLD MEDAL**
1920 Belgium 2 Czechoslovakia 0

# MACEDONIA

Another country to emerge from the breakup of Yugoslavia in the 1990s, Macedonia's first qualifying competition was an unsuccessful attempt to reach Euro '96. Its greatest triumphs so far include a 2–2 draw against England in 2003, followed by a 2–0 win over Croatia four years later.

Goran Pandev (far right) is Macedonia's most dangerous player. He plays his club soccer in Italy for Lazio and his two goals in a friendly match against Spain in 2009 finally pushed him past Macedonia's previous highest scorer, Gjorgji Hristov.

**FACT FILE**

**TOP GOAL SCORER**
Goran Pandev 19 (2001–present)
**MOST APPEARANCES**
Goce Sedloski 94 (1996–present)

**TROPHIES/HONORS**
none

# ISRAEL

Israel competed as part of Asia until 1994, when FIFA allowed the team to join UEFA. Israel's finest hour came in qualifying for the 1970 World Cup, where it excelled with draws against Italy and Sweden. Recently it's pushed much bigger soccer nations close in qualifying campaigns, but is still waiting for a breakthrough.

**FACT FILE**

**TOP GOAL SCORER**
Mordechai Spiegler 32 (1963–1977)
**MOST APPEARANCES**
Arik Benado 95 (1995–present)

**TROPHIES/HONORS**
**AFC ASIAN CUP**
1964 (round-robin league tournament)

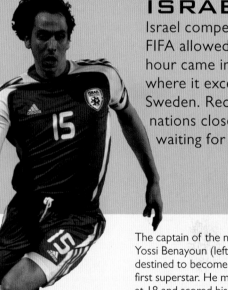

The captain of the national side, Yossi Benayoun (left) looks destined to become Israeli soccer's first superstar. He made his debut at 18 and scored his first international hat trick against San Marino less than a year later. A player with great skill, vision, and agility, he plays his club soccer for English club Liverpool.

Mordechai Spiegler (far left) is Israel's leading scorer and his goals were the chief reason Israel made it to the 1970 World Cup Finals. He played most of his club soccer in Israel, but finished his career alongside Pelé playing for the New York Cosmos in the US.

ISRAEL DREAM TEAM?    1. Avi Ran 2. Alon Harazi 3. Avi Cohen 4. Giora Spiegel 5. Arik Benado 6. Nir Klinger 7. Eyal Berkovic 8. Avi Nimni 9. Mordechai Spiegler 10. Yehoshua Feigenbaum 11. Yossi Benayoun

# NORTHERN IRELAND

Northern Ireland has made it to the World Cup Finals three times, reaching the quarterfinals in 1958 and famously beating Spain 1–0 in 1982. The team has yet to make it to the European Championships, but it can claim to be British champions. It won the 1984 British Home Championships the last time it was contested.

Despite being one of the world's greatest players, George Best (right) never made it to a major championship. He played 37 times for the national side and scored nine goals. The 1968 European Player of the Year, Best played his most successful club soccer for Manchester United. Two-footed, he had it all—pace, great dribbling skills, and a powerful shot.

Pat Jennings (left) was Northern Ireland's first choice goalkeeper for an amazing 22 years. He played more than 1,000 games for clubs and country and was famous for his monstrous goal kicks. In fact, he actually scored directly from a goal kick in 1967.

In September 2006, David Healy (far right) scored the winner in a famous 3–2 win over Spain. Since then he's kept on scoring, and now has nearly three times as many goals as any other Northern Irishman.

**FACT FILE**

**TOP GOAL SCORER**
David Healy 35 (2000–present)

**MOST APPEARANCES**
Pat Jennings 119 (1964–1986)

**TROPHIES/HONORS**
none

**NORTHERN IRELAND DREAM TEAM?** 1. Pat Jennings 2. Jimmy Nicholl 3. Mal Donaghy 4. Terry Neill 5. Danny Blanchflower 6. Martin O'Neill 7. George Best 8. Sammy McIlroy 9. David Healy 10. Norman Whiteside 11. Billy Bingham

## MALTA

Malta has only won four competitive games in its history, but is showing signs of recent progress.

**FACT FILE**

**TOP GOAL SCORER**
Carmel Busuttil 23 (1982–2001)

**MOST APPEARANCES**
David Carabott 121 (1987–2005)

Michael Mifsud (above, right) scored five times for Malta when it thrashed Liechtenstein 7–1 in a friendly match.

## AZERBAIJAN

Although it is still finding its feet in world soccer, Azerbaijan's team did beat Liechtenstein 2–0 in the 2010 World Cup qualifiers.

**FACT FILE**

**TOP GOAL SCORER**
Gurban Gurbanov 12 (1992–2006)

**MOST APPEARANCES**
Aslan Kerimov 75 (1994–2007)

Rugged defender Rashad Sadygov (above, left) has over 50 appearances for his country and was voted Azerbaijan's Player of the Year in 2004 and 2005.

## SAN MARINO

San Marino has the smallest population of any UEFA country (about 30,000) and have never won a competitive match.

**FACT FILE**

**TOP GOAL SCORER**
Andy Selva 8 (1998–present)

**MOST APPEARANCES**
Damiano Vannucci 50 (2001–present)

Italian-born Andy Selva is the bright light in the San Marino team.

## FAROE ISLANDS

The Faroe Islands began playing competitive games in 1990 and immediately pulled off a massive shock by beating Austria 1–0.

**FACT FILE**

**TOP GOAL SCORER**
Rogvi Jacobsen 10 (1999–present)

**MOST APPEARANCES**
Óli Johannesen 83 (1992–2007)

Defender Óli Johannesen (above, left) was a huge influence on the team during its early years.

# CZECH REPUBLIC

When the 1989 "Velvet Revolution" divided Czechoslovakia into two nations, the Czech Republic emerged as the stronger soccer team of the two. The team was runner-up in the 1996 European Championships and reached the semifinals in 2004. However, neighbor Slovakia beat it to a place in the 2010 World Cup Finals.

Skilled midfielder Pavel Nedved (above, left) is regarded as the best Czech player of his generation. He certainly had it all—power, skill, and stamina. He scored 19 times in 91 games for the national team and also enjoyed huge success in Italy with Lazio and Juventus.

Tomáš Rosický (left) is one of the most skillful players in world soccer. A true midfield maestro, his passing is sublime and he can orchestrate a match with sweeping cross field balls. He is also the national team captain and was snapped up by Arsenal in 2006.

Josef Masopust led Czechoslovakia into the 1962 World Cup final against Brazil. He gave the Czechs the lead (above), but the South Americans came back to win the match 3–1.

**FACT FILE**
**TOP GOAL SCORER**
Jan Koller 55 (1999–present)
**MOST APPEARANCES**
Karel Poborský 118 (1994–2006)

**TROPHIES/HONORS**
(Competing as Czechoslovakia)
**UEFA EUROPEAN CHAMPIONSHIP**
1976 Czechoslovakia 2 West Germany 2
Czechoslovakia won 5–3 on penalties
(Competing as Czech Republic)
none

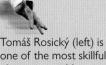

CZECH REPUBLIC DREAM TEAM? 1. Petr Cech 2. Karol Dobiaš 3. Marek Jankulovski 4. Miroslav Kadlec 5. Tomáš Ujfaluši 6. Josef Masopust 7. Pavel Nedved 8. Karel Poborský 9. Jan Koller 10. Antonin Puc 11. Tomáš Rosický

# LITHUANIA

Lithuania has acquitted itself well since gaining independence from the USSR. Under current Portuguese coach José Couceiro, it chalked up some impressive wins in its 2010 World Cup qualifying campaign. However, despite an historic 3–0 victory in Romania and a stunning 2–1 defeat of group winners Serbia, Lithuania failed to qualify for the finals in South Africa.

Captain Tomas Danileviius is Lithuania's all-time leading scorer and his goals have been crucial in Lithuania's recent success. At club level, Danilevicius is something of a journeyman—he has worn the colors of 10 different sides, playing for four separate clubs in 2000 alone.

**FACT FILE**
**TOP GOAL SCORER**
Tomas Danilevicius 17 (1998–present)
**MOST APPEARANCES**
Andrius Skerla 75 (1996–present)

**TROPHIES/HONORS**
none

# FINLAND

Skiing, running, and a type of baseball called Pesäpallo are the most popular sports in Finland, so it's no surprise that the team has never set the soccer world ablaze. However, strong performances in 2007 saw it reach 33 in the FIFA rankings.

The most capped player in Finnish history, Jari Litmanen (right) is also team captain and record goal scorer. He's still playing, despite making his debut in 1989.

Sami Hyypia (above) is a big, solid center back, with more than 100 appearances for Finland, as well as over 450 for former club Liverpool.

**FACT FILE**
**TOP GOAL SCORER**
Jari Litmanen 31 (1989–present)
**MOST APPEARANCES**
Jari Litmanen 126 (1989–present)

**TROPHIES/HONORS**

## GEORGIA

Former USSR state Georgia has yet to qualify for a major tournament and did not win any of its qualifiers for South Africa 2010.

Kakha Kaladze (above) has been voted Georgia's Player of the Year four times, and has played over 200 games for AC Milan.

**FACT FILE**

**TOP GOAL SCORER**
Shota Arveladze 26 (1992–2007)

**MOST APPEARANCES**
Levan Kobiashvili 87 (1996–present)

## LIECHTENSTEIN

With a population of just 35,000, this tiny nation has yet to make a mark on the world stage. However, in 2004, it beat the more populous Luxembourg 4–0.

Liechtenstein's Michael Stocklasa (right) vies for the ball with Finland's Jonatan Johansson (far right) during a 2010 World Cup qualifier.

**FACT FILE**

**TOP GOAL SCORER**
Mario Frick 14 (1993–present)

**MOST APPEARANCES**
Mario Frick 91 (1993–present)

## MOLDOVA

Moldova was bottom of its 2010 World Cup qualifying group after drawing with Greece but lost to Luxembourg.

Versatile Radu Rebeja (above, left) could play in midfield or defense, and won 74 caps for his country.

**FACT FILE**

**TOP GOAL SCORER**
Serghei Clescenco 11 (1991–2006)

**MOST APPEARANCES**
Radu Rebeja 74 (1991–2008)

## ALBANIA

Albania is a small but improving team and has recorded promising draws against Sweden, Denmark, and Portugal.

Albania's Lorik Cana (above, left) fights for the ball with Bruno Alves of Portugal.

**FACT FILE**

**TOP GOAL SCORER**
Alban Bushi 14 (1995–2007)

**MOST APPEARANCES**
Foto Strakosha 73 (1990–2005)

## DENMARK

Traditionally, Denmark was known for producing fine players but had never made much of an international impact as a team. That all changed at Euro '92, when Denmark caused a major upset by beating Germany 2–0 in the final in Gothenburg. Since then Denmark has not made the same impact, despite a few major quarterfinal appearances.

Michael Laudrup (right), and his younger brother Brian, are two of Denmark's greatest players. Playing as attacking midfielders, they won a combined total of 186 caps and scored 58 goals for their country.

**FACT FILE**

**TOP GOAL SCORER**
Poul 'Tist' Nielsen 52 (1910–1925)

**MOST APPEARANCES**
Peter Schmeichel 129 (1987–2001)

**TROPHIES/HONORS**
UEFA EUROPEAN CHAMPIONSHOP
1992 Denmark 2 Germany 0
CONFEDERATIONS CUP
1995 Denmark 2 Argentina 0

Peter Schmeichel (left) was Denmark's number one for 14 years. At club level he played over 400 games for Manchester United, and was regularly voted the Best Keeper in the World. He also scored eleven goals during his career.

Denmark only made it to Sweden for Euro '92 after Yugoslavia was barred from the competition, and then a late goal against France helped it edge through the group stages. Denmark beat the Netherlands in a semifinal penalty shootout to set up a final against Germany. To the amazement of the soccer world, the Danes eased to a 2–0 victory and took the trophy.

**DENMARK DREAM TEAM?** 1. Peter Schmeichel 2. Thomas Helveg 3. John Sivebaek 4. Morten Olsen 5. Lars Olsen 6. Thomas Gravesen 7. Michael Laudrup 8. Nicklas Bendtner 9. Jon Dahl Tomasson 10. Brian Laudrup 11. Allan Simonsen

# SLOVAKIA

Formed in 1993 after the breakup of Czechoslovakia, Slovakia will make its first-ever appearance at a major championship at the 2010 World Cup Finals. It achieved that feat in style, topping a qualifying group that included neighbors and rivals the Czech Republic.

**FACT FILE**
**TOP GOAL SCORER**
Szilárd Németh 22 (1996–present)
**MOST APPEARANCES**
Miroslav Karhan 94 (1995–present)
**TROPHIES/HONORS**
none

Aggressive, quick, and great in the air, Martin Škrtel (left, wearing white) is a rock at the center of Slovakia's defense. He was voted Slovak player of the Year in 2007 and 2008, and is a regular member of English club Liverpool's defense.

Arguably Slovakia's greatest ever player is Szilárd Németh. He is Slovakia's leading goal scorer, with 22 goals and spent four years in the English Premiership scoring goals for Middlesbrough.

**SLOVAKIA DREAM TEAM?** 1. Miroslav König 2. Karol Dobias 3. Dusan Tittel 4. Miroslav Karhan 5. Martin Škrtel 6. Ján Popluhár 7. Marián Masný 8. Marek Hamšík 9. Robert Vittek 10. Adolf Scherer 11. Szilárd Németh

# MONTENEGRO

International soccer's newest addition played its first match in 2007 and beat Hungary 2–1.

**FACT FILE**
**TOP GOAL SCORER**
Mirko Vucinic 7 (2006–present)
**MOST APPEARANCES**
Vukašin Poleksic 20 (2007–present)

Stevan Jovetic (above, left) is a skillful and exciting winger who plays his club soccer for Fiorentina in Italy.

# ARMENIA

Formerly part of the USSR, Armenia played its first international game in 1992. Its most notable victory is 2–1 over Belgium in 2009.

**FACT FILE**
**TOP GOAL SCORER**
Arthur Petrosyan 11 (1992–2005)
**MOST APPEARANCES**
Sargis Hovsepyan 109 (1992–present)

Sargis Hovsepyan (right, top) is Armenia's captain. He has more than 100 caps and has been playing for nearly 20 years.

# KAZAKHSTAN

Kazakhstan has only been playing in European competitions since 2002, after previously competing in the Asian confederation.

Kazakhstan celebrates after scoring against Ukraine during their 2010 World Cup qualifier. It eventually lost the match 2–1.

**FACT FILE**
**TOP GOAL SCORER**
Viktor Zubarev 12 (1997–2004)
**MOST APPEARANCES**
Ruslan Baltiev 67 (1997–present)

# LUXEMBOURG

With a population of under half a million, Luxembourg struggles to make an impression on the world soccer scene.

Luxembourg's Ben Payal (right) vies for the ball with Israel's midfielder Yossi Benayoun.

**FACT FILE**
**TOP GOAL SCORER**
Léon Mart 16 (1933–1946)
**MOST APPEARANCES**
Jeff Strasser 94 (1993–present)

# AUSTRIA

Austria could claim to be the sleeping giants of European soccer. The team finished third in the 1954 World Cup, but has not gone beyond the second round since. In 2008, it cohosted the European Championships with neighbors Switzerland. However, the Austrians were knocked out early on with just one point.

Toni Polster (right) was Austria's star striker in the 1990s. He led the attack during short-lived trips to that decade's World Cups in Italy and France. His tally of 44 goals in 95 games is still a national record. Now retired from soccer, Polster sings in a rock band.

**FACT FILE**

**TOP GOAL SCORER**
Anton "Toni" Polster 44 (1982–2000)

**MOST APPEARANCES**
Andreas Herzog 103 (1998–2003)

**TROPHIES/HONORS**
none

# NORWAY

Norwegian soccer is on the rise, thanks to stars such as John Arne Riise and Morten Gamst Pedersen. In fact, it is the only team in the world to have played Brazil and never lost—so far, the team has drawn two and won two of its four encounters.

John Arne Riise (right) is a marauding left back and owner of one of the game's most ferocious shots. His younger brother, Bjørn Helge Riise, also plays midfield for Norway.

Ole Gunnar Solskjær (above, right) played 61 times for Norway, scoring 21 goals. He also spent over 11 years at Manchester United.

**FACT FILE**

**TOP GOAL SCORER**
Jørgen Juve 33 (1928–1937)

**MOST APPEARANCES**
Thorbjørn Svenssen 104 (1947–1962)

**TROPHIES/HONORS**
none

# WALES

Despite the popularity of rugby, Welsh soccer has enjoyed a recent boom. However, the 1958 World Cup Finals is Wales' only visit so far and the national side continues to just miss out on major tournaments. Great players to pull on the famous Welsh shirt include Cliff Jones, Mark Hughes, and Neville Southall.

Ian Rush (right) was a goal-scoring machine. He netted 28 times for Wales and an incredible 346 times for Liverpool, making him the top scorer for both club and country. He combined great anticipation with lethal finishing and formed a partnership with Scotland's Kenny Dalglish at club level.

John Charles (above, left) is probably the best Welsh all-around player ever. He could play equally well at center back or center forward, and scored 15 goals in 38 games for Wales. He was only the second British player ever to sign for a foreign club, joining Juventus from Leeds United in 1957.

Although he was captain of England as a schoolboy, Ryan Giggs (right) switched to Wales at senior level. Another world-class player never to reach the finals of a major tournament, Giggs' 16 years as an international player saw him capped 64 times and score 12 goals. He retired from Wales in 2007 but is a key player for Manchester United.

**FACT FILE**

**TOP GOAL SCORER**
Ian Rush 28 (1980–1996)

**MOST APPEARANCES**
Neville Southall 92 (1990–2006)

**TROPHIES/HONORS**
none

| WALES DREAM TEAM? | 1. Neville Southall 2. Alf Sherwood 3. Joey Jones 4. Gary Speed 5. John Charles 6. Kevin Ratcliffe 7. Cliff Jones 8. Ivor Allchurch 9. Ian Rush 10. John Toshack 11. Ryan Giggs |
|---|---|

# NORTH AMERICA

**"FOOTBALL IS FULL OF SURPRISES."**

FORMER TRINIDAD AND TOBAGO
CAPTAIN DWIGHT YORKE

St. Lucia, the Bahamas, the British Virgin Islands... this may sound like a list of dream vacation destinations but, in fact, they are all members of the soccer confederation that unites North and Central America and the Caribbean. In addition to including some of the world's most exotic soccer outposts, it also represents some serious contenders for international glory, such as Mexico and the United States. Beach soccer is also popular in this region and an annual tournament is hotly contested among teams from the South American confederation.

The Confederation of North American, Central American, and Caribbean Association Football (CONCACAF) came together in 1961. It produced four qualifiers in the 2006 World Cup. The best-ever World Cup result for a CONCACAF member is the United States' semifinal in 1930.

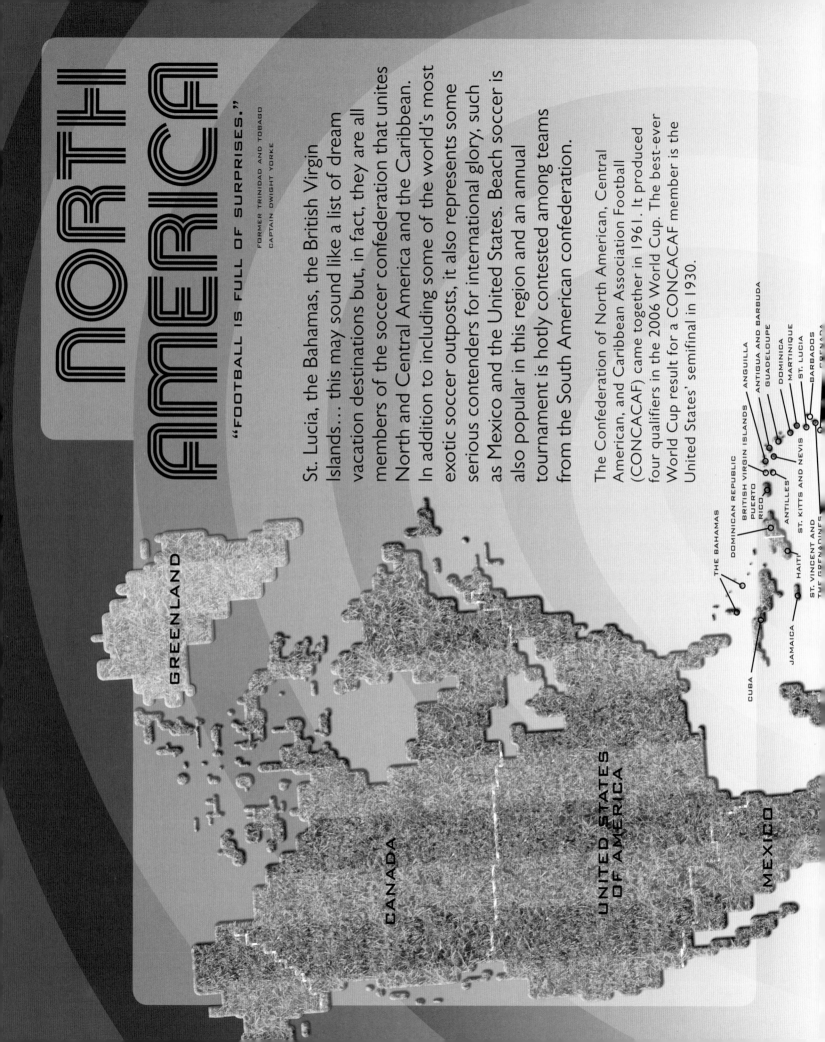

GREENLAND

CANADA

UNITED STATES
OF AMERICA

MEXICO

THE BAHAMAS

DOMINICAN REPUBLIC

BRITISH VIRGIN ISLANDS

PUERTO
RICO

ANGUILLA

ANTIGUA AND BARBUDA

GUADELOUPE

DOMINICA

MARTINIQUE

ST. LUCIA

BARBADOS

ANTILLES

ST. KITTS AND NEVIS

HAITI

JAMAICA

CUBA

ST. VINCENT AND
THE GRENADINES

# SOUTH AMERICA

**"NOT MUCH OCCURS IN LATIN AMERICA THAT DOESN'T BEAR DIRECTLY OR INDIRECTLY ON FOOTBALL."**

URUGUAYAN HISTORIAN AND AUTHOR
EDUARDO GALEANO

The nations and star names of this region read like a list of reasons to get excited about the beautiful game. Pelé, Ardiles, Maradona, Romário, Ronaldinho, Messi, and a flood of other attractive exports have illuminated soccer clubs across the globe. This stronghold of soccer has seen a team within its own federation win the coveted World Cup every time it has hosted the tournament, so hopes are high for the 2014 World Cup Finals, in Brazil.

The Confederación Sudamericana de Fútbol (South American Football Confederation) is also known as CONMEBOL or CSF. It was founded in 1916 by Argentina, Brazil, Chile, and Uruguay. It has 10 member nations and has produced the World Cup winners on nine occasions. CONMEBOL has four guaranteed World Cup places, plus a chance to playoff with the fourth place team from the CONCACAF group.

South American soccer fans have blazed a flamboyant trail for the rest of the world to follow. Traditions like fiesta (street partying) and samba (music and dance), have given them a head start in knowing how to support their heroes in awesome style!

TRINIDAD AND TOBAGO
SURINAM
FRENCH GUIANA
BELIZE
HONDURAS
GUATEMALA
EL SALVADOR
NICARAGUA
COSTA RICA
PANAMA
GUYANA
VENEZUELA
COLOMBIA
ECUADOR
PERÚ
BOLIVIA
BRAZIL
PARAGUAY
CHILE
ARGENTINA
URUGUAY

# BRAZIL

## "BEAUTY COMES FIRST. VICTORY IS SECONDARY. WHAT MATTERS IS JOY."
SÓCRATES, BRAZIL MIDFIELDER 1979–1986

Magical, mesmeric, spellbinding—these terms aren't often lavished on soccer teams, except for Brazil. Universally admired for its scintillating style and breathtaking skills, Brazil is the most successful soccer nation of all time and has won the World Cup a record five times. It has also given the game arguably its greatest-ever player—the legendary Pelé—and blazed a glorious trail for others to follow. For Brazil, soccer really is "the beautiful game"!

The Confederação Brasileira de Futebol (Brazilian Football Confederation) was founded in 1914.

Team captain, Dunga, collects the trophy in 1994. Since retiring, he has successfully managed the national team.

Pelé's real name is Edson Arantes do Nascimento.

## WORLD CUP

Brazil's World Cup triumphs include 1958, when a 17-year-old Pelé scored twice in a 5–2 win over Sweden and 1970, when victory over Italy meant it could keep the Jules Rimet trophy. Surprisingly, the 2–0 win over Germany in the 2002 final was the first-ever competitive clash between these international

## BEST EVER?

Voted FIFA Footballer of the Century in the year 2000, Pelé is the only player ever to be part of three World Cup-winning squads and he scored 77 goals in 92 appearances for his country. A sensational dribbler with an unstoppable shot, he was also an unselfish and inspired playmaker. Pelé's talent and sportsmanship made him universally loved, even by his opponents.

Many argue that Brazil's finest player was actually Garrincha, not Pelé. Despite a deformed spine and one leg longer than the other, he was a mesmerizing dribbler. Garrincha won the World Cup in 1958 and 1962.

Zico is possibly the greatest Brazilian never to have won the World Cup. In 1982 and 1986, teams featuring Zico, Sócrates, Falcão and Junior were a joy to watch, but lost out. In the 2006 World Cup Finals Zico faced Brazil as manager of Japan.

## DID YOU KNOW?

Brazil hasn't always played in yellow and blue. The famous uniform was designed for the team by a 19-year-old fan in a competition to give the team a makeover after the nation turned against the unlucky white gear it wore in the 1950 World Cup.

BRAZIL DREAM TEAM? 1. Gílmar 2. Cafu 3. Nílton Santos 4. Didi 5. Lúcio 6. Bellini 7. Garrincha 8. Leônidas 9. Ronaldo 10. Pelé 11. Rivelino

**RONALDO** follows in an illustrious tradition of great Brazilian strikers. Although he has been criticized for his weight, and his poor performance in the 1998 World Cup final, his record is undeniable. He is the World Cup Finals' top scorer, with 15 goals in four World Cups, and was voted the FIFA World Player of the Year in 1996, 1997, and 2002.

## FACT FILE: BRAZIL

### NICKNAMES
A Seleção (The Selected), Canarinho (Little Canary)

### TOP GOAL SCORERS
1. Pelé 77 (1957–1971)
2. Ronaldo 62 (1994–2006)
3. Romário 55 (1987–2005)
4. Zico 52 (1971–1989)
5. Bebeto 39 (1985–1998)

### MOST APPEARANCES
1. Cafu 142 (1990–2006)
2. Roberto Carlos 125 (1992–2006)
3. Cláudio Taffarel 101 (1987–1998)
4. Djalma Santos 98 (1952–1968)
5. Ronaldo 97 (1994–2006)

### TROPHIES/HONORS

#### FIFA WORLD CUP
2002 Brazil 2 Germany 0
1994 Brazil 3 Italy 2
1970 Brazil 4 Italy 1
1962 Brazil 3 Czechoslovakia 1
1958 Brazil 5 Sweden 2

#### COPA AMÉRICA
2007 Brazil 3 Argentina 0
2004 Brazil 4 Argentina 2
1999 Brazil 3 Uruguay 0
1997 Brazil 3 Bolivia 1
1989 Brazil 1 Uruguay 0
1949 Brazil 7 Paraguay 0
1922 Brazil 3 Paraguay 0
1919 Brazil 1 Uruguay 0

## KAKÁ

Midfielder Kaká is one of the best players in the world today and the second most expensive, after joining Real Madrid from AC Milan for £56 million in June 2009. His vision, range of passing, and forceful shooting make him equally comfortable playing deep in midfield or pushing up into attack.

*Kaká got his nickname as a child because he was unable to say his real name, Ricardo.*

**RONALDINHO** was voted FIFA World Player of the Year in 2004 and 2005 and was part of the World Cup winning team in 2002. Famous for his close control and dribbling skills, he is also a powerful and prolific shooter, despite not being an out-and-out striker. However, it is Ronaldinho's mastery of the unexpected—his ability to pull off a pass, move, feint, or shoot to stun even the best of defenders—that has won him many fans around the world.

Robinho burst out of Kaká and Ronaldinho's shadows when he scored six goals and was named Player of the Tournament as Brazil won the 2007 Copa América. The former Santos and Real Madrid winger signed for Manchester City in August 2009 for an English record price of over $51 million.

# ARGENTINA

*"IF YOU PLAY WELL AND SHOW THE ARGENTINIAN PEOPLE WHAT THEY WANT TO SEE, THEY'LL THANK YOU FOR IT ALL YOUR LIFE."*

HÉCTOR ENRIQUE, PART OF ARGENTINA'S '86 TEAM

The first Argentinian soccer association was founded by Glaswegian teacher Alexander Hutton in 1891. It laid the foundations for the modern Argentine Football Association.

The team lost the first-ever World Cup 4–2 to Uruguay, but has made up for it since, with two World Cups and 14 Copa Américas. Many heroes have played a part in Argentina's dramatic history. "El Gran Capitan," Daniel Passarella, was the first Argentine to touch the World Cup, while Leopoldo Luque lit up the 1978 finals with his sensational long-range efforts at goal scoring. Today, it can call upon some of the world's finest attackers, including Lionel Messi, Gonzalo Higuaín, and Diego Milito.

## HISTORIC MOMENT

Argentina came of age in spectacular style when it hosted and won its first World Cup in 1978. It was a torrid tournament, full of controversy. Argentina bested Brazil in the final on goal difference, after beating Peru 6–0 in the final round-two match. Argentina overpowered the Netherlands' "Total Soccer" in the final.

*Daniel Passarella triumphantly holds the World Cup aloft in 1978.*

*Argentina beat West Germany 3–2 in the 1986 World Cup final.*

Mario Kempes won the 1978 World Cup for Argentina with two goals in a 3–1 overtime victory over the Netherlands. He scored six goals in the Finals and was South American Player of the Year.

Maradona's talent was epitomized by the 1986 World Cup quarterfinal when he took out the whole England defense with a surging, spellbinding dribble to score the "Goal of the Century."

## MARADONA

Diego Maradona scored 34 goals in 91 internationals. His squat, muscular frame gave him a low center of gravity, which made him difficult to knock off the ball. He scored five goals in the 1986 World Cup Finals and inspired his side to victory. Despite a career dogged by controversy both on and off the field, Maradona was appointed Argentina coach in 2008, but his team found World Cup qualification unexpectedly difficult.

ARGENTINA DREAM TEAM? 1. Ubaldo Fillol 2. Javier Zanetti 3. Silvio Marzolini 4. Omar Sívori 5. Daniel Passarella 6. Roberto Ayala 7. José Manuel Moreno 8. Ángel Labruna 9. Alfredo Di Stéfano 10. Diego Maradona 11. Mario Kempes

## STAR STRIKER

Prolific goal scorer Gabriel Batistuta (left) hit 56 goals in 78 games for Argentina, which earned him the nickname "Batigol." He hit four goals in USA '94, and five in France '98—tournaments in which his team as a whole achieved relatively little success. When Batistuta retired from the national team, Hernán Crespo took over as the main striker. Despite competition from younger players such as Messi, Tévez, and Saviola, Crespo's record of more than a goal every other game speaks for itself.

## NEW MARADONA?

Lionel Messi is a big game player. A visionary passer of the ball and scorer of special goals, he is on the way to fulfilling Maradona's prediction that he has a true successor at last. Messi scored two goals and created more in Argentina's 2007 Copa América campaign. Now recognized as one of the world's finest players, Messi won the 2009 European Player of the Year award.

Sergio Agüero is an up-and-coming striker whose goals — including two in the semifinal against Brazil—proved crucial as Argentina won gold again at the 2008 Beijing Olympics. Agüero is nicknamed "Kun" after a Japanese cartoon character with a similar hairstyle.

A powerful and hardworking striker with a deft touch, Carlos Tévez is no stranger to controversy. Signed by Corinthians of Brazil in 2005, he braved a media storm and fan opposition to become South American Player of the Year. Tévez made headlines again in 2009 when he left Manchester United for local rivals Manchester City.

## FACT FILE: ARGENTINA
### NICKNAMES
Albicelestes (White and Sky Blues),
Los Gauchos (The Cowboys)

### TOP GOAL SCORERS
1. Gabriel Batistuta 56 (1991–2002)
2. Hernán Crespo 36 (1995–2007)
3. Diego Maradona 34 (1977–1994)
4. Luis Artime 24 (1961–1967)
5. Daniel Passarella 22 (1976–1986)
= Leopoldo Luque 22 (1975–1981)

### MOST APPEARANCES
1. Javier Zanetti 136 (1994–present)
2. Roberto Ayala 115 (1994–2007)
3. Diego Simeone 106 (1988–2002)
4. Oscar Ruggeri 97 (1983–1994)
5. Diego Maradona 91 (1977–1994)

### TROPHIES/HONORS
#### FIFA WORLD CUP
1986 Argentina 3 West Germany 2
1978 Argentina 3 Netherlands 1 (aet)

#### COPA AMÉRICA
1993 Argentina 2 Mexico 1
1991 (round robin, then final round of four teams in a mini league)
1959, 1957, 1955, 1947, 1946, 1945, 1941, 1937, 1929, 1927, 1925, 1921 (round robin league tournaments)

#### CONFEDERATIONS CUP
1992 Argentina 3 Saudi Arabia 1

#### OLYMPIC GAMES
2004 Argentina 1 Paraguay 0

## DID YOU KNOW?

*Daniel Passarella (see p. 72) had a thick mop of hair when he led Argentina to glory at the 1978 World Cup, but as coach in 1994, he ordered all his players to have their hair cut short. He even condemned striker Claudio Caniggia for having "girl's hair."*

# SOUTH AMERICAN TEAMS

**"OUR FOOTBALL COMES FROM THE HEART, THEIRS COMES FROM THE MIND."** PELÉ COMPARES THE GAME IN SOUTH AMERICA AND EUROPE

South America has so much more to offer than just Brazil and Argentina. From historically illustrious teams such as Uruguay, to optimistic minnows such as Venezuela, this diverse continent captures everything that is fascinating about the world game. South America often produces a dark horse to illuminate a World Cup.

*Recoba is famous for his dribbling, technique, and strong, accurate left-foot shot.*

## FACT FILE

**TOP GOAL SCORER**
Héctor Scarone 31 (1917–1930)
**MOST APPEARANCES**
Rodolfo Rodríguez 78 (1976–1986)

### TROPHIES/HONORS
**FIFA WORLD CUP**
1950 Uruguay topped a four team final group
1930 Uruguay 4 Argentina 2
**COPA AMÉRICA**
1995 Uruguay 1 Brazil 1 (Uruguay won 5–3 in a penalty shoot-out)
1987 Uruguay 1 Chile 0
1983 Uruguay 3 Brazil 1 (agg)
1967, 1959, 1956, 1942, 1935, 1926, 1924, 1923, 1920, 1917, 1916 (round robin league tournaments)
**OLYMPIC GAMES**
1928 Uruguay 2 Argentina 1 (replay)
1924 Uruguay 3 Switzerland 0

## URUGUAY

The Asociación Uruguaya de Fútbol was founded in 1900 and was one of the founder members of CONMEBOL. Although it is one of the few nations to have won the World Cup more than once, Uruguay has been through a lengthy lean spell in recent years which has unfortunately coincided with the upsurge of their local rivals Argentina. In 2006, Uruguay didn't even qualify for the World Cup Finals—it missed out after losing a nail-biting playoff to Australia.

**ÁLVARO RECOBA**, has scored 11 goals in 69 internationals. He managed to upstage Brazilian striker Ronaldo on its shared debut for Inter Milan. The Uruguayan scored two late goals, one a 35-yard rocket.

Victory in the first ever World Cup is not Uruguay fans' fondest memory—securing the trophy in 1950 at the expense of hosts Brazil was an even sweeter triumph.

## PARAGUAY

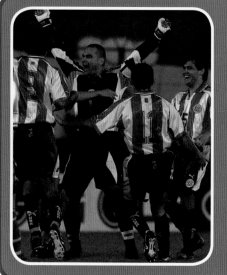

Although overshadowed by more glamorous neighbors, Paraguay has come close to causing major World Cup upsets. In round two in 1998, it was only squeezed out by a "golden goal" in the 114th minute by ultimate winners, France. In 2002, it was a round-two exit again, this time 1–0 to eventual finalists, Germany. Paraguay was a comfortable qualifier for the 2010 World Cup, unlike some traditional South American giants.

Inspired, impulsive, and often controversial, José Luis Chilavert combined daring goalkeeping with a talent for scoring free-kicks and penalties. He scored eight goals in international matches and an amazing 62 throughout his career.

## FACT FILE

**TOP GOAL SCORER**
José Cardozo 25 (1991–2006)
**MOST APPEARANCES**
Carlos Gamarra 110 (1993–2006)

### TROPHIES/HONORS
**COPA AMÉRICA**
1979 and 1953 (round-robin league tournaments)

---

**SOUTH AMERICA DREAM TEAM?** 1. José Luis Chilavert (Paraguay) 2. Víctor Rodríguez Andrade (Uruguay) 3. José Nasazzi (Uruguay) 4. Obdulio Varela (Uruguay) 5. Héctor Chumpitaz (Peru) 6. Elías Figueroa (Chile) 7. Carlos Valderrama (Colombia) 8. Juan Alberto Schiaffino (Uruguay) 9. Alberto Spencer (Ecuador/Uruguay) 10. Teófilo Cubillas (Peru) 11. Leonel Sánchez (Chile)

## COLOMBIA

A 1–0 victory over Mexico in the 2001 Copa América is the only major trophy for this under-achieving side. Although Colombia impressed at Italia '90 when it was the only side to avoid defeat against eventual winners Germany, its most recent World Cup appearance was at France '98, where it managed just one win, 1–0 against Tunisia.

Carlos Valderrama was a gifted playmaker with a style all his own. In 111 internationals, his unhurried style and classy touch made the toughest game look like a walk in the park. No other Colombian has matched Valderrama's feat of being named South American Footballer of the Year—a prize he picked up twice, in 1987 and 1993.

*Valderrama was instantly recognizable thanks to his hairstyle.*

Fiery striker Faustino Asprilla (far left) notched up an impressive 20 goals in 57 appearances. Among his memorable displays was Colombia's legendary 5–0 thrashing of Argentina in 1993. Red cards, fights, and great stories for the press were never far away when "Tino" was involved.

### FACT FILE
**TOP GOAL SCORER**
Arnoldo Iguarán 25 (1979–1993)
**MOST APPEARANCES**
Carlos Valderrama 111 (1983–1998)

**TROPHIES/HONORS**
COPA AMÉRICA
2001 Colombia 1 Mexico 0

## VENEZUELA

Venezuela is the only side in the CONMEBOL never to have qualified for a World Cup Finals. Recently it has showed signs of progress, by impressively hosting the 2007 Copa América and by beating Brazil for the first time in June 2008.

### FACT FILE
**TOP GOAL SCORER**
Giancarlo Maldonado 19 (2003–present)
**MOST APPEARANCES**
José Manuel Rey 106 (1997–present)

**TROPHIES/ HONORS**
none

## BOLIVIA

Bolivia participated in the first World Cup in 1930 and again in 1950, but in recent years it has had little impact on the tournament, apart from a trip to the Finals in the US in 1994.

### FACT FILE
**TOP GOAL SCORER**
Joaquín Botero 20 (1999–2009)
**MOST APPEARANCES**
Marco Antonio Sandy 93 (1993–2003)
= Luis Héctor Cristaldo 93 (1989–2005)
**TROPHIES/HONORS**
COPA AMÉRICA
1963 (round-robin tournament)

## ECUADOR

Traditionally regarded as South American lightweights, Ecuador impressed at the 2006 World Cup Finals, beating Poland and Costa Rica before losing to England in the second round.

### FACT FILE
**TOP GOAL SCORER**
Agustín Delgado 31 (1994–present)
**MOST APPEARANCES**
Iván Hurtado 166 (1992–present)

**TROPHIES/ HONORS**
none

## PERU

Between 1970 and 1982 Peru's flowing football was admired across the globe. Teófilo Cubillas scored 5 goals in 2 World Cups, but a 1970 quarterfinal was its best result and Peru has not graced the Finals for 24 years.

### FACT FILE
**TOP GOAL SCORER**
Teófilo Cubillas 26 (1968–1982)
**MOST APPEARANCES**
Roberto Palacios 124 (1992–present)

**TROPHIES/HONORS**
COPA AMÉRICA
1975 Peru 3 Colombia 1 (agg)
1939 (round-robin league tournament)

Héctor Chumpitaz (above, far left) played in two World Cup Finals and helped his side lift the Copa América in 1975.

## CHILE

Established in 1895, the Federación de Fútbol de Chile was also one of the founding members of CONMEBOL. As host of the 1962 World Cup Finals, Chile recorded a best-ever third place. In 1998, Marcelo Salas' goals brightened its World Cup. He scored twice in a 2–2 draw with Italy as well as in their 4–1 defeat to Brazil in the second round.

Matías Fernández was voted South American Footballer of the Year in 2006. This attacking midfielder is also a free kick specialist.

### FACT FILE
**TOP GOAL SCORER**
Marcelo Salas 37 (1994–2009)
**MOST APPEARANCES**
Leonel Sánchez 84 (1955–1968)

**TROPHIES/HONORS**
none

# USA

*"TEN YEARS AGO COUNTRIES LAUGHED AT US AND WE DIDN'T GET RESPECT, BUT IT IS COMPLETELY DIFFERENT NOW. YOU CAN JUST SENSE THAT IT IS A BIG GAME TO PLAY US."*

FORMER US CAPTAIN CLAUDIO REYNA

The United States Soccer Federation was formed in 1913 and it was affiliated to FIFA in the same year. It was actually called the US Football Federation until 1945, when the name was changed to soccer.

Once known for bringing razzmatazz, cheerleaders, and big-screen replays to soccer—aka footfall—the US now boasts a robust national team. Eyebrows were raised when the US was allocated the 1994 World Cup, but qualification for every World Cup since has silenced critics. A "clean sheet" here may be called a "shutout" elsewhere, but the fresh blood and new ideas from the US have invigorated the world game.

*Bart McGhee (left) and Bert Patenaude (right)*

## HISTORY MAKERS

The US exceeded expectations at the 1930 World Cup and reached the semifinals. American Bart McGhee scored the first-ever goal in a World Cup Finals in a 3–0 win against Belgium and his teammate Bert Patenaude is generally credited with scoring the first-ever World Cup hat trick against Paraguay.

## MODERN SUCCESS

In 2007, the US overcame the rest of North and Central America to triumph in the CONCACAF Gold Cup. Also the host country, the US beat Mexico 2–1 in the final.

USA DREAM TEAM? 1. Kasey Keller 2. Eddie Pope 3. Paul Caligiuri 4. Tab Ramos 5. Marcelo Balboa 6. Walter Bahr 7. Claudio Reyna 8. John Harkes 9. Joe Gaetjens 10. Landon Donovan 11. Brian McBride

## COBI JONES

Along with Earnie Stewart, John Harkes, and Alexi Lalas, lively winger Cobi Jones was one of the host country's heroes when the US reached the second round of the 1994 World Cup Finals. More than five years since he retired, Jones remains by far and away his country's player with the most appearances.

### FACT FILE: USA
#### NICKNAMES
The Stars and Stripes,
The Red, White, and Blue

#### TOP GOAL SCORERS
1. Landon Donovan 42 (2000–present)
2. Eric Wynalda 34 (1990–2000)
3. Brian McBride 30 (1993–2006)
4. Joe-Max Moore 24 (1992–2002)
5. Bruce Murray 21 (1985–1993)

#### MOST APPEARANCES
1. Cobi Jones 164 (1992–2004)
2. Jeff Agoos 134 (1988–2003)
3. Marcelo Balboa 128 (1988–2000)
4. Landon Donovan 120 (2000–present)
5. Claudio Reyna 112 (1994–2006)

## TEAM LEADER

So far, US captain Landon Donovan has scored 35 goals in 99 appearances. He was US Soccer's Male Athlete of the Year in 2003 and 2004, and was honored with a place in the MLS All-Time Best Team. He plays his club soccer for LA Galaxy, alongside David Beckham.

*Since Claudio Reyna's retirement, Donovan has been the USA's first choice No.10.*

The first American ever to be named in a World Cup All-Tournament team (2002), Claudio Reyna (112 caps) appeared in four USA World Cup squads from 1994 to 2006. He preceded Donovan as US captain, and his leadership skills and battling midfield style earned him the nickname "Captain America."

#### TROPHIES/HONORS
##### CONCACAF GOLD CUP
2007 USA 2 Mexico 1
2005 USA 0 Panama 0 (USA won 3–1 in a penalty shoot-out)
2002 USA 2 Costa Rica 0
1991 USA 0 Honduras 0 (USA won 4–3 in a penalty shoot-out)

Clint Dempsey greatly enhanced his reputation as a versatile attacker as the US reached the final of the 2009 FIFA Confederations Cup. He was goal-scoring Man of the Match in the semifinal victory over Spain, ending the European champions' 15-match record winning run. He struck again in the final, although Brazil eventually won 3–2.

## DID YOU KNOW?

*In the 1950 World Cup the US beat England 1–0 in one of the greatest upsets of all time, thanks to goalkeeper Frank Borghi and goal scorer Joe Gaetjens.*

*In 1984, the national side, then known as Team America, played in the North American Soccer League. It was believed that regular competition would improve the side, but it finished bottom of the league.*

## MICHAEL BRADLEY

His father Bob may be coach of the national team, but midfielder Michael Bradley is in the team on talent alone. His tenacious tackling and never-say-die spirit help make him one of the country's most exciting soccer prospects.

# CONCACAF TEAMS

*"WHOEVER INVENTED FOOTBALL SHOULD BE WORSHIPED AS A GOD."*

FORMER MEXICO COACH AND STRIKER HUGO SANCHEZ

The CONCACAF has 40 members and is dominated by Mexico and the US. The federation also includes three South American nations—Guyana, Suriname, and French Guiana. Since 1991, CONCACAF's showpiece tournament has been the Gold Cup. While Mexico has won the CONCACAF championship more times than anyone else, the US has been catching up fast—only for Mexico to thrash its archrivals 5–0 in the most recent final.

*Rafa Márquez is Mexican soccer's modern superstar.*

## MEXICO

Since the 1990s, Mexico has established itself as a regional and world soccer power. The team combines a direct, physical approach with individual brilliance. Striker Hugo Sánchez is widely regarded as the greatest Mexican player of all time and was the national coach until April 2008.

Goalkeeper Antonio Carbajal made his World Cup Finals debut as a 21-year-old in 1950, and 16 years later became the first player to appear in five consecutive Finals tournaments. He was respected for his safe hands and his leadership, but in all his 11 games at the Finals he ended up on the winning side only once.

## CUBA

With baseball as the national sport, Cuba has never been a major soccer power. However, the national team has shown greater promise in recent times, reaching the last four of the CONCACAF Gold Cup in 2003 and only narrowly missing out on qualification for the 2006 World Cup Finals in Germany.

### FACT FILE

**TOP GOAL SCORER**
Information unknown

**MOST APPEARANCES**
Information unknown

**TROPHIES/HONORS**
none

Rafael Márquez is Mexico's captain. He plays as a defender or midfielder and made his international debut at 17-years-old. He became the first Mexican to win a UEFA Champions League medal when his club, Barcelona, won the title in 2006.

### FACT FILE

**TOP GOAL SCORER**
Jared Borgetti 46 (1997–present)

**MOST APPEARANCES**
Claudio Suárez 178 (1992–2006)

**TROPHIES/HONORS**
CONCACAF CHAMPIONSHIP AND GOLD CUP
2009 Mexico 5 USA 0
2003 Mexico 1 Brazil 0
1998 Mexico 1 USA 0
1996 Mexico 2 Brazil 0
1993 Mexico 4 USA 0
1977 (top World Cup qualifying team awarded trophy)
1971, 1965 (round-robin team tournaments)

MEXICO DREAM TEAM?  1. Antonio Carbajal 2. Salvador Carmona 3. Ramón Ramírez 4. Pável Pardo 5. Claudio Suárez 6. Rafael Márquez 7. Luis de la Fuente 8. Cuauhtémoc Blanco 9. Jared Borgetti 10. Hugo Sánchez 11. Luis Hernández

## COSTA RICA

First successful in the early 1960s, Costa Rica suffered a slump in the 1970s and 1980s. The national team has reemerged as a force in the 1990s and 2000s and qualified for three World Cups. Only Mexico and the USA have been crowned CONCACAF champions more often than Costa Rica's 'Los Ticos'.

**FACT FILE**
**TOP GOAL SCORER**
Rolando Fonseca 47 (1992–present)
**MOST APPEARANCES**
Wálter Centeno 135 (1995–present)

**TROPHIES/HONORS**
**CONCACAF CHAMPIONSHIP AND GOLD CUP**
1989 (top World Cup qualifying team awarded trophy)
1969, 1963 (round-robin team tournaments)

With 45 goals in 73 international games, Paolo Wanchope is one of Costa Rica's most prolific strikers. He has played club soccer in England, Spain, Japan and the US.

## HAITI

A golden age in the late 1960s and 1970s saw Haiti reach the 1974 World Cup Finals. However, political and social problems led to a decline in the national soccer team. Now playing some home games at Miami, the future is looking slightly brighter. Haiti drew with the US at the 2009 CONCACAF Gold Cup and reached the quarterfinals.

**FACT FILE**
**TOP GOAL SCORER**
Golman Pierre 23 (1996–2003)

**MOST APPEARANCES**
Pierre-Richard Bruny 83 (1998–present)

**TROPHIES/HONORS**
none

## HONDURAS

Hondurans are passionate about soccer and in 1970 the result of a game led to a war against El Salvador. After appearing at the 1982 World Cup Finals, Honduras endured a long barren spell before a Carlos Pavon goal clinched qualification for the 2010 tournament in South Africa.

**FACT FILE**
**TOP GOAL SCORERS**
Carlos Pavón 56 (1993–present)

**MOST APPEARANCES**
Amado Guevara 129 (1994–present)

**TROPHIES/HONORS**
none

## TRINIDAD AND TOBAGO

Nicknamed the "Soca Warriors," Trinidad and Tobago are the Caribbean's most successful national team. However, a row over bonus payments following Trinidad and Tobago's first ever World Cup in 2006 means that many of the team's stars no longer play for their country.

**FACT FILE**
**TOP GOAL SCORER**
Stern John 69 (1995–present)
**MOST APPEARANCES**
Angus Eve 117 (1994–2005)

**TROPHIES/HONORS**
none

One-time T&T captain Dwight Yorke played in Manchester United's famous 1999 treble-winning side.

## CANADA

Victory in the 2000 CONCACAF Gold Cup was seen to be Canada's big breakthrough, but the weakness of Canadian club soccer has been blamed for failures to reach the 2006 or 2010 World Cup Finals.

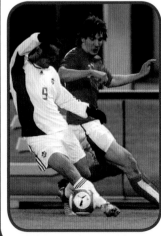

Canada striker Tomasz Radzinski (far left) has played at the top level in England and Belgium.

**FACT FILE**
**TOP GOAL SCORERS**
John Catliff 19 (1984–1994)
Dale Mitchell 19 (1980–1993)
**MOST APPEARANCES**
Randy Samuel 82 (1983–1997)

**TROPHIES/HONORS**
**CONCACAF CHAMPIONSHIP AND GOLD CUP**
2000 Canada 2 Colombia 0
1985 (top World Cup qualifying team awarded trophy)

## JAMAICA

Known as the "Reggae Boyz," Jamaica made its first visit to the World Cup Finals in 1998. However, the team has struggled recently, despite unexpected wins over Mexico and Honduras in 2010 World Cup qualifiers and an increasingly strong domestic league.

**FACT FILE**
**TOP GOAL SCORER**
Paul Young 28 (unknown)
**MOST APPEARANCES**
Ian Goodison 113 (1996–present)

**TROPHIES/HONORS**
none

One of Jamaica's leading scorers, midfielder Theodore Whitmore was his country's Footballer of the Year in 1998.

Captain Anthony Modeste (above, right) plays in defense but has a nose for goal.

## GRENADA

The improving "Spice Boyz" of Grenada qualified for their first ever CONCACAF Gold Cup in 2009.

**FACT FILE**

TOP GOAL SCORER
Ricky Charles 29 (1995–present)

MOST APPEARANCES
Information not available

## US VIRGIN ISLANDS

It may be one of the world's weakest teams, but the team is looking to improve by investing in youth.

**FACT FILE**

TOP GOAL SCORER
Kevin Sheppard 2 (2002–present)

MOST APPEARANCES
Dwight Ferguson (unknown)

## PANAMA

The 21st century has seen Panama make progress. It only lost the 2005 CONCACAF Gold Cup final to the US on penalties and has since beaten Bolivia, Colombia, and South Africa.

Versatile defender and team captain Felipe Baloy (right) has big-match experience from playing in Brazil and Mexico.

**FACT FILE**

TOP GOAL SCORER
José Luis Garcés 25 (2000–present)

MOST APPEARANCES
José Antony Torres 85 (2000–present)

## MONTSERRAT

Montserrat rarely plays internationals due to the threat of volcanic activity on an island of just 5,000 people.

**FACT FILE**

TOP GOAL SCORER
Information not available

MOST APPEARANCES
Information not available

## ANTIGUA AND BARBUDA

Although their passion is cricket, these islands are embracing soccer, with games at the Sir Vivian Richards Cricket Stadium.

**FACT FILE**

TOP GOAL SCORER
Information not available

MOST APPEARANCES
Information not available

## SURINAME

Many great Dutch players have links to this former Dutch colony, including Ruud Gullit, Edgar Davids, and Frank Rijkaard.

**FACT FILE**

TOP GOAL SCORER
Clifton Sandvliet 79 (2000–present)

MOST APPEARANCES
Clifton Sandvliet 68 (2000–present)

## PUERTO RICO

Puerto Rico went 14 years without a win, before reaching the second round of CONCACAF's 2010 World Cup qualifiers.

**FACT FILE**

TOP GOAL SCORER
Raphael Ortiz 4 (2006–present)

MOST APPEARANCES
Information not available

## GUYANA

The "Golden Jaguars" sunk to 181st in the FIFA rankings in 2004, but rose dramatically to 90th three years later.

**FACT FILE**

TOP GOAL SCORER
Information not available

MOST APPEARANCES
Information not available

## NICARAGUA

Nicaragua made its first trip to a major international tournament with the CONCACAF Gold Cup in 2009.

**FACT FILE**

TOP GOAL SCORER
Emilio Palacios 11 (unknown–present)

MOST APPEARANCES
Carlos Alonso 36 (unknown–present)

## BERMUDA

Bermudan Clyde Best was a popular striker in England, the US, and Netherlands before becoming a coach.

**FACT FILE**

TOP GOAL SCORER
Information not available

MOST APPEARANCES
Information not available

Striker Robin Nelisse had a healthy strike rate in the Dutch Eredivisie.

## NETHERLANDS ANTILLES

Officially part of the Netherlands, and made up of two island groups, this area's football future is in doubt.

**FACT FILE**

TOP GOAL SCORER
Information not available

MOST APPEARANCES
Information not available

## ST. VINCENT AND THE GRENADINES

Goalkeeper Melvin Andrews is closing in on 150 caps for one of the Caribbean's tiniest countries.

**FACT FILE**

TOP GOAL SCORER
Shandel Samuel 16 (2004–present)

MOST APPEARANCES
Melvin Andrews 145 (1996–present)

## TURKS AND CAICOS ISLANDS

Ecstatic crowds enjoyed a first World Cup win against St. Lucia in 2008, starring LA Galaxy's Gavin Glinton.

**FACT FILE**

TOP GOAL SCORER
Gavin Glinton 4 (2004–present)

MOST APPEARANCES
Duane Glinton 7 (2004–2008)
Charles Cook 7 (2000–2008)
Errion Charles 7 (1999–2004)

Among the team's most creditable recent results have been a win over Costa Rica and a draw with Northern Ireland.

## BARBADOS

The "Bajan Braves" have been recruiting European-based players, such as Wigan Athletic's Emmerson Boyce.

**FACT FILE**

TOP GOAL SCORER
Information not available

MOST APPEARANCES
Information not available

## CAYMAN ISLANDS

A first World Cup appearance remains a distant dream for the team of these sun-kissed islands.

**FACT FILE**

TOP GOAL SCORER
Lee Ramoon (unknown)

MOST APPEARANCES
Lee Ramoon (unknown)

## BELIZE

A tiny country, with few soccer pros, Belize made the second round of CONCACAF's 2010 World Cup qualifiers.

**FACT FILE**

TOP GOAL SCORER
Dion Frazer 3 (2000–2008)

MOST APPEARANCES
Vallan Symms 25 (unknown)

## BAHAMAS

Dubbed the "Rake'n'Scrape Boyz" after a local style of music, this tropical paradise's players have had little to sing about so far.

**FACT FILE**

TOP GOAL SCORER
Nesley Jean 3 (2004–present)

MOST APPEARANCES
Lionel Haven (unknown)

## BRITISH VIRGIN ISLANDS

The "Nature Boyz" were unfortunate to be knocked out of 2010 World Cup qualifiers without losing a game.

**FACT FILE**

TOP GOAL SCORER
Avondale Williams 5 (unknown)

MOST APPEARANCES
Information not available

## DOMINICAN REPUBLIC

Soccerl fans in the Dominican Republic have an uphill task trying to replace baseball in the nation's affections.

**FACT FILE**

TOP GOAL SCORER
Information not available

MOST APPEARANCES
Information not available

## ST. LUCIA

English league veteran Ken Charlery is the biggest name to have turned out for St. Lucia, which relies on home-based amateurs.

**FACT FILE**

TOP GOAL SCORER
Information not available

MOST APPEARANCES
Information not available

## ST. KITTS AND NEVIS

National pride rests on the goal-scoring "Sugar Boyz" abroad—Keith Gumbs in Indonesia and Atiba Harris in the US.

**FACT FILE**

TOP GOAL SCORER
Keith Gumbs 47 (1989–present)

MOST APPEARANCES
Keith Gumbs 131 (1989–present)

## DOMINICA

Dominica's development was stalled by a 17 months run without any games, before entering the 2010 World Cup qualifiers.

**FACT FILE**

TOP GOAL SCORER
Information not available

MOST APPEARANCES
Information not available

## ARUBA

The island of Aruba has been striving for progress since splitting from the Netherland Antilles in 1986.

**FACT FILE**

TOP GOAL SCORER
Information not available

MOST APPEARANCES
Information not available

## EL SALVADOR

El Salvador holds the record for heaviest World Cup Finals defeat—10–1 to Hungary in 1982. It lost all three games at the tournament, but brave displays in the 2010 qualifiers inspired hopes for future success.

Dynamic winger Eliseo Quintanilla (right) is today's fan-favorite.

**FACT FILE**

TOP GOAL SCORER
Jorge "Mágico" Gonzáles 41 (1979–1998)

MOST APPEARANCES
Luis Guevara Mora 89 (1979–1996)

## GUATEMALA

Guatemala came close to reaching the 2006 World Cup Finals, but the 1967 CONCACAF championship was its greatest day.

**FACT FILE**

TOP GOAL SCORER
Carlos Ruiz 41 (1998–present)

MOST APPEARANCES
Guillermo Ramírez 91 (1997–present)

Carlos Ruíz (above) was a big hit in US with LA Galaxy.

## ANGUILLA

Plucky Anguilla field mostly non-league players from England and play its biggest games in US stadia.

**FACT FILE**

TOP GOAL SCORER
Information not available

MOST APPEARANCES
Information not available

# AFRICA

*"WHEREVER YOU GO THERE [AFRICA], THEY'RE ALL PLAYING FOOTBALL ALL THE TIME. EVERYWHERE."*

CARLOS BILARDO, FORMER LIBYA AND ARGENTINA COACH

CAPE VERDE ISLANDS

The Confederation of African Football was formed in 1957 and was allocated its first guaranteed World Cup place in 1970. The first African Cup of Nations took place in the same year but featured only three teams. Today, the CAF has 53 members and Africa has five World Cup Finals places. (This will rise to six in 2010, since South Africa qualifies automatically as host.)

When the Brazilian legend Pelé said that an African nation would win the World Cup by the year 2000, his prediction was a little premature. However, his remarks helped to bring African soccer to the world's attention. During the last decade, the soccer world has had to sit up and take notice of Africa. Skillful and entertaining teams such as Ghana, Senegal, and Egypt have emerged, as well as talented individuals such as Ivory Coast's Didier Drogba and Cameroon's Samuel Eto'o. In this diverse continent, soccer has a power beyond politics or religion to unite divided nations and bring a shared sense of identity.

## AFRICAN STYLE

Blowing your own horn is common to all soccer fans, but in Africa a deafening bray can often be heard from the passionate supporters who love to make themselves heard. As elsewhere in the world, soccer fanaticism provides an opportunity for celebration that everyday life sometimes fails to deliver.

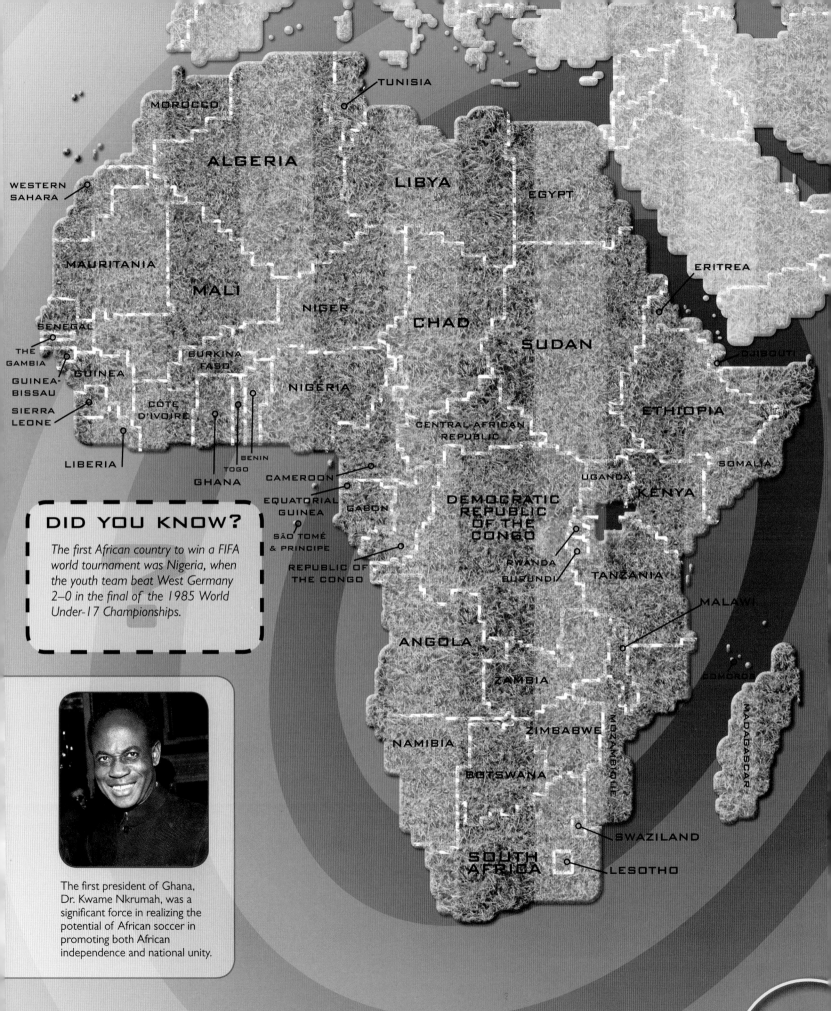

TUNISIA

MOROCCO

ALGERIA

LIBYA

EGYPT

WESTERN
SAHARA

MAURITANIA

ERITREA

MALI

NIGER

CHAD

SUDAN

SENEGAL

THE
GAMBIA

GUINEA

BURKINA
FASO

DJIBOUTI

GUINEA-
BISSAU

CÔTE
D'IVOIRE

NIGERIA

ETHIOPIA

SIERRA
LEONE

CENTRAL AFRICAN
REPUBLIC

SOMALIA

BENIN

UGANDA

KENYA

LIBERIA

TOGO

GHANA

CAMEROON

EQUATORIAL
GUINEA

GABON

DEMOCRATIC
REPUBLIC
OF THE
CONGO

SÃO TOMÉ
& PRINCIPE

RWANDA

BURUNDI

TANZANIA

REPUBLIC OF
THE CONGO

MALAWI

## DID YOU KNOW?

The first African country to win a FIFA
world tournament was Nigeria, when
the youth team beat West Germany
2–0 in the final of the 1985 World
Under-17 Championships.

ANGOLA

ZAMBIA

COMOROS

ZIMBABWE

MOZAMBIQUE

MADAGASCAR

NAMIBIA

BOTSWANA

SWAZILAND

SOUTH
AFRICA

LESOTHO

The first president of Ghana,
Dr. Kwame Nkrumah, was a
significant force in realizing the
potential of African soccer in
promoting both African
independence and national unity.

# SOUTH AFRICA

**"2010 IS ON EVERYONE'S LIPS AND THE PEOPLE OF SOUTH AFRICA ARE LOOKING FORWARD TO GIVING THE WORLD A WARM AFRICAN WELCOME."**

MOLEFI OLIPHANT, PRESIDENT OF THE SOUTH AFRICAN FA

South Africa is proudly pioneering a new era of African soccer after spending three decades in sporting exile. In 1962, the country was expelled by FIFA for refusing to field a mixed-race team and was only allowed back when the apartheid (racial segregation) regime ended in 1992. South Africa celebrated by beating Cameroon 1–0 in its comeback match, thanks to a late penalty by Theophilus "Doctor" Khumalo. In 2010, the "Bafana Bafana" welcome the World Cup to Africa for the first time.

The South African Football Association was founded in 1991. The team play in yellow and green, the same colors adopted for Zakumi, the 2010 World Cup's leopard mascot.

## SUCCESS!

For many South Africans, it was enough simply to host the African Cup of Nations in 1996, but to win was unbelievable, especially for the 80,000 home fans. A year later Phil Masinga's winning goal against Congo saw South Africa qualify for their first World Cup.

Super sub Mark Williams (above, right) secured a place in South African sporting history with the only two goals in the 1996 African Cup of Nations final. Although he traveled widely as a player, his career was overshadowed by that 1996 tournament, where he scored five goals in total— one more than strike partner John "Shoes" Moshoeu.

*Aaron Mokoena in action against Ghana in 2006.*

## YOUNG CAPTAIN

Aaron Mokoena became South Africa's youngest player, when he made his debut against Botswana in 1999 aged 18 years and 56 days. The versatile player, known as "The Ax," is now his country's captain and most-capped player, closing in on a century of caps.

Star striker Benni McCarthy has had impressive spells with Ajax Cape Town, Ajax Amsterdam, Celta Vigo, Porto and Blackburn Rovers, but his international career has been disrupted by disputes with coaches. Despite quitting the team three times, McCarthy is South Africa's leading scorer and remains a folk hero in his native country.

SOUTH AFRICA DREAM TEAM? 1. Andre Arendse 2. Aaron Mokoena 3. Neil Tovey 4. Jomo Sono 5. Lucas Radebe 6. Mark Fish 7. 'Doctor' Khumalo 8. Patrick Ntsoelengoe 9. Steve Mokone 10. Benni McCarthy 11. Kaizer Motaung

Orlando Pirates and Leeds United supporters admired central defender Lucas Radebe for his inspiring leadership and strength. He captained South Africa's World Cup teams in 1998 and 2002. Since retiring from the game he has become an anti-racism campaigner, FIFA Fair Play Award winner and children's charity worker.

## FACT FILE: SOUTH AFRICA
### NICKNAME
Bafana Bafana (The Boys)

### TOP GOAL SCORERS
1. Benni McCarthy 31 (1997–present)
2. Shaun Bartlett 29 (1995–2005)
3. Phil Masinga 18 (1992–2001)
4. Siyabonga Nomvethe 15 (1999–present)
5. Sibusiso Zuma 13 (1998–2008)

### MOST APPEARANCES
1. Aaron Mokoena 90 (1999–present)
2. Benni McCarthy 76 (1997–present)
3. Shaun Bartlett 74 (1995–2005)
4. John Moshoeu 73 (1993–2004)
5. Delron Buckley 72 (1998–present)

### TROPHIES/HONORS
**AFRICAN NATIONS CUP**
1996 South Africa 2 Tunisia 0

*Pienaar is happy playing wide on either wing or drifting inside.*

## STEVEN PIENAAR

Midfielder Steven Pienaar's nimble skills and passing precision have won him many fans in England, where he plays his club soccer with Everton, and brought him hero status back home in South Africa. Alongside the more robust presence of MacBeth Sibaya in midfield, Pienaar provides the South Africa national team's best attacking impetus.

## 2010
The World Cup Finals are on their way to Africa at last. Just one FIFA delegate's vote denied South Africa the chance to host the 2006 tournament, but now the pressure is on to bring the ambitious plans for 2010 to life. Of the 10 venues, five will be entirely new ones with more seats promised per match than at any World Cup since 1994.

Host South Africa defied the odds by reaching the semifinals of the 2009 FIFA Confederations Cup. Joel Santana's side almost sneaked a draw against European champions Spain in the third-place playoff, thanks to a spectacular late brace by striker Katlego Mphela (above, right). Although Spain won 3–2, Mphela and other home-based talents such as Teko Modise and Siphiwe Tshabalala offered South Africa fans plenty to applaud.

# IVORY COAST

"WHEN WE PLAY, ALL OF IVORY COAST IS HAPPY."

MIDFIELDER YAYA TOURÉ

Ivory Coast's (also known as Côte d'Ivoire) first visit to the World Cup Finals in 2006 earned "the Elephants" many admirers, even if their entertaining soccer was not quite enough to reach the second round. Since 2006, Ivory Coast has continued to emerge as a force in world soccer, and many Ivoirian talents can be seen at the world's most prestigious clubs.

The FIF (Fédération Ivoirienne de Football) was founded in 1960. The orange shirts, white shorts, and green socks reflect the three colors of the Ivoirian flag.

## FACT FILE: IVORY COAST

### NICKNAME
Les Éléphants (The Elephants)

### TOP GOAL SCORERS
1. Didier Drogba 41 (2002–present)
2. Information not available
3. Information not available
4. Information not available
5. Information not available

### MOST APPEARANCES
1. Didier Zokora 75 (2000–present)
2. Didier Drogba 52 (2002–present)
3. Cyrille Domoraud 51 (1995–present)
= Bonaventure Kalou 51 (1998–present)
5. Kolo Touré 45 (2000–present)

### TROPHIES/HONORS

AFRICAN CUP OF NATIONS
1992 Côte d'Ivoire 0 Ghana 0
(Côte d'Ivoire won 11–10 in a penalty shoot-out)

*Drogba not only played but helped coach the Ivory Coast team at the 2008 African Cup of Nations after manager Uli Stielike's son tragically died.*

## DROGBA

Didier Drogba is one of the most prolific strikers in the world today. His pace and power terrify defenders, while his finishing is as graceful as it is clinical. Drogba also uses his status as a sporting hero in his work as a UN Goodwill Ambassador.

Although Didier Zokora shook Dutch goalkeeper Edwin van der Sar's woodwork at the 2006 World Cup scoring is not his priority, instead the Ivory Coast's most-capped player is much happier scrapping as a holding midfielder.

## TOP TALENT

Kolo Touré (right) and his younger brother Yaya (left) are products of the Ivory Coast's flourishing youth academies. Kolo is a versatile defender, while Yaya is a surging midfielder. Youngest brother Ibrahim is a striker, but he has yet to win a cap.

## DID YOU KNOW?

*Laurent Pokou held the record as top African Cup of Nations goal scorer for 38 years. He scored six at the 1968 tournament and then eight more two years later, including five in a single gmae. Pokou's record was broken in 2008 by Cameroon's Samuel Eto'o.*

CÔTE D'IVOIRE DREAM TEAM? 1. Alain Gouaméné 2. Emmanuel Eboué 3. Dominique Sam Abou 4. Didier Zokora 5. Kolo Touré 6. Cyrille Domoraud 7. Salomon Kalou 8. Yaya Touré 9. Laurent Pokou 10. Didier Drogba 11. Youssouf Falikou Fofana

# GHANA

*"FOOTBALL IS NOT SIMPLY THE MOST POPULAR SPORT IN GHANA, IT'S LIKE A RELIGION."*

OTTO PFISTER, COACH OF GHANA'S U-17
WORLD CUP WINNERS IN 1991

The Ghana Football Association was founded in 1957. The "Black Stars" play in an all white uniform, although change colors add red, yellow, or green shades.

Ghana has a reputation for developing dynamic young teams. It won the Under-17s World Cup in 1991 and 1995 and a bronze medal at the 1992 Olympic Games. Only Egypt has won the African Cup of Nations more times and like its neighbors and rivals, Ivory Coast, Ghana made its World Cup Finals debut in 2006.

## FACT FILE: GHANA

**NICKNAME**
The Black Stars

**TOP GOAL SCORERS**
1. Abédi "Pelé" Ayew 33 (1981–1998)
2. Anthony Yeboah 29 (1985–1997)
3. Karim Abdul Razak 25 (unknown)
4. Information not available
5. Information not available

**MOST APPEARANCES**
1. Abédi "Pelé" Ayew 73 (1981–1998)
2. Karim Abdul Razak 70 (unknown)
3. Yaw Preko 68 (1992-2007)
4. Richard Kingson 62 (1996–present)
5. John Mensah 61 (2001–present)

**TROPHIES/HONORS**
**AFRICAN CUP OF NATIONS**
1982 Ghana 1 Libya 1 (Ghana won 7–6 in a penalty shootout)
1978 Ghana 2 Uganda 0
1965 Ghana 3 Tunisia 2 (aet)
1963 Ghana 3 Sudan 0

*Muntari scored the first goal in Ghana's 2–0 victory over the Czech Republic in the 2006 World Cup Finals.*

## DRIVING FORCE

Midfielder Sulley Muntari is already a firm favorite with Ghana fans thanks to his dazzling dribbling skills and combative playing style. Despite an often fiery temperament, Muntari is a vital part of the Ghana team.

Michael Essien (right) and captain Stephen Appiah were the midfield motors as Ghana—the youngest squad at the 2006 World Cup—became the only African side in the second round. The versatile Essien has long been seen as a future African Footballer of the Year—a prize won by flamboyant Ghana midfielders Ibrahim Sunday in 1971 and Karim Abdul Razak in 1978.

## DID YOU KNOW?

*The world's first black professional player, Arthur Wharton, was born in what is now Accra, Ghana. He played for various teams in the English leagues from 1885 to 1902.*

Three-time African Footballer of the Year Abédi "Pelé" Ayew (left) is arguably one of the greatest ever African players and surely worthy of his illustrious nickname. He is Ghana's most capped player as well as the top scorer and he was one of the first African players to enjoy success in Europe, in particular with French side Olympique Marseille.

**GHANA DREAM TEAM?**
1. Robert Mensah 2. Ofei Ansah 3. Kwasi Appiah 4. Michael Essien 5. Samuel Kuffour 6. Charles Addo Odametey 7. Baba Yara 8. Karim Abdul Razak 9. Opoku 'Bayie' Afriyie 10. Abédi 'Pelé' Ayew 11. Mohammed 'Polo' Ahmed

### TOP GOAL SCORERS
1. Samuel Eto'o 43 (1996–present)
2. Patrick Mboma 33 (1995–2004)
3. Roger Milla 28 (1978–1994)
4. Information not available
5. Information not available

### MOST APPEARANCES
1. Rigobert Song 131 (1993–present)
2. Roger Milla 102 (1978–1994)
3. Information not available
4. Information not available
5. Information not available)

### TROPHIES/HONORS
#### AFRICAN CUP OF NATIONS
2002 Cameroon 0 Senegal 0 (aet)
(Cameroon won 3–2 on penalties)
2000 Cameroon 2 Nigeria 2 (aet)
(Cameroon won 4–3 on penalties)
1988 Cameroon 1 Nigeria 0
1984 Cameroon 3 Nigeria 1

#### OLYMPIC GOLD MEDAL
2000 Cameroon 2 Spain 2
(Cameroon won 5–3 on penalties)

Fédération Camerounaise de Football was founded in 1959. The "Indomitable Lions" traditionally play in green shirts, red shorts and yellow socks.

# CAMEROON

## "IT'S THANKS TO FOOTBALL THAT A SMALL COUNTRY COULD BECOME GREAT."
CAMEROON LEGEND ROGER MILLA

Cameroon captivated the world when they opened Italia '90 by defeating reigning champions Argentina. It went on to reach the quarterfinals—becoming the first African side ever to do so. Although Cameroon surprisingly missed out on the 2006 World Cup Finals, a young side, inspired by Samuel Eto'o, is bouncing back confidently for 2010.

## STAR STRIKER
Samuel Eto'o made his international debut at age 15 and has gone on to captain his country. The striker combines dynamic pace with deadly accuracy in the penalty area. Eto'o is Cameroon's all-time top goal scorer and has won more major trophies than any other African player.

Eto'o's honors include an unprecedented hat trick of African Footballer of the Year prizes.

Cameroon fans are cheering a different Song with the emergence of Rigobert's nephew, Alexandre. The talented youngster made his debut at the 2008 African Cup of Nations and was part of the "team of the tournament." Versatile Song can play in central defence or midfield.

Roger Milla (left) came out of semi-retirement to become the hero of the 1990 World Cup Finals. At the age of 38, the veteran striker scored four times and celebrated each goal in unique style. Four years later, at USA '94, Milla became the World Cup's oldest scorer with a goal against Russia.

Rigobert Song (right) became the youngest player to be red-carded in a World Cup in 1994, aged 17. He was sent off again four years later but the rugged defender recovered to become Cameroon's most-capped and most reliable player.

**CAMEROON DREAM TEAM?** 1. Thomas Nkono 2. Rigobert Song 3. Lauren 4. Marc-Vivien Foé 5. Stephen Tataw 6. Emmanuel Kundé 7. Geremi 8. Théophile Abega 9. Patrick Mboma 10. Roger Milla 11. Samuel Eto'o

# NIGERIA

**"WE ARE STILL THE TEAM TO BEAT IN AFRICA. EVERY GAME FOR US IS LIKE A FINAL."**

FORMER NIGERIA CAPTAIN JAY-JAY OKOCHA

The Nigeria Football Association was founded in 1945. Nigeria's long-standing choice of home uniform means they the team is often known as not just "Super Eagles," but "Green Eagles" instead.

When the "Super Eagles" are soaring, they inspire dreams of a first African World Cup winner. They certainly have the potential: Nigeria's "Golden Eaglets" won the U-17 World Championships in 1985, 1993 and 2007. The senior team won Olympic gold in 1996 but so far has not gone beyond the second round of the World Cup Finals.

## MIKEL JOHN OBI

Hopes are high for a Nigerian resurgence with plenty of young, talented players coming through the ranks. Mikel John Obi is a powerhouse in midfield for English giants Chelsea, and if he can recreate his club form for Nigeria, the Eagles could indeed be Super.

*Mikel was named second best player as Nigeria finished runners-up at the 2005 FIFA World Youth Cup, beaten by Lionel Messi and Argentina on both counts.*

## FACT FILE: NIGERIA

**NICKNAME**
Super Eagles

**TOP GOAL SCORERS**
1. Rashidi Yekini 37 (1984–1998)
2. Segun Odegbami 23 (1976–1981)
3. Yakuba Aiyegbeni 18 (2000–present)
4. Daniel Amokachi 14 (1990–1999)
= 'Jay-Jay' Okocha 14 (1993–2006)
= Julius Aghahowa 14 (1999–2006)

**MOST APPEARANCES**
1. Mudashiru Lawal 86 (1975–1985)
2. Nwankwo Kanu 80 (1994–present)
3. 'Jay-Jay' Okocha 75 (1993–2006)
4. Peter Rufai 68 (1981–1998)
5. Finidi George 66 (1991–2002)

**TROPHIES/HONORS**
**AFRICAN CUP OF NATIONS**
1994 Nigeria 2 Zambia 1
1980 Nigeria 3 Algeria 0

**OLYMPIC GOLD MEDAL**
1996 Nigeria 3 Argentina 2

Victor Obinna (above right) was captain and top scorer when Nigeria narrowly lost to Argentina in the 2008 Olympics final. Along with another promising young Nigerian striker, Chinedu Obasi, Obinna plays his club football in Europe and hopes to emulate the success of Nigeria team-mates such as Obafemi Martins.

All-time top scorer, Rashidi Yekini (left) scored Nigeria's first ever World Cup Finals' goal in USA '94, in a 3–0 win over Bulgaria. Strikers Yekini and Daniel Amokachi, plus wingers Tijani Babandiga and Finidi George, inspired Nigeria to the second round of the tournament.

Striker Nwankwo Kanu (right) is one of Africa's most successful players, boasting two African Player of the Year awards and an Olympic gold medal, plus UEFA Champions League, UEFA Cup, Nigerian Premier League, Eredivisie, English Premier League and English FA Cup winners' medals at club level.

**NIGERIA DREAM TEAM?**
1. Peter Rufai 2. Christian Chukwu 3. Taribo West 4. Augustine 'Jay-Jay' Okocha 5. Stephen Keshi 6. Uche Okechukwu 7. Finidi George 8. Segun Odegbami 9. Rashidi Yekini 10. Nwankwo Kanu 11. Emmanuel Amuneke

# EGYPT

Egypt wears red shirts, black shorts, and white socks, with a green change uniform. They are, predictably, nicknamed "The Pharaohs."

Consistently one of Africa's highest ranked teams, Egypt has reigned supreme in the African Nations Cup, a record six times. It has also flown the flag for Africa at two World Cups, but was beat out for the 2010 World Cup by Algeria.

In 2008, Egypt became the first country to win the African Nations Cup six times, thanks to a 1–0 win over Cameroon. In 2006 it won on home soil (pictured right), beating the Ivory Coast on penalties.

## FACT FILE: EGYPT

### NICKNAME
The Pharaohs

### TOP GOAL SCORERS
1. Hossam Hassan 69 (1985–2006)
2. Mahmoud El Khatib 39 (1974–1986)
3. Magdi Abdelghani 34 (1980–1990)
4. Emad Moteab 27 (2005–present)
5. Amr Zaki 26 (2004–present)

### MOST APPEARANCES
1. Hossam Hassan 169 (1985–2006)
2. Ahmed Hassan 162 (1995–present)
3. Ibrahim Hassan 125 (1989–2004)
4. Hany Ramzy 124 (1988–2003)
5. Magdi Abdelghani 123 (1980–1990)

### TROPHIES/HONORS
**AFRICAN CUP OF NATIONS**
2008 Egypt 1 Cameroon 0
2006 Egypt 0 Ivory Coast 0 (Egypt won 4–2 in a penalty shoot-out)
1998 Egypt 2 South Africa 0
1986 Egypt 0 Cameroon 0 (Egypt won 5–4 in a penalty shootout)
1959 Egypt 2 Sudan 1
1957 Egypt 4 Ethiopia 0

Hossam Hassan is the fifth highest international goal scorer of all time.

## HOSSAM HASSAN

Hossam Hassan (right) enjoyed a phenomenal soccer career. In addition to an unparalleled 169 caps and 69 goals for Egypt, he also won a record 14 Egyptian league titles. Hassan's twin brother Ibrahim also won 125 caps for the Pharaohs.

## DID YOU KNOW?

Egypt has eight players with more than 100 international caps, which is more than any other African nation.

Hazem Emam (right) was one of Egypt's greatest players. An attacking midfielder, he starred in Egypt's 1998 African Cup of Nations triumph and was voted one of the players of the tournament four years later. He spent most of his club career with Zamalek, one of the giants of African soccer.

EGYPT DREAM TEAM? 1. Thabet El-Batal 2. Ibrahim Hassan 3. Ashraf Kasem 4. Wael Gomaa 5. Ibrahim Youssef 6. Hany Ramzy 7. Ahmed Hassan 8. Mohamed Aboutrika 9. Mahmoud Mokhtar 10. Hossam Hassan 11. Mahmoud El Khatib.

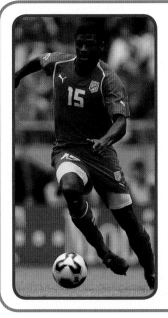

# TUNISIA

Tunisia made history in 1978 when it became the first African country to win a match at a World Cup Finals. The team came from behind to beat Mexico 3–1 in a tournament hosted by Argentina. It took 20 years to return to the Finals, but was the only African team there in both 2002 and 2006. Tunisia's first African Cup of Nations triumph came in 2004.

A powerful player, who is excellent in the air, Radhi Jaïdi (left) has been a regular in the Tunisia team for the last 10 years. He has won more than 100 caps for his country, and played club soccer for Bolton Wanderers, Birmingham City and Southampton in England.

**FACT FILE**
**TOP GOAL SCORER**
Francileudo dos Santos 28 (2004–present)
**MOST APPEARANCES**
Sadok Sassi "Attouga" 110 (1964–1978)
**TROPHIES/HONORS**
**AFRICAN CUP OF NATIONS**
2004 Tunisia 2 Morocco 1

Brazil-born striker Francileudo dos Santos scored four times for Tunisia at the 2004 African Cup of Nations, including this opener in the final against Morocco (pictured left).

# ALGERIA

Despite a shock 2–1 win over West Germany in the 1982 World Cup Finals, Algeria was denied the chance of being the first African team to make it to the second round thanks to Germany's win over Austria in the final group game. Algeria returned to the Finals in 1986, and also in 2010.

**FACT FILE**
**TOP GOAL SCORER**
Rabah Madjer 31 (1978–1992)
**MOST APPEARANCES**
Mahieddine Meftah 107 (1990–2002)

**TROPHIES/HONORS**
**AFRICAN CUP OF NATIONS**
1990 Algeria 1 Nigeria 0

Rabah Madjer (left) was one of the best forwards in the world in the 1980s and played club soccer for FC Porto.

Madjid Bougherra (above, left) is the lynchpin for Algeria. A formidable defender who can also operate in midfield, he plays his club soccer for Glasgow Rangers.

Lakhdar Belloumi (left) scored that famous winner against Germany in 1982 and went on to play over 100 times for Algeria, notching 32 goals in the process. One of Africa's greatest ever players, he was pivotal to Algeria's success of the 1980s.

# GABON

Gabon is one of Africa's most improved soccer nations. However, after a promising start to the 2010 World Cup qualifying campaign, it eventually lost out to Cameroon.

**FACT FILE**
**TOP GOAL SCORER**
François Amégasse (unknown)
**MOST APPEARANCES**
François Amégasse (unknown)

**TROPHIES/HONORS**
none

National team captain and star striker Daniel Cousin (above, left) made his name in France before enjoying success in Scotland with Rangers. In 2008 he joined English Premiership side Hull City.

The Aubameyangs certainly believe in keeping it in the family. Pierre-Emerick (far right) is following in the footsteps of his father, Pierre, and two older brothers, Catilina and Willy, by pulling on a shirt for Gabon. Striker Pierre-Emerick scored on his senior debut for his country, unlike his father, a defender, who failed to hit the back of the net in over 80 appearances for the Black Panthers!

## MOROCCO

In 1986 Morocco became the first African team to top a World Cup first round group. It finished ahead of England, Poland, and Portugal to qualify for the second round. It lost 1–0 to eventual tournament runner-up West Germany. Morocco's sole African Cup of Nations triumph came in 1976.

A tall, strong striker who's powerful in the air, Marouane Chamakh (right) has played over 50 times for Morocco. A regular scorer for his French team, Bordeaux, Chamakh has attracted interest from a lot of top European clubs.

**FACT FILE**

**TOP GOAL SCORER**
Salaheddine Bassir 27 (unknown–2005)

**MOST APPEARANCES**
Noureddine Naybet 115 (1990–2006)

**TROPHIES/HONORS**
AFRICAN CUP OF NATIONS
1976 (round robin league tournament)

## LIBERIA

They have not yet reached the World Cup Finals, but George Weah put Liberian football on the world map. He has also coached and funded the team.

Striker George Weah is the only African so far to become FIFA World Player of the Year (in 1995).

**FACT FILE**

**TOP GOAL SCORERS**
James Debbah 42 (1988–2004)

**MOST APPEARANCES**
Kelvin Sebwe 73 (1986–2009)

## BURKINA FASO

Known as Upper Volta until 1984, Burkina Faso is yet to make it to the final stages of a World Cup. However, it did manage fourth place when it hosted the African Cup of Nations in 1998, only losing out to eventual winners Egypt. Star player Moumouni Dagano averages a goal every other game for "Les Etalons" (The Stallions).

**FACT FILE**

**TOP GOAL SCORER**
Moumouni Dagano 21 (1999–present)

**MOST APPEARANCES**
Information not available

## TOGO

Togo's first World Cup Finals in 2006 involved three defeats. However, just reaching the Finals tournament was a positive sign for this tiny West African nation.

Goal machine Emmanuel Adebayor (right) is the national team captain and was African Footballer of the Year in 2008.

**FACT FILE**

**TOP GOAL SCORER**
Emmanuel Adebayor 30 (2000–present)

**MOST APPEARANCES**
Jean-Paul Abalo 66 (1992–2006)

## MALI

Mali played its first World Cup qualifier in 2000, but despite several star players, it has failed to live up to its promise in recent years.

Real Madrid's Mahamadou Diarra (above) is the defensive rock in Mali's midfield.

Fredi Kanouté (left) is a consistent goal scorer for Mali and was joint top scorer at the 2004 African Cup of Nations. He has played club soccer in France, England, and Spain.

**FACT FILE**

**TOP GOAL SCORER**
Information not available

**MOST APPEARANCES**
Information not available

## SENEGAL

Senegalese soccer seemed to burst from nowhere in 2002 when the team reached its first African Cup of Nations final and then beat holders France 1–0 in the opening game of the World Cup Finals. The "Lions of Teranga" made it to the quarterfinals in that tournament, but hasn't really made an impact at a major competition since.

**FACT FILE**

**TOP GOAL SCORER**
Henri Camara 29 (1999–present)

**MOST APPEARANCES**
Henri Camara 99 (1999–present)

Kalusha Bwalya (above, right) is a Zambian soccer legend, with more goals and more appearances than any other player.

## ZAMBIA

Despite being a regular at the African Cup of Nations, Zambia has yet to make it to the World Cup Finals.

**FACT FILE**

TOP GOAL SCORER
Kalusha Bwalya 50 (1983–2004)

MOST APPEARANCES
Kalusha Bwalya 100 (1983–2004)

## LIBYA

Libya's finest hour came in 1982. As hosts of the African Cup of Nations, it reached the final, losing to Ghana on penalties.

**FACT FILE**

TOP GOAL SCORER
Information not available

MOST APPEARANCES
Tarik El Taib 48 (1998–2008)

## NAMIBIA

Namibia played its first international in 1990 and by 2008 was good enough to reach the finals of the ACN.

**FACT FILE**

TOP GOAL SCORER
Gervatius Uri Khob 12 (unknown)

MOST APPEARANCES
Johannes Hindjou 69 (unknown)

## MOZAMBIQUE

Veteran striker Tico-Tico is Mozambique's most capped player, top goal scorer and team captain.

**FACT FILE**

TOP GOAL SCORER
Manuel José Luis 'Tico-Tico' Bucuane 28 (1992–present)

MOST APPEARANCES
Manuel José Luis 'Tico-Tico' Bucuane 82 (1992–present)

## BENIN

Despite a lack of star players, "The Squirrels" have made it to the final stages of the last three ACN tournaments.

**FACT FILE**

TOP GOAL SCORER
Information not available

MOST APPEARANCES
Information not available

## REPUBLIC OF CONGO

Blackburn Rovers' Christopher Samba is one of Congo's key players as they chase a first trophy since 1972.

**FACT FILE**

TOP GOAL SCORER
Information not available

MOST APPEARANCES
Information not available

TROPHIES/HONORS
AFRICAN CUP OF NATIONS
1972 Congo 3 Mali 2

## SUDAN

In 1965, Sudan recorded one of the biggest ever international victories, thrashing Oman 15–0.

**FACT FILE**

TOP GOAL SCORER
Haitham Tambal 24 (unknown–present)

MOST APPEARANCES
Haitham Mustafa Karar 98 (unknown–present)

TROPHIES/HONORS
AFRICAN CUP OF NATIONS
1970 Sudan 1 Ghana 0

## TANZANIA

The 1980 ACN was Tanzania's only appearance so far and it earned a draw with Ivory Coast.

**FACT FILE**

TOP GOAL SCORER
Information not available

MOST APPEARANCES
Information not available

## GUINEA

Guinea awaits a World Cup Finals debut and hope to emerge from the shadows of famous neighbors such as Mali.

**FACT FILE**

TOP GOAL SCORER
Shabani Nonda 19 (2000–present)

MOST APPEARANCES
Information not available

## GAMBIA

Sadly for fans of "The Scorpions," Gambia has yet to qualify for a major championship.

**FACT FILE**

TOP GOAL SCORER
Information not available

MOST APPEARANCES
Information not available

## ANGOLA

Angola made its World Cup Finals debut in 2006 and earned creditable draws with Mexico and Iran. However, it lost 1–0 to former colonial rulers Portugal and went out in the group stage.

Striker Akwá (right) bagged 36 goals in 80 starts for the "Black Antelopes."

**FACT FILE**

TOP GOAL SCORER
Fabrice "Akwa" Maieco 36 (1995–2006)

MOST APPEARANCES
Fabrice "Akwa" Maieco 80 (1995–2006)

**FACT FILE**

TOP GOAL SCORER
Information not available

MOST APPEARANCES
Information not available

TROPHIES/HONORS
AFRICAN CUP OF NATIONS
1968 Zaire (now DR Congo) 1 Ghana 0
1974 Zaire (now DR Congo) 2 Zambia 0

## CONGO DR

Democratic Republic of Congo's golden age came way back in 1974. Under its former name, Zaire, it won its second African Cup of Nations and made its only World Cup Finals appearance so far.

## UGANDA

A runner-up medal at the 1978 African Cup of Nations has so far been the pinnacle for Ugandan soccer.

**FACT FILE**

TOP GOAL SCORER
Information not available

MOST APPEARANCES
Information not available

Kenya's Mulinge Ndeto (left) battles with Aymen Damit and Jemal Amar of Tunisia during a World Cup qualifier.

## KENYA

Kenya or the "Harambee Stars" best result was in 1961 when it thrashed Zanzibar 10–0.

**FACT FILE**

**TOP GOAL SCORER**
Information not available

**MOST APPEARANCES**
Information not available

## ZIMBABWE

"The Warriors" only qualified for the African Cup of Nations in 2004. The team's biggest win came against its neighbors Botswana in 1980, when it dished out a 7–0 thrashing.

Maverick former Liverpool goalkeeper Bruce Grobbelaar (above) made 32 appearances for Zimbabwe in the 1980s.

**FACT FILE**

**TOP GOAL SCORER**
Peter Ndlovu 38 (1991–2006)

**MOST APPEARANCES**
Information not available

Zimbabwe's Peter Ndlovu (above, right) spent most of his club career in England.

## RWANDA

Its one and only visit to the African Cup of Nations so far saw Rwanda beat Congo DR 1–0 in 2004.

**FACT FILE**

**TOP GOAL SCORER**
Information not available

**MOST APPEARANCES**
Information not available

## SOMALIA

The Ocean Stars are currently banned from playing any matches at home because of an ongoing civil war.

**FACT FILE**

**TOP GOAL SCORER**
Cisse Aadan Abshir 15 (2003–present)

**MOST APPEARANCES**
Information not available

## CHAD

Chad's current star player and inspiration is Misdongard Betoligar, who plays for FC Metalac in Serbia.

**FACT FILE**

**TOP GOAL SCORER**
Information not available

**MOST APPEARANCES**
Information not available

## BURUNDI

Nicknamed "Les Hirondelles" (The Swallows) US-based David Habarugira is Burundi's highest flyer.

**FACT FILE**

**TOP GOAL SCORER**
Information not available

**MOST APPEARANCES**
Information not available

## MALAWI

Malawi's "Flames" were certainly on fire in 1992 when some good results saw them reach 53rd in FIFA's rankings.

**FACT FILE**

**TOP GOAL SCORER**
Information not available

**MOST APPEARANCES**
Information not available

## ETHIOPIA

Although it won the African Cup of Nations in 1950, Ethiopia hasn't made much impression since then.

**FACT FILE**

**TOP GOAL SCORER**
Getu Tilahun (unknown)

**MOST APPEARANCES**
Luciano Vassallo (unknown)

Botswana's Dipsy Selolwane (above) is an experienced forward who has played in the US and South Africa.

## BOTSWANA

The Zebras were bottom of their 2010 World Cup qualifying group, despite a shock 1–1 draw with Ivory Coast.

**FACT FILE**

**TOP GOAL SCORER**
Diphetogo "Dipsy" Selolwane 11 (1999–present)

**MOST APPEARANCES**
Diphetogo "Dipsy" Selolwane 34 (1999–present)

## NIGER

Niger is one of the weaker teams in West Africa and has never qualified for a World Cup Finals.

**FACT FILE**

**TOP GOAL SCORER**
Information not available

**MOST APPEARANCES**
Information not available

## MADAGASCAR

Despite beating Egypt 1–0 in the qualification rounds of the 2004 ACN, it has never reached beyond the qualifying rounds.

**FACT FILE**

**TOP GOAL SCORER**
Information not available

**MOST APPEARANCES**
Information not available

Striker Mohamed Kallon (above, left) made his international debut when he was just 15-years-old.

## SIERRA LEONE
Many Sierra Leone internationals play their soccer abroad, mostly in the English lower divisions and in the US.

**FACT FILE**

TOP GOAL SCORER
Mohamed Kallon (1995–present)

MOST APPEARANCES
Musa Kallon (unknown)

## ERITREA
Eritrea has never won a match by more than one goal. The top club, with six league titles, is Red Sea FC.

**FACT FILE**

TOP GOAL SCORER
Information not available

MOST APPEARANCES
Information not available

## MAURITANIA
Mauritania's only success was as runner-up in the 1995 Amílcar Cabral Cup, a competition for West African teams.

**FACT FILE**

TOP GOAL SCORER
Information not available

MOST APPEARANCES
Information not available

## CENTRAL AFRICAN REPUBLIC
Africa's lowest ranked team, CAR stars include Boris Sandjo and Marcelin Tamboulas.

**FACT FILE**

TOP GOAL SCORER
Information not available

MOST APPEARANCES
Information not available

## CAPE VERDE ISLANDS
This team really does punch above its weight, and many of its players have been signed up by European clubs.

**FACT FILE**

TOP GOAL SCORER
Joao Pedro da Veiga (unknown)

MOST APPEARANCES
Bubista (unknown)

Macedo Elves shields the ball from Mozambique's Cumaio Arlindo.

## MAURITIUS
Mauritius scored three goals during South Africa 2010 qualifying, with Wesley Marquette scoring two of them.

**FACT FILE**

TOP GOAL SCORER
Information not available

MOST APPEARANCES
Information not available

## GUINEA-BISSAU
Guinea-Bissau was knocked out in the first round of qualifying for SA 2010 after losing to Sierra Leone.

**FACT FILE**

TOP GOAL SCORER
Information not available

MOST APPEARANCES
Information not available

## DJIBOUTI
Poor Djibouti ended its 2010 World Cup qualifying campaign with a goal difference of -28, from six games.

**FACT FILE**

TOP GOAL SCORER
Ahmed Daher 7 (2007–present)

MOST APPEARANCES
Information not available

## DID YOU KNOW?
Sierra Leone star Mohamed Kallon is so famous in his homeland that they've actually named a team after him, Kallon FC. And what's more, he recently signed up to play for them!

## SWAZILAND
In 2008 Swaziland had a 1–0 win over Togo, but suffered a 6–0 thrashing in the return fixture.

**FACT FILE**

TOP GOAL SCORER
Sibusiso Dlamini 26 (unknown)

MOST APPEARANCES
Mlungisi Ngubane (unknown)

## COMOROS
This small island has only been part of FIFA since 2005, but has already beaten neighbor Seychelles.

**FACT FILE**

TOP GOAL SCORER
Information not available

MOST APPEARANCES
Information not available

## EQUATORIAL GUINEA
With automatic entry to the 2012 African Cup of Nations as joint hosts, things are looking up for this West African team.

**FACT FILE**

TOP GOAL SCORER
Information not available

MOST APPEARANCES
Information not available

## SEYCHELLES
More famous for its beaches, Seychelles' part-timers were recently beaten 2–1 by Comoros.

**FACT FILE**

TOP GOAL SCORER
Philip Zialor 10 (unknown)

MOST APPEARANCES
Information not available

## LESOTHO
Lehlohonolo Seema is the star of the Lesotho team. He also captains top South African side Orlando Pirates.

**FACT FILE**

TOP GOAL SCORER
Information not available

MOST APPEARANCES
Information not available

MONGOLIA

DEMOCRATIC PEOPLES REPUBLIC OF KOREA

UZBEKISTAN

KYRGYZSTAN

TURKMENISTAN

TAJIKISTAN

CHINA

SYRIA
LEBANON
JORDAN

IRAQ

IRAN

AFGHANISTAN

REPUBLIC OF KOREA

KUWAIT

PAKISTAN

BHUTAN

QATAR

NEPAL

SAUDIA ARABIA

UNITED ARAB EMIRATES

INDIA

TAIWAN

OMAN

BANGLADESH

LAOS

BURMA

VIETNAM

YEMEN

THAILAND

CAMBODIA

BRUNEI

SRI LANKA

MALAYSIA

SINGAPORE

INDONESIA

# ASIA

**"THE FUTURE IS ASIA."**

AFC MOTTO

When co-host the Republic of Korea (also known as South Korea) lined up to play Germany in the semifinal of the 2002 World Cup Finals it was the first time an Asian side had reached that stage of the tournament. Although Korea lost the match 1–0, it proved that Asian teams were serious international contenders. Making a bigger impact on the world stage is a prime objective for this region, and a major plan is under way to revitalize the domestic leagues in ambitious countries such as China, Japan, Iran, and of course, the Republic of Korea.

Founded in 1954, the AFC (Asian Football Confederation) is divided into four subgroups: East Asia, containing the Republic of Korea, Democratic People's Republic of Korea, China, and Japan; West Asia, covering the Middle East; Central and South Asia, including India and Pakistan; and the ASEAN representing Southeast Asia and, since 2006, Australia.

# OCEANIA

**"WE HAVE SHOWN THAT THE SOUTH PACIFIC CAN PRODUCE EXCEPTIONAL FOOTBALL TALENT."**
OFC PRESIDENT REYNALD REMARII

Formed in 1966, by Australia, New Zealand and Fiji, the OFC (Oceania Football Confederation) is the smallest and also the weakest of the world's soccer confederations. Of its current eleven members, only one has ever qualified for the World Cup Finals—New Zealand, which failed to get past the group stage in 1982.

Beautiful tropical paradises are not generally noted for their soccer success, but places like the Solomon Islands, Tahiti, and Fiji provide stunning locations for the beautiful game to thrive in. Since the departure of Australia in 2006, many of the Oceania federation national teams hover dangerously close to the bottom of FIFA's rankings. However, even in this success-starved region, the game of soccer can boast many passionate followers.

JAPAN · NORTHERN MARIANA ISLANDS · PHILIPPINES · GUAM · FEDERATED STATES OF MICRONESIA · REPUBLIC OF THE MARSHALL ISLANDS · PALAU · NAURU · PAPUA NEW GUINEA · KIRIBATI · INDONESIA · SOLOMON ISLANDS · TUVALU · SAMOA · AMERICAN SAMOA · COOK ISLANDS · FIJI · NIUE · VANUATU · TONGA · TAHITI · NEW CALEDONIA · AUSTRALIA · NEW ZEALAND

## SUPER-POLITE FANS

This eye-catching South Korean is a member of a fan group known as the Red Devils and dresses accordingly. However, despite their devilish tastes in clothes, South Korean supporters are universally admired for their politeness and respect for opposing fans.

# AUSTRALIA

### "THE FUTURE IS ALWAYS BRIGHT FOR AUSTRALIAN FOOTBALL."

MIDFIELDER HARRY KEWELL

The Australian Soccer Association was founded in 1961 and is now called Football Federation Australia. Like the Australian rugby team, the Socceroos play in yellow shirts and green shorts.

Like the US, Australia is not yet as dominant in soccer as it is in other sports. The team failed to score in its first World Cup Finals in 1974, but after a long wait it returned in 2006 and only an injury-time penalty for Italy denied Australia a place in the quarterfinals. After years of record wins in Oceania, Australia left to join the more competitive AFC in 2006.

Cahill was named Oceania Footballer of the Year in 2004.

As a 17-year-old, Harry Kewell left the Australian Academy of Sport to join England's Leeds United. A nimble and dangerous honor, Kewell's career has been hampered by injury in recent years, but his reputation as perhaps the most talented Australian player of all time remains.

## TIM CAHILL

Tim Cahill has the knack of ghosting from midfield at just the right moment to score. In a dramatic 3–1 win over Japan in 2006, he came off the bench to become the first Australian goal scorer at a World Cup Finals. A short time later, he also became the second.

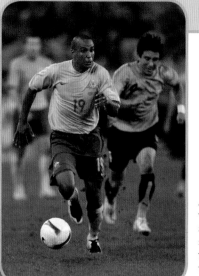

Archie Thompson (far left) scored a record 13 goals when Australia beat poor American Samoa 31–0 in a World Cup qualifier in April 2001. Yet Thompson still missed the Socceroos' next game, and Australia failed to reach the 2002 World Cup, despite also trouncing Tonga 22–0 and Samoa 11–0.

Livewire winger Mark Bresciano (left) has scored plenty of spectacular goals, for Australia as well as Italian club sides Empoli, Parma, and Palermo. But perhaps his most significant was the equalizer in Australia's 2006 World Cup qualifying playoff against Uruguay.

## FACT FILE: AUSTRALIA

**NICKNAME**
Socceroos

**TOP GOAL SCORERS**
1. Damian Mori 29 (1992–2002)
2. John Aloisi 27 (1997–present)
3. John Kosmina 25 (1976–1988)
= Attila Abonyi 25 (1967–1977)
4. Archie Thompson 21 (2001–present)
= David Zdrilic 21 (1997–present)

**MOST APPEARANCES**
1. Alex Tobin 87 (1988–1998)
2. Paul Wade 84 (1986–1996)
3. Tony Vidmar 76 (1991–2006)
4. Mark Schwarzer 72 (1993–present)
5. Brett Emerton 71 (1998–present)

**TROPHIES/HONORS**
OFC NATIONS CUP
2004 Australia 11 Solomon Islands 1 (agg)
2000 Australia 2 New Zealand 0
1996 Australia 11 Tahiti 0 (agg)
1980 Australia 4 Tahiti 2

## DID YOU KNOW?

*Australian-born players who opted to play international soccer for other countries include Tony Dorigo (England), Saša Ilic (Serbia) and Josip Šimunic (Croatia).*

Ukraine-born Nikita Rukavytsya's early performances at the 2008 Olympics and for Dutch team FC Twente have inspired hopes he may successfully fill the striking shoes of Mark Viduka or John Aloisi.

*Veteran striker Mark Viduka captained Australia at the 2006 World Cup, where it gave eventual champions Italy a run for its money.*

## SOCCEROOS

Australia lost World Cup playoffs to Argentina in 1993, Iran in 1997, and Uruguay in 2001. When it finally beat Uruguay in 2005 to qualify for the 2006 World Cup Finals, its long-suffering fans were ecstatic.

*Mark Bresciano was one of nine Australians to play in all four of their games at the 2006 World Cup.*

AUSTRALIA DREAM TEAM? 1. Mark Schwarzer 2. Joe Marston 3. Tony Vidmar 4. Tim Cahill 5. Peter Wilson 6. Craig Moore 7. Mark Bresciano 8. Johnny Warren 9. Frank Farina 10. Mark Viduka 11. Harry Kewell

# REPUBLIC OF KOREA

## "KOREAN PEOPLE LOVE THE NATIONAL TEAM AND THEIR SUPPORT... IS INCREDIBLE."
AFSHIN GHOTBI, ASSISTANT COACH AT THE 2002 AND 2006 WORLD CUPS

## FACT FILE: REPUBLIC OF KOREA

**NICKNAMES**
Taeguk Warriors, Tigers, Red Devils

**TOP GOAL SCORERS**
1. Cha Bum-Kun 55 (1972–1986)
2. Seon-Hong Hwang 50 (1993–2002)
3. Choi Soon-Ho 30 (1980–1991)
4. Huh Jung-Moo 29 (1974–1986)
= Kim Do-Hoon 29 (1994–2003)

**MOST APPEARANCES**
1. Hong Myung-Bo 136 (1990–2002)
2. Lee Woon-Jae 123 (1994–present)
= Yoo-Sang-Chul 123 (1994–2005)
3. Cha Bum-Kun 121 (1972–1986
4. Lee Young-Pyo 108 (1999–present)

**TROPHIES/HONORS**
**AFC ASIAN CUP**
1960 Republic of Korea 1 China 0
1956 Republic of Korea 4 Taiwan 1 (agg)

The Republic of Korea found unexpected glory in 2002 when it co-hosted the World Cup Finals. Thanks to manager Guus Hiddink's astute leadership, exciting young, players and passionate fans, the team reached the semifinals. Life since has been a bit of an anticlimax, but South Korean soccer continues to earn respect worldwide.

The Korea Football Association was founded in 1928. The team plays in red shirts and "Be the Reds" became the rallying cry of a fervent nation at the 2002 World Cup Finals.

*Park Ji-Sung was a hero when his volley beat Portugal in the 2002 World Cup.*

## CHA BUM-KUN
Cha Bum-Kun (above) was nicknamed "Cha Boom," and any goalkeeper who tried to stop one of his shots knew why. The striker's move to Germany in 1977 paved the way for other Asian players to move to Europe, but few could emulate Cha's ability and his achievements. Many young Germans grew up idolizing him, including Michael Ballack, Jürgen Klinsmann, and Oliver Kahn.

## PARK JI-SUNG
Manchester United's Park Ji-Sung played under manager Guus Hiddink for both South Korea and PSV Eindhoven. In fact, it was Hiddink who made the wise decision to switch Park from a defensive midfield role to the wing.

### DID YOU KNOW?
*In the 1977 Park's Cup, Korea were losing 4–1 to Malaysia before Cha Bum-Kun scored an amazing seven-minute hat trick to level the score.*

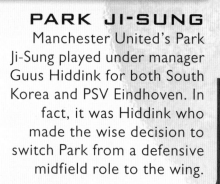

Striker Park Chu-Young (left) and midfielders Lee Chung-Yong and Ki Sung-Yong are part of a new generation determined to emulate the 2002 heroes. Park struck four goals in 2010 World Cup qualifiers, which led to a move to French club AS Monaco.

Ahn Jung-Hwan paid a high price for the greatest moment of his soccer career—the golden goal that knocked Italy out of the 2002 World Cup in the second round. His Italian employers Perugia fired the striker, saying he had "ruined Italian soccer."

| REPUBLIC OF KOREA DREAM TEAM? | 1. Lee Woon-Jae 2. Choi Jin-Cheul 3. Lee Young-Pyo 4. Kim Nam-Il 5. Hong Myung-Bo 6. Kim Tae-Young 7. Park Ji-Sung 8. Song Chong-Gug 9. Cha Bum-Kun 10. Kim Joo-Sung 11. Seol Ki-Hyeon |

# JAPAN

*"OUR FANS ARE AMONG THE BEST IN THE WORLD."* TAKESHI OKADA, JAPAN MANAGER AT THE '98 WORLD CUP

The Japan Football Association was formed in 1921. Japan currently plays in blue shirts, but in the past it has favored red and white instead, after the national flag.

After decades living in the shadow of baseball, table-tennis, and martial arts, Japanese soccer came of age in 1993 when the J.League was launched. A successful co-hosting of the World Cup Finals in 2002 plus AFC Asian Cups in 2000 and 2004, has elevated soccer to the second most popular sport in Japan.

## KAZU

After leaving for Brazil aged 15 and playing for Pelé's old team Santos, Kazuyoshi Miura (left) returned to Japan in 1990. Known as "Kazu," the super striker won the first two J.League Championships with Verdy Kawasaki, before becoming 1993 Asian Footballer of the Year and then joining Genoa in Italy. Kazu famously performed a unique dance when he scored a great goal.

*Nakamura was the first Japanese player to score a UEFA Champions League goal.*

Keiji Tamada (right) may be one of international soccer's more slightly built strikers— but he has a ferocious left foot. China discovered this to its cost in the 2004 AFC Asian Cup final which Japan won 3–1, Tamada scoring the third goal. He also scored against Brazil in a World Cup Finals first-round clash two years later, although Brazil went on to win the match 4–1.

## NAKAMURA

Shunsuke Nakamura is a midfield playmaker and free-kick specialist. He was Japan's star performer in its 2004 Asian Cup victory and scored Japan's opening goal against Australia in the 2006 World Cup.

*Nakamura's left foot can unleash delicate through-balls or devastating set-pieces.*

Central midfielder Hidetoshi Nakata (left) was a key part of Japan's soccer boom. Although Junichi Inamoto scored more goals and Kazuyuki Toda had even brighter dyed hair, it was Nakata who captured the hearts of the Japanese people. His 2001 Serie A title with AS Roma was celebrated across Japan, but his decision to retire after the 2006 World Cup at the age of 29 was a major shock.

## DID YOU KNOW?

*Kunishige Kamamoto's seven goals made him the top scorer at the 1968 Summer Olympics in Mexico City, where Japan won the bronze medal. Kamamoto is Japan's all-time top scorer and has now swapped soccer for politics.*

JAPAN DREAM TEAM? 1. Yoshikatsu Kawaguchi 2. Akira Kaji 3. Koji Nakata 4. Hidetoshi Nakata 5. Tsuneyasu Miyamoto 6. Masami Ihara 7. Junichi Inamoto 8. Shunsuke Nakamura 9. Kunishige Kamamoto 10. Kazuyoshi Miura 11. Yasuhiko Okudera

# CHINA

## "FOOTBALL IS VERY MUCH IN THE HEARTS OF THE CHINESE PEOPLE."

ARIE HAAN, CHINA MANAGER 2002–2004

The Chinese Football Association was originally founded in 1924, but it was replaced by a new body in 1949, after the country became the People's Republic of China.

Over the years, China has struggled to make a significant impact on the world of soccer. However, recent years have brought encouraging signs, such as qualifying for its first World Cup in 2002—although it lost all three games without scoring. A professional domestic league is also gaining ground and soccer is rapidly becoming a popular sport among a population of 1.3 billion.

Striker Qu Bo's goals were not enough to take China to the 2010 World Cup Finals, but he took part in their 2002 debut. Although teammates Dong Fangzhuo and Lee Dong-Gook moved to England, Bo remained in China with Qingdao Jonoon.

## HAO HAIDONG

Talented striker Hao Haidong (far left) scored a record 41 goals in 115 appearances for his country. His status as China's greatest soccer figure is challenged only by fellow forward Lee Wei Tong, captain of the country's 1936 Olympic team and later a vice president of FIFA.

China has twice finished AFC Asian Cup as runner-up, but perhaps the country's finest achievement was to hold then world champions Brazil to a 0–0 draw in 2002. Ronaldo, Ronaldinho, and Rivaldo could find no way past inspired goalkeeper Liu Yunfei, while Sun Jihai came agonizingly close to a glorious winner.

## FACT FILE: CHINA

### NICKNAMES
Team China, Guozu (National Foot), Guojia Dui (National Team)

### TOP GOAL SCORERS
1. Hao Haidong 41 (1992–2004)
2. Liu Haiguang 36 (1983–1990)
3. Ma Lin 33 (1984–1990)
4. Li Hui 28 (1983–1988)
5. Su Maozhen 26 (1992–2002)
= Li Jinyu 26 (1996–present)

### MOST APPEARANCES
1. Li Ming 141 (1992–2004)
2. Jia Xiuquan 136 (1982–1992)
3. Fan Zhiyi 132 (1992–2002)
4. Xie Yuxin 120 (1987–1996)
5. Li Fusheng 119 (1976–1984)

### TROPHIES/HONORS
none

## ZHENG ZHI

He calls himself the best Chinese player of his generation, and Zheng Zhi's confidence is matched by his versatility. Although he is best known as a goal-scoring midfielder and occasional forward, he began his international career as a defender.

Zheng Zhi's work rate makes him an ideal captain.

## DID YOU KNOW?

In China an estimated TV audience of 250 million people watched their team lose 3–1 to Japan in the 2004 Asian Cup final, a Chinese record for a sporting event.

CHINA DREAM TEAM? 1. Ou Chuliang 2. Zheng Zhi 3. Sun Jihai 4. Li Ming 5. Fan Zhiyi 6. Jia Xiuquan 7. Li Tie 8. Shao Jiayi 9. Hao Haidong 10. Lee Wei Tong 11. Yang Chen

# SAUDI ARABIA

Saudi Arabia has won the Asian Cup three times and first visited the World Cup Finals in 1994, where it reached the second round. Wealthy Saudi investors may be eyeing up high-profile European clubs, but the national team missed out on the 2010 World Cup after losing a playoff to Bahrain.

Al-Qahtani top-scored at the 2007 AFC Asian Cup.

2007 Asian Footballer of the Year Yasser Al-Qahtani (left) succeeded long-serving striker Sami al-Jaber as the country's soccer focal point. Nicknamed "the Sniper," Al-Qahtani is lethal in front of goal.

## FACT FILE

**TOP GOAL SCORER**
Majed Abdullah 67 (1977–1994)
**MOST APPEARANCES**
Mohamed Al-Deayea 181 (1990–2006)

**TROPHIES/HONORS**
**AFC ASIAN CUP**
1996 Saudi Arabia 0 United Arab Emirates 0
(Saudi Arabia won 4–2 in a penalty shoot-out)
1988 Saudi Arabia 0 Korea Republic 0
(Saudi Arabia won 4–3 in a penalty shoot-out)
1984 Saudi Arabia 2 China 1

Saeed Al-Owairan's surging 70-yard solo effort against Belgium in 1998 was one of the World Cup's greatest-ever goals.

Adventurous right-back Mehdi Mahdavikia (left), the 2003 Asian Footballer of the Year, plays his club soccer in Germany. He is a versatile player and often plays as an attacking wing back.

# IRAN

Iranian soccer entered a golden age in 1968 with three consecutive Asian Cups: gold at the 1974 Asian Games and a draw with Scotland at the 1978 World Cup Finals. Modern-day heroes Javad Nekounam and Andranik Teymourian hope to emulate that success.

When Iran faced the US at the 1998 World Cup Finals, the two teams symbolically exchanged flowers before kickoff. Iran won 2–1, thanks to goals from Hamid Reza Estili and Mehdi Mahdavikia.

## ALI DAEI

Striker Ali Daei (left) scored more international goals than any man on Earth—109 in 149 games since his international debut in 1993. He had a disappointing stint as national coach from March 2008 to March 2009.

## FACT FILE

**TOP GOAL SCORER**
Ali Daei 109 (1993–2006)
**MOST APPEARANCES**
Ali Daei 149 (1993–2006)

**TROPHIES/HONORS**
**AFC ASIAN CUP**
1976 Iran 1 Kuwait 0
1972 Iran 2 Republic of Korea 1 (aet)
1968 (round-robin league tournament)

# KOREA DPR

North Korea had an astounding 1966 World Cup Finals. Its all-out attacking style knocked out Italy and the team raced into a 3–0 lead against Portugal, only to lose 5–3. International obscurity followed, until North Korea qualified for the 2010 World Cup Finals.

## FACT FILE

**TOP GOAL SCORER**
Information not available
**MOST APPEARANCES**
Information not available

**TROPHIES/HONORS**
none

Pak Doo-Ik's right foot drilled home one of the World Cup's most startling goals—the one that sent Italy home early from the 1966 World Cup.

## JONG TAE-SE

Jong Tae-Se was born in Japan and held South Korean citizenship, but chose to represent the country that provided much of his education—North Korea. The 2010 World Cup is the first time both North and South Korea have qualified for the finals.

Jong Tae-Se is a bustling center-forward with a mighty shot.

## KUWAIT

Kuwait won the Asian Cup in 1980 and also created one of the World Cup's most bizarre moments in 1982, when the team stormed off the field until a French "goal" was disallowed for offside.

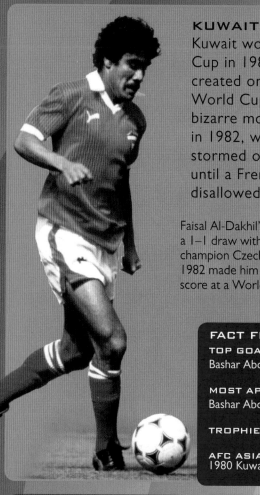

Faisal Al-Dakhil's (left) equalizer in a 1–1 draw with European champion Czechoslovakia in 1982 made him the first Kuwaiti to score at a World Cup Finals.

**FACT FILE**

TOP GOAL SCORER
Bashar Abdullah 75 (1995–2006)

MOST APPEARANCES
Bashar Abdullah 134 (1995–2006)

TROPHIES/HONORS

AFC ASIAN CUP
1980 Kuwait 3 Korea Republic 0

## MONGOLIA

Subzero temperatures make soccer impossible between October and June. The country played no international matches between 1960 and 1998.

**FACT FILE**

TOP GOAL SCORER
Ganbaatar Tugsbayar 6 (unknown)

MOST APPEARANCES
Information not available

## SRI LANKA

Cricket still rules, but Sri Lanka's players were South Asian champions in 1995 and performed well in 2006 World Cup qualifying.

**FACT FILE**

TOP GOAL SCORER
Bob Surendran (unknown)

MOST APPEARANCES
Information not available

## UZBEKISTAN

Uzbekistan is Asia's strongest ex-Soviet state and the team were quarterfinalists in the 2004 and 2007 Asian Cups. Star striker Maksim Shatskikh has proved a worthy successor to Andriy Shevchenko at Ukraine's Dinamo Kiev.

**FACT FILE**

TOP GOAL SCORER
Maksim Shatskikh 30 (1999–present)

MOST APPEARANCES
Mirjalol Qosimov 65 (1992–2005)
Andrei Fyodorov 65 (1994–2006)

## VIETNAM

Vietnam returned to international soccer in 1991. As co-hosts, it reached the quarterfinals of the 2007 AFC Asian Cup.

**FACT FILE**

TOP GOAL SCORER
Lê Huynh Dúc 30 (1995–2002)

MOST APPEARANCES
Lê Huynh Dúc 63 (1995–2002)

## TURKMENISTAN

Ex-Soviet state Turkmenistan's peak achievement so far has been reaching the 2004 AFC Asian Cup.

**FACT FILE**

TOP GOAL SCORER
Charyar Mukhadov 13 (1992–1999)

MOST APPEARANCES
Information not available

A'ala Hubail shot to prominence as joint top-scorer at the 2004 Asian Cup.

## BAHRAIN

Bahrain was FIFA's most improved side in 2004, after it finished a best-ever fourth at the Asian Cup. The team contested World Cup qualifying playoffs in 2006 and 2010.

**FACT FILE**

TOP GOAL SCORER
Husain Ali 33 (1998–present)

MOST APPEARANCES
Abdulrazzaq Mohamed 102 (unknown)

## OMAN

Although Oman is still yet to reach the World Cup Finals or get through the Asian Cup's first round, it is ranked in FIFA's top 100 teams.

Agile goalkeeper Ali Al-Habsi did not concede once as Oman won the 2009 Gulf Cup of Nations.

**FACT FILE**

TOP GOAL SCORER
Imad Al-Hosni 32 (2003–present)

MOST APPEARANCES
Sulaiman Al Mazroui (1992–present)

## MYANMAR

Myanmar played its first World Cup qualifier in 2007. It won the Asian Games in 1966 and 1970, and was a finalist in the 1968 Asian Cup.

**FACT FILE**

TOP GOAL SCORER
Information not available

MOST APPEARANCES
Information not available

## LEBANON

Lebanon joined FIFA in 1935 but has had little to cheer about, aside from a successful hosting of the 2000 AFC Asian Cup Finals.

**FACT FILE**

TOP GOAL SCORER
Roda Antar 48 (2000–present)

MOST APPEARANCES
Roda Antar 48 (2000–present)

## QATAR

Qatar's long-awaited emergence seemed to be underway when striker Khalfan Ibrahim was named the 2006 Asian Footballer of the Year. In 2004 Qatar triumphed in the Arab world's Gulf Cup and won the Asian Games in 2006.

Sebastián Soria (left) was born in Uruguay but now plays up-front for his adopted homeland Qatar.

### FACT FILE

**TOP GOAL SCORER**
Mansour Muftah 53 (unknown)

**MOST APPEARANCES**
Adel Khamis Al-Noubi 110 (unknown)

## GUAM

Guam is AFC's smallest member country. It conceded 35 goals to Iran and Tajikstan, during games two days apart in 2000.

### FACT FILE

**TOP GOAL SCORER**
Zachary Pangelinan 11 (2005-present)

**MOST APPEARANCES**
Information not available

## SYRIA

Syria's finest hour so far came when it won the 1994 AFC Youth Championship by beating Japan 2–1 in the final.

Syria's captain striker Firas Al-Khatib (above, in green) made his debut at aged 17 and has been a regular on the scoresheet ever since.

### FACT FILE

**TOP GOAL SCORER**
Information not available

**MOST APPEARANCES**
Information not available

## MALAYSIA

Malaysian soccer had its heyday in the 1970s and early 1980s, with Mokhtar Dahari dynamic up front and R Arumugam often unbeatable in goal.

### FACT FILE

**TOP GOAL SCORER**
Mokhtar Dahari 125 (1972–1985)

**MOST APPEARANCES**
Soh Chin Aun 252 (1970–1985)

## THAILAND

Thailand has been South-East Asian Games soccer champions 12 times but is still striving for a big international breakthrough. In September 2009, Thailand appointed former England captain Bryan Robson as manager, having previously employed two other ex-England internationals, Peter Withe and Peter Reid.

### FACT FILE

**TOP GOAL SCORER**
Piyapong Piew-on 103 (1981–1997)

**MOST APPEARANCES**
Tawan Sripan 145 (1993–2007)

## IRAQ

Iraqi players, officials, and fans were happy just to reach the 2007 AFC Asian Cup, after years of repression under the Ba'ath regime. But in one of soccer's biggest upsets, the team beat Saudi Arabia 1–0 in the final.

Iraq captain Younis Mahmoud scored the winning goal in the 2007 Asian Cup final. Goalkeepr Noor Sabri also put in a match-winning performance.

### FACT FILE

**TOP GOAL SCORER**
Hussein Saeed 63 (1976–1990)

**MOST APPEARANCES**
Hussein Saeed 126 (1976–1990)

**TROPHIES/HONORS**

**AFC ASIAN CUP**
2007 Iraq 1 Saudi Arabia 0

## NEPAL

Soccer was banned in Nepal during the 1930s but is now a popular sport, despite little international success.

### FACT FILE

**TOP GOAL SCORER**
Information not available

**MOST APPEARANCES**
Information not available

## YEMEN

The North Yemen and South Yemen soccer teams were unified for the first time in 1990.

### FACT FILE

**TOP GOAL SCORER**
Information not available

**MOST APPEARANCES**
Information not available

## UNITED ARAB EMIRATES

Although nearly 85 percent of the United Arab Emirates' population are foreign citizens, the national team still managed to reach the 1990 World Cup Finals. However, Brazilian coach Mario Zagallo was fired just before the tournament and the UAE lost all three games. The UAE also lost the 1996 Asian Cup final to Saudi Arabia in a penalty shootout.

### FACT FILE

**TOP GOAL SCORER**
Adnan Al-Talyani 53 (1983–1997)

**MOST APPEARANCES**
Adnan Al-Talyani 164 (1983–1997)

## INDIA

Soccer was brought to India by British army officers in the mid-19th century and the Durand Cup, established in 1888, is the third-oldest soccer competition in the world. The World Cup remains a distant prospect for India. Although it qualified in 1950, the team later withdrew after refusing to wear soccer cleats.

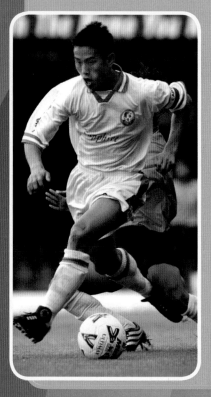

Despite his short stature, Baichung Bhutia is a giant of Indian soccer— his country's captain, top scorer, and ambassador for the game.

**FACT FILE**

TOP GOAL SCORER
Baichung Bhutia 43 (1995–present)

MOST APPEARANCES
Baichung Bhutia 102 (1995–present)

## TAJIKISTAN

This ex-Soviet state won the first AFC Challenge Cup in 2006, which aims to raise standards of the region's weaker teams.

**FACT FILE**

TOP GOAL SCORER
Takhir Muminov 10 (unknown)

MOST APPEARANCES
Information not available

## LAOS

The Laotian leagues are largely amateur, but soccer was the main draw for the 2009 South East Asian Games held in Laos.

**FACT FILE**

TOP GOAL SCORER
Information not available

MOST APPEARANCES
Information not available

## INDONESIA

As Dutch East Indies, Indonesia was the World Cup Finals' first Asian competitor, losing 6–0 to Hungary in 1938. Impassioned, 90,000-strong crowds packed Jakarta's Gelora Bung Karno stadium when Indonesia co-hosted the 2007 Asian Cup.

Bambang Pamungkas (right) is Indonesia's goalscoring talisman.

**FACT FILE**

TOP GOAL SCORER
Bambang Pamungkas 36 (1999–present)

MOST APPEARANCES
Bambang Pamungkas 64 (1999–present)

## BHUTAN

On the day of the 2002 World Cup final, Bhutan beat Montserrat 4–0, in a friendly game. It has been slowly on the rise since then.

**FACT FILE**

TOP GOAL SCORER
Wangay Dorji 5 (unknown)

MOST APPEARANCES
Information not available

## TIMOR-LESTE

Timor-Leste gained independence from Indonesia in 2002. The team played its first World Cup qualifiers in 2007.

**FACT FILE**

TOP GOAL SCORER
Emílio da Silva 4 (2004–present)

MOST APPEARANCES
Diamantino Leong 12 (2004–present)

The Singapore team (above) held Australia to a surprise goalless draw in March 2008, and almost won but captain Indra Sahdan Daud hit the woodwork instead.

## SINGAPORE

Home-born Shahril Ishak and naturalized citizen Egmar Goncalves (Brazil), are the stars for Singapore.

**FACT FILE**

TOP GOAL SCORER
Fandi Ahmad 55 (1978–1997)

MOST APPEARANCES
Malik Awab (unknown)

Goalkeeper Samreth Seiha (above) is only just out of his teens but is already looking comfortable as Cambodia's number one.

## CAMBODIA

As the country recovers from humanitarian crises of the 1970s and 1980s, Cambodia's players are gaining in ambition.

**FACT FILE**

TOP GOAL SCORER
Hok Sochetra 42 (unknown)

MOST APPEARANCES
Information not available

## KYRGYZSTAN

The national team draws many players from Dordoi Dynamo Naryn, league champions for five straight years since 2004.

**FACT FILE**

TOP GOAL SCORER
Sergey Kutsov 3 (1996–2001)
Sergey Chikishev 3 (2003–2004)
Zamirbek Jumagulov 3 (1992–2003)

MOST APPEARANCES
Vyacheslav Amin 33 (2000–2007)

## MACAU

Macau has a national team, despite now being a Chinese territory. It has won just three World Cup qualifiers since 1982.

**FACT FILE**

TOP GOAL SCORER
Information not available

MOST APPEARANCES
Information not available

## MALDIVES

This island group is yet to make its first Asian Cup, but won the South Asian Football Federation Cup by beating India in 2008.

**FACT FILE**

**TOP GOAL SCORER**
Ali Ashfaq 14 (2002–present)

**MOST APPEARANCES**
Ibrahim Fazeel 14 (1999–present)

## AFGHANISTAN

The war-ravaged nation returned to international soccer in 2003, after a 19-year absence. Bashir Ahmad Saadat is leading the team.

**FACT FILE**

**TOP GOAL SCORER**
Mohammad Saber Rohparwar 25 (unknown–1980)

**MOST APPEARANCES**
Hafizullah Qadami 25 (2005–2007)

## BRUNEI DARUSSALAM

This sultanate has been trying to boost its experience and skills by contesting matches in Malaysia's top division.

**FACT FILE**

**TOP GOAL SCORER**
Information not available

**MOST APPEARANCES**
Information not available

## JORDAN

Jordan achieved its highest FIFA ranking of 37 in 2004, after qualifying for its first-ever Asian Cup and then reaching the quarterfinals.

Despite some bright displays in qualifying, midfielder Amer Deeb (right) and Jordan fell short of reaching the 2010 World Cup Finals.

**FACT FILE**

**TOP GOAL SCORER**
Information not available

**MOST APPEARANCES**
Information not available

## CHINESE TAIPEI

Baseball may be the number one sport, but Taiwan's women's team was Asia's best in the 1970s and 1980s. The men have yet to catch up.

**FACT FILE**

**TOP GOAL SCORER**
Information not available

**MOST APPEARANCES**
Information not available

## PHILIPPINES

The country's greatest player is Paulino Alcántara, who remains Barcelona's record scorer after 80 years.

**FACT FILE**

**TOP GOAL SCORER**
Information not available

**MOST APPEARANCES**
Information not available

### DID YOU KNOW?

Palestine became the first Asian nation to play a World Cup qualifier in 1934, although the territory was under British control at that time.

Ex-manager Peter Withe was once suspended by Thailand's soccer federation over his preference for wearing shorts, rather than a suit, during matches.

## BANGLADESH

Bangladesh has had a professional league since 2007. The nation's star player is Kazi Salahuddin who was later national team coach.

**FACT FILE**

**TOP GOAL SCORER**
Kazi Salahuddin (unknown)

**MOST APPEARANCES**
Kazi Salahuddin (unknown)

## PALESTINE

FIFA recognized Palestine as an independent soccer association in 1998. A troubled homeland means that the team plays in Qatar and trains in Egypt.

**FACT FILE**

**TOP GOAL SCORER**
Ziyad Al-Kord 15 (1998-2006)

**MOST APPEARANCES**
Saeb Jendeya 70 (1998-present)

## PAKISTAN

Soccer fever is strong in Pakistan, despite the sport being overshadowed by cricket. Gradual progress is aided by the likes of ex-Premiership defender Zesh Rehman, former Manchester United youngster Adnan Ahmed, and current captain Muhammad Essa.

Leading goal scorer and playmaker Muhammad Essa (right) is not only today's idol, but is encouraging tomorrow's stars through his own soccer academy.

## HONG KONG

Although Hong Kong has been reunified with China since 1997, it has a separate national team. Playing as Hong Kong China, the team's biggest win was 15–0 against Guam in 2005.

**FACT FILE**

**TOP GOAL SCORER**
Au Wai Lun 26 (1989–2005)

**MOST APPEARANCES**
Lee Wai Man 68 (1993–2006)

Striker Chan Siu Ki (above, right) is Hong Kong's most reliable source of goals, after the 2005 retirement of ex-captain Au Wai Lun.

**FACT FILE**

**TOP GOAL SCORER**
Muhammad Essa 20 (2000–present)

**MOST APPEARANCES**
Jaffar Khan 59 (2001–present)

# OCEANIA TEAMS

"PEOPLE KNEW WE'D GIVEN OUR ALL AND IN A COUNTRY DOMINATED BY RUGBY THEY BEGAN TO UNDERSTAND HOW BIG FOOTBALL IS IN THE REST OF THE WORLD."

STEVE SUMNER, NZ CAPTAIN AT THE 1982 WORLD CUP FINALS

The landscapes in the Oceania region are picturesque, but the horizons are usually cloudy when it comes to international soccer. Little wonder, if you consider how small populations can be. Yet, while Oceania's teams struggle to make a mark on the global game, local pride ensures a range of continental tournaments are always hotly contested.

*Ryan Nelsen won the Defender of the Year award when he played for US team DC United.*

## RYAN NELSEN

Blackburn Rovers defender Ryan Nelsen provides the rugged backbone of the New Zealand team. He returned after a lengthy injury absence to captain his country at the 2008 Olympics, and will follow in the footseps of 1982 captain Steve Sumner when he leads the "All-Whites" at the 2010 World Cup Finals in South Africa.

## NEW ZEALAND

The "All Whites" may lack the prestige of the country's cricket and rugby teams, but players such as defender Ryan Nelsen and striker Shane Smeltz hope to change that. Moreover, Australia's transfer to the AFC has left New Zealand as Oceania's dominant team and boosted its chances of representing the region at future World Cup Finals. Sure enough, New Zealand booked its place at the 2010 World Cup Finals in a playoff against Bahrain.

New Zealand Football was founded in 1891 and was one of the founding members of the Oceania federation.

## FACT FILE

**TOP GOAL SCORER**
Vaughan Coveny 28 (1992–2007)

**MOST APPEARANCES**
Vaughan Coveny 65 (1992–2009)

## TROPHIES/HONORS

**OFC NATIONS CUP**
2008 (round-robin league tournament)
2002 New Zealand 1 Australia 0
1998 New Zealand 1 Australia 0
1973 (round-robin league tournament)

New Zealand soccer owes much to the 1957 emigration of England international Ken Armstrong (right). The ex-Chelsea midfielder helped the game gain popularity while also playing for several clubs. He made 13 appearances for his adopted country.

**NEW ZEALAND DREAM TEAM?** 1. Richard Wilson 2. Ryan Nelsen 3. Adrian Elrick 4. Steve Sumner 5. Ivan Vicelich 6. Ken Armstrong 7. Ricki Herbert 8. Wynton Rufer 9. Vaughan Coveny 10. Shane Smeltz 11. Chris Killen

## FACT FILE
**TOP GOAL SCORER**
Esala Masi 23 (1997–2005)
**MOST APPEARANCES**
Esala Masi 35 (1997–2005)

# FIJI
Fiji finished third at the OFC Nations Cup in 1998 and 2008, and claimed the South Pacific Games crown in 1991 and 2003. Young forwards Roy Krishna and Osea Vakatalesau dominate the goal scoring.

# TONGA
Tonga often finds itself near the bottom of the world rankings. However, soccer in the area is receiving a boost from FIFA's Goal Project which provides resources for cash-strapped countries.

## FACT FILE
**TOP GOAL SCORER**
Unaloto Ki-Atenoa Feao 5
**MOST APPEARANCES**
Kilifi Uele (unknown)

# NEW CALEDONIA
Five-time South Pacific Games winner, New Caledonia is rapidly emerging as the main threat to New Zealand's supremacy in Oceania. It ran the "All Whites" a close second at the 2008 OFC Nations Cup. French World Cup-winner Christian Karembeu was born in New Caledonia.

## FACT FILE
**TOP GOAL SCORER**
Information not available
**MOST APPEARANCES**
Information not available

# COOK ISLANDS
The Cook Islands were one of the first teams to be ruled out of qualification for the 2010 World Cup, three years before the finals! Although, with a population of just 21,000, it's not surprising.

## FACT FILE
**TOP GOAL SCORER**
Stentor Mani 2 (unknown)
Nikorima Te Miha 2 (unknown)
Teariki Mateariki 2 (unknown)
**MOST APPEARANCES**
Tony Jamieson 18 (unknown)

Commins Menapi (far left) scored both Solomon Islands' goals in the draw with Australia in 2004.

# SOLOMON ISLANDS
The Solomon Islands best results were a 2–2 draw with Australia and a creditable second place finish at the 2004 OFC Nations Cup.

## FACT FILE
**TOP GOAL SCORER**
Commins Menapi 34 (2000–present)
**MOST APPEARANCES**
Batram Suri 48 (1992–present)

# AMERICAN SAMOA
American Samoa has not won a game since 1983, and has been on the wrong side of some impressive score lines since then.

Goalkeeper Nicky Salapu had to pick the ball out of the net a record 31 times when American Samoa lost to Australia in 2001.

## FACT FILE
**TOP GOAL SCORER**
Samuel Hayward 3 (unknown)
**MOST APPEARANCES**
Nicky Salapu 8 (unknown)
Ramin Ott 8 (unknown)
Samual Hayward 8 (unknown)

# PAPUA NEW GUINEA
Papua New Guinea's women won the 2007 South Pacific Games and almost reached the 2008 Olympics, but the men's team has been one of the world's least active in recent years and failed to even enter 2010 World Cup qualifiers.

## FACT FILE
**TOP GOAL SCORER**
Reginald Davani (unknown)
**MOST APPEARANCES**
Richard Daniel (unknown)

# TAHITI
Tahiti finished runner-up in the first three installments of the OFC Nations Cup, but has seen little match action since the turn of the century, let alone success.

## FACT FILE
**TOP GOAL SCORER**
Felix Tagawa 14 (unknown)
**MOST APPEARANCES**
Information not available

# SAMOA
Another country funded by FIFA's Goal Project, Samoa boasts Chris Cahill—the brother of Australian superstar Tim—as its captain.

## FACT FILE
**TOP GOAL SCORER**
Information not available
**MOST APPEARANCES**
Information not available

# VANUATU
Jean Victor Maleb and Etienne Mermer were the team leaders as Vanuatu stunned New Zealand 4–2 at the 2004 OFC Nations Cup, in perhaps the country's greatest victory. Vanuatu also won bronze at the 2007 South Pacific Games.

## FACT FILE
**TOP GOAL SCORER**
Information not available
**MOST APPEARANCES**
Information not available

*German soccer fans watch a penalty shoot-out in the quarterfinal match against Argentina in the 2006 World Cup Finals. Germany won the shootout 4–2.*

# FAMOUS COMPETITIONS

**"IF YOU DON'T WANT SUCCESS IT'S NOT WORTH PLAYING—WINNING TROPHIES IS THE MAIN THING."**

ENGLAND AND LIVERPOOL
MIDFIELDER STEVEN GERRARD

From the FIFA World Cup to the African Cup of Nations, each international competition has its own special magic. Agonizing months, even years, of nail-biting qualifying matches played in far-flung stadia all seem worth it when you realize your team has a shot at the big prize. That's the best thing about cup soccer—it gives lesser-known teams a chance to step up and show the world who they are and allows the big teams to dazzle and delight a worldwide audience. Unfortunately, there can only ever be one winner. Until next time, of course.

# FIFA WORLD CUP™

*"FIRST AND FOREMOST, THE WORLD CUP SHOULD BE A FESTIVAL OF FOOTBALL."*
FRANZ BECKENBAUER

The World Cup is seen by many as the greatest sporting event on Earth. Held every four years, it brings together the top international teams after three years of qualifying matches. The 2006 final in Germany was watched by a global audience of 715 million. In the 18 tournaments played, only seven nations have ever won the title: Argentina, Brazil, England, France, Germany, Italy, and Uruguay.

## THE CUP

The current FIFA World Cup trophy was first awarded in 1974. It replaced the Jules Rimet trophy that Brazil was allowed to keep after its third tournament win in 1970. The bottom of the trophy bears the name and year of every winner since West Germany in 1974. The trophy will need to be replaced in 2038 because there will be no more space!

*Designed by Italian Silvio Gazzaniga, the trophy is 14 in (36cm) high, weighs just over 13 lb (6kg), and is made of 18-carat gold.*

## FACT FILE:
## FIFA WORLD CUP™ FINALS

### TOP GOAL SCORERS
1. Ronaldo (Brazil) 15 (1994–2006)
2. Gerd Müller (West Germany) 14 (1966–74)
3. Just Fontaine (France) 13 (1958)
4. Pelé (Brazil) 12 (1958–70)
5. Jürgen Klinsmann (Germany) 11 (1990–98)
= Sándor Kocsis (Hungary) 11 (1954)

### FASTEST GOALS
1. Hakan Sükür (Turkey) v South Korea 2002—11 seconds
2. Václav Mašek (Czechoslovakia) v Mexico 1962—15 seconds
3. Pak Seung-Zin (North Korea) v Portugal 1966—23 seconds
4. Ernst Lehner (Germany) v Austria 1934—24 seconds
5. Bryan Robson (England) v France 1982—27 seconds

*Ronaldo beat Gerd Müller's record with a goal against Ghana in the 2006 Finals. Former Brazil captain Cafu also holds the record for most appearances in the World Cup final with three, and Brazil is the only team to be present at every World Cup Finals.*

**JULES RIMET** was president of FIFA for an incredible 33 years—from 1921 to 1954—and was instrumental in making soccer the world game. It was thanks to this Frenchman that the first Finals were held in 1930. In 1946, the original trophy was renamed the Jules Rimet Trophy in his honor.

*The trophy was stolen in 1983 and has never been recovered. It is thought to have been melted down by the thieves.*

## GREATEST GOALS

The World Cup Finals have been blessed with many amazing goals, from 17-year-old Pelé's stunning volley against Sweden in 1958 to Netherlands' Arie Haan's long range strike against West Germany in 1978. Here are two of the very best of all time:

In one glorious minute of the 1986 quarterfinal, Argentina's Diego Maradona dribbled 55 yards (50 meters), passing four England players, to score the goal voted FIFA's Greatest World Cup Goal in a 2002 poll.

Carlos Alberto's goal in the 1970 final epitomises Brazil's extraordinary skill. Nine players dribbled and passed the ball the length of the pitch before defender Alberto charged into space and powered home Pelé's pass from the edge of the area.

## CONTROVERSY

Since the very beginning, World Cup Finals have never been short of talking points both on and off the field. From arguments over the choice of hosts to controversial goals, disputed decisions, and violent tackles, the World Cup has seen it all.

In 1986, Maradona claimed his first goal against England was due "a little to the head of Maradona, a little to the hand of God." Other people just say it was handball!

In the 1966 final, a close-range shot from England's Geoff Hurst hit the bar, bounced down and back into play. The linesman ruled that it was a goal and England went on to win the match. However, many people argue that the whole of the ball did not cross the line—meaning it wasn't a goal.

Italy versus Chile in the 1962 Finals was one of the dirtiest matches ever, as players fought and police had to break up mass brawls. It became known as the "Battle of Santiago."

WORLD CUP WINNERS **Brazil:** 5 times—1958, 1962, 1970, 1994, 2002 **Italy:** 4 times—1934, 1938, 1982, 2006 **Germany:** 3 times—1954, 1974, 1990 **Argentina:** twice—1978, 1986 **Uruguay:** twice—1930, 1950 **England:** once—1966 **France:** once—1998

*This is the actual size of the World Cup trophy.*

## 1930 URUGUAY

**FINAL:**
Uruguay 4 Argentina 2

**THIRD PLACE:**
Not awarded

**GOLDEN BOOT:**
Guillermo Stábile 8 (Argentina)

**GOLDEN BALL:** Guillermo Stábile (Argentina)

### ALL STAR TEAM
1. Enrique Ballesteros (Uruguay) 2. José Nasazzi (Uruguay) 3. Milutin Ivkovic (Yugoslavia) 4. Luis Monti (Argentina) 5. Álvaro Gestido (Uruguay) 6. José Andrade (Uruguay) 7. Pedro Cea (Uruguay) 8. Héctor Castro (Uruguay) 9. Héctor Scarone (Uruguay)10. Guilliermo Stábile (Uruguay) 11. Bert Patenaude (USA)

### FINAL
Host Uruguay provided a thrilling climax to the very first World Cup Finals, with a second-half comeback against arch rival Argentina. Both teams wanted to use their own match ball, so they were allowed 45 minutes each. Argentina took a 2–1 lead at half-time, using its own ball, only for Pedro Cea's equalizer (pictured above) to turn the game around.

## 1934 ITALY

**FINAL:**
Italy 2 Czechoslovakia 1 (aet)

**THIRD PLACE:**
Germany

**GOLDEN BOOT:**
Oldrich Nejedlý 5 (Czechoslovakia)

**GOLDEN BALL:** Giuseppe Meazza (Italy)

### ALL STAR TEAM
1. Ricardo Zamora (Spain) 2. Jacinto Quincoces (Spain) 3. Eraldo Monzeglio (Italy) 4. Luiz Monti (Italy) 5. Attilio Ferraris (Italy) 6. Leonardo Cilaurren (Spain) 7. Giussepe Meazza (Italy) 8. Raimundo Orsi (Italy) 9. Enrique Guaita (Italy) 10. Matthias Sindelar (Austria) 11. Oldrich Nejedlý (Czechoslovakia)

## 1950 BRAZIL

**FINAL:**
Uruguay 2 Brazil 1

**THIRD PLACE:**
Sweden

**GOLDEN BOOT:**
Ademir 9 (Brazil)

**GOLDEN BALL:** Zizinho (Brazil)

### ALL STAR TEAM
1. Roque Máspoli (Uruguay) 2. Erik Nilsson (Sweden) 3. José Parra (Spain) 4. Schubert Gambetta (Uruguay) 5. Obdulio Varela (Uruguay) 6. Walter Bahr (USA) 7. Alcides Ghiggia (Uruguay) 8. Zizinho (Brazil) 9.Ademir (Brazil) 10. Jair (Brazil) 11. Schiaffino (Uruguay)

### FINAL
Alcides Ghiggia's late winner (above) gave Uruguay a shock victory over the host, and favorite, Brazil. There was no official trophy presentation—the cup was smuggled into captain Obdulio Varela's hands, and the new champions hid in their dressing room until it was deemed safe to come out.

## 1954 SWITZERLAND

**FINAL:**
West Germany 3 Hungary 2

**THIRD PLACE:**
Austria

**GOLDEN BOOT:**
Sándor Kocsis 11 (Hungary)

**GOLDEN BALL:** Sándor Kocsis (Hungary)

### ALL STAR TEAM
1. Gyula Grosics (Hungary) 2. Ernst Ocwirk (Austria) 3. József Bozsik (Hungary) 4. José Santamaria (Uruguay) 5. Fritz Walter (West Germany) 6. Bauer (Brazil) 7. Helmut Rahn (West Germany) 8. Nándor Hidegkuti (Hungary) 9. Ferenc Puskás (Hungary) 10. Sándor Kocsis (Hungary) 11. Zoltán Czibor (Hungary)

## 1962 CHILE

**FINAL**
Brazil 3 Czechoslovakia 1

**THIRD PLACE:**
Germany

**GOLDEN BOOT:**
Garrincha 4 (Brazil), Vavá 4 (Brazil), Leonel Sánchez 4 (Chile), Dražan Jerkovic 4 (Yugoslavia), Valentin Ivanov 4 (USSR), Flórián Albert 4 (Hungary)

**GOLDEN BALL:** Garrincha (Brazil)

### ALL STAR TEAM
1. Antonio Carbajal (Mexico) 2. Djalma Santos (Brazil) 3. Cesare Maldini (Italy) 4. Valeriy Voronin (USSR) 5. Karl-Heinz Schnellinger (West Germany) 6. Zagallo (Brazil) 7. Zito (Brazil) 8. Josef Masopust (Czechoslovakia) 9. Vavá (Brazil) 10. Garrincha (Brazil) 11. Leonel Sánchez (Brazil)

### FINAL
1962 truly was Garrincha's World Cup, especially after Pelé withdrew early through injury. Garrincha was actually sent off for fighting in the semifinal, but appealed against suspension to pull the strings in the final. Pelé's replacement Amarildo, Zito (above), and Vavá got the goals this time.

## 1966 ENGLAND

**FINAL:**
England 4 West Germany 2

**THIRD PLACE:**
Portugal

**GOLDEN BOOT:**
Eusébio 9 (Portugal)

**GOLDEN BALL:** Bobby Charlton (England)

### ALL STAR TEAM
1. Gordon Banks (England) 2. George Cohen (England) 3. Bobby Moore (England) 4. Valeriy Voronin (USSR) 5. Silvio Marzolini (Argentina) 6. Franz Beckenbauer (West Germany) 7. Mário Coluna (Portugal) 8. Bobby Charlton (England) 9. Flórián Albert (Hungary) 10. Uwe Seeler (West Germany) 11. Eusébio (Portugal)

**FINAL**
Uruguay did not defend its title, staying away in protest after only four European sides had turned up in 1930. Raimondo Orsi, a runner-up with Argentina four years earlier but now an Italian citizen scored Italy's (above) first in the final, before a clincher by Angelo Schiavio.

## 1938 FRANCE

**FINAL:**
Italy 4 Hungary 2

**THIRD PLACE:**
Brazil

**GOLDEN BOOT:**
Leônidas da Silva 7 (Brazil)

**GOLDEN BALL:** Leônidas da Silva (Brazil)

### ALL STAR TEAM
1. František Plánicka (Czechoslovakia) 2. Pietro Rava (Italy) 3. Alfredo Foni (Italy) 4.Domingos da Guia (Brazil) 5. Michele Andreolo (Italy) 6. Ugo Locatelli (Italy) 7. Silvio Piola (Italy) 8. Gino Colaussi (Italy) 9. György Sárosi (Hungary) 10. Gyula Zsengellér (Hungary) 11. Leônidas da Silva (Brazil)

**FINAL**
Luigi Colaussi and brute-strength goal machine Silvio Piola each bagged a brace as Italy retained its World Cup title. They achieved it with more of a flourish then they had on home turf four years earlier. Vittorio Pozzo is still the only person to win the World Cup twice as manager, in 1934 and 1938.

**FINAL**
Hungary crushed West Germany 8–3 in the first round, only to throw away a two-goal lead in the final against the same opponents. Ferenc Puskás saw a late "equalizer" dubiously ruled out for offside and Helmut Rahn's 84th-minute strike stole what the Germans still call "The Miracle of Berne."

## 1958 SWEDEN

**FINAL:**
Brazil 5 Sweden 2

**THIRD PLACE:**
France

**GOLDEN BOOT:**
Just Fontaine 13 (France)

**GOLDEN BALL:** Raymond Kopa (France)

### ALL STAR TEAM
1. Lev Yashin (USSR) 2. Djalma Santos (Brazil) 3. Bellini (Brazil) 4. Nílton Santos (Brazil) 5. Danny Blanchflower (Northern Ireland) 6. Didi (Brazil) 7. Pelé (Brazil) 8. Garrincha (Brazil) 9. Just Fontaine (France) 10. Raymond Kopa (France) 11. Gunnar Gren (Sweden)

**FINAL**
A 17-year-old named Pelé (far right) emerged as the hero, as Brazil finally broke its World Cup duck. The teenager, along with dazzling winger Garrincha, stayed in the stands for Brazil's opening game, deemed not mature enough by team doctors. But the hosts had no answer to the irrepressible duo in the final, nor the sumptuous passing of midfield maestro Didi.

**FINAL**
Arguments still rage about whether Geoff Hurst's second, and England's third, goal against West Germany in the 1966 final should have been allowed after bouncing off the crossbar. Hurst made sure of a famous win in the last minute, completing the only hat trick to be scored, so far, in a World Cup final.

## 1970 MEXICO

**FINAL:**
Brazil 4 Italy 1

**THIRD PLACE:**
West Germany

**GOLDEN BOOT:**
Gerd Müller 10 (West Germany)

**GOLDEN BALL:** Pelé (Brazil)

### ALL STAR TEAM
1. Ladislao Mazurkiewicz (Uruguay) 2. Carlos Alberto Torres (Brazil) 3. Piazza (Brazil) 4. Franz Beckenbauer (West Germany) 5. Giacinto Facchetti (Italy) 6. Gérson (Brazil) 7. Gianni Rivera (Italy) 8. Bobby Charlton (England) 9. Pelé (Brazil) 10. Gerd Müller (West Germany) 11. Jairzinho (Brazil)

**FINAL**
Ask most people what is the greatest team ever, and they will answer "Brazil, 1970." Pelé, Jairzinho, Rivelino, and Carlos Alberto were all imperious—but the final against Italy was tight and finely-balanced at 1–1, when midfielder Gérson swept this shot into the net from distance. The rest is history.

## 1974 WEST GERMANY

**FINAL:**
West Germany 2 Netherlands 1

**THIRD PLACE:**
Poland

**GOLDEN BOOT:**
Grzegorz Lato 7 (Poland)

**GOLDEN BALL:** Johan Cruyff (Netherlands)

**ALL STAR TEAM**
1. Jan Tomaszewski (Poland) 2. Berti Vogts (West Germany) 3. Wim Suurbier (Netherlands) 4. Franz Beckenbauer (West Germany) 5. Marinho Chagas (Brazil) 6. Wolfgang Overath (West Germany) 7. Kazimierz Deyna (Poland) 8. Johan Neeskens (Netherlands) 9. Rob Rensenbrink (Netherlands)10. Johan Cruyff (Netherlands) 11. Grzegorz Lato (Poland)

**FINAL**
It doesn't always happen, but the two best teams in the world went head to head in the 1974 final, and the two best players, too. In the end, it was West Germany's Franz Beckenbauer (above, with the rest of the German team) hoisting the trophy instead of Dutch counterpart Johan Cruyff, thanks to goal-poacher supreme Gerd Müller.

## 1978 ARGENTINA

**FINAL:**
Argentina 3 Netherlands 1

**THIRD PLACE:**
Brazil

**GOLDEN BOOT:**
Mario Kempes 6 (Argentina)

**GOLDEN BALL:** Mario Kempes (Argentina

**ALL STAR TEAM**
1. Ubaldo Fillol (Argentina) 2. Berti Vogts (West Germany) 3. Ruud Krol (Netherlands) 4. Daniel Passarella (Argentina) 5. Alberto Tarantini (Argentina) 6. Dirceu ( Brazil) 7. Franco Causio (Italy) 8. Rob Rensenbrink (Netherlands) 9. Teófilo Cubillas (Peru) 10.Daniel Bertoni (Argentina) 11. Mario Kempes (Argentina)

## 1986 MEXICO

**FINAL:**
Argentina 3 West Germany 2

**THIRD PLACE:**
France

**GOLDEN BOOT:**
Gary Lineker 6 (England)

**GOLDEN BALL:** Diego Maradona (Argentina)

**ALL STAR TEAM**
1. Harald Schumacher (West Germany) 2. Josimar (Brazil) 3. Manuel Amoros (France) 4. Maxime Bossis (France) 5. Jan Ceulemans (Belgium) 6. Felix Magath (West Germany) 7. Michel Platini (France) 8. Diego Maradona (Argentina) 9. Preben Elkjær-Larsen (Denmark) 10. Emilio Butragueño (Spain) 11. Gary Lineker (England)

**FINAL**
Few players have dominated a World Cup as Diego Maradona (above) did in 1986. Many saw the champions as a one-man team, but José Luis Brown, Jorge Valdano, and Jorge Burruchaga scored the goals in the final. Burrachaga's winner was made by a perfect defense-splitting through-ball from Maradona.

## 1990 ITALY

**FINAL:**
West Germany 1 Argentina 0

**THIRD PLACE:**
Italy

**GOLDEN BOOT:**
Salvatore Schillaci 6 (Italy)

**GOLDEN BALL:** Salvatore Schillaci (Italy)

**ALL STAR TEAM**
1. Sergio Goycochea (Argentina) 2. Andreas Brehme (West Germany) 3. Paolo Maldini (Italy) 4. Franco Baresi (Italy) 5. Diego Maradona (Argentina) 6. Lothar Matthäus (West Germany) 7. Roberto Donadoni (Italy) 8. Paul Gascoigne (England) 9. Salvatore Schillaci (Italy) 10. Roger Milla (Cameroon) 11. Tomáš Skuhravý (Czechoslovakia)

## 1998 FRANCE

**FINAL:**
France 3 Brazil 0

**THIRD PLACE:**
Croatia

**GOLDEN BOOT:**
Davor Šuker 6 (Croatia)

**GOLDEN BALL:** Ronaldo (Brazil)

**STAR PLAYERS**
**Goalkeepers:** Fabien Barthez (France), José Luis Chilavert (Paraguay) **Defenders:** Roberto Carlos da Silva (Brazil), Marcel Desailly (France), Lilian Thuram (France), Frank de Boer (Netherlands), Carlos Gamarra (Paraguay) **Midfielders:** Dunga (Brazil), Rivaldo (Brazil), Michael Laudrup (Denmark), Zinedine Zidane (France), Edgar Davids (Netherlands) **Forwards:** Ronaldo (Brazil), Davor Šuker (Croatia) Brian Laudrup (Denmark), Dennis Bergkamp (Netherlands)

**FINAL**
France won its first World Cup on home turf. After being sent off earlier in the tournament, Zinedine Zidane redeemed himself with two emphatic finishes (the second pictured above), before Emmanuel Petit added a third in the closing seconds. Brazil was visibly subdued after star striker Ronaldo suffered a pregame fit.

## 2002 REPUBLIC OF KOREA & JAPAN

**FINAL:**
Brazil 2 Germany 0

**THIRD PLACE:**
Turkey

**GOLDEN BOOT:**
Ronaldo 8 (Brazil)

**GOLDEN BALL:** Oliver Kahn (Germany)

**STAR PLAYERS**
**Goalkeepers:** Oliver Kahn (Germany), Rüstü Reçber (Turkey) **Defenders:** Roberto Carlos (Brazil), Sol Campbell (England), Fernando Hierro (Spain), Hong Myung-Bo (South Korea), Alpay Özalan (Turkey) **Midfielders:** Rivaldo (Brazil), Ronaldinho (Brazil), Michael Ballack (Germany), Yoo Sang-Chul (South Korea) **Forwards:** Ronaldo (Brazil), Miroslav Klose (Germany), El Hadji Diouf (Senegal), Hasan Sas (Turkey)

**FINAL**

Argentina won its first world crown in Buenos Aires' Monumental stadium. Attacking midfielder Mario Kempes (above, left) was the tournament's revelation, scoring six goals, including two in the final. The unlucky Dutch, without Johan Cruyff, fell just short in the final once again.

## 1982 SPAIN

**FINAL:**
Italy 3 West Germany 1

**THIRD PLACE:**
Poland

**GOLDEN BOOT:**
Paolo Rossi 6 (Italy)

**GOLDEN BALL:** Paolo Rossi (Italy)

### ALL STAR TEAM
1. Dino Zoff (Italy) 2. Claudio Gentile (Italy)
3. Luizinho (Brazil) 4. Fulvio Collovati (Italy)
5. Júnior (Brazil) 6. Zbigniew Boniek (Poland)
7. Falcão (Brazil) 8. Michel Platini (France)
9. Zico (Brazil) 10. Paolo Rossi (Italy)
11. Karl-Heinz Rummenigge (Brazil)

**FINAL**

Marco Tardelli's long-range strike (above) was Italy's second in a comfortable 3–1 defeat of West Germany. This victory drew Italy level with Brazil on three World Cup triumphs each. The championship in Spain was the first in 48 years to be expanded, featuring 24 teams instead of 16.

**FINAL**

Italia '90 was settled by a late Andreas Brehme penalty, after a dubious refereeing decision. German joy on the soccer field (above) came as East and West Germany prepared to celebrate reunification.

## 1994 USA

**FINAL:**
Brazil 0 Italy 0 (aet)
Brazil won 3–2 on penalties

**THIRD PLACE:**
Sweden

**GOLDEN BOOT:**
Hristo Stoichkov 6 (Bulgaria), Oleg Salenko 6 (Russia)

**GOLDEN BALL:** Romário (Brazil)

### ALL STAR TEAM
1. Michel Preud'homme (Belgium) 2. Jorginho (Brazil) 3. Márcio Santos (Brazil) 4. Paulo Maldini (Italy) 5. Dunga (Brazil) 6. Krasimir Balakov (Bulgaria) 7. Gheorghe Hagi (Romania) 8. Thomas Brolin (Sweden) 9. Romário (Brazil) 10. Hristo Stoichkov (Bulgaria) 11. Roberto Baggio (Italy)

The 1994 final was the first to be settled on penalties. Brazil came out on top, with Italy's genius Roberto Baggio surprisingly ballooning the decisive spot-kick over the bar. Italy defender Franco Baresi, perhaps man of the match despite playing with an injury, had also missed a penalty.

**FINAL**

After a World Cup where France, Argentina, and Italy all crashed out early, the final itself featured two of international soccer's stalwarts. Ronaldo put his 1998 misery behind him with two clinical finishes. Lifting the cup marked a unique achievement for captain Cafu—playing in a World Cup final for the third time.

## 2006 GERMANY

**FINAL:**
Italy 1 France 1 (aet)
Italy won 5–3 on penalties

**THIRD PLACE:**
Germany

**GOLDEN BOOT:**
Miroslav Klose 5 (Germany)

**GOLDEN BALL:** Zinedine Zidane (France)

### STAR PLAYERS
**Goalkeepers:** Gianluigi Buffon (Italy), Jens Lehmann (Germany), Ricardo (Portugal) **Defenders:** Roberto Ayala (Argentina), John Terry (England), Lilian Thuram (France), Philipp Lahm (Germany), Fabio Cannavaro (Italy), Gianluca Zambrotta (Italy), Ricardo Carvalho (Portugal) **Midfielders:** Zé Roberto (Brazil), Patrick Vieira (France), Zinedine Zidane (France), Michael Ballack (Germany), Andrea Pirlo (Italy), Gennaro Gattuso (Italy), Luis Figo (Portugal), Cristiano Ronaldo (Portugal), **Forwards:** Hernán Crespo (Argentina), Thierry Henry (France), Miroslav Klose (Germany), Francesco Totti (Italy), Luca Toni (Italy)

**FINAL**

Italy's 2006 success was a vindication of strength in depth—only the two reserve goalkeepers were unused squad members. Fabio Grosso's penalty won the shootout, after France's David Trezeguet hit the bar, six years after his "golden goal" beat Italy in the Euro 2000 final.

# UEFA EUROPEAN CHAMPIONSHIP

## "FOOTBALL UNITES AND TRANSCENDS EUROPE."

UEFA PRESIDENT AND EUROPEAN CHAMPIONSHIP-
WINNING FRANCE MIDFIELDER MICHEL PLATINI

The UEFA European Championship ranks second only to the World Cup for prestige and popularity in international soccer. More than 50 countries enter the qualifying stages, while the major nations of the continent vie for supremacy. Held every four years, the tournament began in 1960 with a four-team competition, but has grown to become a month-long contest involving 16 teams.

### AN IDEA
Henri Delaunay, former secretary of the French FA, first suggested the idea of a European Championship in 1927 but the first tournament did not take place until 1960.

### 2008
The European Championship trophy was named in Henri Delaunay's honor. A new trophy was created for the 2008 tournament in Austria and Switzerland with a sturdier base and more space for the winners' names. However, the trophy looks very similar to the old one and retains Delaunay's name.

*Jürgen Klinsmann celebrates scoring a goal against Russia during Euro '96 in England.*

### FIRST CHAMPIONSHIPS
The USSR defeated Yugoslavia 2–1 in the first European Championship final in Paris. Led by the legendary goalkeeper Lev Yashin, the Soviets needed extra time to complete their victory, with the winning goal scored by Viktor Ponedelnik.

### GERMAN SKILL
Germany is the most successful team in the European Championship. As West Germany and the reunified side, it won the tournament three times and was runner-up twice. The last triumph in 1996 came when the Germans beat the much favored host England in a thrilling semifinal, before a 2–1 overtime victory over the Czech Republic in the final.

### DID YOU KNOW?
Oliver Bierhoff's 94th minute winner for Germany in the 1996 final was the first time a major international tournament was decided by a "golden goal." The rule stated that in extra time, the game would end immediately if one team scored a goal. This way of deciding the outcome of a game became known as a "golden goal."

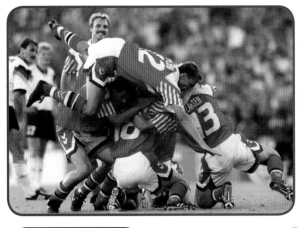

One of the most famous tournaments was in 1992 when outsider Denmark beat favorite Germany 2–0 in Gothenburg's Ullevi stadium, thanks to goals from John Jensen and Kim Vilfort. The Danes were only at the finals because of the late withdrawal of Yugoslavia, who had to pull out of the competition due to civil war.

Michel Platini (above) holds the record for the most goals scored by one player in a European Championship. He scored nine on the way to France's triumph in 1984, including the opener in the 2–0 defeat of Spain in the final. This total also makes him the Championship's all-time top scorer.

### FACT FILE: UEFA EUROPEAN CHAMPIONSHIP

(see p. 182 for complete list of winners)

**TOP GOAL SCORERS**
1. Michel Platini (France) 9
2. Alan Shearer (England) 7
3. Nuno Gomes (Portugal) 6
= Thierry Henry (France) 6
= Patrick Kluivert (Netherlands) 6
= Ruud van Nistelrooy (Netherlands) 6
4. Milan Baroš (Czech Republic) 5
= Jürgen Klinsmann (West Germany/Germany) 5
= Savo Milošević (Yugoslavia/Serbia) 5
= Marco van Basten (Netherlands) 5
= Zinédine Zidane (France) 5

**MOST SUCCESSFUL TEAMS**
1. Germany (3 wins)
2. France (2 wins)
= Spain (2 wins)
3. USSR (1 win)
= Czechoslovakia (1 win)
= Italy (1 win)
= Netherlands (1 win)
= Denmark (1 win)
= Greece (1 win)

*Spain was captained to glory by goalkeeper Iker Casillas (left).*

When Greece beat host Portugal 2–1 in the opening game of Euro 2004, no one would have predicted that three weeks later the same teams would be in the final. Greece won that final 1–0, with a goal from Angelos Charisteas (above, left). In the semifinal, Greece's Traianos Dellas had also headed a winning "silver goal" against Czech Republic, the only time a championship game has ended in that way.

## EURO 2008

Spain ended its 44-year wait for a trophy in 2008. The final win over Germany was more comfortable than the 1–0 scoreline suggests, as the free-flowing Spanish claimed their just rewards. Euro 2008 was also the first tournament to be played in two host countries—Austria and Switzerland.

# COPA AMÉRICA

**"THE COPA AMÉRICA IS MORE DIFFICULT THAN THE WORLD CUP BECAUSE OF THE RIVALRY THAT EXISTS IN SOUTH AMERICA."** DUNGA, WHO WON THE COPA WITH BRAZIL AS A PLAYER AND AS COACH

The Copa América is the oldest—and most fiercely contested—international tournament. It was introduced in 1916, to mark a century of Argentina's independence from Spain. The format, name and frequency of the competition have varied greatly over the years, but it is now established as a 12-team tournament held every four years, with hosting rights rotated between the 10 CONMEBOL countries.

The actual Copa América trophy was first introduced in 1917, a year after Uruguay had won the first tournament.

Argentina's glory in 1957, including a 3–0 destruction of archrival Brazil (left), gave coach Guillermo Stabile the trophy for a sixth and final time. No other manager has won it more than twice.

*Argentine hard-man Oscar Ruggeri was a South American champion in 1991 and 1993, as well as a World Cup winner in 1986.*

Enzo Francescoli (above, pictured in 1995) was the architect of Uruguay's 1983, 1987, and 1995 victories.

Uruguay's players spoiled host Argentina's independence centenary celebrations by winning the first organized Copa América in 1916 (above). Argentina had beaten Uruguay in an unofficial South American championship clash in 1910. The two countries are currently even, with 14 tournaments each.

## DID YOU KNOW?

*The 1919 final between Brazil and Uruguay lasted for 150 minutes, including 60 minutes of overtime. The deadlock was only broken by Arthur Friedenreich's 122nd-minute winner for Brazil.*

*Argentina striker Martín Palermo missed three penalties during Colombia's 3–0 win in the 1999 Copa América—an international record.*

## ARGENTINA

Victory in 1993 brought Argentina its 14th Copa América, and its last international trophy to date. Oscar Ruggeri (left) captained the team and two goals from Gabriel Batistuta proved too much for guest Mexico in the final. Argentina was runner-up to Brazil in 2004 and 2007 and is still chasing a 15th Copa América to take it ahead of Uruguay.

Two men named Córdoba were crucial to Colombia's first—and, so far, only—Copa América title, in 2001. On home turf, Captain Iván Córdoba (far left) scored the only goal of the final against Mexico. He was also the mainstay of the first defense to go through an entire Copa América without conceding, with Óscar Córdoba (no relation) keeping the shutouts in goal.

## FACT FILE: COPA AMÉRICA
(See p. 182 for complete list of winners)

### TOP GOAL SCORERS
1. Norberto Méndez (Argentina) 17
= Zizinho (Brazil) 17
2. Teodoro Fernández (Peru) 15
= Severino Varela (Uruguay) 15

### MOST SUCCESSFUL TEAMS
1. Argentina (14 wins)
= Uruguay (14 wins)
2. Brazil (8 wins)
3. Paraguay (2 wins)
= Peru (2 wins)

In 2004, Argentina had its hands on the trophy until three minutes into stoppage-time in the final, when Brazilian center-forward Adriano (right, center) struck his seventh goal of the tournament. Brazil's Seleção went on to win on penalties, becoming the first country to hold both World Cup and Copa América crowns at the same time.

Two or three CONCACAF guest nations are invited to the Copa América tournament. In 2001, guests Honduras (right) stunned Brazil 2–0 in the quarterfinal. Mexico also finished runner-up in that year.

*Robinho's six goals made him the tournament's top scorer.*

*Victory in 2007 meant that Brazil retained the trophy it had also won in 2004.*

## BRAZIL
In 2007, the result seemed a foregone conclusion. Brazilian stars such as Kaká and Ronaldinho were absent, while Riquelme and Messi lit up a majestic Argentina side. However, Brazil outmuscled its old rival 3–0 in the final to win the Copa for the eighth time.

# CONCACAF GOLD CUP

BOB BRADLEY, US COACH SINCE 2006

CONCACAF's showpiece has had a varied history and throughout the 1980s it was chiefly used to decide World Cup places. In 1990, it was rebranded as the CONCACAF Gold Cup and since then the tournament has enjoyed greater prestige. Although the competition is dominated by Mexico and the US, the 2009 event brought encouraging displays from Honduras, Guadeloupe, Haiti, and Panama.

### CANADA
Although Jason de Vos and Carlo Corazzin got the goals to conquer Colombia in the final, Canada's victory in 2000 owed much to goalkeeper Craig Forrest (above, right). Forrest saved two penalties, including one in the semifinal against Trinidad and Tobago, and was voted the competition's most valuable player.

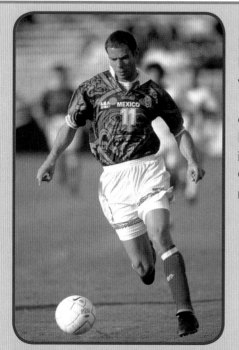

### GOAL LEGENDS
In 1993, striker Zaguinho (left) inspired Mexico to a famous victory. Zaguinho, whose real name is Luis Roberto Alves, hit 12 goals in that tournament, scoring seven of them in a 9–0 first-round thrashing of Martinique. Mexican-born but brought up in Brazil by Brazilian parents, Zaguinho's CONCACAF Gold Cup goal scoring remains a tournament record.

Landon Donovan (right) has been on the roster for three of the US's four CONCACAF championship-winning campaigns, including a game-turning penalty against Mexico in the 2007 final. His four goals in one game against Cuba helped him finish joint top scorer in the 2003 championship.

### USA
In 2007, new coach Bob Bradley helped the US to continue its good record in the 21st century by winning the CONCACAF Gold Cup final 2–1 against Mexico (pictured left.) The US had also won in 2002 and 2005, as well as way back in 1991.

Former Barcelona wonderkid Giovani dos Santos (right) lived up to the highest of Mexican expectations when he lit up the 2009 CONCACAF Gold Cup. The 20-year-old winger scored one and set up two more for Mexico in the final, which earned him the prize for the tournament's best player. Victory in the final also marked Mexico's first away win against the US in 10 years.

## FACT FILE: CONCACAF GOLD CUP

(See p. 182 for complete list of winners)

**TOP GOAL SCORERS**
1. Zaguinho (Mexico) 13
2. Landon Donovan (USA) 12
3. Carlos Pavón (Honduras) 9
= Eric Wynalda (USA) 9
4. Paulo Wanchope (Costa Rica) 8
= Walter Centeno (Costa Rica) 8
= Brian McBride (USA) 8

**MOST SUCCESSFUL TEAMS**
1. Mexico (8 wins)
2. USA (4 wins)
3. Costa Rica (3 wins)
4. Canada (2 wins)

## DID YOU KNOW?

*Champion Canada only got past the first round in 2000 by the toss of a coin. It had finished its group level on points and goal difference with guest team, Republic of Korea.*

*In 2007, US goalkeeper Kasey Keller appeared in a record sixth CONCACAF Gold Cup.*

*The 2009 Gold Cup was played at 13 stadiums. The US was host for the third time in a row.*

*All five of Mexico's goals in the final were scored in the second half.*

## 2009 GOLD CUP

After watching rival US take the two previous titles, Mexico—under new coach Javier Aguirre—romped to a 5–0 victory over host, USA, in the 2009 final. Mexico striker Miguel Sabah won the 2009 Golden Boot, despite only making his international debut two months before the tournament.

*This was Mexico's fifth title since an overhaul of the competition in 1991, giving it a record eight championships.*

# AFRICAN CUP OF NATIONS

Just three teams (Egypt, Sudan, and Ethiopia) took part in the first CAF African Cup of Nations in Sudan in 1957. However, it is now a prestigious biennial event with 16 teams participating in the 2008 tournament in Ghana. The competition is usually held in January, but with many African players playing in European leagues, pressure is growing to move it to the summer.

The current ACN trophy (above) is the third. Ghana was allowed to keep the original Abdelaziz Abdallah Salem Trophy after its third triumph in 1978, and the African Unity Cup was kept by Cameroon in 2000.

### SOUTH AFRICA

Mark Williams' two goals in the last 17 minutes of the 1996 tournament gave host South Africa its most glorious moment in soccer so far. President Nelson Mandela was there as South Africa made the most of it, after stepping in as a late replacement for original host, Kenya.

*Goal-scoring hero Mark Williams (right) proudly holds the trophy aloft.*

## DID YOU KNOW?

*No player has scored more goals in one African Cup of Nations than Ndaya Mulamba's nine for Zaire (now DPR Congo) in 1974.*

### GHANA

Ghana's "Black Stars" put African soccer on the map by winning the 1963 and 1965 tournaments in irresistible style. A third win in 1978 entitled Ghana to keep the trophy, but there have been lengthy, impatient waits between victories since then. Abédi "Pelé" Ayew announced himself as a 17-year-old wonder in Ghana's fourth success in 1982. However, he was suspended for the epic 11–10 shootout defeat to Ivory Coast 10 years later.

### TUNISIA

Tunisia's one and only ACN triumph came in 2004, in front of a home crowd, at the Stade 7 Novembre in Radès. Ziad Jaziri struck a memorable winner in the final against Morocco. Former France manager Roger Lemerre was in charge, Riadh Bouazizi led from midfield as captain, while Brazilian-born Tunisia striker Francileudo Santos ended the tournament as joint top scorer.

## CAMEROON

Although much of the world first discovered the delights of Cameroon's soccer at the 1990 World Cup Finals, the seeds of the team's success were sown in the early 1980s. The "Indomitable Lions" made three consecutive finals that decade and won two of them, most notably beating Nigeria 3–1 in the 1984 final. Cameroon also captured the first two titles of the 21st century, thanks to the team's calmness in penalty shootouts. Cameroon's third victory in 2000 earned it the right to keep the trophy.

### FACT FILE: AFRICAN CUP OF NATIONS
(See p. 182 for complete list of winners)

**TOP GOAL SCORERS**
1. Samuel Eto'o (Cameroon) 16
2. Laurent Pokou (Ivory Coast) 14
3. Rashidi Yekini (Nigeria) 13
4. Hassan El-Shazly (Egypt) 12
5. Hossam Hassan (Egypt) 11
= Patrick Mboma (Cameroon) 11

**MOST SUCCESSFUL TEAMS**
1. Egypt (6 wins)
2. Ghana (4 wins)
= Cameroon (4 wins)
3. Congo DR (2 wins)
= Nigeria (2 wins)

*Aboutrika plays his club soccer for Al-Ahly in Egypt.*

## EGYPT

The "Pharaohs" won the first two ACN titles—Raafat Ateya scored the first-ever ACN goal in 1957 and Al-Diba hit all four goals in that year's final. Egypt has won the title six times, including a 1–0 victory over Cameroon in 2008 (pictured above.)

Skillful playmaker Mohamed Aboutrika scored the decisive penalty in Egypt's 2006 shootout victory over Ivory Coast, as well as the only goal of the final against Cameroon as Egypt retained the title two years later.

# AFC ASIAN CUP

**"THIS IS NOT JUST ABOUT FOOTBALL... THIS HAS BROUGHT GREAT HAPPINESS TO A WHOLE COUNTRY."**

JORVAN VIEIRA, BRAZILIAN COACH OF 2007 AFC ASIAN CUP WINNERS IRAQ

The AFC Asian Cup was first held in 1956 in Hong Kong and won by the Republic of Korea. The competition was then held every four years until 2007, when the AFC brought the tournament forward a year to avoid clashing with the Olympics and the European Championship. For the first time, the competition was co-hosted by four nations (Indonesia, Malaysia, Vietnam, and Thailand)—and AFC newcomer Australia made its debut.

The first Asian Cup was won in 1956, just two years after the AFC was formed. Only four teams competed for the title back then, compared to the 16 finalists taking part today.

Iran won every game in the 1968, 1972, and 1976 tournaments to take three consecutive trophies. However, in recent years the team has struggled to rediscover this form despite the goal-scoring efforts of Javad Nekounam (left, center) in 2007.

Saudi Arabia is a three-time winner and three-time runner-up, although its last title came in 1996 (pictured above,) when Mohammed Al-Deayea's penalty saves a frustrated United Arab Emirates in the final.

Republic of Korea was the first AFC Asian Cup winner, in 1956 and 1960. However, it has failed to win the tournament since then, despite the best efforts of players such as former Middlesbrough striker Lee Dong-Gook (above)—Golden Boot winner in 2000 and second top scorer four years later.

## JAPAN

In 2004 Shunsuke Nakamura's man-of-the-match display helped Japan to its third win since 1992. Japan beat China 3–1 in the final and captain Tsuneyasu Miyamoto proudly lifted the trophy (left).

Veteran midfielder Li Ming (right), alongside Shao Jiayi, provided the driving force behind host country China's surge to the final of the 2004 AFC Asian Cup. It was China's best performance for 20 years and Li Ming scored in the Beijing final, which proved to be his international swansong. However, China ultimately fell short against Japan in the final.

## FACT FILE: AFC ASIAN CUP
(See p. 182 for complete list of winners)

### TOP GOAL SCORERS
1. Ali Daei (Iran) 14
2. Lee Dong-Gook (Republic of Korea) 10
3. Naohiro Takahara (Japan) 9
4. Jassem Al Houwaidi (Kuwait) 8
5. Choi Soon-Ho (Republic of Korea) 7
= Behtash Fariba (Iran) 7
= Hossein Kalani (Iran) 7

### MOST SUCCESSFUL TEAMS
1. Saudi Arabia (3 wins)
= Iran (3 wins)
= Japan (3 wins)
2. Republic of Korea (2 wins)
3. Israel (1 win)
= Kuwait (1 win)
= Iraq (1 win)

Much-traveled Brazilian coach Jorvan Vieira (left) took charge of Iraq just two months before leading it to the title—its first—in 2007. He had only got the job after three other contenders pulled out. Despite quitting immediately after winning in 2007, Vieira returned for a second spell in charge the following year.

*Younis Mahmoud lifts the Asian Cup after Iraq's 2007 victory in Jakarta, Indonesia.*

## FIRST-TIME CHAMP

Australia was the favorite in 2007, but outside-bet Iraq, led by captain and crucial goal scorer Younis Mahmoud, was the surprise winner. Goalkeeper Noor Sabri was another Iraqi hero, conceding just twice—both times in the first round—and saving a decisive penalty in a semifinal shootout against Republic of Korea.

# WOMEN'S COMPETITIONS

The female game's flagship competition, the Women's World Cup, was only staged for the first time in 1991, but has already attracted strong challenges from five continents. The 2007 contest enjoyed a higher profile than ever before as Brazil's path to the final upset the usual US/European dominance. Interest in the women's game is growing and with 26 million female players around the world, the sky is the limit for women's soccer.

*In 2007, Birgit Prinz proudly holds the World Cup trophy as Germany retains the title it won in 2003.*

## THE OLYMPIC GAMES

Women's soccer debuted at the Olympic Games in 1996 and the US has won gold on three out of four occasions. At the Beijing Olympics in 2008 the US beat Brazil 1–0 in the final (pictured above.) However, Norway made the US settle for a rare silver medal in the 2000 games.

## THE WORLD CUP

The first FIFA Womens' World Cup was held in 1991 and won by the US. Germany was a worthy world champion in 2007 and did not concede a goal in the entire tournament. Germany started its campaign with an 11–0 thrashing of Argentina in which striker and team captain Birgit Prinz scored a hat trick. Prinz also scored in the final, in a 2–0 victory over Brazil where German goalkeeper Nadine Angerer saved a penalty.

## AFC WOMEN'S ASIAN CUP

The AFC Women's Asian Cup is one of the longest-running international women's competitions. It was introduced in 1975 and won by New Zealand. China has dominated the competition since then, winning eight times. However, in 2008 North Korea surprised China with a 2–1 victory in the final (right).

## EUROPEAN CHAMPIONSHIP

Germany won the first UEFA Women's Championship in 1991. The team beat Norway 3–1 in that final and the same teams played out an identical scoreline in England in 2005. Germany won again in 2009, thrashing England 6–2, with goals from Prinz (2), Grings (2), Behringer, and Kulig (far left). In fact, Norway's narrow victory over Italy in 1993 was the only time Germany has failed to take the title.

## OTHER WOMEN'S COMPETITIONS

Beginning in 1991, the first four Sudamericano Femenino contests were won by Brazil. However, Argentina finally turned the tables on Brazil in 2006, despite a talented team that included the legendary Marta. Argentina beat its old rival 2–0 in the final, thanks to goals from Eva Nadia González and María Belén Potassa.

At the other end of the world, in the Oceania region, the OFC Women's Championship has been shared between New Zealand and Australia, with three wins each. Chinese Taipei is following close behind with two trophies, in 1986 and 1989. New Zealand won the tournament in 2007, scoring 21 goals in three games.

## CONCACAF WOMEN'S GOLD CUP

The US has enjoyed a secure grip on the CONCACAF Women's Gold Cup, winning six out of seven contests. 1998 champion Canada was beaten in the 2006 final by a last-minute penalty from Kristine Lilly (pictured right, player on far left.)

## CAF WOMEN'S CHAMPIONSHIP

Nigeria and Ghana have competed in three CAF Women's Championship finals and all of them have been won by Nigeria. In fact, Nigeria has won all seven CAF tournaments. In the 2006 final (pictured right), Nigeria beat Ghana 1–0, thanks to Perpetua Nkwocha's early goal. Success in the CAF Championships meant that both countries qualified for the 2007 Women's World Cup.

FC Porto and Manchester United players shake hands before the 2009 UEFA Champions League quarterfinal second leg at the Dragao Stadium in Portugal.

# CLUB SOCCER

"IN HIS LIFE, A MAN CAN CHANGE WIVES, POLITICAL PARTIES, OR RELIGIONS, BUT HE CANNOT CHANGE HIS FAVORITE FOOTBALL TEAM."

URUGUAYAN AUTHOR EDUARDO GALLEANO

Supporting your favorite club can be a roller-coaster ride. The highs are glorious, but when results are bad and your local rival has inflicted yet another painful defeat, you might wonder why you ever chose your team in the first place. Somehow, you just can't stop yourself from caring—once you've given your heart to a team, that's it. After all, there's always next season...

# UEFA CHAMPIONS LEAGUE

**"THE CHAMPIONS LEAGUE IS THE COMPETITION EVERYONE WANTS TO BE IN."** STEVEN GERRARD, LIVERPOOL'S TROPHY-WINNING CAPTAIN IN 2005

The Champions League is possibly the most prestigious club competition in the world. Originally called the European Cup, it changed its name in 1992 and adopted a league-and-knockout format. The spectacular season-long competition features the best club sides from Europe and many of the world's finest players and generates huge television and sponsorship deals.

The original trophy was donated by French magazine *L'Équipe*, whose editor Gabriel Hanot suggested the competition. The current cup is the sixth as Real Madrid, Ajax, AC Milan, Bayern Munich, and Liverpool have all been allowed to keep the trophy.

*Cruyff won the European Cup three times as an Ajax player, and once as Barcelona manager.*

### AJAX

The great Ajax side of Johan Cruyff, Johnny Rep, Arie Haan, and co. reigned supreme during the early 1970s, winning three European Cups in a row, thanks to victories over Panathinaikos (1971), Inter (1972), and Juventus (1973.) Opponents had no answer to Ajax's philosophy of "Total Soccer" (see p. 47.)

*Captain Paolo Maldini lifts the trophy after Milan's 2–1 defeat of Liverpool in 2007.*

### AC MILAN

Italy's most successful European Cup/Champions League club is AC Milan, with seven victories, most recently in 2007. Arguably Milan's finest win was the 4–0 humiliation of Barcelona in 1994. The team, managed by Fabio Capello, produced a performance viewed by some as the best ever by a club team.

### BAYERN MUNICH

Bayern Munich also achieved three consecutive triumphs, between 1974 and 1976. Great players such as Franz Beckenbauer (above, right), Uli Hoeness, Georg Schwarzenbeck, Sepp Maier, Paul Breitner, and Gerd Müller were key to the team's success. Bayern secured its fourth trophy in 2001, beating Valencia on penalties as former Borussia Dortmund coach Ottmar Hitzfeld became only the second manager to lead two different teams to the title.

## REAL MADRID

Real Madrid is the most successful team in Europe's top competition, with nine wins. The team has won the first five European Cups (1956–1960), lifted the trophy again in 1966, and has brought the Champions League title back to Spain on a another three occasions (1998, 2000, and 2002). Here, Manuel Sanchís and his teammates celebrate the club's 2000 victory (right).

## LIVERPOOL

Losing 3–0 to AC Milan at halftime during the 2005 final in Istanbul, four-time winner Liverpool looked doomed. But the English team launched an unforgettable comeback, inspired by captain Steven Gerrard (left, scoring Liverpool's first goal.) Unbelievably, Liverpool drew level with Milan and then earned a fifth trophy, thanks to a nail-biting 3–2 win in the penalty shootout. However, two years later Milan had its revenge and defeated Liverpool 2–1 in a much more straightforward final.

### FACT FILE: UEFA CHAMPIONS LEAGUE
(See p. 184 for complete list of winners)

**TOP GOAL SCORERS**
1. Raúl (Real Madrid) 61
2. Andriy Shevchenko (Dinamo Kiev, AC Milan, Chelsea) 59
3. Ruud van Nistelrooy (PSV Eindhoven, Manchester United, Real Madrid) 57
4. Thierry Henry (Monaco, Arsenal, Barcelona) 53
5. Alfredo Di Stéfano (Real Madrid) 49

**MOST SUCCESSFUL TEAMS**
1. Real Madrid (Spain) 9 wins
2. AC Milan (Italy) 7 wins
3. Liverpool (England) 5 wins
4. Ajax (Netherlands) 4 wins
= Bayern Munich (Germany) 4 wins

## MANCHESTER UNITED

Manchester United became the first English winner of the European Cup in 1968 and also emerged as champion by beating Chelsea on penalties in the first all-English final, 40 years later (pictured, left.) The second of its three titles came in 1999, thanks to two stoppage-time goals by Teddy Sheringham and Ole Gunnar Solskjær against Bayern Munich.

*Lionel Messi (celebrating below, left with Xavi) scored nine goals in the 2008-2009 Champions League, including a rare header in the final.*

## BARCELONA

Barcelona enjoyed a comfortable 2–0 victory over defending champions Manchester United in the 2009 final, three years after the Catalans had defeated another English club—Arsenal—at the same stage. The 2008—2009 season was the first as a coach for Pep Guardiola, who had been a Barcelona midfielder when it claimed its first European Cup in 1992.

(See p. 185 for complete list of winners)

## FACT FILE: UEFA EUROPA LEAGUE

**TOP GOAL SCORERS**
1. Henrik Larsson 40
2. Dieter Müller 29
3. Shota Arveladze 27
4. Alessandro Altobelli 25
5. Jupp Heynckes 23

**MOST SUCCESSFUL TEAMS**
**3 WINS**
   Internazionale (Italy)
   Juventus (Italy)
   Liverpool (England)
**2 WINS**
   Borussia Mönchengladbach (Germany)
   Feyenoord (Netherlands)
   IFK Gothenburg (Sweden)
   Parma (Italy)
   Real Madrid (Spain)
   Sevilla (Spain)
   Tottenham Hotspur (England)

# UEFA EUROPA LEAGUE

### "WINNING THE UEFA CUP WAS THE HIGHLIGHT OF MY CAREER." HAKAN SÜKÜR, WINNER WITH GALATASARAY IN 2000

Europe's second most important club competition has been rebranded several times. What began in 1955 as the Inter-Cities Fairs Cup became the UEFA Cup in 1971 and the Europa League in 2009. Teams qualify on the basis of domestic league position. Domestic cup winners have taken part ever since the UEFA Cup Winners' Cup was scrapped in 1999 and later rounds also include unsuccessful Champions League teams.

## FAMOUS VICTORY

Porto's Deco (right) and Nuno Valente (left) hold the UEFA Cup aloft after their team won a wonderfully exciting 2003 final 3–2 against Celtic in Seville. Porto triumphed after scoring a "silver goal" (see p. 203) in overtime. A year later, Porto won the Champions League.

## SHAKHTAR DONETSK

Shakhtar Donetsk's 2–1 win over Werder Bremen in May 2009 made it the first Ukrainian victor and the last club to lift the old UEFA Cup. Success was especially sweet for Shakhtar as the team beat domestic rivals Dinamo Kiev in the semifinals.

Italian giant Juventus has won the trophy a record three times. The team's first triumph was in 1977 against Athletic Bilbao and victory in 1990 (celebrated left) came when it defeated fellow Italians Fiorentina 3–1 on aggregate. Juventus last won the trophy in 1993.

*Brazilian midfielder Jádson scored Shakhtar's overtime winner.*

## CUP WINNERS' CUP

Italian team Lazio has held the European Cup Winners' Cup for more than 10 years. However, this is because the Roman side got to keep the trophy after winning the last competition in 1999. The ECWC had run for 38 seasons, but came to an end when it was absorbed into the UEFA Cup. Lazio beat Mallorca 2–1, thanks to goals from Christian Vieri (right, center) and Pavel Nedved (far right.)

# CONCACAF CHAMPIONS LEAGUE

*"CONCACAF HAS BECOME BETTER AND BETTER EACH AND EVERY YEAR, AT ALL LEVELS."*

CHIVAS USA SPORTING DIRECTOR THOMAS RONGEN

The CONCACAF Champions Cup was first introduced in 1962, but the US did not participate until 1997, when CONCACAF granted the recently formed MLS (Major League Soccer) two places in the tournament. The cup is contested by the leading club sides in the region, and has so far been dominated by clubs from Mexico. The competition was renamed the CONCACAF Champions League in 2009, a group stage was introduced, and the number of competing clubs was tripled from eight to 24.

## FACT FILE: CONCACAF CHAMPIONS LEAGUE

(See p. 186 for complete list of winners)

**TOP GOAL SCORERS**
1. Information not known
2. Information not known
3. Information not known
4. Information not known
5. Information not known

**MOST SUCCESSFUL TEAMS**
1. Club América (Mexico) 5 wins
= Cruz Azul (Mexico) 5 wins
2. Saprissa (Costa Rica) 3 wins
= UNAM Pumas (Mexico) 3 wins
= Pachuca (Mexico) 3 wins

### LA GALAXY

In 2000, Los Angeles Galaxy became only the second US team to take the trophy, beating Honduran side Olimpia 3–2 in the final. Defender Ezra Hendrickson was the surprise two-goal hero in California, with Cobi Jones (far left) also scoring. DC United had been the first North American winners in 1998, only a year after US teams first entered the competition.

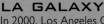

### MEXICO

Mexican teams Club América and Cruz Azul have both won the competition a record five times. Mexican star striker Cuauhtémoc Blanco (far right) and defender Duilio Davino (right) helped Club América to ther last victory in 2006.

### NECAXA

Ecuadorian midfielder Álex Aguinaga (second right) was opening scorer and player of the tournament when Mexico's Necaxa won its first CONCACAF Champions' Cup in 1999. Necaxa beat LD Alajuelense of Costa Rica 2–1 in the final, three years after it had finished runner-up to Cruz Azul in a mini-league final system.

### DEPORTIVO SAPRISSA

Costa Rica's Saprissa recorded its third CONCACAF victory as Rónald Gómez and Christian Bolaños helped defeat UNAM Pumas of Mexico 3–2 in a two-leg final. Saprissa is nicknamed "El Monstruo Morado" (The Purple Monster) because of its purple uniform, which is said to be the result of the team's original red shirts and blue shorts mixing in the wash in 1937.

*Atlante's goalkeeper and captain Federico Vilar (celebrating, right, with Giancarlo Maldonado) had shutouts in both legs of the final.*

## 2009

The first Champions League season, in 2008–2009, brought a second championship for Atlante and the 26th for a Mexican club. Atlante beat compatriots Cruz Azul 2–0 on aggregate in a two-legged final.

# COPA LIBERTADORES

### "WHEN I ARRIVED AT RIVER [PLATE] MY DREAM WAS TO WIN THE COPA LIBERTADORES."

ARGENTINA STRIKER HERNÁN CRESPO, WHO WON
THE TROPHY WITH RIVER PLATE IN 1996

The trophy is named after the "liberators" including Simón Bolívar, who won independence for many South American countries from Spain in the 19th century.

The Copa Libertadores was introduced in 1960 as South America's challenge to the European Cup (now UEFA Champions League), and this exciting annual contest certainly seems to guarantee more goals per game than its European counterpart. The format is similar to the Champions League, with the top teams from each country competing for the trophy. It began with just nine clubs, but now 38 clubs compete for the Copa.

## BOCA JUNIORS

Argentina's Boca Juniors has dominated the Copa in the 21st century. In 2007, Juan Román Riquelme (on loan from Spain's Villareal) inspired a 5–0 two-leg triumph over Brazil's Grêmio, netting three goals himself.

## TOP SCORER

Ecuador's Alberto Spencer (above, left) was the Libertadores' most lethal striker, with 54 goals in 77 games between 1960 and 1972. He earned three winners' medals with Peñarol of Uruguay.

A 2004 rule change permitted clubs from the same country to contest the final. This resulted in two all-Brazil showdowns in a row. In 2005, São Paulo beat Atlético Paranaense 5–1 over two legs (pictured above) but the following year the team could only finish runner-up after losing 4–3 on aggregate to fellow Brazilians Internacional.

## INDEPENDIENTE

No Argentine team has dominated quite like Independiente, whose 4–1 playoff victory over Peñarol in 1965 (pictured above) was the second of seven wins. The most recent came in 1984.

### FACT FILE: COPA LIBERTADORES

(See p. 185 for complete list of winners)

### TOP GOAL SCORERS

1. Alberto Spencer (Peñarol, Barcelona) 54
2. Fernando Morena (Peñarol) 37
3. Pedro Virgílio Rocha (Peñarol, São Paulo, Palmeiras) 36
4. Daniel Onega (Club Atlético River Plate) 31
5. Julio Morales (Nacional) 30

### MOST SUCCESSFUL TEAMS

1. Independiente (Argentina) 7 wins
2. Boca Juniors (Argentina) 6 wins
3. Peñarol (Uruguay) 5 wins
4. Estudiantes LP (Argentina) 4 wins
5. Nacional (Uruguay) 3 wins
= São Paulo (Brazil) 3 wins
= Olimpia (Paraguay) 3 wins

## ESTUDIANTES 2009

Argentine team Estudiantes claimed the 2009 Copa Libertadores with a two-legged victory over Cruzeiro of Brazil. Juan Sebastián Verón was the midfield playmaker for Estudiantes, 41 years after goals from his father Juan Ramón Verón had given the same side its first Copa title.

# CAF CHAMPIONS LEAGUE

### FACT FILE: CAF CHAMPIONS LEAGUE
(See p. 186 for complete list of winners)

#### TOP GOAL SCORERS
1. Information not available
2. Information not available
3. Information not available
4. Information not available
5. Information not available

#### MOST SUCCESSFUL TEAMS
1. Al-Ahly (Egypt) 6 wins
2. El Zamalek (Egypt) 5 wins
3. Raja Casablanca (Morocco) 3 wins
= Canon Yaoundé (Cameroon) 3 wins
= Hafia Conakry (Guinea) 3 wins

Africa's main club championship has followed closely in the footsteps of its European counterpart, from its introduction in the 1960s to its Champions League revamp and expansion in the 1990s. However, Europe cannot match the openness of the African version, which has been won by 25 clubs from 12 different countries. It is only in recent years that North African teams have begun to dominate.

### ÉTOILE
Having won every other continental trophy, Tunisia's Étoile Sahel lost the CAF Champions League final in 2004 and 2005. However, it made it third time lucky by beating favorite Al-Ahly in the 2007 climax. Mohamed Ali Nafkha (far right) was among the goal scorers.

*Captain Tresor Mputu scored TP Mazembe's decisive away goal in Nigeria, his sixth strike of the 2009 tournament.*

### AL-AHLY
Egyptian giant Al-Ahly's sixth African championship in 2008 (celebrated above) was a 4–2 aggregate victory over Cameroon's Cotonsport Garoua. It edged the team one ahead of archrival Zamalek as the tournament's most successful team. Before TP Mazembe, the last winner from outside North Africa was Nigeria's Enyimba, which won the trophy in 2003 and 2004.

### TP MAZEMBE

TP Mazembe of the Democratic Republic of Congo lifted the trophy for the third time in 2009 with an away-goals victory over Nigeria's Heartland. It was the team's first Champions League title since 1968, when it was known as Englebert.

# AFC CHAMPIONS LEAGUE

**"WE ARE NOT ACCEPTING ANYTHING LESS THAN WHAT EXISTS IN THE TOP LEAGUES IN EUROPE."**

ASIAN FOOTBALL CONFEDERATION PRESIDENT MOHAMMED BIN HAMMAM

The idea of an Asian club championship has been established since 1967, but it had many teething problems, including a 15-year break between 1971 and 1986. The launch of the AFC Champions League in 2002 has brought much more effective promotion and participation, and is yet another sign of the Asian region's growing ambition for its soccer.

## FACT FILE: AFC CHAMPIONS LEAGUE
(See p. 187 for complete list of winners)

**TOP GOAL SCORERS**
1. Zaynitdin Tadjiyev (Pakhtakor Tashkent) 13
2. Magno Alves (Gamba Osaka, Al-Ittihad and Umm-Sala) 12
= Anvarjon Soliev (Pakhtakor Tashkent and Bunyodkor) 12
= Kim Do-Hoon (Jeonbuk Hyundai Motors and Seongnam Ilhwa Chunma) 12

**MOST SUCCESSFUL TEAMS**
**2 WINS**
Al-Hilal   (Saudi Arabia)
Esteghlal (Iran)
Al-Ittihad (Saudi Arabia)
Suwon Samsung Bluewings (Republic of Korea)
Pohang Steelers (Republic of Korea)
Thai Farmers Bank   (Thailand)
Maccabi Tel Aviv   (Israel)*

*Israel no longer belong to the AFC

### BIG WIN
Fathallah Hamzah Saeed and Lee Ki-Hyung battle for a 50-50 ball (left) but few final games have been as one-sided as Al-Ittihad's 5–0 demolition of Republic of Korea's Seongnam Ilhwa Chunma in 2004. It gave the Saudi side a 6–3 aggregate win and the first of its two titles.

### 2009 CHAMPS
Pohang Steelers became the first club to complete a hat trick of AFC Champions League triumphs in 2009 (below). It beat Al-Ittihad 2–1, with man of the match No Byung-Jun opening the scoring.

# ENGLISH CLUBS

There are 92 senior clubs in the English Football League. The Premier League is the top division and is made up of 20 teams.

England is often seen as the home of soccer. It has the oldest soccer association (1863), the oldest professional league (1888), and what borders on a national obsession with the game. English soccer is famous for its fast and physical style, and the arrival of foreign players has helped raise the standard of technical skill. In 1992, the top 20 clubs formed the Premier League, which brought major changes to the English game. Factors such as new stadiums, bigger crowds, and rich foreign owners have brought huge financial success, particularly for the biggest clubs such as Manchester United and Arsenal. Every team is desperate to remain in the Premier League, but each season three clubs are promoted from the division below and three are relegated.

## ARSENAL
EMIRATES STADIUM, LONDON

Arsenal is by far London's most successful club, with 13 league titles and 10 FA Cups. The modern team has been transformed under Frenchman Arsene Wenger, with young stars such as Spain's Cesc Fàbregas (right) and England's Theo Walcott (left) producing entertaining and free-flowing soccer.

## LEEDS UNITED
ELLAND ROAD, LEEDS

Leeds United reached the Champions League semifinals in 2001, but within six years had dropped to English soccer's third tier. Yet between 1965 and 1974, Don Revie's Leeds were England's dominant team and never finished outside of the top four. It won two league titles, the FA Cup, the League Cup, and two Inter-Cities Fairs Cups.

## TOTTENHAM HOTSPUR
WHITE HART LANE, LONDON

Spurs have struggled in recent years but they are famous for being the only "non-league" team to win the FA Cup (1901), the first British club to win a European trophy (1963), and the first to win the "Double" (the league title and the FA Cup) in the 20th century (1961, right).

## CHELSEA
STAMFORD BRIDGE, LONDON

Since buying the club in 2003, billionaire Roman Abramovich has helped Chelsea to become one of England's most successful teams. It has twice won the league (2005 and 2006), FA Cup (2007 and 2009), and League Cup (2005 and 2007). Didier Drogba (above, in yellow) scored one of the goals in a 2–1 win over Everton in 2009.

## PRESTON NORTH END
DEEPDALE, PRESTON, LANCASHIRE

Preston North End was the first winner of the Football League in 1889 and by winning the FA Cup the same year became the only club to secure the prestigious "Double" for more than 70 years. The modern team has yet to feature in the Premier League, despite reaching the Championship playoffs three times.

## EVERTON
GOODISON PARK, LIVERPOOL

With nine league titles and five FA Cup wins, Everton is one of England's most successful clubs of all time and fierce local rivals of Liverpool. Despite a lack of recent glory, Goodison Park is still one of the best grounds in England for exciting atmosphere.

## LIVERPOOL
ANFIELD, LIVERPOOL

"The Mighty Reds" are England's most successful club, with 18 league titles, five European Cups, and 17 other major trophies. The 1984 team (above) almost won every competition it played in, including the European Cup, the League title, and the League Cup. However, the team lost in the fourth round of the FA Cup that year.

## MANCHESTER CITY
EASTLANDS, MANCHESTER

Manchester City is usually overshadowed by local rival, United. Even when City won its last league title in 1968, United went one better and won England's first European Cup. However, a big money takeover in 2008 transformed City into the world's richest club, attracting stars such as Tévez, Adebayor, and Robinho.

## MANCHESTER UNITED
OLD TRAFFORD, MANCHESTER

With millions of fans across the globe, United is one of the world's biggest clubs. Current boss Sir Alex Ferguson is the most successful British manager of all time, with more than 20 major trophies won by his team, including the Premier League title in 2009 (celebrated, below).

| MOST SUCCESSFUL CLUBS | LEAGUE TITLES | FA CUP | LEAGUE CUPS | EUROPEAN TROPHIES* |
| --- | --- | --- | --- | --- |
| LIVERPOOL | 18 | 7 | 7 | 8 |
| MANCHESTER UNITED | 18 | 11 | 3 | 4 |
| ARSENAL | 13 | 10 | 2 | 2 |
| ASTON VILLA | 7 | 7 | 5 | 1 |
| TOTTENHAM HOTSPUR | 2 | 8 | 4 | 3 |
| EVERTON | 9 | 5 | - | 1 |
| CHELSEA | 3 | 5 | 4 | 2 |
| NEWCASTLE UNITED | 4 | 6 | - | 1 |
| LEEDS UNITED | 3 | 1 | 1 | 2 |
| BLACKBURN ROVERS | 3 | 6 | 1 | - |
| MANCHESTER CITY | 2 | 4 | 2 | 1 |
| WOLVERHAMPTON WANDERERS | 3 | 4 | 2 | - |
| SHEFFIELD WEDNESDAY | 4 | 3 | 1 | - |
| SUNDERLAND | 6 | 2 | - | - |
| WEST BROMWICH ALBION | 1 | 5 | 1 | - |
| HUDDERSFIELD TOWN | 3 | 1 | - | - |
| PORTSMOUTH | 2 | 2 | - | - |
| PRESTON NORTH END | 2 | 2 | - | - |
| BURNLEY | 2 | 1 | 1 | - |
| DERBY COUNTY | 2 | 1 | - | - |

*Total number of European trophies includes UEFA Champions League, UEFA Europa League, and European Cup Winners' Cup only.

## ASTON VILLA
VILLA PARK, BIRMINGHAM

Birmingham-based Aston Villa has won seven league titles and seven FA Cups, and its win over Bayern Munich in 1982 kept the European Cup in England for a sixth consecutive season. Current manager Martin O'Neill keeps faith in homegrown talent including England internationals James Milner, Ashley Young, and Gabriel Agbonlahor.

# FRENCH CLUBS

### "FOOTBALL IS A FANTASTIC AND INTELLIGENT GAME THAT TEACHES US HOW TO LIVE TOGETHER."
UEFA PRESIDENT MICHEL PLATINI

The French League (Le Championnat) has produced legends such as Just Fontaine, Michel Platini, and Zinedine Zidane. Attacking flair and technical ability are features of the French game, and coaches such as Aimé Jacquet, Gérard Houllier, and Guy Roux have built strong youth development systems. However, despite their undeniable talent, French teams have a repuation for underachieving in European competitions.

The French League began in 1932 and is split into two divisions, Ligues 1 and 2, each with 20 teams.

## FC GIRONDINS DE BORDEAUX
STADE CHABAN DELMAS, BORDEAUX

Some of the biggest names in modern French soccer have played for the five-times champions Bordeaux, including Alain Giresse, Christophe Dugarry, Eric Cantona, Jean Tigana, and Zinedine Zidane. After a slump in the early 1990s, Bordeaux's Ligue 1 and League Cup double in 2009 has made it one of France's dominant forces once more.

## OLYMPIQUE LYONNAIS
STADE GERLAND, LYON

Lyon is the most successful French club of modern times, winning all seven Ligue 1 titles between 2002 and 2007—a French record. Despite domestic success "Les Gones" (The Kids) has never got past the quarterfinal of any European competition.

## FC SOCHAUX
STADE AUGUSTE BONAL, MONTBÉLIARD

FC Sochaux was France's first professional club. Formed in 1928, it enjoyed early success and won the league in 1935 and 1938. After years of underachievement, a young, talented team has reemerged, winning the French Cup in 2007.

## AS ST. ÉTIENNE
STADE GEOFFROY-GUICHARD, ST ÉTIENNE

"Les Verts" (The Greens) dominated French soccer in the 1960s and 70s, thanks to great players such as Michel Platini (left,) but did not achieve the same success in Europe.

*Wide-man Sidney Govou has been a constant factor, and goal-scoring threat, throughout Lyon's 21st-century Ligue 1 dominance.*

# OLYMPIQUE MARSEILLE
### STADE VÉLODROME, MARSEILLE

France's best-supported club, Marseille has won eight league titles, a record ten French Cups, and in 1993 became the only ever French Champions League winner. A corruption scandal saw OM relegated in 1994 but the team has bounced back in recent years. Legendary players include Jean-Pierre Papin (left) and Didier Deschamps.

## LEAGUE TROPHY

The Ligue 1 trophy was first contested in 1932–1933, when it was won by Olympique Lillois (now Lille). St. Étienne, with 10 titles, is the most successful club.

| MOST SUCCESSFUL CLUBS FRANCE | LIGUE 1 | COUPE DE FRANCE | LEAGUE CUP | EUROPEAN TROPHIES* |
|---|---|---|---|---|
| OLYMPIQUE DE MARSEILLE | 8 | 10 | - | 1 |
| AS SAINT-ÉTIENNE | 10 | 6 | - | - |
| AS MONACO FC | 7 | 5 | 1 | - |
| PARIS SAINT-GERMAIN | 2 | 7 | 3 | 1 |
| OLYMPIQUE LYONNAIS | 7 | 4 | 1 | - |
| GIRONDINS DE BORDEAUX | 6 | 3 | 3 | - |
| FC NANTES ATLANTIQUE | 8 | 3 | - | - |
| LOSC LILLE METROPOLE | 3 | 5 | - | - |
| FC SOCHAUX-MONTBÉLIARD | 2 | 2 | 4 | - |
| OGC NICE | 4 | 3 | - | - |
| AJ AUXERRE | 1 | 4 | - | - |
| RC LENS | 1 | - | 2 | - |
| STADE RENNAIS FC | - | 2 | - | - |
| AS NANCY-LORRAINE | - | 1 | 1 | - |

*Total number of European trophies includes UEFA Champions League, UEFA Europa League, and European Cup Winners' Cup only.

# EN AVANT DE GUINGAMP
### STADE DU ROUDOUROU, GUINGAMP

The tiny Brittany town of Guingamp brought romance to the French Cup in 2009, by becoming only the second non-top-flight team to lift the trophy. Brazilian striker Eduardo's two late goals stunned favorites Rennes, thereby raising him to hero status alongside ex-Guingamp stars such as Didier Drogba, Jean-Pierre Papin, and Florent Malouda.

# FC NANTES ATLANTIQUE
### LA BEAUJOIRE-LOUIS FONTENEAU, NANTES

Now languishing in Ligue 2, Nantes has won eight league titles since 1965. The Canaries are famed for their one-touch soccer, and for a youth system that produced players of the quality of Marcel Desailly and Didier Deschamps.

# AS MONACO
### STADE LOUIS II, MONACO

The club from the tiny country of Monaco is one of the most successful teams in French soccer. It has won seven French titles and reached the final of the UEFA Champions League in 2004.

*South Korea's Park Chu-Young and Brazil's Nene offer Monaco plenty to smile about with their dynamism down both flanks and up-front.*

# PARIS ST.-GERMAIN
### PARC DES PRINCES, PARIS

Formed in 1970 by the merger of two Paris clubs—Paris FC and Stade Saint-Germain—PSG rapidly established a reputation as a cup team, winning the French Cup seven times. The club has featured such stars as David Ginola (above), Youri Djorkaeff, and George Weah.

# ITALIAN CLUBS

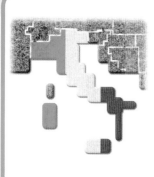

Italian league soccer is split into four divisions, with a total of 78 clubs.

*"FOOTBALL IS A PHENOMENON IN ITALY. IT'S ALL THEY TALK ABOUT. IT'S CRAZY!"* DAVID TREZEGUET, FRANCE AND JUVENTUS STRIKER

Italian soccer, or "calcio," has few rivals when it comes to passion, intensity, and success. Big clubs like AC Milan, Internazionale, Roma, and Juventus play in famous stadiums, field many of the world's finest players, and enjoy fanatical support. Italian teams are famed for an organized, defensive style combined with exciting individual flair. In the 1980s and 1990s Serie A could claim to be the best division in the world, as foreign stars such as Maradona, van Basten, Papin, and Gullit, plus homegrown talents such as Franco Baresi, Roberto Mancini, and Gianluca Vialli lit up the Italian game. Recent corruption scandals and crowd trouble have tarnished the reputation of Italian soccer, but Italian clubs still rank among the greats.

## LAZIO
### STADIO OLIMPICO, ROME

Lazio shares its ground with fierce local rival Roma. It has won two league titles (1974 and 2000), five Italian cups, and one European Cup Winners' Cup (1999). Lazio beat Sampdoria on penalties to take the 2009 Coppa Italia (below.)

## AC MILAN
### SAN SIRO, MILAN

Mighty AC Milan has won the European Cup no less than seven times and the scudetto (league) on 17 occasions. Pictured above (left) is the club's legendary defender Paolo Maldini, who finally retired at the age of 40.

## JUVENTUS
### STADIO OLIMPICO DI TORINO, TURIN

Italy's most popular club is followed by supporters from Sicily to the Alps. Nicknamed "La Vecchia Signora" (The Old Lady), the club has won two European Cups and 27 scudetti and has a history of producing brilliant players such as Alessandro del Piero (left).

## GENOA
### STADIO LUIGI FERRARIS, GENOA

Genoa has had its ups and downs in recent years, including a fifth place in 2009, but the club can lay claim to being the first of Italy's great teams, winning nine league titles or "scudetti" between 1898 and 1924.

## TORINO
### STADIO OLIMPICO DI TORINO, TURIN

Torino was the finest Italian side of the 1940s. The team won four consecutive league titles (1946–49) before tragedy struck in the Mount Superga disaster of 1949, when a plane carrying the team crashed, killing 18 players.

*Inter players celebrate winning the 2009 Serie A title.*

## INTERNAZIONALE
### SAN SIRO, MILAN

Internazionale was founded when some members split away from AC Milan in 1908. Pioneering the defensive style known as "catenaccio" (meaning "door bolt") Internazionale dominated during the 1960s and won the European Cup twice. It is also known as Inter or Inter Milan.

| MOST SUCCESSFUL CLUBS ITALY | COPPA ITALIA | SERIE A CHAMPIONS | EUROPEAN TROPHIES* |
|---|---|---|---|
| JUVENTUS | 9 | 27 | 6 |
| AC MILAN | 5 | 17 | 9 |
| INTERNAZIONALE | 5 | 17 | 2 |
| AS ROMA | 9 | 3 | 1 |
| TORINO | 5 | 7 | - |
| GENOA | 1 | 9 | - |
| AS LIVORNO CALCIO | 6 | 2 | 1 |
| AFC FIORENTINA | 6 | 2 | - |
| LAZIO | 5 | 2 | 1 |
| NAPOLI | 3 | 2 | 1 |
| PARMA FC | 3 | - | 2 |
| UC SAMPDORIA | 4 | 1 | - |
| BOLOGNA FC 1909 | 2 | 2 | - |
| ATALANTA BC | 1 | - | - |
| CAGLIARI CALCIO | 1 | - | - |
| HELLAS VERONA FC | - | 1 | - |

*Total number of European trophies includes UEFA Champions League, UEFA Europa League, and European Cup Winners' Cup only.

## AS ROMA
### STADIO OLIMPICO, ROME

Wearing Rome's ancient wolf symbol on its shirts, the "Giallorossi" (the Yellow-Reds) has won a total of three titles and nine Italian Cups. Captain and all-time leading scorer Francesco Totti (right) is a Roman icon, having spent his entire career with the club.

## NAPOLI
### STADIO SAN PAOLO, NAPLES

For many fans, Napoli is not just the pride of Naples, but of all of southern Italy. During the delirious days of the 1980s, Diego Maradona helped Napoli win two Serie A titles and a UEFA Cup. But one of the western world's oldest cities now boasts some of soccer's most admired young talents, such as Slovakia's Marek Hamšík and Argentina's Ezequiel Lavezzi.

# GERMAN CLUBS

### "THERE ARE NO RIGHT OR WRONG, OR FAIR RESULTS. THERE'S JUST THE FINAL SCORE."

GREECE MANAGER OTTO REHHAGEL

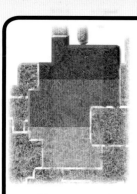

Three teams are relegated from the Bundesliga and three promoted each season.

The modern Bundesliga was formed in 1963, for teams in what was then West Germany. After the country's unification in 1991, the East and West German leagues were merged, but the top tier is still dominated by clubs from the former West Germany. Soccer is hugely popular in Germany, and German clubs attract some of the largest crowds in the world. Germany's two professional divisions, the Bundesliga and the 2. Bundesliga, each have 18 teams.

## SCHALKE 04
### VELTINS-ARENA, GELSENKIRCHEN

Founded in 1904, Schalke won the league six times between 1934 and 1942 and was a significant force in German soccer. Aside from its seventh league win in 1958 (its last to date) major success eluded Schalke for most of the second half of the 20th century. However, victory in the 1997 UEFA Cup final—its first in Europe—signaled the start of Schalke's revival. So far in the 21st century, Schalke has been Bundesliga runner-up three times and has won the German Cup twice.

## BAYERN MUNICH
### ALLIANZ ARENA, MUNICH

Germany's most successful club, with 21 national championships and four European Cups, Bayern Munich is also the world's third biggest, after Real Madrid and Barcelona of Spain. Recent challenges in a highly competitive division have seen Bayern splash out on the likes of Franck Ribéry (above, top, far left) Arjen Robben (above, bottom left), and Italy's Luca Toni.

## BAYER LEVERKUSEN
### BAYARENA, LEVERKUSEN

Bayer emerged as a force in the late 1980s, but so far has won only one German Cup and a UEFA Cup. Bayer Leverkusen was set up and is still run by the Bayer pharmaceutical company. Former players include Rudi Völler and Michael Ballack.

## WERDER BREMEN
### WESERSTADION, BREMEN

Four-time German champion Werder Bremen established itself as a soccer powerhouse under coach Otto Rehhagel in the 1980s. Now a regular Champions League competitor, it has a reputation for attractive soccer. Werder fell just short in the 2009 UEFA Cup final but won the 2009 German Cup (celebrated, right.)

## VFL WOLFSBURG
VOLKSWAGEN ARENA, WOLFSBURG

The "Wolves" of Wolfsburg emerged as champion in one of Europe's most open title contests in 2008–2009, largely thanks to a Bundesliga record run of 10 wins in a row, and the goals of Brazilian Grafite and Bosnian Edin Džeko. Wolfsburg's first-ever championship rewarded ambitious investment by club owners, Volkswagen.

*Striker Grafite (pictured) paired up with Edin Džeko to score more goals in the 2008-2009 season than any other strike duo in Bundesliga history.*

| MOST SUCCESSFUL CLUBS GERMANY | BUNDESLIGA CHAMPIONS | DFB-POKAL CHAMPIONS | EUROPEAN TROPHIES* |
|---|---|---|---|
| BAYERN MUNICH | 21 | 14 | 6 |
| FC NÜRNBERG | 9 | 4 | 1 |
| SCHALKE 04 | 7 | 4 | 1 |
| HAMBURG | 7 | 3 | 2 |
| WERDER BREMEN | 4 | 6 | 1 |
| BORUSSIA DORTMUND | 6 | 2 | 2 |
| BORUSSIA MÖNCHENGLADBACH | 5 | 3 | 2 |
| VFB STUTTGART | 5 | 3 | - |
| KÖLN | 3 | 4 | - |
| EINTRACHT FRANKFURT | 1 | 4 | 1 |
| DRESDNER SC | 2 | 2 | - |
| 1860 MUNICH | 1 | 2 | - |
| KARLSRUHER FC | - | 2 | - |
| VFL WOLFSBURG | 1 | - | - |

*Total number of European trophies includes UEFA Champions League, UEFA Europa League, and European Cup Winners' Cup only.

## VFB STUTTGART
GOTTLIEB-DAIMLER-STADION, STUTTGART

2007 league champion Stuttgart has won a total of five national titles, but is yet to enjoy sustained European success. The club has one of the most successful youth development programs in Germany and has also featured world-class names such as Jürgen Klinsmann, Jon Dahl Tomasson, and Aliaksandr Hleb.

## FC NÜRNBERG
EASYCREDIT-STADION, NUREMBERG

In the 1920s, nine-time champion Nürnberg was Germany's most popular and successful team. Since then, the team has endured lean times—a German Cup win in 2007 (left) was followed by relegation the following season.

## BORUSSIA DORTMUND
SIGNAL IDUNA PARK, DORTMUND

After initial success in the 1950s and 1960s, Dortmund reemerged as a major club in the 1990s. Winner of six German titles and the Champions League in 1997, its average home attendance of 80,000 is the highest in Europe.

*Matthias Sammer (right) played for Borussia Dortmund from 1993 to 1998 and later managed the club.*

## HAMBURGER SV
HSH NORDBANK ARENA, HAMBURG

The only club never to have been relegated from the top division, Hamburg has won seven national titles and was European Champion in 1983.

# DUTCH CLUBS

*"FOOTBALL IS SIMPLE. BUT THE HARDEST THING IS TO PLAY FOOTBALL IN A SIMPLE WAY."* JOHAN CRUYFF

The Netherlands' top Dutch league, the Eredivisie, has 18 clubs; the second tier, the Eerste Divisie, has 20.

Dutch soccer is dominated by three clubs: Ajax, PSV Eindhoven, and Feyenoord. Since 1965, only one team outside this big three has taken the league title, although in recent years smaller teams such as AZ Alkmaar, FC Twente, and SC Herenveen have shown themselves to be an increasing threat. The Dutch game is traditionally played in an open, attacking style, which brought Dutch sides their greatest success in Europe in the 1970s. But the country's small size means its clubs can't compete financially with the big leagues of Spain, Italy, Germany, and England, and top players now rarely spend more than two or three seasons in the Netherlands before transferring abroad.

## FC TWENTE
### DE GROLSCH VESTE, ENSCHEDE
Encouraging displays both at home and in European competitions have given Twente fans hope of finally ending the team's lengthy wait for an Eredivisie title. Former England coach Steve McClaren led the club to a surprise runner-up finish in 2008–2009, only the second time it had finished so high.

## AJAX
### AMSTERDAM ARENA, AMSTERDAM
Ajax has won a record 29 titles plus four European Cups. In 1995, it won both the Eredivisie title and the European Cup (above,) but it was the great Ajax team of the 1966–73 era that pioneered the concept of "Total Soccer" under coach Rinus Michels. The number 14 shirt has been retired in honor of the club's most famous player, the great Johan Cruyff.

## PSV EINDHOVEN
### PHILIPS STADION, EINDHOVEN
In 1988, PSV became one of only three Dutch teams to win the European Cup (now the Champions League.) Dutch champion 21 times, including 2007 and 2008, PSV has featured famous names such as Ruud van Nistelrooy, Philip Cocu, and Ronaldo. Before starring for Chelsea, Real Madrid, and Bayern Munich, speedy winger Arjen Robben tormented defenders while playing for PSV (above, right.)

## FEYENOORD
### FEYENOORD STADION OR "THE KUIP," ROTTERDAM
Feyenoord won the Netherlands' first European trophy when it lifted the European Cup in 1970. The biggest club in the Netherlands' second city of Rotterdam, Feyenoord has a passionate rivalry with Ajax Amsterdam. Veteran Dutch internationals Giovanni van Bronckhorst and Roy Makaay are current Feyenoord favorites.

| MOST SUCCESSFUL CLUBS HOLLAND | EREDIVISIE CHAMPIONS | KNVB CUP | EUROPEAN TROPHIES* |
|---|---|---|---|
| AJAX | 29 | 17 | 6 |
| PSV EINDHOVEN | 21 | 8 | 2 |
| FEYENOORD | 14 | 11 | 3 |
| SPARTA ROTTERDAM | 6 | 3 | - |
| KON HVV | 8 | - | - |
| QUICK | 1 | 5 | - |
| AZ ALKMAAR | 2 | 3 | - |
| WILLEM II | 3 | 2 | - |
| ADO DEN HAAG | 2 | 2 | - |
| HFC HAARLEM | 1 | 3 | - |
| HBS | 2 | 2 | - |
| GO AHEAD EAGLES | 4 | - | - |
| UTRECHT | 1 | 3 | - |
| FC TWENTE | 1 | 2 | - |
| RAP | 2 | 1 | - |

*Total number of European trophies includes UEFA Champions League, UEFA Europa League, and European Cup Winners' Cup only.

## WILLEM II
### WILLEM II STADION, TILBURG

Named after a 19th century Dutch king, Willem II has not been league champion since 1955, but is now establishing a presence in European competition for the first time. Famous former players include Marc Overmars, Jaap Stam, and Finland's Sami Hyypiä.

## SPARTA ROTTERDAM
### HET KASTEEL, ROTTERDAM

The Netherlands' oldest club was formed in 1888 and, inspired by England's Sunderland FC, adopted a red and white striped uniform in 1889. League champions six times before 1960, Sparta Rotterdam regained its place in the top division in 2005 after a three year absence.

## AZ ALKMAAR
### DSB STADION, ALKMAAR

Founded in 1967, AZ is the only side outside the big three (Ajax, PSV, and Feyenoord) to win the league since 1964. The team won it in 1981 but was relegated from the Eredivisie in 1988. Since its return in 1998, it has enjoyed a remarkable revival, finally winning a second league title in 2009 with the formidable Louis Van Gaal as coach.

*AZ was a comfortable champion in 2009, 11 points clear of its nearest challengers.*

# SPANISH CLUBS

**"FOOTBALL IS AN EXCUSE TO MAKE US HAPPY."**

JORGE VALDANO, FORMER REAL ZARAGOZA AND REAL MADRID STRIKER

Spain's top professional division is La Liga, with 20 teams. The next level is the Segunda División, with 22 teams.

Spain's La Liga is one of the world's top leagues, and it has a reputation for thrilling, attacking soccer. First contested in 1928, it has only ever been won by nine clubs. For years, the big two of Real Madrid (31 titles) and Barcelona (19 titles) have dominated, but recently the league has become more competitive, with teams such as Sevilla FC, Real Sociedad, and Valencia CF challenging for the title.

## VALENCIA CF
**ESTADIO MESTELLA, VALENCIA**

Champions in the 1940s, 1970s, and twice since 2000, Valencia attracts passionate support bettered only by the big two. Its current success has been based on a defensive style at odds with Spanish league tradition, but the emergence of lethal striker David Villa (above) has injected a touch of flair.

## FC BARCELONA
**CAMP NOU, BARCELONA**

Founded in 1899, and never relegated, Barcelona is one of the biggest clubs in the world. With a reputation for flamboyant, entertaining soccer, Barça has nearly 2,000 supporter clubs worldwide and is an integral part of the Catalan region of Spain. Its motto is "Més que un club" (More than a club.) Under former captain and rookie coach Josep "Pep" Guardiola, the team has won the triple of league, cup, and Champions League in 2009—the first Spanish club to do so.

*Barcelona's dynamic winger Lionel Messi scores as many goals as he creates.*

## VILLAREAL CF
**EL MADRIGAL, VILLAREAL**

For a town containing fewer than 50,000 people, and whose soccer team only reached the top division for the first time in 1998, Villareal's recent rise has been phenomenal. The so-called "Yellow Submarine" reached the 2006 Champions League semifinals and has run Real Madrid and Barcelona closer than anyone in recent seasons.

## ATLÉTICO MADRID
### VICENTE CALDERÓN, MADRID

In the 1960s and 1970s, only Atlético challenged the dominance of city neighbor Real. (Above, Atlético as champion in 1973.) It remains Spain's third most successful club, although the team has struggled in recent years.

| MOST SUCCESSFUL CLUBS SPAIN | LA LIGA | COPA DEL REY | EUROPEAN TROPHIES* |
|---|---|---|---|
| REAL MADRID | 31 | 17 | 11 |
| FC BARCELONA | 19 | 25 | 10 |
| ATHLETIC BILBAO | 8 | 23 | 1 |
| ATLÉTICO MADRID | 9 | 9 | 1 |
| VALENCIA CF | 6 | 7 | 4 |
| REAL ZARAGOZA | - | 6 | 2 |
| SEVILLA FC | 1 | 4 | 2 |
| RCD ESPANYOL | - | 4 | - |
| REAL BETIS | 1 | 2 | - |
| REAL SOCIEDAD | 2 | 2 | - |

*Total number of European trophies includes UEFA Champions League, UEFA Europa League, and European Cup Winners' Cup only.

## REAL MADRID
### SANTIAGO BERNABÉU, MADRID

The richest club in the world, Real has won a record nine European Cups and 31 La Liga titles, including a dramatic last-day victory in 2007. Over the years, legends such as Alfredo di Stéfano, Ferenc Puskás, Emilio Butragueño, David Beckham, and Ronaldo have worn the famous white shirt. The big-money arrivals of Cristiano Ronaldo (top right), Kaká (bottom right,) and Karim Benzema (top, third from left) in 2009 signaled the start of a new "Galácticos" (Superstars) era.

## SEVILLA FC
### RAMÓN SÁNCHEZ PIZJUÁN, SEVILLE

Champion only once (in 1946,) Sevilla returned to La Liga in 2000. It won the Spanish Cup in 2007 and back-to-back UEFA Cups in 2006 and 2007 (pictured left) with a skillful, high-tempo style of play.

## ATHLETIC BILBAO
### SAN MAMÉS, BILBAO

Eight-time champion Bilbao is one of only three Spanish sides never to be relegated from La Liga, and the team has won the Spanish Cup more times than any other club, except Barcelona. Bilbao has a long-standing policy known as "cantera," where it only signs players from the Basque region. In recent years, the team has drifted around the mid-table, putting the cantera policy under pressure.

# EUROPEAN CLUBS

*"LET FOOTBALL REMAIN THE GAME THAT HAS BEEN THE DREAM OF GENERATIONS, THAT FILLS CHILDREN WITH WONDER, AND UNITES EUROPEANS."* MICHEL PLATINI

Although European club competition, particularly the Champions League, may be dominated by teams from just a few nations, the rest of the continent is also home to some famous clubs, fiercely contested leagues, zealous fans, and historic rivalries.

## DINAMO KIEV
LOBANOVSKY DINAMO STADIUM, KIEV, UKRAINE

Since Ukraine became an independent country in 1991, Dinamo Kiev has dominated domestic soccer, winning 12 league titles and nine Ukrainian Cups.

Vladislav Vashchuk (front, left) and Valentin Belkevich (front, right) celebrate winning the 2007 Ukrainian Cup.

## ANDERLECHT
CONSTANT VANDEN STOCK STADIUM, BRUSSELS, BELGIUM

Anderlecht is the biggest club in Belgium by some margin, with 29 domestic titles and three victories in European competition—twice in the Winners' Cup (1976 and 1978) and once in the UEFA Cup (1983).

## FENERBAHÇE AND GALATASARAY
SÜCRÜ SARACOGLU, STADYUMU, ISTANBUL, TURKEY

The Istanbul game between archrivals Fenerbahçe and Galatasaray is one of the world's fieriest. Honors are even in terms of league titles (17 each), but Galatasaray is the only Turkish team to win a European trophy, after beating Arsenal in the 2000 UEFA Cup final.

## RANGERS AND CELTIC
RANGERS: IBROX, GLASGOW, SCOTLAND
CELTIC: CELTIC PARK, GLASGOW, SCOTLAND

The "Old Firm" rivalry between Glasgow giants Celtic and Rangers is one of the oldest in world soccer. The Rangers have 52 Scottish league titles to its neighbor's 42, but Celtic became the first British team to win the European Cup, in 1967.

## CSKA SOFIA
BALGARSKA ARMIA STADIUM, SOFIA, BULGARIA

Historically backed by Bulgaria's army, CSKA Sofia has lost a little ground to rival Levski Sofia in recent years. However, CSKA still holds the Bulgarian record for league titles (31), despite losing stars such as Stoichkov, Berbatov, and Stilian Petrov to bigger European nations.

## SPARTAK MOSCOW
LUZHNIKI STADIUM, MOSCOW, RUSSIA

The Russian capital boasts six different clubs in Russia's Premier League, but it was Spartak—nicknamed "The Meat"—who won nine of the first 10 post-Soviet league titles. Spartak plays many of its home games on the plastic field of the 78,000 -capacity Luzhniki Stadium, but the team once played a friendly game in Red Square.

Czech center-back Martin Jiránek is the Spartak captain, a team desperate to clinch its first league championship since 2001.

## PORTO
ESTÁDIO DO DRAGÃO, PORTO, PORTUGAL

Porto has eclipsed Sporting and Benfica in the 21st century, thanks to a 2004 Champions League triumph, under manager Jose Mourinho. Six of Porto's 24 league titles have been won in the past seven years.

## MACCABI HAIFA
KIRYAT ELIEZER, HAIFA, ISRAEL

Maccabi Haifa was the first Israeli club to reach the Champions League group stage in 2002–2003, after a 3–0 win over Manchester United. Back at home, it leads closest challengers Beitar Jerusalem by six Israeli Premier League titles to two.

## RED STAR BELGRADE
STADION CRVENA ZVEZDA, BELGRADE, SERBIA

Serbia's finest remains the last Eastern European club to lift the European Cup, when the 1991 team of Robert Prosinecki, Dejan Savicevic, and Siniša Mihajlovic beat Marseille. But its elite status in domestic competition is under threat from neighbor Partizan Belgrade.

## RAPID VIENNA
GERHARD HANAPPI STADION, VIENNA, AUSTRIA

During a golden age in the 1920s and 1930s, Rapid competed in three finals of the Mitropa Cup (a forerunner of the European Cup) and won one. Continental success has been more scarce since then, but the team has won a record 32 domestic league titles.

## SPORTING CP AND BENFICA
SPORTING: ESTÁDIO JOSÉ ALVALADE, LISBON, PORTUGAL
BENFICA: ESTÁDIO DA LUZ, LISBON, PORTUGAL

Benfica became the first team to wrench the European Cup from Real Madrid's clutches, in 1961, and retained the trophy 12 months later. Both victories were inspired by Eusébio, who had been controversially recruited from Lisbon rivals Sporting. Competition in the Portuguese capital remains fierce, although Benfica has 31 league titles to Sporting's 18.

Striker Nuno Gomes (right) has had two spells at Benfica, from 1997 to 2000 and from 2002 to the present time.

Raúl Bravo celebrates Olympiacos' 3–1 victory over Werder Bremen in the Champions League in 2007.

## OLYMPIACOS
GEORGIOS KARAISKAKIS STADIUM, ATHENS, GREECE

Olympiacos is the best supported and most successful of the three major Athens sides. The team has won the Greek national championship a record 37 times.

## IFK GOTHENBURG
ULLEVI STADIUM, GOTHENBURG, SWEDEN

IFK Gothenburg is one of the biggest clubs in Sweden, and it is certainly the most successful, with 18 league titles. IFK is also the only Swedish team ever to lift a trophy in European competition, with two UEFA Cup triumphs, in 1982 and 1987.

## DINAMO ZAGREB
MAKSIMIR STADIUM, ZAGREB, CROATIA

Zagreb has been a reliable production line for many of Croatia's greats, such as Zvonimir Boban and Luka Modric. Dinamo—briefly known as Croatia Zagreb in the 1990s—has won the Prva HNL league eleven times, to archrival Hajduk Split's six.

## SPARTA PRAGUE
GENERALI ARENA, PRAGUE, CZECH REPUBLIC

Sparta was a successful team in the old Czechoslavakian league. It has also dominated the new Czech Republic premier league since its formation in 1993, with ten victories in 16 seasons.

Sparta Prague players celebrate winning the Czech league in 2007.

Steaua Bucharest line up before a 2009 Europa League match against Turkey's Fenerbahçe.

## STEAUA BUCHAREST
STADIONUL GHENCEA, BUCHAREST, ROMANIA

Steaua can take pride in being the first Eastern European club to win the European Cup, in 1986. It also went 104 matches unbeaten between 1986 and 1989 and has won 23 league titles.

## WISLA KRAKÓW
STADION MIEJSKI, KRAKÓW, POLAND

Wisla has recently edged ahead of Legia Warsaw as Poland's highest-achieving team, winning six of the last nine league championships. Known as "The White Star," Wisla played 73 home games without defeat between 2001 and 2006.

# BRAZILIAN CLUBS

## "IF ONE COUNTRY HAS TWO EXCEPTIONAL PLAYERS, THEN BRAZIL WILL HAVE FIVE."

1958 WORLD CUP-WINNING PLAYER AND
1970 WORLD CUP-WINNING COACH MÁRIO ZAGALLO

Few fans are more exuberant, players more extravagant, and coaches more vulnerable to getting fired than in Brazil. A national championship only started in 1971, but the longer-running annual state championships are often judged as just as important. These 23 local contests are played between January and May each year. São Paulo's "Paulista" tournament is the oldest (1902) and only Rio's "Carioca" rivals it for prestige.

In 2003, end-of-season playoffs were abandoned and the trophy given to whichever team finishes top of the league after everyone has played each other twice.

*São Paulo midfielder Hernanes is widely tipped to be Brazil's next superstar, with Barcelona showing a keen interest in him.*

## CORINTHIANS
ESTÁDIO DO PACAEMBU, SÃO PAULO

The Corinthians are on the way back up after a financial meltdown and relegation in 2007. In addition to four national league titles, the team also leads the Paulista field with 26 state championships. The great Ronaldo (above, center) is back in his homeland, and his goals clinched the 2009 Copa do Brasil for the Corinthians.

## SANTOS
ESTÁDIO VILA BELMIRO, SANTOS

Many people claim that Pelé never tested himself outside Brazil, but his Santos side of the 1960s endured a relentless schedule of international matches. World Cup winners such as Gilmar and Zito were co-stars, as Santos scooped Copa Libertadores and Intercontinental Cup trophies in both 1962 and 1963.

## SÃO PAULO
ESTÁDIO DO MORUMBI, SÃO PAULO

São Paulo was formed in 1935 and quickly made its mark by winning five state championships in the 1940s. The 1990s brought even more notable glory, under much-loved coach Telê Santana and with Sócrates' younger brother Raí pulling the strings on the field. In the 2000s, São Paulo became the first Brazilian club to win three consecutive Brazilian league titles, from 2006 to 2008—taking it to a record-breaking six overall. Brazilian hero Kaká also made his name at the club.

| MOST SUCCESSFUL CLUBS BRAZIL | CAMPEONATO BRASILEIRO | COPA DO BRASIL | SOUTH AMERICAN TROPHIES* |
|---|---|---|---|
| SANTOS | 2 | 5 | 2 |
| SÃO PAULO | 6 | - | 3 |
| GRÊMIO | 2 | 4 | 2 |
| PALMEIRAS | 4 | 3 | 1 |
| CRUZEIRO | 1 | 5 | 2 |
| CORINTHIANS | 4 | 3 | - |
| FLAMENGO | 5 | 2 | 1 |
| INTERNACIONAL | 3 | 1 | 2 |
| BAHIA | 1 | 1 | - |
| SPORT CLUB RECIFE | 1 | 1 | - |
| FLUMINENSE | 1 | 1 | - |
| BOTAFOGO | 1 | 1 | - |
| ATLÉTICO PARANAENSE | 1 | - | - |

*Total number of South American trophies includes Copa Libertadores and Copa Sudamericana only.

# FLAMENGO
### ESTÁDIO DA GÁVEA, RIO DE JANEIRO / ESTÁDIO DO MARACANÃ, RIO DE JANEIRO

Brazil's best-supported club, Flamengo's great rivals are Fluminense. One match between the two clubs in 1963 attracted a club world record crowd of 177,656. Striker Adriano (above, right) is rebuilding his career with "The Vulture" after a stint in Europe and his goals helped them to take the 2009 league title.

# GRÊMIO
### OLÍMPICO MONUMENTAL, PORTO ALEGRE

It was at Grêmio that a dazzling young playmaker named Ronaldinho was introduced to the world, although he was just a trainee when the team won its second South American championship in 1995. The Porto Alegre-based club has also featured 1970 World Cup-winning defender Everaldo and Manchester United midfielder Anderson.

# CRUZEIRO
### ESTÁDIO MINEIRÃO, BELO HORIZONTE

Cruzeiro won its first national league title in 2003, and also added the Copa Brasil and the Minas Gerais state championship to become the first Brazilian club to complete that triple win in one year. 1970 World Cup idol Tostão is its record scorer, with 249 goals, and Ronaldo also began his professional career at Cruzeiro.

# PALMEIRAS
### ESTÁDIO PALESTRA ITÁLIA, SÃO PAULO

Djalma Santos and Vavá in the 1960s, Roberto Carlos and Rivaldo in the 1990s and Vagner Love and Edmílson in recent times have all worn the famous green shirts of four-time Brazilian champion Palmeiras. The club was founded among São Paulo's Italian community in 1914 and won its first—and so far only—Copa Libertadores in 1999, managed by future World Cup-winning coach Luiz Felipe Scolari. Matches against local rivals Corinthians are always full-blooded confrontations.

# INTERNACIONAL
### ESTÁDIO BEIRA-RIO, PORTO ALEGRE

Grêmio's local rival Internacional is the only side to have won the world club championship, as well as the Brazilian league and South America's two major continental club trophies (Copa Libertadores and Copa Sudamericana). Its finest moment was beating Spain's Barcelona in the 2006 FIFA Club World Cup (pictured right), with a team showcasing 17-year-old prodigy Alexandre Pato, now of AC Milan.

# ARGENTINIAN CLUBS

*"WHEN YOU COME FROM THE COUNTRY OF THE TANGO, YOU AREN'T ASHAMED TO SHOW THAT YOU POSSESS THE ART OF DANCING."*

FORMER RIVER PLATE, HURACÁN AND ARGENTINA FORWARD ALFREDO DI STÉFANO

Argentine club soccer can be as confusing, chaotic, and thrilling as any on Earth and the "Big Five" of Bocca Juniors, River Plate, San Lorenzo, Independiente, and Racing tend to dominate the national game. Clubs currently get two opportunities for league glory each calendar year—with an opening "Apertura" championship followed by a separate, "Clausura" (closing) campaign. The Apertura runs from August to December and the Clausura follows the next year, from February until June.

Club form can fluctuate: River Plate was Clausura champion in June 2008, but bottom of the Apertura pile six months later.

## ESTUDIANTES DE LA PLATA

ESTADIO JORGE LUIS HIRSCHI, LA PLATA

Estudiantes was one of Argentina's famous Intercontinental Cup-winning clubs of the 1960s, combining tough tackling and cunning ploys with efficient soccer. The team returned to grace in 2009 by winning the Copa Libertadores (pictured below). It was the club's fourth Copa, but its first since 1970.

*Former Inter and Manchester United midfielder Juan Sebastián Verón has thrived since going back to first club Estudiantes, becoming South American Footballer of the Year in 2009.*

## HURACÁN

ESTADIO TOMÁS ADOLFO DUCÓ, BUENOS AIRES

Formed in 1908, Huracán remains one of Argentina's oldest and most cherished clubs, despite just one league title to its name (1973). Famous former players include Osvaldo Ardiles, who left Huracán for England's Tottenham Hotspur after helping Argentina win the 1978 World Cup and then returned to Huracán as coach 29 years later.

## RACING CLUB DE AVELLANEDA

EL CILINDRO DE AVELLANEDA, BUENOS AIRES

Racing fans enjoy a roller-coaster ride. The club was crowned Argentina's first world club champion in 1967 (left), but it was brought to the edge of bankruptcy in 1999. It then bounced back in 2001 to clinch the Apertura title, but recent seasons have involved struggles near the bottom of the rankings.

## INDEPENDIENTE

ESTADIO LIBERTADORES DE AMÉRICA, BUENOS AIRES

No club has been South American champion more often than the "Red Devils" of Independiente, whose seven Copa Libertadores triumphs include four in a row between 1972 and 1975. Its last five were won during Independiente icon Ricardo Bochini's unbroken 20 years' service (1971–1991). The lively "Avellaneda" clashes with local rival Racing can divide families—in the early years of the 21st century, Independiente center-back Gabriel Milito would have to mark his brother Diego up-front for Racing.

# RIVER PLATE
### EL MONUMENTAL, BUENOS AIRES

River Plate plays in the national stadium and holds the record for league titles, with 33. The famous team of 1986 captured the South American and world club championships the same year Argentina won the World Cup.

Former wonderkid Ariel Ortega is now an elder statesman of the River Plate midfield, after returning to where he began his career.

| MOST SUCCESSFUL CLUBS ARGENTINA | PRIMERA DIVISION CHAMPIONS | SOUTH AMERICAN TROPHIES* |
|---|---|---|
| RIVER PLATE | 33 | 2 |
| BOCA JUNIORS | 24 | 8 |
| INDEPENDIENTE | 14 | 7 |
| SAN LORENZO | 10 | 1 |
| VÉLEZ SÁRSFIELD | 7 | 1 |
| RACING CLUB | 7 | 1 |
| ESTUDIANTES | 4 | 4 |
| NEWELL'S OLD BOYS | 5 | - |
| ROSARIO CENTRAL | 4 | - |
| ARGENTINOS JUNIORS | 2 | 1 |
| FERRO CARRIL OESTE | 2 | - |
| QUILMES | 1 | - |
| HURACÁN | 1 | - |
| CHACARITA JUNIORS | 1 | - |

*Total number of South American trophies includes Copa Libertadores and Copa Sudamericana only.

# BOCA JUNIORS
### "LA BOMBONERA," BUENOS AIRES

Boca has enjoyed bragging rights over rival River Plate in recent years, winning four of its six Copa Libertadores and two of its three world championships this century alone. Diego Maradona's favorite club (he had two spells at the club) has lifted 18 international trophies in all, a world record it shares with Italy's AC Milan.

Playmaker Juan Román Riquelme is one of many top players produced by Boca's much-admired youth academy.

# NEWELL'S OLD BOYS
### ESTADIO NEWELL'S OLD BOYS, OR "EL COLOSO DEL PARQUE," ROSARIO

British club names such as Newell's Old Boys reflect the men who first brought the game of soccer to Argentina, in the late 19th and early 20th centuries. Newell's is named after its first coach, Isaac Newell, an English principal. "Old boys" who have graduated impressively from the five-time Argentine champion include Jorge Valdano, Gabriel Batistuta, and Lionel Messi.

# SAN LORENZO DE AMAGRO
### ESTADIO PEDRO BIDEGAIN, OR "EL NUEVO GASÓMETRO," BUENOS AIRES

Of Argentina's "Big Five," San Lorenzo is the only club still waiting to win a Copa Libertadores. Coach Diego Simeone and star signing Kily González hope to add this missing silverware to its 10 league titles. Nicknamed "The Crows" and "The Cyclone," San Lorenzo compete in "el clásico del Barrio" with southern Buenos Aires neighbor Huracán.

# LANÚS
### ESTADIO LANÚS, BUENOS AIRES

The home stadium known as "The Fortress" lived up to its nickname as unfashionable Lanús claimed its first league title in 2007, by winning the opening championship.

Striker José Sand (above, center) was the hero of 2007, hitting 15 goals in as many games.

# SOUTH AMERICA

## "FOOTBALL IS PASSION, MULTITUDE, THE JOY OF LIVING."

FORMER ARGENTINA FOOTBALLER AND PLAYERS' UNION
GENERAL SECRETARY JORGE DOMÍNGUEZ

Although lack of financial muscle means many top stars leave for Europe, there is no doubting the flair and excitement of the region's game or the passion of South American soccer fans. Uruguayan clubs were pioneers in continental and intercontinental clashes of the 1960s, but recent decades have brought encouraging progress elsewhere, especially Paraguay, Chile, and Ecuador.

### CLUB OLIMPIA

ESTADIO MANUEL FERREIRA, ASUNCIÓN, PARAGUAY

Paraguay's oldest club celebrated its centenary in 2002 with its third Copa Libertadores. However, domestically Paraguay's oldest club is suffering something of a drought. Paraguyan stars who started at Olimpia include Roque Santa Cruz and Carlos Paredes.

Julio César Enciso raises the Copa Libertadores trophy in 2002, after beating Brazil's São Caetano on penalties.

### UNIVERSITARIO DE DEPORTES

ESTADIO MONUMENTAL, LIMA, PERU

Founded by students and academics in 1924, Universitario battles it out for glory and popularity with Lima rival Alianza. Universitario now leads in league titles won and was Peru's first team to contest a Copa Libertadores final, in 1972.

Peñarol's Jose Maria Franco heads the ball during a game against Nacional.

### PEÑAROL

ESTADIO CENTENARIO, MONTEVIDEO, URUGUAY

Peñarol won the inaugural Copa Libertadores in 1960 and has won it four more times since. It has also won the Uruguayan league 36 times.

Midfielder Macnelly Torres is a major talent for Colo-Colo and the Colombia national team.

### COLO-COLO

ESTADIO MONUMENTAL DAVID ARELLANO, SANTIAGO, CHILE

Colo-Colo has won more league titles (28) than any other team, and is the only Chilean team to win the Copa Libertadores (in 1991). The club's name comes from the Chilean name for a wildcat, and the team has a variety of nicknames such as Los Albos (the Snow Whites), El Indio (the Indian), and El Popular (the Popular).

### AMÉRICA DE CALI

ESTADIO OLIMPICO PASCUAL GUERRERO, CALI, COLOMBIA

Colombian champion América boasts one of the smallest strikers in the game. 5ft 2in Anthony De Ávila is the team's top scorer and part of the team that lost three Copa Libertadores finals in a row in the mid-1980s.

Marwin Pita (above, right) of El Nacional in action against Eduardo Piris of Paraguay's Nacional in the Copa Libertadores in 2009.

## CLUB DEPORTIVO EL NACIONAL
ESTADIO OLIMPICO ATAHUALPA, QUITO, ECUADOR

Owned by the country's military, El Nacional only fields players of Ecuadorian nationality. The team colors (red, light blue, and dark blue) represent the three branches of the military. With 13 domestic titles, it is jointly Ecuador's most successful team, an honor it shares with Barcelona Sporting Club of Guayaquil.

## ALIANZA LIMA
ESTADIO ALEJANDRO VILLANUEVA, LIMA, PERU

Although local rival Universitario de Deportes has won more league titles (24) than Alianza (22), Alianza lost its entire team in an air crash in 1987, and the club is still recovering.

## CERRO PORTEÑO
ESTADIO GENERAL PABLO ROJAS, ASUNCIÓN, PARAGUAY

The proclaimed "working people's club" of Paraguay reclaimed the league title in 2009 after four years without it, taking its tally to 28 and inching ever closer to rival Olimpia's record haul of 38.

## CLUB NACIONAL DE FOOTBALL
PARQUE CENTRAL, MONTEVIDEO, URUGUAY

Uruguayan giant Nacional has won 42 domestic titles and is three-time world club champion. The first-ever World Cup Finals match was played at its stadium in 1930.

## CLUB BOLÍVAR
ESTADIO LIBERTADOR SIMON BOLÍVAR, LA PAZ, BOLIVIA

Named after the country's founder, Simon Bolívar, the La Paz team has won 16 titles, making it the most successful team in the professional league era (1977 onward).

## MILLONARIOS
ESTADIO EL CAMPIN, BOGOTÁ, COLOMBIA

Colombia's Millonarios could claim to be soccer's first "Galácticos," putting together an all-star 1950s team with the likes of Alfredo di Stéfano and Adolfo Pedernera. The so-called "Blue Ballet" shares the record for league titles with América de Cali (13).

## CARACAS FC
COCODRILOS SPORTS PARK, CARACAS, VENEZUELA

The 10-time domestic league champion is the most successful team in Venezuelan history, with all 10 titles won in the last two decades. Its nickname is "Los Rojos" (the Reds). Amazingly, the club only turned professional in 1984.

## SPORTING CLUB DE BARCELONA
ESTADIO MONUMENTAL BANCO PICHINCHA, GUAYAQUIL, ECUADOR

It is named after one of the world's most famous clubs and the birthplace of the club founder. Despite a domestic title drought since 1997, Ecuador's Barcelona has won a joint record 13 league championships and reached two Copa Libertadores finals.

*Franklin Lucena of Caracas FC (right, front) vies for the ball with Grêmio's Tcheco in a 2009 Copa Libertadores game.*

159

# NORTH AMERICA

*"AMERICA IS A GREAT PLACE TO PLAY AND THE STANDARD IS IMPROVING ALL THE TIME."*

LA GALAXY MIDFIELDER DAVID BECKHAM

The 15 MLS clubs are split into two divisions, the Eastern and Western Conferences. The top four teams from each reach the playoffs and the winners of those contest the MLS Cup—US soccer's most prestigious prize. The Supporters' Shield is awarded to the team that had the most points during the regular season.

The US first launched a professional soccer league in 1968. Known as the NASL (North American Soccer League), it lasted until 1984 and boasted stars such as Pelé, Franz Beckenbauer, and George Best and helped to raise soccer's profile in North America, particularly among young people. Ten years after the demise of the NASL, the US successfully hosted the World Cup Finals, and in 1996 Major League Soccer was launched. Since then, the MLS has flourished, attracting big-money sponsorship and world-class players.

## EASTERN CONFERENCE

### D.C. UNITED
RFK STADIUM, WASHINGTON, D.C.

The team from the US capital quickly became a power base of the MLS, winning four League Championships, including a 1996 league and cup double.

### NEW YORK RED BULLS
RED BULL ARENA, HARRISON, NEW JERSEY

New York has captured big-name recruits such as Lothar Matthäus and Youri Djourkaeff, as well as home-grown talents including Tim Howard, Jozy Altidore, and Claudio Reyna. But despite great expectations, the team has underachieved so far.

### NEW ENGLAND REVOLUTION
GILLETTE STADIUM, FOXBOROUGH, MASSACHUSETTS

Never mind a revolution, perhaps New England just needs a change of luck—former Scottish international Steve Nicol has coached the team to four MLS Cup finals in six years, but it has lost them all.

New England captain Steve Ralston (right) has played more MLS games than any other current player.

### CHICAGO FIRE
TOYOTA PARK, BRIDGEVIEW, ILLINOIS

Chicago Fire was hot stuff in its debut season in 1998, lifting the MLS Cup. With Mexico's Cuauhtémoc Blanco and US legend Brian McBride now on board, more silverware looks likely.

### TORONTO FC
BMO FIELD, TORONTO, ONTARIO, CANADA

Toronto was the first Canadian entrant to the MLS in 2007 and its passionate support leads to sell-out crowds at almost every game.

Columbus Crew beat New York Red Bulls 3–1 to take the 2008 MLS Cup (above).

### COLUMBUS CREW
COLUMBUS CREW STADIUM, COLUMBUS, OHIO

One of the MLS' founding clubs, the Crew bills itself as "America's hardest-working club." It was finally rewarded with the MLS Cup in 2008 and Argentine midfielder Guillermo Barros Schelotto was named the season's Most Valuable Player.

### KANSAS CITY WIZARDS
COMMUNITYAMERICA BALLPARK, KANSAS CITY, KANSAS

The Wizards' most passionate fans occupy a section of the stadium known as "The Cauldron" and had plenty to cheer about when their team won the 2000 MLS Cup. Goalkeeper Tony Meola set new records for shoutouts.

# WESTERN CONFERENCE

## COLORADO RAPIDS
### DICK'S SPORTING GOODS PARK, COMMERCE CITY, COLORADO

The Rapids have notched up more changes in uniform colors than championship titles, but have attracted such flamboyant figures as Colombia's Carlos Valderrama. Owner Stan Kroenke has forged close links with Arsenal, the English club in which he holds a large stake.

## CHIVAS USA
### THE HOME DEPOT CENTER, CARSON, CALIFORNIA

California's cultural heritage is well-represented by Chivas USA, which shares strong links with the "Chivas" of Mexico's CD Guadalajara. It shares a stadium with LA Galaxy, as well as a fiery rivalry.

## SEATTLE SOUNDERS
### QWEST FIELD, SEATTLE, WASHINGTON

After a long wait for admission, the Seattle Sounders became the 15th MLS franchise in 2009. Goalkeeper-captain Kasey Keller led the team into the playoffs in its debut season. The Sounders enjoy sold-out crowds for every home game, although its 52-member marching band might claim some of the credit.

## REAL SALT LAKE
### RIO TINTO STADIUM, SANDY, UTAH

The Utah-based franchise only arrived in the MLS in 2005. It has fostered friendly links with inspirational namesakes Real Madrid and the two clubs share responsibility for a promising youth academy and play annual friendly matches. Real Salt Lake highlighted its progress by winning the MLS Cup for the first time in 2009, beating LA Galaxy on penalties.

## LA GALAXY
### THE HOME DEPOT CENTER, CARSON, CALIFORNIA

LA Galaxy mixes Hollywood glamour with good, old-fashioned successful soccer. The team has won the MLS Championship twice and the CONCACAF Champions' Cup once, in 2000. LA Galaxy was the first MLS club to record a profit.

Former England captain David Beckham (far left) brought glamour and pinpoint set-pieces to the MLS in 2007. He also necessitated a rule change in which each club is allowed one "marquee player" who can break the league's salary cap.

## SAN JOSE EARTHQUAKES
### BUCK SHAW STADIUM, SANTA CLARA, CALIFORNIA OR OAKLAND-ALAMEDA COUNTY COLISEUM, OAKLAND, CALIFORNIA

Starting out as San Jose Clash, the Earthquakes won the MLS Cup in 2001 and 2003. The team lost its franchise in 2005 (see below) but regained it in 2008 and returned to the Western Conference.

## HOUSTON DYNAMO
### ROBERTSON STADIUM, HOUSTON, TEXAS

Houston Dynamo took over the San Jose Earthquakes franchise in 2005, which meant that it kept the same players but changed the team's name and moved to a different state (Texas, from California). The side won the 2006 MLS Cup in its first season and retained the trophy in 2007.

Jeff Cunningham (above, right) has scored more than a century of MLS goals.

## FC DALLAS
### PIZZA HUT PARK, FRISCO, TEXAS

Hugo Sánchez signed in 1996, and Denílson—once the world's most expensive player—followed 11 years later. The franchise formerly known as Dallas Burn awaits its first MLS title, but did give the MLS one of its most prolific scorers of all time, Jason Kreis.

# CONCACAF CLUBS

**"IT'S FAIR TO SAY THAT CONCACAF TEAMS ARE IMPROVING ACROSS THE BOARD."**

USA MANAGER BOB BRADLEY

Mexican clubs have the history and heritage, the supporter bases, and the TV money, and have dominated recent CONCACAF championships. However, the unusually close qualification for the 2010 World Cup is matched by rising standards at club level across the Central American region. The launch of a CONCACAF Champions League in 2008 has helped expose more clubs to more intense—and more lucrative—competitive action.

## FC VILLA CLARA
ESTADIO AUGUSTO CESAR SANDINO, SANTA CLARA, CUBA

Villa Clara is Cuba's leading team, with 10 league titles to its name. Unusually, the country's championship is decided by splitting clubs into four groups of four, then staging semifinals and a final for the best performers.

Pachuca celebrate beating Costa Rica's Deportivo Saprissa in the 2008 CONCACAF Champions Cup final.

## CF PACHUCA
ESTADIO HIDALGO, PACHUCA, MEXICO

In the last decade Mexico's oldest club CF Pachuca has outshone rival Cruz Azul and Club América to win five championships and three CONCACAF Champions' Cups.

## JOE PUBLIC
MARVIN LEE STADIUM, TUNAPUNA, TRINIDAD AND TOBAGO

Joe Public is Trinidad and Tobago's most prominent side. It was among the founding members of the country's first professional league in 1997, winning three championships since then and competing with honor in the 2008–2009 CONCACAF Champions League.

*Emmanuel Villa, a young Argentine striker signed in summer 2009, began his Cruz Azul career with 16 goals in his first 16 games as the team sought its first league title since 1997.*

## CLUB AMÉRICA
ESTADIO AZTECA, MEXICO CITY, MEXICO

Mexico's wealthiest club set new standards in the 1980s, when five of its ten league titles were captured in consecutive seasons. Progress since the mid-Nineties has been patchy, although producing national hero Cuauhtémoc Blanco was a highlight, as was its fifth CONCACAF Champions' Cup in 2006.

## CRUZ AZUL
ESTADIO AZUL, MEXICO

Cruz Azul shares the record for most CONCACAF championship triumphs with Club América (five). It is also the only Mexican club to reach a Copa Libertadores final—as invited guest it lost to Boca Juniors on penalties in 2001.

## SV TRANSVAAL
ANDRÉ KAMPERVEEN STADIUM, PARAMARIBO, SURINAME

Rivals SV Transvaal and SV Robinhood have held the balance of power in Suriname's national league since it was set up in 1924. Transvaal trails by 19 league titles to 24, but was CONCACAF champion in 1973 and 1981—a feat its rivals have never achieved.

## DEPORTIVO SAPRISSA

ESTADIO RICARDO SAPRISSA AYMÁ, SAN JOSÉ, COSTA RICA

Saprissa has a record 28 domestic titles as well as three CONCACAF Champions' Cups. Its home ground, nicknamed "Monster's Cave," is the biggest in Costa Rica.

Ronald Gomez (above, left) of Saprissa celebrates the goal against Al-Ittihad that earned Saprissa third place at the 2005 FIFA Club World Cup.

## DEFENSE FORCE

HASELEY CRAWFORD STADIUM, PORT OF SPAIN, TRINIDAD AND TOBAGO

Since Defense Force's foundation in 1974 many players have been drawn from the Armed Forces. The team has marched its way to a record 20 league titles, six domestic cups, and the CONCACAF championship in 1978 and 1985. Carlos Edwards and Jason Scotland both graduated from here en route to the English Premier League.

## CSD MUNICIPAL

ESTADIO MATEO FLORES, GUATEMALA CITY, GUATEMALA

Municipal has won 26 league titles and has never been relegated. It became Guatemala's only CONCACAF champion, in 1974. Current captain Juan Carlos Plata has scored more than 400 goals for Municipal since 1990.

## FAS

ESTADIO OSCAR QUITEÑO, SANTA ANA, EL SALVADOR

Jorge "Magico" González not only helped conjure up five of FAS's record 16 Salvadoran league titles, but also the 1979 CONCACAF championship—the country's only triumph at that level.

## ALAJUELENSE 40

ESTADIO ALEJANDRO MORERA SOTO, ALAJUELA, COSTA RICA

Saprissa has four more league titles, but Alajuelense's 24 are spread across every single decade since it was formed in 1919. It became Costa Rica's first CONCACAF club champions in 1986, and then reclaimed that crown 18 years later.

## CLUB DEPORTIVO GUADALAJARA

ESTADIO JALISCO, GUADALAJARA, MEXICO

Fielding only Mexican-born players, Deportivo has won a record 11 Mexican league titles. Nicknamed "Chivas" (Goats), it also has a California franchise that takes part in the MLS.

## CLUB DEPORTIVO OLIMPIA

ESTADIO TIBURCIO CARIAS ANDINO, TEGUCIGALPA, HONDURAS

Olimpia is Honduras' most dominant club, scooping a record 22 league titles and launching the careers of talents such as striker David Suazo, midfielder Wilson Palacios, and defender Maynor Figueroa.

*Brazilian forward Allan Kardec dos Santos (right) fired Olimpia toward its 22nd league triumph in 2009.*

## RC HAÏTIEN

STADE SYLVIO CATOR, PORT-AU-PRINCE, HAITI

Ten-time league champion RC Haïtien leads the domestic field in Haiti. However, its 1963 CONCACAF Champions' Cup triumph was matched 21 years later by rival Violette.

# AFRICAN CLUBS

**"IT'S ALL ABOUT FOOTBALL, FOOTBALL, FOOTBALL, FOOTBALL—THE WHOLE OF AFRICA, WE LOVE FOOTBALL."** NIGERIA CAPTAIN AND STRIKER NWANKWO KANU

Despite some of the greatest talents being tempted away by rich European clubs, Africa has an impressive soccer culture. Rowdy rivalries, noble histories, and some of the loudest, proudest fans on the planet— African club soccer has all the right ingredients. The African Cup of Champions kicked off in 1964 and became the CAF Champions League in 1997.

## RAJA CASABLANCA
STADE MOHAMED V, CASABLANCA, MOROCCO

Founded in 1949, the "people's club" took 26 years to win a trophy. However, it won the CAF Champions League in 1989, 1997, and 1999. Along with local rival Wydad Casablanca, it is Morocco's most powerful club.

*Defender Abdellatif Jrindou is the current Raja Casablanca captain.*

## CANON YAOUNDÉ
STADE OMNISPORTS, YAOUNDÉ, CAMEROON

Canon Yaoundé is one of the most successful clubs in Cameroon. It has won nine league titles, three CAF Champions Leagues (1971, 1978, 1980), and one CAF Cup Winners' Cup.

## AL-AHLY
CAIRO INTERNATIONAL STADIUM, CAIRO, EGYPT

Named the CAF's "Club of the Century" in 2000, Al-Ahly's record of six CAF Champions League titles and 34 Egyptian titles is unrivaled. It did not lose a single game from 1974 to 1977.

*Al-Ahly's captain Shady Mohamed (left) celebrates winning the Egyptian Super Cup in 2008.*

## AS DOUANES
STADE LEOPOLD SENGHOR, DAKAR, SENEGAL

AS Douanes gave good warning of its ascent to the top in Senegal when it lifted the domestic cup four years in a row to 2005, before notching a hat trick of league titles from 2006 to 2008.

## JS KABYLIE
STADE 1ER NOVEMBRE, TIZI OUZOU, ALGERIA

JS Kabylie has more than twice as many domestic titles as any rival. Key internationals Mahieddine Meftah, Djamel Menad, and Moussa Saib are among those to wear the yellow of Kabylie's "Canaries."

## MAMELODI SUNDOWNS
ATTERIDGEVILLE SUPER STADIUM, TSHWANE, SOUTH AFRICA

Having a billionaire owner helps, but Mamelodi Sundowns was already a rising power in South Africa before Patrice Mosepe's 2003 takeover. It has won five league titles since 1998.

The Sundowns edged out Orlando Pirates for South Africa's Supa 8 Cup in 2007.

Enyimba players (left) celebrate beating Sharks FC in the final of the Nigerian Federation Cup in Lagos in 2009.

## EL ZAMALEK
### CAIRO STADIUM, CAIRO

El Zamalek and Al-Ahly is Egypt's answer to the Glasgow "Old Firm" (see p. 152), and foreign referees are brought in to oversee its fierce local rivalry games. Zamalek has won the league 11 times and its five CAF Champions League titles put it just one behind rivals Al-Ahly. It topped FIFA's club rankings in 2003.

El Zamalek's Amr Zaki (far right) and El Ettehad's Ahmed Bakry fight for the ball in 2009.

## ENYIMBA
### ENYIMBA INTERNATIONAL STADIUM, ABA, NIGERIA

In 2003, Enyimba, whose name means "Elephant," brought the CAF Champions League trophy to Nigeria for the first time, 13 years after turning professional.

## ÉTOILE SPORTIVE DU SAHEL
### STADE OLYMPIQUE DE SOUSSE, SOUSSE, TUNISIA

Tunisia's oldest club, Sahel has won an array of CAF trophies to add to eight domestic league titles, thanks to Tunisian heroes such as midfielder Kaies Ghodhbane and Brazil-born striker Francileudo Santos, backed by big-name imports such as Ivoirian forward Kader Keïta.

## ASANTE KOTOKO
### BABA YARA STADIUM, KUMASI, GHANA

Ghana's most formidable club, nicknamed "the Porcupine Warriors," was originally called Rainbow FC. It won African club championships in 1970 and 1983 and is narrowly ahead of rival Hearts of Oak, with 21 league titles.

## INVINCIBLE ELEVEN
### ANTOINETTE TUBMAN STADIUM, MONROVIA, LIBERIA

Invincible Eleven shares a stadium with rival Mighty Barolle. Both teams have won the league 13 times, but the 1986-1987 season stands out as George Weah scored 24 goals in 23 games to give the IE "Yellow Boys" the glory.

## ASEC MIMOSAS
### STADE FÉLIX HOUPHOUËT-BOIGNY, ABIDJAN, CÔTE D'IVOIRE

Its 22 league titles to 2007 is an awesome record, but just as impressive is the youth academy created by Jean-Marc Guillou that has produced Emmanuel Eboué, Bonaventure and Salomon Kalou, and Kolo and Yaya Touré.

## HAFIA FC
### STADE 28 SEPTEMBRE, CONAKRY, GUINEA

Guinea's greatest got to keep the first African championship trophy after its third win in 1977, and it won the Guinean league 15 times (including titles won under its previous name Conakry II). However, success has eluded Hafia in recent years, with clubs such as Horoya AC and AS Kaloum Star rising to the top instead.

## DJOLIBA AC 34
### COMPLEX SPORTIF HÉRÉMAKONO, BAMAKO, MALI

Djoliba AC and Stade Malien have fought out a fierce tussle for supremacy in Mali since both clubs were founded in 1960. Djoliba has the edge, with 20 league titles, to Stade Malien's 15.

Kouakou N'doua (left) of ASEC Mimosas vies with Housam Ashour of Al-Ahly in a 2008 African Champions League match.

# ASIA AND OCEANIA

### "ASIAN FOOTBALL IS IN THE PROCESS OF MAKING A BIG STEP FORWARD."

FRENCH SUPERSTAR ZINEDINE ZIDANE

The A-League (Australia), I-League (India), J.League (Japan), and K-League (Republic of Korea) are just some of the logically named club championships of Asia and Oceania. Over the years, their up-and-coming teams have lured many notable players, such as Kazuyoshi Miura and Dwight Yorke (Australia), Hristo Stoichkov, Patrick Mboma, and Gary Lineker (Japan), and Alpay (Republic of Korea). The future looks bright for this rapidly developing soccer region.

Jeonbuk's players after winning the AFC Champions League 2006 trophy.

## JEONBUK FC

### JEONJU WORLD CUP STADIUM, JEONJU, REPUBLIC OF KOREA

Jeonbuk was the first South Korean team to win the AFC Champions League, in 2006. Despite domestic cup success, it still awaits its first K-League title, since the league has been largely monopolized by Seongnam Ilhwa Chunma.

## DEMPO SPORTS CLUB

### FATORDA PANDIT JAWARHARLAL NEHRU STADIUM, MARGAO, INDIA

Dempo won two of the last three titles of India's National Football League. The NFL finished in 2007 and was replaced by a new league, the I-League, which Dempo also won in its first season.

Tough-tackling ex-Australia captain Kevin Muscat (right) returned to Melbourne in 2002 after ten years in the UK.

## MELBOURNE VICTORY FC

### DOCKLANDS STADIUM, MELBOURNE, AUSTRALIA

Sydney FC won the first A-League in 2006, but captain Kevin Muscat (left) helped take the title to Melbourne the next year. Victory also added the Championship trophy after the top four played off in the Finals Series. Then, after a barren season, the team reclaimed both trophies in 2009.

## GOLD COAST UNITED

### ROBINA STADIUM, QUEENSLAND, AUSTRALIA

Gold Coast United only joined Australia's A-League in the 2009 season, but the newcomer soon showed its intent by tempting Australian international Jason Culina back home from Dutch giants PSV Eindhoven.

NZ striker Shane Smeltz (above) scored nine goals on his Gold Coast debut.

## ARBIL FC

### FRANSO HARIRI STADIUM, ARBIL, IRAQ

Arbil has emerged as the supreme force in Iraqi soccer, despite being based away from the capital, Baghdad. It took its first league title in 2007, adding two more in a row, thanks to such talents as AFC Asian Cup-winning homegrown forward Luay Salah.

## WELLINGTON PHOENIX

### WESTPAC STADIUM, WELLINGTON, NEW ZEALAND

Wellington Phoenix was formed in 2007 to replace New Zealand Knights in Australia's A-League. It lost star striker Shane Smeltz to Gold Coast United in 2009 and is still chasing its first trophy.

## WAPDA FC
### PUNJAB STADIUM, LAHORE, PAKISTAN

The water company-backed club, nicknamed "The Watermen," has displaced Pakistan Army FC as the country's leading team, with seven league titles. It went through the 2007–2008 league campaign without losing a single game.

## ESTEGHLAL FC
### AZADI STADIUM, TEHRAN, IRAN

Local rival Persepolis has won a couple more league titles and shares the same 90,000-capacity home, but 2009 league champions Esteghlal can also boast of being Asian club champions in 1971 and 1991, and runner-up in 1999.

*Al-Hilal striker Yasser Al-Qahtani is also the captain of the Saudi Arabia national team.*

*Takuya Nozawa (above) holds the trophy as Kashima Antlers won its second straight J.League title in 2008.*

## KASHIMA ANTLERS
### KASHIMA STADIUM, KASHIMA, JAPAN

Kashima Antlers clinched the J.League's most eye-catching transfer coup by signing Brazilian star Zico in 1993. The six-time league champion peaked in 2000, with a triple of the J.League, J.League Cup, and the Emperor's Cup.

## CHURCHILL BROTHERS SC
### FATORDA STADIUM, MARGAO, GOA, INDIA

Mohun Bagan is India's most-loved club, and one of the oldest in Asia, but it was beaten to the I-League title in 2009 by Churchill Brothers SC, which had been in existence for a mere 21 years.

## DALIAN SHIDE
### DALIAN PEOPLE'S STADIUM, DALIAN, CHINA

Dalian Shide is the most successful team in China. It won seven out of 10 Jia league titles and has, so far, won the new Super League once.

## JÚBILO IWATA
### YAMAHA STADIUM, IWATA, SHIZUOKA, JAPAN

World Cup-winning Brazil captain Dunga and Golden Boot-winning Italian Salvatore Schillaci helped establish Júbilo Iwata in Japan's J.League, in the 1990s. It later went on to win the J.League three times and was Asian club champion in 1999.

## AL-HILAL
### KING FAHD INTERNATIONAL STADIUM, RIYADH, SAUDI ARABIA

The Al-Hilal trophy cabinet has been crammed with 48 cups since 1957, thanks to talents such as Brazilian World Cup-winner Rivelino, who played for them from 1978–1981.

## SEONGNAM ILHWA CHUNMA
### TANCHEON SPORTS COMPLEX, SEONGNAM, REPUBLIC OF KOREA

Despite moving cities three times in four years, (from Seoul to Cheonan in 1995 and from Cheonan to Seongnam in 1999) Ilhwa Chunma has won seven K-League titles. It also won the 1996 Asian club championship, with a Lee Tae Hong goal against Saudi Arabia's Al Nassr.

## AL-ZAWRAA
### AL-ZAWRAA STADIUM, BAGHDAD, IRAQ

Arguably Iraq's best player Ahmed Radhi—1988 Asian Footballer of the Year—had three jubilant spells with the country's biggest club, Al-Zawraa. The Baghdad team has won the league a record 11 times, but a single goal by Japan's Shimizu S-Pulse denied it the Asian Cup Winners' Cup in 2000.

# WOMEN'S CLUBS

**"WE HAVE COME A LONG WAY IN DEVELOPING THE NATIONAL TEAMS—NOW THE TIME HAS COME TO WORK EVEN HARDER TO DEVELOP THE CLUBS."**

SUSANNE ERLANDSSON OF THE UEFA
WOMEN'S FOOTBALL COMMITTEE

As relatively recently as the end of the 20th century, women were banned from playing soccer in many countries, such as Brazil. However, in the 21st century things are slowly improving—the international game is gaining in popularity and domestic leagues are now flourishing, especially in Northern Europe and the US. Brazil's second place at the 2007 Women's World Cup has even prompted promises to set up a league there.

## L.LEAGUE
### JAPAN
Introduced in 1989, Japan's amateur L.League thrived thanks to big-money sponsorship and star players such as the US's Tiffeny Milbrett (Shiroki Serena) and Norway's Hege Riise (Nikko Securities Dream Ladies).

## FRAUEN-BUNDESLIGA
### GERMANY
Two clubs have dominated German women's soccer since the women's semi-pro league was founded in 1990—1. FFC Frankfurt and 1. FFC Turbine Potsdam. Domestic and European success, particularly for Frankfurt, has provided the foundation for Germany's many international triumphs.

FFC Frankfurt clinched its third UEFA Women's Cup in 2008 (left) with a win over Sweden's Umeå IK, the same club it beat for its first win six years earlier.

Goal ace Anja Mittag (right) has helped fire 1. FFC Turbine Potsdam to three Bundesliga titles, as well as the 2005 UEFA Women's Champions League.

## TOPPSERIEN
### NORWAY
Scandinavia has long been a stronghold for women's soccer and Norway first established a women's league in 1984. It began as three regional divisions, which then merged three years later to form a single league. The majority of titles have been shared between Trondheims-Ørn and Asker SK. In fact, during the 1998 season Asker SK won all of its 18 games!

## AROUND THE WORLD
Despite boasting one of the world's finest female teams at international level, **Brazil** has had no national league since 2001. However, clubs still participate in cup contests such as the Copa Libertadores. **Argentina** has a better established league, with the Campeonato de Fútbol Feminino set up in 1991 and dominated since then by Boca Juniors (16 league titles) and River Plate (nine). Other long-running leagues include **Denmark's** Elitedivisionen, founded in 1973, and **Italy's** Serie A, whose first season was 1985–1986. As the women's game grows worldwide, new arrivals include the Eredivisie in the **Netherlands** and **Mexico's** Super Liga Femenil de Fútbol, both introduced in 2007. **Australia's** new W-League also crowned Brisbane Roar as inaugural champion in 2008–2009.

Captain Christie Rampone (above, left) and striker Natasha Kai celebrate after New Jersey-based Sky Blue FC seized the first WPS championship in a 2009 playoff, after finishing fourth in the league.

## USA WPS-LEAGUE
USA

The US made history by setting up the world's first professional league for women in 2000. Although the Women's United Soccer Association folded after just three years, a relaunched version known as Women's Professional Soccer got underway in 2009. Former WUSA stars returning to the fray, after the six-year hiatus, have included USA internationals Kristine Lilly and Tiffeny Milbrett, Canada's Christine Latham, and England's Kelly Smith.

## SUPERLIGA FEMININA
SPAIN

The women's league clubs in Spain have maintained close links to their male counterparts since kicking off in 1983. As in La Liga's early years, the front-runner is Athletic Bilbao. However, in the women's game, Real Madrid remains absent from the top divison and Barcelona was relegated in 2006–2007.

Arsenal Ladies (above) lifted the FA Women's Cup for a record tenth time in 2009, beating Sunderland 2–1 to claim its fourth triumph in a row.

## PREMIER LEAGUE
ENGLAND

When Arsenal Ladies beat Sweden's Umeå IK to capture the UEFA Women's Cup in 2007 it was England's first victory in that competiton. It marked a clean sweep of trophies for the London club and also brought positive signs for the development of the women's game in England.

*Los Angeles Sol's Brazilian wonder Marta lived up to her top billing in the US's new professional league, by finishing top scorer in the opening 2009 season.*

## DAMALLSVENSKAN
SWEDEN

Sweden seems to develop women's soccer better than anywhere else in the world. The Swedish league, known as the Damallsvenskan, dates back to 1973 and has attracted leading names such as the US's Kristine Lilly, China's Ma Xiaoxu, and Brazil's Marta, combining with the finest homegrown talents such as Hanna Ljungberg. Today's stars include German goalkeeper Nadine Angerer and top team Umeå IK has twice been UEFA Women's Cup champion. Despite club success, Sweden remains international soccer's runner-up, losing four major international finals.

## RIVELINO
### BRAZIL

The midfielder's performances for Brazil between 1965 and 1978 earned him legendary status. Famed for his graceful play and thunderous left foot, Rivelino is unofficially credited with scoring the fastest ever goal—directly from the kickoff.

## JAIRZINHO
### BRAZIL

This powerful winger scored in every game of the 1970 World Cup tournament, the only player so far ever to achieve this feat. Immensely talented, Jairzinho made his professional debut at 15 and his international debut in 1964, at the age of 19.

## MATTHIAS SINDELAR
### AUSTRIA

Widely regarded as Austria's greatest player ever, center forward Matthias Sindelar was known as "the Paper Man" because of his fragile build. He is famous for his refusal to play for the unified German team after the Nazis' annexation of Austria in 1938.

## PATRICK VIEIRA
### FRANCE

Midfielder Patrick Vieira was one of the stalwarts of the French team that won the 1998 World Cup and Euro 2000. Although he is a defensive midfielder, reknowned for his tackling and authority on the field, Vieira also has great attacking vision.

# HALL OF FAME

"THE CLEVEREST DO MATH, THE NEXT-BEST WRITE BOOKS. DANCERS ARE THE CLEVEREST WITH THEIR FEET, NEXT ARE FOOTBALLERS." JOHAN CRUYFF

In this book we have set out to select the greatest players and best teams in world soccer. Sadly, it is impossible to include absolutely everyone and many soccer legends have not managed to squeeze onto our pages. However, there are some heroes—old and new and from all around the world—that we simply had to find space for. This is our Hall of Fame.

## JORGE VALDANO
### ARGENTINA

The striker played for his country between 1975 and 1986, and also achieved fame as a player and coach with Real Madrid. Valdano's soccer knowledge and opinions of the game have earned him the nickname "The Philosopher of Football."

## SÓCRATES
### BRAZIL

Skillful, inspirational, and a fine reader of the game, Sócrates captained his country in the 1982 and 1986 World Cups. His trademark move was the blind heel pass, which involved passing the ball with his heel while looking in the opposite direction.

## JOHAN NEESKENS
### NETHERLANDS

A technically gifted midfielder, Neeskens provided the base for the master Johan Cruyff to work his magic in the great Dutch "Total Soccer" side of the 1970s. He played club soccer for Ajax and Barcelona and was known for his powerful penalty kicks.

## FERNANDO HIERRO
### SPAIN

A tough defender with superior passing ability, Hierro was a stalwart for Spain for more than a decade. He scored an impressive 29 goals for his country in 89 appearances and also helped Real Madrid to five league titles between 1989 and 2002.

## OLIVER KAHN
### GERMANY

This recently retired goalkeeper was nicknamed "King Kahn." He was regarded as the world's number one after the 2002 World Cup Finals, when he became the first goalkeeper in history to win the Golden Ball for best player.

## OMAR SÍVORI
### ARGENTINA/ITALY

A wonderfully gifted, audacious forward who loved to dribble the ball and delighted in nutmegging defenders, his speed and invention make him one of the finest players ever. Sívori played for both Argentina and Italy between 1956 and 1962.

## ADNAN AL-TALYANI
### UNITED ARAB EMIRATES
UAE forward Adnan Al-Talyani is among an elite group of players with more than a century of caps for his country. He scored 53 goals in 164 appearances, making him his country's leading scorer and most capped player. He retired in 1997.

## MARCEL DESAILLY
### FRANCE
Between 1993 and 2004, Desailly won every major club and international honor in the game with AC Milan, Chelsea, and France. Chelsea fans voted him their greatest ever center-back, with John Terry, but he also played in central midfield for Milan.

## HONG MYUNG-BO
### REPUBLIC OF KOREA
A classy center-back and rallying captain, Hong Myung-Bo was the firm foundation of Republic of Korea's 2002 World Cup team. He was the first Asian player to play in four consecutive World Cup finals tournaments and is his country's most capped player.

## SIR BOBBY CHARLTON
### ENGLAND
Graceful, athletic, quick, with a thunderbolt shot and fierce sense of fair play, Bobby Charlton's exploits with Manchester United and England during the 1950s and 1960s make him one of the greatest players of all time. He is still England's top scorer.

## JIMMY GREAVES
### ENGLAND
In the 1960s, no one was better at scoring goals than striker Jimmy Greaves. He scored on every debut and netted 44 times in 57 England games—including six hat tricks. He also played for Chelsea, AC Milan, Tottenham Hotspur, and West Ham.

## MICHELLE AKERS
### USA
Dubbed "the Pelé of women's soccer" and voted FIFA's Woman Player of the Century in 2002, Akers was part of the first-ever US women's team in 1985. She was top scorer in the first women's World Cup in 1991, scoring twice in the final win over Norway.

## DENIS LAW
### SCOTLAND
The only Scotsman ever to be European Footballer of the Year, (in 1964), this fiercely competitive striker was a supreme goal scorer, incisive passer, and intelligent reader of the game. A legend at Manchester United, he also played for Manchester City.

## FRANCO BARESI
### ITALY
Able to play as a central defender or sweeper, Baresi was famous for his tough tackling. He captained Italy at the 1994 World Cup Finals. He was also a rock in the AC Milan defense for 20 years and AC Milan's No. 6 shirt has been retired in his honor.

## LILIAN THURAM
### FRANCE
France's most capped player was a skilled defender who also played some of Europe's top clubs, including Monaco, Parma FC, Juventus, and FC Barcelona. Since his retirement from soccer in 2008, Thuram has become an campaigner against racism.

## SIR STANLEY MATTHEWS
### ENGLAND
A classic winger, Matthews played for an astonishing 33 years—until he was 50! He was the first-ever European Footballer of the Year and the first soccer player to be knighted. Matthews was a true gentleman of the game and never received a single booking.

## ALI KARIMI
### IRAN
Often called "the Asian Maradona" or the "Wizard of Tehran," Ali Karimi is an Iranian attacking player. He is able to play on the wing or as a forward and was 2004 Asian Footballer of the Year. He retired from international soccer in 2009.

## ERIC CANTONA
### FRANCE
One of the most influential players of the 1980s and 1990s, Cantona had everything. Dubbed "The King" by Man United fans, he could score goals or create them, displayed superb ball control and breathtaking vision—a true entertainer.

### ROBERTO AYALA
**ARGENTINA**

This much-capped central defender is good in the air, a tenacious tackler and an excellent passer of the ball. Ayala inherited the nickname of "El Ratón" (Mouse) from Argentine 1974 World Cup player Rubén Ayala, although they are not related.

### KRISTINE LILLY
**USA**

The US's legendary captain has played 340 games for the national side—a world record for men or women. Nicknamed "Iron Woman," Lilly is a tireless worker who can score and create goals. She is the first woman to play in five World Cup Finals.

### MARK SCHWARZER
**AUSTRALIA**

Australia's undisputed No.1, goalkeeper Mark Schwarzer has everything—height, agility, presence, and great reactions. He is a consistently strong performer for both his country and his club, Fulham, where he was named Player of the Year in 2009.

### ALFREDO DI STÉFANO
**ARGENTINA/SPAIN**

Considered by many the greatest player ever, di Stéfano's fitness and versatility saw him play in most outfield positions. Best known as a deadly center-forward, he inspired Real Madrid to five successive European Cups between 1956 and 1960.

### BRIAN MCBRIDE
**USA**

Hard-working striker Brian McBride has won many fans during his playing career in the US and Europe. He was Fulham's Player of the Year in 2005 and 2006 and is the only American so far to score goals in more than one World Cup Finals, doing so in 1998 and 2002.

### ROMÁRIO
**BRAZIL**

This gifted center-forward, who retired in 2008 at over 40 years old, claimed a career total of more than 1,000 goals. His technique and sharpness in the box fired PSV and Barcelona to success, as well as Brazil. Romário won the Golden Ball at the '94 World Cup Finals.

### FRITZ WALTER
**GERMANY**

Named by the German soccer associations as the country's most outstanding player, this forward captained Germany to its first World Cup success in 1954. His ability to read the game and to control the ball kept him two steps ahead of opponents.

### MAHMOUD EL-KHATIB
**EGYPT**

A true legend of Egyptian soccer, striker El-Khatib was an accomplished goal scorer between 1972 and 1988. Nicknamed "Bibo," El-Khatib holds the dubious honor of sustaining the most injuries in the history of the Egyptian game.

### DANNY BLANCHFLOWER
**NORTHERN IRELAND**

A great passer and tactician, midfielder Danny Blanchflower was part of Tottenham Hotspur's famous team of the 1960s. He was English Footballer of the Year in 1958 and 1961 and captained his country at to the 1958 World Cup quarterfinals.

### DINO ZOFF
**ITALY**

One of the finest goalkeepers ever, Zoff holds the record for not conceding an international goal—1,142 minutes between 1972 and 1974. He captained Italy, most famously at the 1982 World Cup, and was a key member of the great Juventus team of the 1970s.

### "JAY-JAY" OKOCHA
**NIGERIA**

A skillful midfielder renowned for his dazzling stepovers, Okocha helped establish his country as a world force in the 1990s and played for club sides across Europe. His fans at Bolton Wanderers used to say he's, "so good they named him twice."

### "DOCTOR" KHUMALO
**SOUTH AFRICA**

The man who made his country and his club side, Kaizer Chiefs, tick in the 1980 and 1990s, Khumalo's passing and movement were so good that he could run the game from his midfield position. He was also an accomplished ball juggler!

## KASEY KELLER
### USA

One of the US's best soccer exports, goalkeeper Kasey Keller played in the English Premier League and the German Bundesliga before returning home to the Seattle Sounders. Keller's finest game for his country was the United States' 1–0 victory over Brazil in 1998.

## RUUD KROL
### NETHERLANDS

A legend of the 1970s "Total Soccer" sides of Ajax and the Netherlands, Krol was a technically gifted defender who could play across the back line, as a sweeper or defensive midfielder. He captained his country after Johan Cruyff retired.

## JÜRGEN KLINSMANN
### GERMANY

Jürgen Klinsmann was a successful club player across Europe and a World Cup winner in 1990. Noted for his exaggerated dives, he was in fact a superb all-around striker. He later managed Germany and led it to the 2006 World Cup semifinals.

## JAVIER ZANETTI
### ARGENTINA

The versatile Javier Zanetti can play in defense or midfield and he is his country's most capped player. He is also a legend at Italian club Internazionale, for whom he has played more than 450 matches. Inter fans nickname Zanetti "Il Trattore" (the Tractor) for his strength and stamina.

## FRANCISCO GENTO
### SPAIN

Gento's ability to run with the ball and eye for goal-making were central to the success of the Real Madrid side of the 1950s and 1960s. He is still the only man to win six European Cups and was also part of Spain's 1964 European Championship winning side.

## PAOLO MALDINI
### ITALY

Defender Paolo Maldini is a legend of Italian soccer. He played 25 seasons at AC Milan—his entire career—before retiring at the age of 40. He won seven Serie A and five Champions League medals and also captained Italy a record 74 times.

## LI MING
### CHINA

Hard-working midfielder Li Ming's reputation for striking the right balance between attack and defense made him a key part of the Dalian Shide team that won six Chinese league titles in the 1990s. He is also China's most-capped player.

## PAULINO ALCÁNTARA
### PHILIPPINES

Born in the Philippines to a Spanish father, striker Alcántara scored a remarkable 357 goals in 357 games for Barcelona between 1912 and 1927. The first Asian player ever to play for a European club, Alcántara is still Barcelona's top scorer.

## SALIF KEÏTA
### MALI

A hugely talented striker, Keïta was also a soccer pioneer. He was the first African Footballer of the Year (in 1970) and one of the first African players to play in Europe. In 2005, Keïta was elected president of the Malian Federation of Football (FEMAFOOT).

## KARIM ABDUL RAZAK
### GHANA

Midfielder Razak was blessed with superb ball control and ability to read the game. He was African Footballer of the Year in 1978 and was a key part of the Ghana team that won the African Cup of Nations in the same year. Razak is now a top coach in Ghana.

## MASAMI IHARA
### JAPAN

An accomplished sweeper and central defender, Ihara was a fixture in the national team throughout the 1990s. What he lacked in pace he made up for in awareness. His phenomenal record of 122 caps may never be equaled.

## MOHAMMED AL-DEAYEA
### SAUDI ARABIA

A goalkeeper who played for his country in four World Cup Finals, Al-Deayea holds 181 caps, a record for a male player. His penalty saves in the 1996 Asian Cup final helped Saudi Arabia to victory. Al-Deayea has now retired from international soccer.

## ALCIDES GHIGGIA
### URUGUAY/ITALY
Winger Alcides Ghiggia's goal against host Brazil secured the 1950 World Cup trophy for Uruguay. He only played 12 times for Uruguay, but won two league titles with Peñarol before joining Italy's AS Roma. Ghiggia later played five times for Italy.

## BIRGIT PRINZ
### GERMANY
Goal-machine Birgit Prinz has been the mainstay of a virtually all-conquering German women's team since 1994. She has nearly 200 caps for her country, averaging over a goal per game. Prinz was FIFA Women's World Player of the Year in 2003, 2004, and 2005.

## ARTHUR FRIEDENREICH
### BRAZIL
Striker Arthur Friedenreich first played for Brazil in 1914 and was part of the Copa América winning teams in 1919 and 1922. He was one of the first black players to feature for Brazil and it is believed that he scored more than 1,200 career goals.

## PAUL GASCOIGNE
### ENGLAND
Known as "Gazza," midfielder Paul Gascoigne was one of the most gifted midfielders of his generation. Off-field troubles prevented him from fulfilling his potential, but Gazza will be remembered for lighting up Italia '90 with his talent and his tears.

## DUNCAN EDWARDS
### ENGLAND
One of Manchester United's famous "Busby Babes," midfielder Duncan Edwards' promising career was cut short in the 1958 Munich air disaster, which claimed the lives of 23 people. Many believe that Duncan Edwards had the talent to rival Pelé and George Best.

## OSVALDO ARDILES
### ARGENTINA
A World Cup winner with Argentina in 1978, midfielder Osvaldo Ardiles is a popular figure in the game. A competitive and attacking player, he has also managed clubs in England, Japan, Mexico, Australia, Syria, Israel, Argentina, and Uruguay.

## NANDOR HIDEGKUTI
### HUNGARY
Nandor Hidegkuti was one of Hugary's "Magnificent Magyars" of the 1950s. He was one of the first players to play in what is now often called "the hole," i.e., just behind the main striker. Against England in 1953, Hidegkuti scored a hat trick from this position.

## KELLY SMITH
### ENGLAND
Striker Kelly Smith was a key part of the Arsenal Ladies team that dominated English women's soccer, until she moved to USA's Boston Breakers in 2009. A key player for England, Smith is rapidly closing in on Karen Walker's all-time scoring record.

## SAMUEL KUFFOUR
### GHANA
One of Africa's all-time great players, Ghana defender Samuel Kuffour spent the most glorious years of his career at Bayern Munich. He won six league titles and a 2001 UEFA Champions League winner's medal during 11 seasons in Germany.

## GÜNTER NETZER
### GERMANY
When Barcelona signed Johan Cruyff in 1973, rival Real Madrid responded quickly and signed Günter Netzer. Famed for his long passing ability and attacking play, Günter Netzer won two league titles and two domestic cups with Madrid, twice as many as Cruyff.

## HUGO SÁNCHEZ
### MEXICO
Striker Hugo Sánchez spent 12 seasons in Spain's La Liga (from 1981 to 1992 with Atlético and then Real Madrid) and is still the second highest goal scorer in the history of that league. He is generally regarded as Mexico's greatest player of all time.

## JOSÉ NASAZZI
### URUGUAY
Defender José Nasazzi was the captain of the Uruguay team that won the first-ever World Cup tournament in 1930. Nicknamed "el Gran Mariscal" (the Great Marshal), Nasazzi also won two Olympic gold medals and four Copa América titles.

## GIUSEPPE MEAZZA
### ITALY
Giuseppe Meazza started out as a striker, but his passing and dribbling abilities meant that he finished his career as a midfielder. He won back-to-back World Cups with Italy in 1934 and 1938 and also scored more than 200 goals for Internazionale.

## GRAEME SOUNESS
### SCOTLAND
Tough-tackling Scottish midfielder Graeme Souness was captain of the Liverpool team that dominated English soccer in the 1980s. He won five league titles and three European Cups at Liverpool, and later managed the team from 1991–1994.

## MARCELO SALAS
### CHILE
One of Chile's most high-profile players in recent years, Marcelo Salas was famous for his wicked left foot shot. Nicknamed "el Matador" (the Killer) because of it, Salas played club soccer in Chile, Argentina, and Italy before retiring in 2009.

## LUIS MONTI
### ARGENTINA AND ITALY
Defender Luis Monti played in two consecutive World Cup finals, for two different nations. He was on the losing side when Argentina lost to Uruguay in 1930, but on the winning side four years later when adopted country Italy beat Czechoslovakia.

## DIEGO FORLÁN
### URUGUAY
Soccer is a family tradition for Diego Forlán. His father also played for Uruguay, while his grandfather played for Independiente. Striker Forlán has enjoyed his greatest club success in Spain with Villareal and Atlético Madrid and has twice been Europe's top scorer.

## UWE SEELER
### GERMANY
Striker Uwe Seeler was a one-club player. He spent his entire club career at Hamburger SV. A popular player, Seeler's phenomenal goal-scoring record saw him average more than a goal every other game for both club and country.

## DIDI
### BRAZIL
Midfielder Waldyr Pereira, or Didi, had strength, stamina, incredible passing ability, and scored many goals. He played at three World Cups, winning the trophy in 1958 and 1962. He was also the first player ever to score a goal at the Maracanã stadium, in 1950.

## PAULO FUTRE
### PORTUGAL
Paulo Futre played for Portugal's three main clubs—Sporting, Porto, and Benfica. Admired for his speed, dribbling, and wing play, Futre played for a total of 10 clubs, including AC Milan and Atlético Madrid before persistent knee problems led him to retire.

## ROBERTO CARLOS
### BRAZIL
A defender with an explosive shot, Roberto Carlos is also famous for his unstoppable free kicks. Playing as an attacking full back or wing back, Carlos won the 2002 World Cup with Brazil and 13 trophies during his 11 years with Real Madrid.

## KEVIN KEEGAN
### ENGLAND
Goal-scoring forward Kevin Keegan was European Footballer of the Year in 1978 and 1979, while playing for Hamburger SV. He had previously won three First Division titles, two UEFA Cups, two FA Cups, and the European Cup with Liverpool.

## GIACINTO FACCHETTI
### ITALY
One of the first players to demonstrate the attacking potential of full backs, Giacinto Facchetti was a one-club player—Internazionale. He played 634 times for the Italian club and when he died in 2006, Inter retired the No. 3 shirt in his honor.

## TEÓFILO CUBILLAS
### PERU
Not only Peru's greatest ever player, but also one of South America's all-time finest, Teófilo Cubillas was a free-scoring midfielder. He was 1972 South American Footballer of the Year and part of the 1975 Copa América-winning Peru team.

## ITALY V WEST GERMANY
### WORLD CUP SEMIFINAL, JUNE 17, 1970

This game is regarded as one of the greatest World Cup Finals' games of all time. The game finished 1–1 in regular time, after a last-minute equalizer from Germany's Karl-Heinz Schnellinger. An amazing five goals were scored in overtime and Italy ran out 4–3 winners. Italy's team went on to lose to Brazil in the final, with many people claiming that it had been left drained by its epic semifinal match.

## FRANCE V BRAZIL
### WORLD CUP QUARTERFINAL
### JUNE 10, 1986

France and Brazil have faced each other in many crucial matches, including the 1998 World Cup final. However, one of their most intriguing encounters took place in the 1986 World Cup. Their quarterfinal match finished 1–1 after extra time, so the outcome had to be decided on a penalty shootout. Three of the world's greatest players ever missed their penalties—Michel Platini for France and Sócrates for Brazil. Zico scored his (above, right) but France eventually won 4–3 on penalties, with Luis Fernández (left) taking the decisive spot-kick.

## KOREA DPR V PORTUGAL
### WORLD CUP QUARTERFINAL
### JULY 23, 1966

North Korea certainly surprised a few people at the 1966 World Cup Finals in England. The team finished above Italy and Chile in the group stages, earning a quarterfinal place against Portugal. There were even more surprises in store when North Korea stormed into a 3–0 lead in the quarterfinal, after just 25 minutes. However, Portugal hit back quickly with a goal from the great Eusébio. He added another before halftime (a penalty, pictured right) and two more in the second half to turn the game around. A fifth goal from José Augusto sealed Portugal's 5–3 victory and spoiled North Korea's fairy tale.

# GREAT GAMES

"THE GAME IS ABOUT GLORY. IT IS ABOUT DOING THINGS IN STYLE, WITH A FLOURISH, ABOUT GOING TO BEAT THE OTHER LOT, NOT WAITING FOR THEM TO DIE OF BOREDOM."

THE LATE TOTTENHAM HOTSPUR AND NORTHERN IRELAND MIDFIELDER DANNY BLANCHFLOWER

Great games live on in people's memories long after the final whistle has blown. They are usually characterized by unlikely victories, spectacular goals, amazing comebacks, individual brilliance, or contentious decisions by the referee. Take a closer look at some of the most special games the world has seen, so far.

## GREAT BRITAIN V GERMANY
### DECEMBER 25, 1915

Although soccer can be a hot-blooded and contentious game, it can also bring people together at difficult times. This is certainly true of the match played between British and German soldiers on Christmas Day in 1915. Although it was the middle of World War I, both sides called a temporary truce and played a soccer game in "No Man's Land" between the two sets of trenches in northern France. Although the game itself was not a classic—it was more of a large-scale kick-around than a formal 90-minute, 11-a-side game—it has become a symbol of humanity and hope in adversity.

## ROMANIA V ARGENTINA
### WORLD CUP 2ND ROUND, JULY 3, 1994

At the 1994 World Cup Finals in the US, Diego Maradona, the hero of Mexico '86 and Italia '90 was sent home in disgrace after two games. Despite that, Argentina managed to scrape through the group stages in third place and qualify for the knockout stages. It faced Romania and Ilie Dumitrescu scored twice in the first 20 minutes, before Gabriel Batistuta (above, left) pulled a goal back for Argentina with a penalty. Gheorghe Hagi made it 3–1 to Romania after halftime and although Argentina scored once more, Romania held on for a famous victory.

## SCOTLAND V ENGLAND
### INTERNATIONAL FRIENDLY GAME, NOVEMBER 30, 1872

The world's first ever official international game took place between neighboring countries Scotland and England at the West of Scotland Cricket Club's ground in Glasgow, Scotland. The field was damp and heavy after three days of continuous rain, which made playing attractive soccer difficult. Nevertheless, both sides favored the attacking formations that were popular in the 19th century. England had eight forwards, while Scotland opted for a more conservative six up front. Despite this the game ended goalless, although Scotland did have a goal disallowed in the first half.

## ENGLAND V HUNGARY
### INTERNATIONAL FRIENDLY 25TH NOVEMBER 1953,

During the 1950s, Hungary was known as the "Magnificent Magyars" and when it faced England in a friendly game at Wembley in 1953, it had not been beaten for three years. Led by captain Ferenc Puskás, the Hungarians were famous for their attacking style and opened the scoring after 90 seconds, thanks to Nándor Hidegkuti. Hidegkuti went on to score a hat trick, and Puskás added a brace, as Hungary overran England 6–3 in what is sometimes called "The Match of the Century." The game was also England's first home defeat to a non-British side.

## REAL MADRID V EINTRACHT FRANKFURT
### EUROPEAN CUP FINAL, MAY 13, 1960

Few could argue that Real Madrid was a worthy winner of one of the greatest finals ever to grace the European Cup. Boasting stars such as Alfredo Di Stefano, Francisco Gento, and Ferenc Puskás, Madrid played attractive, attacking soccer that brought goals galore. Despite this, it was Frankfurt that took the lead after 18 minutes. Madrid hit back quickly with three goals before halftime and emerged 7–3 winner. Puskás scored four goals and Di Stefano three and they remain two of only three players to have scored a hat trick in a European Cup final.

## IVORY COAST V CAMEROON
### AFRICAN CUP OF NATIONS QUARTERFINAL 2006

Ivory Coast has a reputation for endurance in African Cup of Nations' penalty shootouts. It won the 1992 trophy by defeating Ghana 11–10 on penalties in the final. When it faced Cameroon in a 2006 quarterfinal shootout, it was Les Elephants that held its nerve once again, winning 12–11. Samuel Eto'o missed for Cameroon, before a jubilant Didier Drogba (above, right) won it for Ivory Coast.

## LIVERPOOL V AC MILAN
### CHAMPIONS LEAGUE FINAL MAY 25, 2005

The 2005 UEFA Champions League final in Istanbul did not begin well for England's Liverpool. Italy's AC Milan had a three-goal lead by halftime, thanks to goals from Paolo Maldini and Hernan Crespo (2), and looked to have the trophy in its sights. However, an exhilirating five-minute spell early in the second half turned the game around. Goals from Steven Gerrard (celebrating, left), Vladimir Smicer and Xabi Alonso brought Liverpool back on level terms and took the game to overtime. The game was eventually decided by a penalty shootout, which Liverpool won 3–2, thanks to some heroic goalkeeping from Jerzy Dudek.

## REAL MADRID V BARCELONA
### LA LIGA MATCH, MAY 2, 2009

Known as "el Clásico," the game between Spain's Real Madrid and Barcelona is one of the most watched games in the world. Before their May 2009 meeting, Real Madrid was unbeaten in 18 games, but form counts for nothing in a game of archrivals and Barcelona swept its rival aside with ease. Madrid scored first (Higuain, after 14 minutes) but Barcelona replied quickly through Thierry Henry (above, left) and took control of the game. Barcelona ran out 6–2 winner, thanks to goals from Henry (2), Lionel Messi (2), Carles Puyol, and Gerard Piqué.

### MARCO VAN BASTEN

**NETHERLANDS V USSR
EUROPEAN CHAMPIONSHIPS
FINAL, JUNE 25, 1988**

When the Netherlands faced the USSR in the final of Euro '88 in Germany, few could have predicted what an historical encounter it would turn out to be. Not only was it the last time that the USSR played in the tournament, but it was also the setting for arguably the competition's greatest ever goal. Marco Van Basten's goal in the final was truly spectacular and sealed the Netherlands' 2–0 victory. Arnold Mühren floated a high ball across the penalty area to Van Basten who, despite the seemingly impossible angle, hit it on the volley (left) and smashed the ball past stunned USSR keeper Rinat Dasaev.

### TEÓFILO CUBILLAS

**PERU V SCOTLAND
WORLD CUP FIRST ROUND
JUNE 3, 1978**

Prolific midfielder Teófilo Cubillas scored 10 World Cup Finals goals in total, the most by a midfielder and making him seventh in the list of World Cup all-time top scorers. Two of his most memorable goals came in a game against Scotland at the 1978 tournament. The first was a cracking shot from outside the edge of the Scotland penalty area, and the second was one of Cubillas' specialities—a free kick.

### ZINEDINE ZIDANE

**REAL MADRID V BAYER
LEVERKUSEN
CHAMPIONS LEAGUE FINAL
MAY 15, 2002**

Nine-time European champion Real Madrid met German team Bayer Leverkusen in the 2002 final of the Champions League. Although it was Leverkusen's first Champions League final and the team was not even Bundesliga champion, the game was a closer contest than many anticipated. With the scores tied 1–1 just before halftime, a stunning strike from Zinedine Zidane gave the Spanish team the lead. Zidane met Roberto Carlos' high cross and lashed in a perfect left foot volley from the edge of the penalty area (left). Despite a close-run second half, Real Madrid held on to win 2–1.

# GREAT GOALS

**"IT ONLY TAKES A SECOND TO
SCORE A GOAL."**
BRIAN CLOUGH

What makes a great goal? Individual brilliance? Team work? Spectacular skill? Maybe the sweetest goal could be a simple tap-in if it wins the World Cup, or a fluke shot off a defender's knee if it beats your local rivals for the first time in 50 years. Take a look at some of the most memorable goals ever scored in world soccer and decide whether you think they are great.

### DAVOR ŠUKER

**CROATIA V DENMARK EUROPEAN CHAMPIONSHIPS
FIRST ROUND, JUNE 16, 1996**

One of the challengers to Van Basten's 1988 volley's unofficial status as the best European Championship goal of all time, is Davor Šuker's 1996 effort against defending champion Denmark. Croatia already had a comfortable 2–0 lead when Šuker made sure of the win with a spectacular 90th minute goal. Danish goalkeeper Peter Schmeichel was scrambling to get back into position after joining the attack for a last-ditch Danish corner, when Šuker calmly lobbed the ball straight over the dumbfounded keeper's head.

### PELÉ

**BRAZIL V SWEDEN
WORLD CUP FINAL, JUNE 29, 1958**

Brazil is famous for scoring amazing World Cup goals (see p. 113). Pelé's first (Brazil's third) in the 1958 5–2 victory over Sweden runs Carlos Alberto's 1970 strike close for sheer brilliance. The 17-year-old Pelé, playing in his first World Cup Final, received the ball inside the penalty area, chipped it over the defender, and then smashed it past the helpless Swedish goalkeeper, Kalle Svensson.

## RIVALDO

### BARCELONA V VALENCIA
### LA LIGA, JUNE 2001

The 2000–2001 season doesn't rank up there with any of Barcelona's greatest. Going into the last game of the La Liga season, the best Barcelona could hope for was fourth place, which would at least guarantee it a spot in the next season's Champions League competition. However, it was up against Valencia, that season's losing Champions League finalist, which only needed a point to clinch fourth spot for themselves. Valencia seemed to be in control of the game and heading for the Champions League. Enter Rivaldo to score an unlikely hat trick, including a sweetly struck 90th minute bicycle kick (right) that won the game for Barcelona.

## PAUL GASCOIGNE

### ENGLAND V SCOTLAND EUROPEAN CHAMPIONSHIPS
### FIRST ROUND (GROUP STAGES), JUNE 15, 1996

Ever since England and Scotland played the world's first international game in 1872, there has been a extra-competitive edge whenever the neighboring countries meet. At Euro '96, England took the lead in the second half through Alan Shearer before Scotland's Gary McAllister had his penalty saved. A minute later Paul Gascoigne received the ball on the left of the Scotland penalty area, flicked the ball over the defender with his left foot, and then volleyed the ball into the goal with his right foot.

## DAVID BECKHAM

### MANCHESTER UNITED V WIMBLEDON
### PREMIER LEAGUE
### AUGUST 17, 1996

In 1996, 21-year-old David Beckham was beginning to establish himself as a first-choice in Manchester United's midfield. However, a Premier League game against Wimbledon really made the world sit up and take notice of him. With United 2–0 up, Beckham noticed that the Wimbledon goalkeeper, Neil Sullivan, was off his line. So, Beckham launched a shot from inside his own half, which traveled more than 50 yards (45 meters) and beat the stranded goalkeeper. The Beckham legend was born.

## GEORGE WEAH

### AC MILAN V VERONA
### SERIE A
### SEPTEMBER 8, 1996

After claiming the titles of World, African and European Footballer of the Year in 1995, Liberia's George Weah had the world at his feet. Despite many great games for AS Monaco, Paris Saint-Germain, and AC Milan, probably Weah's greatest moment of individual skill came in a 1996 Serie A match against Verona. Weah collected the ball in the Milan penalty area and then proceeded to dribble the length of the field, evading all challenges, before calmly slotting the ball into the back of the net. Simple!

## DENNIS BERGKAMP

### NETHERLANDS V ARGENTINA
### WORLD CUP QUARTERFINAL, JULY 4, 1998

With three clever touches of his magical right foot, Dennis Bergkamp broke Argentinian hearts and sent the Netherlands through to the semifinals of the 1998 World Cup. Bergkamp leapt to collect Frank De Boer's long pass, controlled it with his first touch, knocked it past defender Robert Ayala with his second, and then slotted it home using the outside of his shoe with his third. The Netherlands went on to lose to Brazil on penalties in the semifinal.

## SAEED AL-OWAIRAN

### SAUDI ARABIA V BELGIUM
### WORLD CUP FIRST ROUND, JUNE 29, 1994

Saudi Arabia reached the World Cup Finals for the first time at USA '94. It lost its first group game 2–1 to the Netherlands, then beat Morocco by the same score. Going into the final group game with Belgium, Saudi Arabia had to win to reach the second round, and it did just that thanks to a brilliant solo goal from Saeed Al-Owairan. The midfielder ran from his own half, through a maze of Belgian players to score and win the game for Saudi Arabia.

### AZTECA
#### MEXICO CITY, MEXICO
Mexico's national stadium is the fifth largest in the world. It is also home to Club América and has a capacity of 105,000. So far, it is the only stadium to host two World Cup final games—Brazil v Argentina in 1970 and Argentina v West Germany in 1986.

### WEMBLEY
#### LONDON, ENGLAND
Originally built in 1923, Wembley Stadium is the home of English soccer. All major home internationals are played there, as well as all domestic finals. In 2007, a new structure was opened and with 90,000 seats it is the second largest stadium in Europe.

### CENTENARIO
#### MONTEVIDEO, URUGUAY
Built for the 1930 World Cup finals and to celebrate the centenary of Uruguay's constitution, the Centenario stadium now has a capacity of 65,000. It was here that Uruguay won the inaugural World Cup in front of an ecstatic home crowd.

### MARACANÃ
#### RIO DE JANEIRO, BRAZIL
The Maracanã is the biggest in South America. It hosted the deciding game of the 1950 World Cup as Brazil lost 2–1 to Uruguay in front of an estimated 210,000 fans, and will also host the final of the 2014 World Cup in front of just under 90,000 fans.

### BERNABÉU
#### MADRID, SPAIN
Named after a former Real Madrid president, the Santiago Bernabéu was built in 1947 and has a capacity of 75,000. Spain's national stadium, it has hosted prestigious matches, such as the 1982 World Cup final and is also the home ground of Real Madrid.

# SUPER STADIUMS

**"DOWN THROUGH ITS HISTORY, ONLY THREE PEOPLE HAVE MANAGED TO SILENCE THE MARACANÃ: THE POPE, FRANK SINATRA AND ME."**

FORMER URUGUAYAN STRIKER, ALCIDES GHIGGIA

The beautiful game can be played virtually anywhere, but the greatest soccer games deserve world-class settings. Once-in-a-lifetime occasions such as the World Cup demand awe-inspiring stadiums, packed to their rafters with passionate fans. Take a tour around some of the world's biggest, loudest, and most famous soccer stadiums.

### ESTÁDIO DA LUZ
#### LISBON, PORTUGAL
The old Estádio da Luz was built in 1954 and was home to the likes of Eusébio and Rui Costa. The new Estádio da Luz (Stadium of Light) was built in time for Euro 2004 and hosted the final, which Portugal lost to Greece. It has a capacity of 65,400.

### HAMPDEN PARK
#### GLASGOW, SCOTLAND
Scotland's national stadium was built in 1903. It regularly housed up to 150,000 people and was the largest stadium in the world of that time. Renovated in 1999, Hampden can now host up to 52,000 fans, and is also home to lowly Queen's Park FC.

### INTERNATIONAL STADIUM
#### YOKAHAMA, JAPAN
Built in 1998 and home to the J. League's Yokohama F. Marinos, the International Stadium stepped into the international spotlight during the 2002 World Cup Finals. It hosted the final between Brazil and Germany.

### SAN SIRO
#### MILAN, ITALY
The Stadio Giuseppe Meazza is more commonly known as the San Siro after the Milan district in which it is located. It is home to both Internazionale and AC Milan who contest fierce local rivalry matches known as "Derby della Madonnina" every season.

### OLD TRAFFORD
#### MANCHESTER, ENGLAND
Nicknamed "Theater of Dreams" by Manchester United legend Bobby Charlton, the Reds' home ground is the second largest in England, after Wembley. Built in 1909, the ground was virtually destroyed during World War II and had to be rebuilt in 1949.

### ALLIANZ ARENA
#### MUNICH, GERMANY
Built for the 2006 World Cup Finals, the Allianz Arena is now home to both Bayern Munich and 1860 Munich. It has a seating capacity of 66,000 and is the first stadium in the world to be able to fully change color on the outside thanks to 2,760 lighting panels.

### LA BOMBONERA
#### BUENOS AIRES, ARGENTINA
Boca Junior's home ground, Estadio Alberto J. Armando, is more commonly known as "La Bombonera" (the Chocolate Box) due to its unusual shape. The stadium has three steep stands and one flat, giving it world famous acoustics.

### STADE DE FRANCE
#### PARIS, FRANCE
France's national stadium hosts both soccer and rugby union, but its greatest moments have undoubtedly been soccer. Built for the 1998 World Cup Finals, Stade de France was the setting for the host nation's famous victory over Brazil in the final.

### STADE VELÓDROME
#### MARSEILLES, FRANCE
Olympique Marseille's home ground is the largest soccer stadium in France. It was a World Cup Finals venue in both 1938 and 1998 and has a capacity of around 60,000. Like Stade de France, Stade Velódrome also hosts international rugby.

### EL MONUMENTAL
#### BUENOS AIRES, ARGENTINA
Estadio Monumental Antonio Vespucio Liberti, El Monumental de Nuñez or River Plate Stadium—Argentina's national stadium has many names. Popularly known as "El Monumental" (the Monument) it is also the great River Plate's home ground.

### LUZHNIKI STADIUM
#### MOSCOW, RUSSIA
The biggest stadium in Russia with a capacity of 78,360, the Luzhniki Stadium is home to both Torpedo Moscow and Spartak Moscow. Famous for its artificial field, grass was specially laid for the 2008 Champions League final between Chelsea and Manchester United.

### CAMP NOU
#### BARCELONA, SPAIN
Barcelona's Camp Nou (translated as "new field") is Europe's biggest stadium. It can hold over 98,000 spectators and over the years stars such as Lionel Messi, Josep Fusté, Romário, and Thierry Henry have played on the famous turf.

### KING FAHD STADIUM
#### RIYADH, SAUDI ARABIA
The King Fahd International Stadium is famous for having the largest roof of any stadium in the world. 24 columns arranged in a circle support a huge umbrella-like roof that provides vital shade for spectators in Saudi Arabia's hot desert climate.

### OLYMPIASTADION
#### BERLIN, GERMANY
Originally built for the 1936 Olympics, the Olympiastadion is also home to Hertha Berlin. It was renovated in time for the 2006 World Cup Finals and hosted the final. The new roof has transparent panels that allow sunlight to stream in during the day.

### WORKERS STADIUM
#### BEIJING, CHINA
It is one of the Ten Great Buildings constructed to honor the 10th anniversary of the People's Republic of China in 1959. It is the home ground of Chinese Super League team Beijing Guoan and hosted matches in the 2008 Olympics.

### AMSTERDAM ARENA
#### AMSTERDAM, NETHERLANDS
Ajax Amsterdam's home ground was built in 1996 and has a retractable roof. In addition to soccer games, it is also a popular venue for music concerts. It was also formerly home to the now defunct Amsterdam Admirals American soccer team.

### SOCCER CITY
#### JOHANNESBURG, SOUTH AFRICA
Built for the 2010 World Cup Finals, the look of the new Soccer City stadium was inspired by African pottery. It can hold up to 94,700 people and is designed so that every spectator will have a great view, not more than 330 ft (100 meters) from the action.

## FIFA WORLD CUP

A competition for national teams of member nations of FIFA, the international ruling body of soccer.

| | |
|---|---|
| 2006 | Italy |
| 2002 | Brazil |
| 1998 | France |
| 1994 | Brazil |
| 1990 | West Germany |
| 1986 | Argentina |
| 1982 | Italy |
| 1978 | Argentina |
| 1974 | West Germany |
| 1970 | Brazil |
| 1966 | England |
| 1962 | Brazil |
| 1958 | Brazil |
| 1954 | West Germany |
| 1950 | Uruguay |
| 1938 | Italy |
| 1934 | Italy |
| 1930 | Uruguay |

## FIFA WOMEN'S WORLD CUP

| | |
|---|---|
| 2007 | Germany |
| 2003 | Germany |
| 1999 | USA |
| 1995 | Norway |
| 1991 | USA |

## UEFA EUROPEAN CHAMPIONSHIP

A competition for national teams of nations governed by UEFA, the ruling body of European soccer.

| | |
|---|---|
| 2008 | Spain |
| 2004 | Greece |
| 2000 | France |
| 1996 | Germany |
| 1992 | Denmark |
| 1988 | Netherlands |
| 1984 | France |
| 1980 | West Germany |
| 1976 | Czechoslovakia* |
| 1972 | West Germany |
| 1968 | Italy |
| 1964 | Spain |
| 1960 | USSR |

* See p. 37 for the current name of Czechoslovakia.

## UEFA WOMEN'S CHAMPIONSHIP

| | |
|---|---|
| 2009 | Germany |
| 2005 | Germany |
| 2001 | Germany |
| 1997 | Germany |
| 1995 | Germany |
| 1993 | Norway |
| 1991 | Germany |

## CONMEBOL COPA AMÉRICA

A competition for national teams of nations governed by CONMEBOL, the ruling body of South American soccer.

| | |
|---|---|
| 2007 | Brazil |
| 2004 | Brazil |
| 2001 | Colombia |
| 1999 | Brazil |
| 1997 | Brazil |
| 1995 | Uruguay |
| 1993 | Argentina |
| 1991 | Argentina |
| 1989 | Brazil |
| 1987 | Uruguay |
| 1983 | Uruguay |
| 1979 | Paraguay |
| 1975 | Peru |
| 1967 | Uruguay |
| 1963 | Bolivia |
| 1959 | Uruguay (December) |
| 1959 | Argentina (April) |
| 1957 | Argentina |
| 1956 | Uruguay |
| 1955 | Argentina |
| 1953 | Paraguay |
| 1949 | Brazil |
| 1947 | Argentina |
| 1946 | Argentina |
| 1945 | Argentina |
| 1942 | Uruguay |
| 1941 | Argentina |
| 1939 | Peru |
| 1937 | Argentina |
| 1935 | Uruguay |
| 1929 | Argentina |
| 1927 | Argentina |
| 1926 | Uruguay |
| 1925 | Argentina |
| 1924 | Uruguay |
| 1923 | Uruguay |
| 1922 | Brazil |
| 1921 | Argentina |
| 1920 | Uruguay |
| 1919 | Brazil |
| 1917 | Uruguay |
| 1916 | Uruguay |

## CONCACAF GOLD CUP*

A competition for national teams of countries governed by CONCACAF, the ruling body of soccer in North America, Central America, and the Caribbean.

| | |
|---|---|
| 2009 | Mexico |
| 2007 | USA |
| 2005 | USA |
| 2003 | Mexico |
| 2002 | USA |
| 2000 | Canada |
| 1998 | Mexico |
| 1996 | Mexico |
| 1993 | Mexico |
| 1991 | USA |
| 1989 | Costa Rica |
| 1985 | Canada |
| 1981 | Honduras |
| 1977 | Mexico |
| 1973 | Haiti |
| 1971 | Mexico |
| 1969 | Costa Rica |
| 1967 | Guatemala |
| 1965 | Mexico |
| 1963 | Costa Rica |

*1963–1989 competition known as CONCACAF Championship; 1991—present competition known as CONCACAF Gold Cup.

## CONCACAF WOMEN'S GOLD CUP

| | |
|---|---|
| 2006 | USA |
| 2002 | USA |
| 2000 | USA |
| 1998 | Canada |
| 1994 | USA |
| 1993 | USA |
| 1991 | USA |

## CAF AFRICAN CUP OF NATIONS

A competition for national teams of African countries, sanctioned by CAF.

| | |
|---|---|
| 2008 | Egypt |
| 2006 | Egypt |
| 2004 | Tunisia |
| 2002 | Cameroon |
| 2000 | Cameroon |
| 1998 | Egypt |
| 1996 | South Africa |
| 1994 | Nigeria |
| 1992 | Ivory Coast |
| 1990 | Algeria |
| 1988 | Cameroon |
| 1986 | Egypt |
| 1984 | Cameroon |
| 1982 | Ghana |
| 1980 | Nigeria |
| 1978 | Ghana |
| 1976 | Morocco |
| 1974 | Zaire |
| 1972 | Congo |
| 1970 | Sudan |
| 1968 | Congo Kinshasa (now DR Congo) |
| 1965 | Ghana |
| 1963 | Ghana |
| 1962 | Ethiopia |
| 1959 | Egypt |
| 1957 | Egypt |

## CAF WOMEN'S CHAMPIONSHIP

| | |
|---|---|
| 2008 | Equatorial Guinea |
| 2006 | Nigeria |
| 2004 | Nigeria |
| 2002 | Nigeria |
| 2000 | Nigeria |
| 1998 | Nigeria |
| 1995 | Nigeria |
| 1991 | Nigeria |

## AFC ASIAN CUP

A competition for national teams of Asian countries, organized by AFC.

| | |
|---|---|
| 2007 | Iraq |
| 2004 | Japan |
| 2000 | Japan |
| 1996 | Saudi Arabia |
| 1992 | Japan |
| 1988 | Saudi Arabia |
| 1984 | Saudi Arabia |
| 1980 | Kuwait |
| 1976 | Iran |
| 1972 | Iran |
| 1968 | Iran |
| 1964 | Israel |
| 1960 | Republic of Korea |
| 1956 | Republic of Korea |

## AFC WOMEN'S ASIAN CUP

| | |
|---|---|
| 2008 | Korea DPR |
| 2006 | China |
| 2003 | Korea DPR |
| 2001 | Korea DPR |
| 1999 | China |
| 1997 | China |
| 1995 | China |
| 1993 | China |
| 1991 | China |
| 1989 | China |
| 1986 | China |
| 1983 | Thailand |
| 1981 | Chinese Taipei |
| 1979 | Chinese Taipei |
| 1977 | Chinese Taipei |
| 1975 | New Zealand |

## OFC NATIONS CUP (OCEANIA)

A competition for national teams of member countries of OFC.

| | |
|---|---|
| 2008 | New Zealand |
| 2004 | Australia |
| 2002 | New Zealand |
| 2000 | Australia |
| 1998 | New Zealand |
| 1996 | Australia |
| 1980 | Australia |
| 1973 | New Zealand |

## FIFA CONFEDERATIONS CUP

A competition for winners of the AFC Asian Cup, the CAF African Cup of Nations, the CONCACAF Gold Cup, the CONMEBOL Copa América, the OFC Nations Cup, the UEFA European Championships, and the World Cup champions and host country.

| | |
|---|---|
| 2009 | Brazil |
| 2005 | Brazil |
| 2003 | France |
| 2001 | France |
| 1999 | Mexico |
| 1997 | Brazil |
| 1995 | Denmark |
| 1992 | Argentina |

## OLYMPIC GAMES— MEN'S SOCCER

A soccer competition that is part of an international event made up of multiple sporting competitions.

| | |
|---|---|
| 2008 | Argentina |
| 2004 | Argentina |
| 2000 | Cameroon |
| 1996 | Nigeria |
| 1992 | Spain |
| 1988 | USSR |
| 1984 | France |
| 1980 | Czechoslovakia* |
| 1976 | East Germany** |
| 1972 | Poland |
| 1968 | Hungary |
| 1964 | Hungary |
| 1960 | Yugoslavia*** |
| 1956 | USSR**** |
| 1952 | Hungary |
| 1948 | Sweden |
| 1936 | Italy |
| 1928 | Uruguay |
| 1924 | Uruguay |
| 1920 | Belgium |
| 1912 | Great Britain |
| 1908 | Great Britain |
| 1904 | Canada |
| 1900 | Great Britain |

*, ***, **** See p. 37 for the current names of Czechoslovakia, Yugoslavia, and the USSR.
** See p. 45 for the current name of East Germany.

## OLYMPIC GAMES— WOMEN'S SOCCER

| | |
|---|---|
| 2008 | USA |
| 2004 | USA |
| 2000 | Norway |
| 1996 | USA |

## FIFA WORLD PLAYER OF THE YEAR*

| | |
|---|---|
| 2008 | Cristiano Ronaldo (Manchester United and Portugal) |
| 2007 | Kaká (AC Milan and Brazil) |
| 2006 | Fabio Cannavaro (Juventus, Real Madrid and Italy) |
| 2005 | Ronaldinho (Barcelona and Brazil) |
| 2004 | Ronaldinho (Barcelona and Brazil) |
| 2003 | Zinedine Zidane (Real Madrid and France) |
| 2002 | Ronaldo (Internazionale, Real Madrid and Brazil) |
| 2001 | Luís Figo (Real Madrid and Portugal) |
| 2000 | Zinedine Zidane (Juventus and France) |
| 1999 | Rivaldo (Barcelona and Brazil) |
| 1998 | Zinedine Zidane (Juventus and France) |
| 1997 | Ronaldo (Barcelona, Internazionale and Brazil) |
| 1996 | Ronaldo (PSV Eindhoven, Barcelona and Brazil) |
| 1995 | George Weah (AC Milan, Paris Saint-Germain, and Liberia) |
| 1994 | Romário (Barcelona and Brazil) |
| 1993 | Roberto Baggio (Juventus and Italy) |
| 1992 | Marco van Basten (AC Milan and Netherlands) |
| 1991 | Lothar Matthäus (Internazionale and Germany) |

*As voted by coaches and captains of international teams.

## EUROPEAN PLAYER OF THE YEAR*

| | |
|---|---|
| 2009 | Lionel Messi (Barcelona and Argentina) |
| 2008 | Cristiano Ronaldo (Manchester United and Portugal) |
| 2007 | Kaká (AC Milan and Brazil) |
| 2006 | Fabio Cannavaro (Real Madrid and Italy) |
| 2005 | Ronaldinho (Barcelona and Brazil) |
| 2004 | Andriy Shevchenko (AC Milan and Ukraine) |
| 2003 | Pavel Nedvěd (Juventus and Czech Republic) |
| 2002 | Ronaldo (Internazionale, Real Madrid and Brazil) |
| 2001 | Michael Owen (Liverpool and England) |
| 2000 | Luís Figo (Real Madrid and Portugal) |
| 1999 | Rivaldo (Barcelona and Brazil) |
| 1998 | Zinedine Zidane (Juventus and France) |
| 1997 | Ronaldo (Barcelona, Internazionale and Brazil) |
| 1996 | Matthias Sammer (Borussia Dortmund and Germany) |
| 1995 | George Weah (Paris Saint-Germain, AC Milan and Liberia) |
| 1994 | Hristo Stoichkov (Barcelona and Bulgaria) |
| 1993 | Roberto Baggio (Juventus and Italy) |
| 1992 | Marco van Basten (AC Milan and Netherlands) |
| 1991 | Jean-Pierre Papin (Marseille and France) |
| 1990 | Lothar Matthäus (Internazionale and West Germany) |
| 1989 | Marco van Basten (AC Milan and Netherlands) |
| 1988 | Marco van Basten (AC Milan and Netherlands) |
| 1987 | Ruud Gullit (PSV Eindhoven and Netherlands) |
| 1986 | Igor Belanov (Dinamo Kiev and USSR) |
| 1985 | Michel Platini (Juventus and France) |
| 1984 | Michel Platini (Juventus and France) |
| 1983 | Michel Platini (Juventus and France) |
| 1982 | Paolo Rossi (Juventus and Italy) |
| 1981 | Karl-Heinz Rummenigge (Bayern Munich and West Germany) |
| 1980 | Karl-Heinz Rummenigge (Bayern Munich and West Germany) |
| 1979 | Kevin Keegan (Hamburg and England) |
| 1978 | Kevin Keegan (Hamburg and England) |
| 1977 | Allan Simonsen (Borussia Mönchengladbach and Denmark) |
| 1976 | Franz Beckenbauer (Bayern Munich and West Germany) |
| 1975 | Oleg Blokhin (Dinamo Kiev and USSR) |
| 1974 | Johan Cruyff (Barcelona and Netherlands) |
| 1973 | Johan Cruyff (Ajax, Barcelona and Netherlands) |
| 1972 | Franz Beckenbauer (Bayern Munich and West Germany) |
| 1971 | Johan Cruyff (Ajax and Netherlands) |
| 1970 | Gerd Müller (Bayern Munich and West Germany) |
| 1969 | Gianni Rivera (AC Milan and Italy) |
| 1968 | George Best (Manchester United and Northern Ireland) |
| 1967 | Flórián Albert (Ferencváros and Hungary) |
| 1966 | Bobby Charlton (Manchester United and England) |
| 1965 | Eusébio (Benfica and Portugal) |
| 1964 | Denis Law (Manchester United and Scotland) |
| 1963 | Lev Yashin (Dinamo Moscow and USSR) |
| 1962 | Josef Masopust (Dukla Prague and Czechoslovakia) |
| 1961 | Omar Sívori (Juventus and Italy) |
| 1960 | Luis Suárez (Barcelona and Spain) |
| 1959 | Alfredo di Stéfano (Real Madrid and Spain) |
| 1958 | Raymond Kopa (Real Madrid and France) |
| 1957 | Alfredo di Stéfano (Real Madrid and Spain) |
| 1956 | Stanley Matthews (Blackpool and England) |

*As voted by France Football magazine.

## SOUTH AMERICAN FOOTBALLER OF THE YEAR*

**2008** Juan Sebastián Verón (Estudiantes and Argentina)
**2007** Salvador Cabañas (Club América and Paraguay)
**2006** Matías Fernández (Colo-Colo and Chile)
**2005** Carlos Tevéz (Corinthians and Argentina)
**2004** Carlos Tevéz (Boca Juniors and Argentina)
**2003** Carlos Tevéz (Boca Juniors and Argentina)
**2002** José Cardozo (Toluca and Paraguay)
**2001** Juan Román Riquelme (Boca Juniors and Argentina)
**2000** Romário (Vasco da Gama and Brazil)
**1999** Javier Saviola (River Plate and Argentina)
**1998** Martín Palermo (Boca Juniors and Argentina)
**1997** Marcelo Salas (River Plate and Chile)
**1996** José Luis Chilavert (Vélez Sársfield and Paraguay)
**1995** Enzo Francescoli (River Plate and Uruguay)
**1994** Cafú (São Paulo and Brazil)
**1993** Carlos Valderrama (Atlético Junior and Colombia)
**1992** Raí (São Paulo and Brazil)
**1991** Oscar Ruggeri (Vélez Sársfield and Argentina)
**1990** Raúl Vicente Amarilla (Olimpia and Paraguay)
**1989** Bebeto (Vasco da Gama and Brazil)
**1988** Rubén Paz (Racing Club and Uruguay)
**1987** Carlos Valderrama (Deportivo Cali and Colombia)
**1986** Antonio Alzamendi (River Plate and Uruguay)
**1985** Romerito (Fluminense and Paraguay)
**1984** Enzo Francescoli (River Plate and Uruguay)
**1983** Sócrates (Corinthians and Brazil)
**1982** Zico (Flamengo and Brazil)
**1981** Zico (Flamengo and Brazil)
**1980** Diego Maradona (Argentinos Juniors and Argentina)
**1979** Diego Maradona (Argentinos Juniors and Argentina)
**1978** Mario Kempes (Valencia and Argentina)
**1977** Zico (Flamengo and Brazil)
**1976** Elías Figueroa (Internacional and Chile)
**1975** Elías Figueroa (Internacional and Chile)
**1974** Elías Figueroa (Internacional and Chile)
**1973** Pelé (Santos and Brazil)
**1972** Teófilo Cubillas (Alianza Lima and Peru)
**1971** Tostão (Cruzeiro and Brazil)

*As voted by El Mundo magazine 1971–1986 and El País 1987–present.

## AFRICAN FOOTBALLER OF THE YEAR*

**2008** Emmanuel Adebayor (Arsenal and Togo)
**2007** Frédéric Kanouté (Sevilla and Mali)
**2006** Didier Drogba (Chelsea and Côte d'Ivoire)
**2005** Samuel Eto'o (Barcelona and Cameroon)
**2004** Samuel Eto'o (Real Mallorca, Barcelona and Cameroon)
**2003** Samuel Eto'o (Real Mallorca and Cameroon)
**2002** El Hadji Diouf (Lens, Liverpool and Senegal)
**2001** El Hadji Diouf (Lens and Senegal)
**2000** Patrick Mboma (Parma and Cameroon)
**1999** Nwankwo Kanu (Arsenal and Nigeria)
**1998** Mustapha Hadji (Deportivo La Coruña and Morocco)
**1997** Viktor Ikpeba (Monaco and Nigeria)
**1996** Nwankwo Kanu (Ajax, Internazionale and Nigeria)
**1995** George Weah (Milan and Liberia)
**1994** Emmanuel Amuneke (Zamalek, Sporting Lisbon and Nigeria)
**1993** Rashidi Yekini (Vitória Setubal and Nigeria)
**1992** Abédi 'Pelé' Ayew (Marseille and Ghana)
**1991** Abédi 'Pelé' Ayew (Marseille and Ghana)
**1990** Roger Milla (Cameroon)
**1989** George Weah (Monaco, Paris Saint-Germain and Liberia)
**1988** Kalusha Bwalya (Cercle Brugge and Zambia)
**1987** Rabah Madjer (Porto and Algeria)
**1986** Badou Zaki (Real Mallorca and Morocco)
**1985** Mohammed Timoumi (FAR Rabat and Morocco)
**1984** Théophile Abega (Toulouse and Cameroon)
**1983** Mahmoud El-Khatib (Al-Ahly and Egypt)
**1982** Thomas Nkono (Espanyol and Cameroon)
**1981** Lakhdar Belloumi (GCR Mascara and Algeria)
**1980** Jean Manga-Onguene (Canon Yaoundé and Cameroon)
**1979** Thomas Nkono (Canon Yaoundé and Cameroon)

**1978** Abdul Razak (Asante Kotoko and Ghana)
**1977** Tarak Dhiab (Espérance and Tunisia)
**1976** Roger Milla (Canon Yaoundé and Cameroon)
**1975** Ahmed Faras (SC Chabab Mohammedia and Morocco)
**1974** Paul Moukila (CARA Brazzaville and People's Republic of Congo)
**1973** Tshimen Bwanga (TP Mazembe and Zaire)
**1972** Cherif Souleymane (Hafia Conakry and Guinea)
**1971** Ibrahim Sunday (Asante Kotoko and Ghana)
**1970** Salif Keïta (Saint-Étienne and Mali)

*As voted by France Football magazine 1970–1992 and CAF 1992–present.

## ASIAN FOOTBALLER OF THE YEAR*

**2009** Yasuhito Endo (Japan and Gamba Osaka)
**2008** Server Djeparov (Bunyodkor and Uzbekistan)
**2007** Yasser Al-Qahtani (Al-Hilal and Saudi Arabia)
**2006** Khalfan Ibrahim (Al-Sadd and Qatar)
**2005** Hamad Al-Montashari (Al-Ittihad and Saudi Arabia)
**2004** Ali Karimi (Al-Ahli and Iran)
**2003** Mehdi Mahdavikia (Hamburg and Iran)
**2002** Shinji Ono (Feyenoord and Japan)
**2001** Fan Zhiyi (Dundee and China)
**2000** Nawaf Al-Temyat (Al-Hilal and Saudi Arabia)
**1999** Ali Daei (Hertha Berlin and Iran)
**1998** Hidetoshi Nakata (Perugia and Japan)
**1997** Hidetoshi Nakata (Bellmare Hiratsuka and Japan)
**1996** Khodadad Azizi (Bahman and Iran)
**1995** Masami Ihara (Yokohama Marinos and Japan)
**1994** Saeed Al-Owairan (Al-Shabab and Saudi Arabia)
**1993** Kazuyoshi Miura (Verdy Kawasaki and Japan)
**1992** Not awarded
**1991** Kim Joo-Sung (Daewoo Royals and Republic of Korea)
**1990** Kim Joo-Sung (Daewoo Royals and Republic of Korea)
**1989** Kim Joo-Sung (Daewoo Royals and Republic of Korea)
**1988** Ahmed Radhi (Al-Rasheed and Iraq)

*Awarded by AFC.

## OCEANIA FOOTBALLER OF THE YEAR*

**2008** Shane Smeltz (Wellington Phoenix and New Zealand)
**2007** Shane Smeltz (Wellington Phoenix and New Zealand)
**2006** Ryan Nelsen (Blackburn Rovers and New Zealand)
**2005** Marama Vahirua (OGC Nice and FC Nantes Atlantique)
**2004** Tim Cahill (Millwall, Everton and Australia)
**2003** Harry Kewell (Leeds United, Liverpool and Australia)
**2002** Brett Emerton (Feyenoord and Australia)
**2001** Harry Kewell (Leeds United and Australia)
**2000** Mark Viduka (Celtic, Leeds United and Australia)
**1999** Harry Kewell (Leeds United and Australia)
**1998** Christian Karembeu (Sampdoria, Real Madrid and France)
**1997** Mark Bosnich (Aston Villa and Australia)
**1996** Paul Okon (Club Brugge, Lazio and Australia)
**1995** Christian Karembeu (Nantes Atlantique, Sampdoria and France)
**1994** Aurelio Vidmar (KSV Waregem, Standard Liège and Australia)
**1993** Robbie Slater (Anderlecht, Lens and Australia)
**1992** Wynton Rufer (Werder Bremen and New Zealand)
**1991** Robbie Slater (Anderlecht, Lens and Australia)
**1990** Wynton Rufer (Werder Bremen and New Zealand)
**1989** Wynton Rufer (Grasshopper Zürich, Werder Bremen and New Zealand)
**1988** Frank Farina (Marconi Fairfield, Club Brugge and Australia)

*As voted by a forum of journalists.

## UEFA CHAMPIONS LEAGUE/EUROPEAN CUP

A competition for the most successful soccer clubs in Europe, organized by UEFA.

**2009** Barcelona (Spain)
**2008** Manchester United (England)
**2007** AC Milan (Italy)
**2006** Barcelona (Spain)
**2005** Liverpool (England)
**2004** Porto (Portugal)
**2003** AC Milan (Italy)
**2002** Real Madrid (Spain)
**2001** Bayern Munich (Germany)
**2000** Real Madrid (Spain)
**1999** Manchester United (England)

**1998** Real Madrid (Spain)
**1997** Borussia Dortmund (Germany)
**1996** Juventus (Italy)
**1995** Ajax (Netherlands)
**1994** AC Milan (Italy)
**1993** Marseille (France)
**1992** Barcelona (Spain)
**1991** Red Star Belgrade (Yugoslavia*)
**1990** AC Milan (Italy)
**1989** AC Milan (Italy)
**1988** PSV Eindhoven (Netherlands)
**1987** Porto (Portugal)
**1986** Steaua Bucharest (Romania)
**1985** Juventus (Italy)
**1984** Liverpool (England)
**1983** Hamburg (West Germany)
**1982** Aston Villa (England)
**1981** Liverpool (England)
**1980** Nottingham Forest (England)
**1979** Nottingham Forest (England)
**1978** Liverpool (England)
**1977** Liverpool (England)
**1976** Bayern Munich (West Germany)
**1975** Bayern Munich (West Germany)
**1974** Bayern Munich (West Germany)
**1973** Ajax (Netherlands)
**1972** Ajax (Netherlands)
**1971** Ajax (Netherlands)
**1970** Feyenoord (Netherlands)
**1969** AC Milan (Italy)
**1968** Manchester United (England)
**1967** Celtic (Scotland)
**1966** Real Madrid (Spain)
**1965** Internazionale (Italy)
**1964** Internazionale (Italy)
**1963** AC Milan (Italy)
**1962** Benfica (Portugal)
**1961** Benfica (Portugal)
**1960** Real Madrid (Spain)
**1959** Real Madrid (Spain)
**1958** Real Madrid (Spain)
**1957** Real Madrid (Spain)
**1956** Real Madrid (Spain)

*See p.37 for current name of Yugoslavia.

## UEFA WOMEN'S CHAMPIONS LEAGUE*

**2008-2009** FCR 2001 Duisburg
**2007-2008** 1. FFC Frankfurt
**2006-2007** Arsenal
**2005-2006** 1. FFC Frankfurt
**2004-2005** FFC Turbine Potsdam
**2003-2004** Umeå IK
**2002-2003** Umeå IK
**2001-2002** 1. FFC Frankfurt

*Formerly known as UEFA Women's Cup

## UEFA EUROPA LEAGUE*

A competition for European soccer clubs, organized by UEFA.

**2008–2009** Shakhtar Donetsk (Ukraine)

**2007–2008** Zenit St. Petersburg (Russia)
**2006–2007** Sevilla (Spain)
**2005–2006** Sevilla (Spain)
**2004–2005** CSKA Moscow (Russia)
**2003–2004** Valencia (Spain)
**2002–2003** Porto (Portugal)
**2001–2002** Feyenoord (Netherlands)
**2000–2001** Liverpool (England)
**1999–2000** Galatasaray (Turkey)
**1998–1999** Parma (Italy)
**1997–1998** Internazionale (Italy)
**1996–1997** Schalke (Germany)
**1995–1996** Bayern Munich (Germany)
**1994–1995** Parma (Italy)
**1993–1994** Internazionale (Italy)
**1992–1993** Juventus (Italy)
**1991–1992** Ajax (Netherlands)
**1990–1991** Internazionale (Italy)
**1989–1990** Juventus (Italy)
**1988–1989** Napoli (Italy)
**1987–1988** Bayer Leverkusen (West Germany)
**1986–1987** IFC Gothenburg (Sweden)
**1985–1986** Real Madrid (Spain)
**1984–1985** Real Madrid (Spain)
**1983–1984** Tottenham Hotspur (England)
**1982–1983** Anderlecht (Belgium)
**1981–1982** IFK Gothenburg (Sweden)
**1980–1981** Ipswich Town (England)
**1979–1980** Eintracht Frankfurt (West Germany)
**1978–1979** Borussia Mönchengladbach (West Germany)
**1977–1978** PSV Eindhoven (Netherlands)
**1976–1977** Juventus (Italy)
**1975–1976** Liverpool (England)
**1974–1975** Borussia Mönchengladbach (West Germany)
**1973–1974** Feyenoord (Netherlands)
**1972–1973** Liverpool (England)
**1971–1972** Tottenham Hotspur (England)
**1970–1971** Leeds United (England)
**1969–1970** Arsenal (England)
**1968–1969** Newcastle United (England)
**1967–1968** Leeds United (England)
**1966–1967** Dinamo Zagreb (Yugoslavia)
**1965–1966** Barcelona (Spain)
**1964–1965** Ferencváros (Hungary)
**1963–1964** Real Zaragoza (Spain)
**1962–1963** Valencia (Spain)
**1961–1962** Valencia (Spain)
**1960–1961** Roma (Italy)
**1958–1960** Barcelona (Spain)
**1955–1958** Barcelona (Spain)

*Before 1971 competition was known as the Inter-Cities Fairs Cup.
From 1971 to 2009 competition known as the UEFA Cup.

## EUROPEAN CUP WINNERS' CUP

A club competition for recent winners of European cup competitions, organized by UEFA.

**1998–1999** Lazio (Italy)
**1997–1998** Chelsea (England)
**1996–1997** Barcelona (Spain)
**1995–1996** Paris Saint-Germain (France)
**1994–1995** Real Zaragoza (Spain)
**1993–1994** Arsenal (England)
**1992–1993** Parma (Italy)
**1991–1992** Werder Bremen (Germany)
**1990–1991** Manchester United (England)
**1989–1990** Sampdoria (Italy)
**1988–1989** Barcelona (Spain)
**1987–1988** Mechelen (Belgium)
**1986–1987** Ajax (Netherlands)
**1985–1986** Dinamo Kiev (USSR)
**1984–1985** Everton (England)
**1983–1984** Juventus (Italy)
**1982–1983** Aberdeen (Scotland)
**1981–1982** Barcelona (Spain)
**1980–1981** Dinamo Tbilisi (USSR)
**1979–1980** Valencia (Spain)
**1978–1979** Barcelona (Spain)
**1977–1978** Anderlecht (Belgium)
**1976–1977** Hamburg (West Germany)
**1975–1976** Anderlecht (Belgium)
**1974–1975** Dinamo Kiev (USSR)
**1973–1974** 1. FC Magdeburg (East Germany)
**1971–1972** Rangers (Scotland)
**1970–1971** Chelsea (England)
**1969–1970** Manchester City (England)
**1968–1969** Slovan Bratislava (Czechoslovakia)
**1967–1968** AC Milan (Italy)
**1966–1967** Bayern Munich (West Germany)
**1965–1966** Borussia Dortmund (West Germany)
**1964–1965** West Ham United (England)
**1963–1964** Sporting Lisbon (Portugal)
**1962–1963** Tottenham Hotspur (England)
**1961–1962** Atlético Madrid (Spain)
**1960–1961** Fiorentina (Italy)

## EUROPEAN SUPER CUP

An annual soccer match played between the current champions of the UEFA Cup and the Champions League.

**2009** Barcelona
**2008** Zenit St. Petersburg (Russia)
**2007** AC Milan (Italy)
**2006** Sevilla (Spain)
**2005** Liverpool (England)
**2004** Valencia (Spain)
**2003** AC Milan (Italy)

**2002** Real Madrid (Spain)
**2001** Liverpool (England)
**2000** Galatasaray (Turkey)
**1999** Lazio (Italy)
**1998** Chelsea (England)
**1997** Barcelona (Spain)
**1996** Juventus (Italy)
**1995** Ajax (Netherlands)
**1994** AC Milan (Italy)
**1993** Parma (Italy)
**1992** Barcelona (Spain)
**1991** Manchester United (England)
**1990** AC Milan (Italy)
**1989** AC Milan (Italy)
**1988** Mechelen (Belgium)
**1987** Porto (Portugal)
**1986** Steaua Bucharest (Romania)
**1985** Not played
**1984** Juventus (Italy)
**1983** Aberdeen (Scotland)
**1982** Aston Villa (England)
**1981** Not played
**1980** Valencia (Spain)
**1979** Nottingham Forest (England)
**1978** Anderlecht (Belgium)
**1977** Liverpool (England)
**1976** Anderlecht (Belgium)
**1975** Dinamo Kiev (USSR)
**1974** Not played
**1973** Ajax (Netherlands)
**1972** Ajax (Netherlands)

## CONMEBOL COPA LIBERTADORES

A competition for the most successful soccer clubs in South America, organized by CONMEBOL.

**2009** Estudiantes (Argentina)
**2008** LDU Quito (Ecuador)
**2007** Boca Juniors (Argentina)
**2006** Internacional (Brazil)
**2005** São Paulo (Brazil)
**2004** Once Caldas (Colombia)
**2003** Boca Juniors (Argentina)
**2002** Olimpia (Paraguay)
**2001** Boca Juniors (Argentina)
**2000** Boca Juniors (Argentina)
**1999** Palmeiras (Brazil)
**1998** Vasco da Gama (Brazil)
**1997** Cruzeiro (Brazil)
**1996** River Plate (Argentina)
**1995** Grêmio (Brazil)
**1994** Vélez Sársfield (Argentina)
**1993** São Paulo (Brazil)
**1992** São Paulo (Brazil)
**1991** Colo-Colo (Chile)
**1990** Olimpia (Paraguay)
**1989** Atlético Nacional (Colombia)
**1988** Nacional (Uruguay)
**1987** Peñarol (Uruguay)
**1986** River Plate (Argentina)
**1985** Argentinos Juniors (Argentina)
**1984** Independiente (Argentina)
**1983** Grêmio (Brazil)
**1982** Peñarol (Uruguay)
**1981** Flamengo (Brazil)
**1980** Nacional (Uruguay)
**1979** Olimpia (Paraguay)

| 1978 | Boca Juniors (Argentina) |
|------|--------------------------|
| 1977 | Boca Juniors (Argentina) |
| 1976 | Cruzeiro (Brazil) |
| 1975 | Independiente (Argentina) |
| 1974 | Independiente (Argentina) |
| 1973 | Independiente (Argentina) |
| 1972 | Independiente (Argentina) |
| 1971 | Nacional (Uruguay) |
| 1970 | Estudiantes (Argentina) |
| 1969 | Estudiantes (Argentina) |
| 1968 | Estudiantes (Argentina) |
| 1967 | Racing Club (Argentina) |
| 1966 | Peñarol (Uruguay) |
| 1965 | Independiente (Argentina) |
| 1964 | Independiente (Argentina) |
| 1963 | Santos (Brazil) |
| 1962 | Santos (Brazil) |
| 1961 | Peñarol (Uruguay) |
| 1960 | Peñarol (Uruguay) |

## CONMEBOL COPA LIBERTADORES DE FUTBOL FEMININO

**2009** Brazil

## FIFA CLUB WORLD CUP

A competition between the winners of the 6 continental federations: UEFA, CONMEBOL, CONCACAF, CAF, AFC and OFC.

| 2008 | Manchester United (England) |
|------|-----------------------------|
| 2007 | AC Milan (Italy) |
| 2006 | Internacional (Brazil) |
| 2005 | São Paulo (Brazil) |
| 2001–2004 | Not played until merged with Intercontinental Cup in 2005 |
| 2000 | Corinthians (Brazil) |

## INTERCONTINENTAL CUP*

A competition between the winners of the UEFA Champions League and the Copa Libertadores.

| 2004 | Porto (Portugal) |
|------|------------------|
| 2003 | Boca Juniors (Argentina) |
| 2002 | Real Madrid (Spain) |
| 2001 | Bayern Munich (Germany) |
| 2000 | Boca Juniors (Argentina) |
| 1999 | Manchester United (England) |
| 1998 | Real Madrid (Spain) |
| 1997 | Borussia Dortmund (Germany) |
| 1996 | Juventus (Italy) |
| 1995 | Ajax (Netherlands) |
| 1994 | Vélez Sársfield (Argentina) |
| 1993 | São Paulo (Brazil) |
| 1992 | São Paulo (Brazil) |
| 1991 | Red Star Belgrade (Yugoslavia**) |
| 1990 | AC Milan (Italy) |
| 1989 | AC Milan (Italy) |
| 1988 | Nacional (Uruguay) |
| 1987 | Porto (Portugal) |
| 1986 | River Plate (Argentina) |


| 1985 | Juventus (Italy) |
|------|------------------|
| 1984 | Independiente (Argentina) |
| 1983 | Grêmio (Brazil) |
| 1982 | Peñarol (Uruguay) |
| 1981 | Flamengo (Brazil) |
| 1980 | Nacional (Uruguay) |
| 1979 | Olimpia (Paraguay) |
| 1978 | Not played |
| 1977 | Boca Juniors (Argentina) |
| 1976 | Bayern Munich (West Germany) |
| 1975 | Not played |
| 1974 | Atlético Madrid (Spain) |
| 1973 | Independiente (Argentina) |
| 1972 | Ajax (Netherlands) |
| 1971 | Nacional (Uruguay) |
| 1970 | Feyenoord (Netherlands) |
| 1969 | AC Milan (Italy) |
| 1968 | Estudiantes (Argentina) |
| 1967 | Racing Club (Argentina) |
| 1966 | Peñarol (Uruguay) |
| 1965 | Internazionale (Italy) |
| 1964 | Internazionale (Italy) |
| 1963 | Santos (Brazil) |
| 1962 | Santos (Brazil) |
| 1961 | Peñarol (Uruguay) |
| 1960 | Real Madrid (Spain) |

* Known as the World Club Championship until 2000. From 2005, competition replaced by FIFA Club World Cup.

** See p.37 for the current names of Yugoslavia.

## CONCACAF CHAMPIONS LEAGUE*

A competition for the most successful soccer clubs in North America, Central America, and the Caribbean, organized by CONCACAF.

| 2008–2009 | Atlante (Mexico) |
|-----------|------------------|
| 2008 | Pachuca (Mexico) |
| 2007 | Pachuca (Mexico) |
| 2006 | Club América (Mexico) |
| 2005 | Deportivo Saprissa (Costa Rica) |
| 2004 | Alajuelense (Costa Rica) |
| 2003 | Toluca (Mexico) |
| 2002 | Pachuca (Mexico) |
| 2001 | Not played |
| 2000 | Los Angeles Galaxy (USA) |
| 1999 | Necaxa (Mexico) |
| 1998 | DC United (USA) |
| 1997 | Cruz Azul (Mexico) |
| 1996 | Cruz Azul (Mexico) |
| 1995 | Deportivo Saprissa (Costa Rica) |
| 1994 | CS Cartaginés (Costa Rica) |
| 1993 | Deportivo Saprissa (Costa Rica) |
| 1992 | Club América (Mexico) |
| 1991 | Puebla (Mexico) |
| 1990 | Club América (Mexico) |
| 1989 | UNAM Pumas (Mexico) |
| 1988 | Olimpia (Honduras) |
| 1987 | Club América (Mexico) |
| 1986 | Alajuelense (Costa Rica) |
| 1985 | Defence Force (Trinidad and Tobago) |
| 1984 | Violette AC (Haiti) awarded the trophy after Guadalajara (Mexico) and New York Freedoms (USA) were disqualified |


| 1983 | Atlante (Mexico) |
|------|------------------|
| 1982 | UNAM Pumas (Mexico) |
| 1981 | Transvaal (Surinam) |
| 1980 | UNAM Pumas (Mexico) |
| 1979 | FAS (El Salvador) |
| 1978 | Universidad de Guadalajara (Mexico), CSD Comunicaciones (Guatemala) and Defence Force (Trinidad and Tobago) all declared joint winners |
| 1977 | Club América (Mexico) |
| 1976 | Aguila (El Salvador) |
| 1975 | Atlético Español (Mexico) |
| 1974 | CSD Municipal (Guatemala) won 4–2 on aggregate |
| 1973 | Transvaal (Surinam) awarded the trophy after Northern and Central region teams withdrew |
| 1972 | Olimpia (Honduras) |
| 1971 | Cruz Azul (Mexico) |
| 1970 | Cruz Azul (Mexico) awarded the trophy after Transvaal (Surinam) and Deportivo Saprissa (Costa Rica) withdrew |
| 1969 | Cruz Azul (Mexico) |
| 1968 | Toluca (Mexico) awarded a walkover win after Aurora (Guatemala) and Transvaal (Surinam) were suspended |
| 1967 | Alianza (El Salvador) |
| 1964–1966 | Not played |
| 1963 | Racing Club (Haiti) awarded the cup after Guadalajara withdrew |
| 1962 | Guadalajara (Mexico) |

*Known as the CONCACAF Champions' Cup until 2008.

## CAF AFRICAN CHAMPIONS LEAGUE*

A competition for the most successful soccer clubs in Africa, organized by CAF.

| 2008 | Al-Ahly (Egypt) |
|------|-----------------|
| 2007 | Étoile du Sahel (Tunisia) |
| 2006 | Al-Ahly (Egypt) |
| 2005 | Al-Ahly (Egypt) |
| 2004 | Enyimba (Nigeria) |
| 2003 | Enyimba (Nigeria) |
| 2002 | Zamalek (Egypt) |
| 2001 | Al-Ahly (Egypt) |
| 2000 | Hearts of Oak (Ghana) |
| 1999 | Raja Casablanca (Morocco) |
| 1998 | ASEC Abidjan (Côte d'Ivoire) |
| 1997 | Raja Casablanca (Morocco) |
| 1996 | Zamalek (Egypt) |
| 1995 | Orlando Pirates (South Africa) |
| 1994 | Espérance (Tunisia) |
| 1993 | Zamalek (Egypt) |
| 1992 | Wydad Casablanca (Morocco) |
| 1991 | Club Africain (Algeria) |
| 1990 | JS Kabylie (Algeria) |
| 1989 | Raja Casablanca (Morocco) |
| 1988 | ES Sétif (Algeria) |
| 1987 | Al-Ahly (Egypt) |
| 1986 | Zamalek (Egypt) |


| 1985 | FAR Rabat (Morocco) |
|------|---------------------|
| 1984 | Zamalek (Egypt) |
| 1983 | Asante Kotoko (Ghana) |
| 1982 | Al-Ahly (Egypt) |
| 1981 | JE Tizi-Ouzou (Algeria) |
| 1980 | Canon Yaoundé (Cameroon) |
| 1979 | Union Douala (Cameroon) |
| 1978 | Canon Yaoundé (Cameroon) |
| 1977 | Hafia Conakry (Ghana) |
| 1976 | MC Algiers (Algeria) |
| 1975 | Hafia Conakry (Ghana) |
| 1974 | CARA Brazzaville (Congo) |
| 1973 | AS Vita Club (Zaire) |
| 1972 | Hafia Conakry (Ghana) |
| 1971 | Canon Yaoundé (Cameroon) |
| 1970 | Asante Kotoko (Ghana) |
| 1969 | Ismaily (Egypt) |
| 1968 | TP Englebert (Zaire) |
| 1967 | Trophy awarded to TP Englebert (Zaire) after Asante Kotoko (Ghana) refused to take part in a play-off |
| 1966 | Stade Abidjan (Côte d'Ivoire) |
| 1965 | Not played |
| 1964 | Oryx Douala (Cameroon) |

*Known as the African Cup of Champions until 1997, and since then as the CAF Champions League.

## CAF AFRICAN CONFEDERATION CUP*

A competition for African Football clubs, organized by CAF.

| 2008 | CS SFaxien (Tunisia) |
|------|----------------------|
| 2007 | CS SFaxien (Tunisia) |
| 2006 | Étoile du Sahel (Tunisia) |
| 2005 | FAR Rabat (Morocco) |
| 2004 | Hearts of Oak (Ghana) |

*Competition was formed when the CAF Cup and the CAF African Cup Winners' Cup merged.

## CAF CUP

A competition for African clubs, organized by CAF.

| 2003 | Raja Casablanca (Morocco) |
|------|---------------------------|
| 2002 | JS Kabylie (Algeria) |
| 2001 | JS Kabylie (Algeria) |
| 2000 | JS Kabylie (Algeria) |
| 1999 | Étoile du Sahel (Tunisia) |
| 1998 | CS Sfaxien (Tunisia) |
| 1997 | Espérance (Tunisia) |
| 1996 | Kawkab Marrakech (Morocco) |
| 1995 | Étoile du Sahel (Tunisia) |
| 1994 | Bendel Insurance (Nigeria) |
| 1993 | Stella Club d' Adbjamé (Côte d'Ivoire) |
| 1992 | Shooting Stars (Nigeria) |

## CAF AFRICAN CUP WINNERS' CUP

A competition for African clubs who were winners of national competitions, organized by CAF.

| | |
|---|---|
| 2003 | Étoile du Sahel (Tunisia) |
| 2002 | Wydad Casablanca (Morocco) |
| 2001 | Kaizer Chiefs (South Africa) |
| 2000 | Zamalek (Egypt) |
| 1999 | Africa Sports (Côte d'Ivoire) |
| 1998 | Espérance (Tunisia) |
| 1997 | Étoile du Sahel (Tunisia) |
| 1996 | Al-Mokawloon al-Arab (Egypt) |
| 1995 | JS Kabylie (Algeria) |
| 1994 | DC Motemba Pemba (Zaire) |
| 1993 | Al-Ahly (Egypt) |
| 1992 | Africa Sports (Côte d'Ivoire) |
| 1991 | Power Dynamos (Zambia) |
| 1990 | BBC Lions (Nigeria) |
| 1989 | Al-Merreikh (Sudan) |
| 1988 | CA Bizertin (Algeria) |
| 1987 | Gor Mahia (Kenya) |
| 1986 | Al-Ahly (Egypt) |
| 1985 | Al-Ahly (Egypt) |
| 1984 | Al-Ahly (Egypt) |
| 1983 | Al-Mokawloon al-Arab (Egypt) |
| 1982 | Al-Mokawloon al-Arab (Egypt) |
| 1981 | Union Douala (Cameroon) |
| 1980 | TP Mazembe (Zaire) |
| 1979 | Canon Yaoundé (Cameroon) |
| 1978 | Horoya AC (Guinea) |
| 1977 | Enugu Rangers (Nigeria) |
| 1976 | Shooting Stars (Nigeria) |
| 1975 | Tonnerre Yaoundé (Cameroon) |

## CAF AFRICAN SUPER CUP

A competition match between the current champions of the CAF Confederation Cup and the CAF Champions League.

| | |
|---|---|
| 2009 | Al-Ahly (Egypt) |
| 2008 | Étoile du Sahel (Tunisia) |
| 2007 | Al-Ahly (Egypt) |
| 2006 | Al-Ahly (Egypt) |
| 2005 | Enyimba (Nigeria) |
| 2004 | Enyimba (Nigeria) |
| 2003 | Zamalek (Egypt) |
| 2002 | Al-Ahly (Egypt) |
| 2001 | Hearts of Oak (Ghana) |
| 2000 | Raja Casablanca (Morocco) |
| 1999 | ASEC Abidjan (Côte d'Ivoire) |
| 1998 | Étoile du Sahel (Tunisia) |
| 1997 | Zamalek (Egypt) |
| 1996 | Orlando Pirates (South Africa) |
| 1995 | Espérance (Tunisia) |
| 1994 | Zamalek (Egypt) |
| 1993 | Africa Sports (Côte d'Ivoire) |

## AFC ASIAN CHAMPIONS LEAGUE*

A competition between champions and cup winners of the top 14 Asian leagues.

| | |
|---|---|
| 2008–2009 | Gamba Osaka (Japan) |

| | |
|---|---|
| 2006–2007 | Urawa Red Diamonds (Japan) |
| 2005–2006 | Jeonbuk Hyundai Motors (Republic of Korea) |
| 2004–2005 | Al-Ittihad (Saudi Arabia) |
| 2003–2004 | Al-Ittihad (Saudi Arabia) |
| 2002–2003 | Al Ain (United Arab Emirates) |

*Competition formed when the Asian Cup Winners' Cup and the Asian Champions Cup merged.

## AFC ASIAN CUP WINNERS' CUP

A competition for Asian domestic cup winners, organized by AFC.

| | |
|---|---|
| 2001–2002 | Al-Hilal (Saudi Arabia) |
| 2000–2001 | Al-Shabab (Saudi Arabia) |
| 1999–2000 | Shimizu S-Pulse (Japan) |
| 1998–1999 | Al-Ittihad (Saudi Arabia) |
| 1997–1998 | Al-Nasr (Saudi Arabia) |
| 1996–1997 | Al-Hilal (Saudi Arabia) |
| 1995–1996 | Bellmare Hiratsuka (Japan) |
| 1994–1995 | Yokohama Flügels (Japan) |
| 1993–1994 | Al-Qadisiya (Saudi Arabia) |
| 1992–1993 | Yokohama Marinos (formerly Nissan) (Japan) |
| 1991–1992 | Nissan (Japan) |
| 1990–1991 | Persepolis (Iran) |

## AFC ASIAN CHAMPIONS CUP*

A competition for champions of Asian leagues.

| | |
|---|---|
| 2001–2002 | Suwon Samsung Bluewings (Republic of Korea) |
| 2000–2001 | Suwon Samsung Bluewings (Republic of Korea) |
| 1999–2000 | Al-Hilal (Saudi Arabia) |
| 1998–1999 | Júbilo Iwata (Japan) |
| 1997–1998 | Pohang Steelers (South Korea) |
| 1996–1997 | Pohang Steelers (Republic of Korea) |
| 1995–1996 | Ilhwa Chunma (South Korea) |
| 1994–1995 | Thai Farmers Bank (Thailand) |
| 1993–1994 | Thai Farmers Bank (Thailand) |
| 1991–1992 | Al-Hilal (Saudi Arabia) |
| 1990–1991 | Esteghlal (Iran) |
| 1989–1990 | Liaoning (China) |
| 1988–1989 | Al-Sadd (Qatar) |
| 1987–1988 | Yomiuri (Japan) awarded the trophy after Al-Hilal (Saudi Arabia) withdrew |
| 1986–1987 | Furukawa Electric (Japan) |
| 1985–1986 | Daewoo Royals (South Korea) |
| 1972–1984 | Not played |
| 1970–1971 | Maccabi Tel Aviv (Israel) awarded the trophy after |

| | |
|---|---|
| 1969–1970 | Al Shorta (Iraq) withdrew Taj (Iran) |
| 1968–1969 | Maccabi Tel Aviv (Israel) |
| 1966–1967 | Hapoel Tel Aviv (Israel) |

* 1967–1971 known as the Asian Club Championship; 1985–2002 known as the Asian Champions Cup. Not played 1967–1968 and 1972–1984.

## AFC ASIAN SUPER CUP

A competition between the winners of the Asian Champions Cup and the Asian Cup Winners' Cup. Came to an end after the Asian Champions League was formed.

| | |
|---|---|
| 2002 | Suwon Samsung Bluewings (Republic of Korea) |
| 2001 | Suwon Samsung Bluewings (Republic of Korea) |
| 2000 | Al-Hilal (Saudi Arabia) |
| 1999 | Júbilo Iwata (Japan) |
| 1998 | Al-Nasr (Saudi Arabia) |
| 1997 | Al-Hilal (Saudi Arabia) |
| 1996 | Ilhwa Chunma (Republic of Korea) |
| 1995 | Yokohama Flügels (Japan) |

## ARAB CHAMPIONS LEAGUE*

A competition for clubs in the Arab world.

| | |
|---|---|
| 2009 | Espérance (Tunisia) |
| 2008 | ES Sétif (Algeria) |
| 2007 | ES Sétif (Algeria) |
| 2006 | Raja Casablanca (Morocco) |
| 2005 | Al-Ittihad (Saudi Arabia) |
| 2004 | CS Sfaxien (Tunisia) |
| 2003 | Zamalek (Egypt) |
| 2002 | Al-Ahli (Saudi Arabia) |
| 2001 | Al-Sadd (Qatar) |
| 2000 | CS Sfaxien (Tunisia) |
| 1999 | Al-Shabab (Saudi Arabia) |
| 1998 | WA Tlemcen (Algeria) |
| 1997 | Club Africain (Algeria) |
| 1996 | Al-Ahly (Egypt) |
| 1995 | Al-Hilal (Saudi Arabia) |
| 1994 | Al-Hilal (Saudi Arabia) |
| 1993 | Espérance (Tunisia) |
| 1992 | Al-Shabab (Saudi Arabia) |
| 1991 | Not played |
| 1990 | Not played |
| 1989 | Wydad Casablanca (Morocco) |
| 1988 | Al-Ittifaq (Saudi Arabia) |
| 1987 | Al-Rasheed (Iraq) |
| 1986 | Al-Rasheed (Iraq) |
| 1985 | Al-Rasheed (Iraq) |
| 1984 | Al-Ittifaq (Saudi Arabia) |
| 1983 | Not played |
| 1982 | Al-Shorta (Iraq) |

* Known as the Arab Club Champions Cup until 2001, when it merged with the Arab Cup Winners' Cup.

New tournament known as the Prince Faysal bin Fahad Tournament for Arab Clubs until 2003.

## ARAB CUP WINNERS' CUP*

A competition between winners of national club competitions in Arab nations.

| | |
|---|---|
| 2001–2002 | Stade Tunisien (Tunisia) |
| 2000–2001 | Al-Hilal (Saudi Arabia) |
| 1999–2000 | Al Ittihad (Qatar) |
| 1998–1999 | MC Oran (Algeria) |
| 1997–1998 | MC Oran (Algeria) |
| 1996–1997 | OC Khouribga (Morocco) |
| 1995–1996 | Club Africain (Tunisia) |
| 1994–1995 | Al-Ahly (Egypt) |
| 1993–1994 | Olympique Casablanca (Morocco) |
| 1992–1993 | Olympique Casablanca (Morocco) |
| 1991–1992 | Olympique Casablanca (Morocco) |
| 1989–1990 | Stade Tunisien (Tunisia) |

* 1990–1991 not played.

## OCEANIA CHAMPIONS LEAGUE*

A competition for Oceanian soccer clubs, organized by OFC.

| | |
|---|---|
| 2009 | Auckland City (New Zealand) |
| 2008 | Waitakere United (New Zealand) |
| 2007 | Waitakere United (New Zealand) |
| 2006 | Auckland City (New Zealand) |
| 2004–2005 | Sydney (Australia) |
| 2001–2004 | Not played |
| 2000–2001 | Wollongong Wolves (Australia) |
| 1999 | South Melbourne (Australia) |
| 1987 | Adelaide City (Australia) |

*Known as Oceania Club Championship until 2007.

## UEFA WOMENS CUP

| | |
|---|---|
| 2007–2008 | 1. FFC Frankfurt (Germany) |
| 2006–2007 | Arsenal (England) |
| 2005–2006 | 1. FFC Frankfurt (Germany) |
| 2004–2005 | Turbine Potsdam (Germany) |
| 2003–2004 | Umeå IK (Sweden) |
| 2002–2003 | Umeå IK (Sweden) |
| 2001–2002 | 1. FFC Frankfurt (Germany) |

# DOMESTIC STATS

## ENGLAND: PREMIER LEAGUE*

| | |
|---|---|
| 2008–2009 | Manchester United |
| 2007–2008 | Manchester United |
| 2006–2007 | Manchester United |
| 2005–2006 | Chelsea |
| 2004–2005 | Chelsea |
| 2003–2004 | Arsenal |
| 2002–2003 | Manchester United |
| 2001–2002 | Arsenal |
| 2000–2001 | Manchester United |
| 1999–2000 | Manchester United |
| 1998–1999 | Manchester United |
| 1997–1998 | Arsenal |
| 1996–1997 | Manchester United |
| 1995–1996 | Manchester United |
| 1994–1995 | Blackburn Rovers |
| 1993–1994 | Manchester United |
| 1992–1993 | Manchester United |
| 1991–1992 | Leeds United |
| 1990–1991 | Arsenal |
| 1989–1990 | Liverpool |
| 1988–1989 | Arsenal |
| 1987–1988 | Liverpool |
| 1986–1987 | Everton |
| 1985–1986 | Liverpool |
| 1984–1985 | Everton |
| 1983–1984 | Liverpool |
| 1982–1983 | Liverpool |
| 1981–1982 | Liverpool |
| 1980–1981 | Aston Villa |
| 1979–1980 | Liverpool |
| 1978–1979 | Liverpool |
| 1977–1978 | Nottingham Forest |
| 1976–1977 | Liverpool |
| 1975–1976 | Liverpool |
| 1974–1975 | Derby County |
| 1973–1974 | Leeds United |
| 1972–1973 | Liverpool |
| 1971–1972 | Derby County |
| 1970–1971 | Arsenal |
| 1969–1970 | Everton |
| 1968–1969 | Leeds United |
| 1967–1968 | Manchester City |
| 1966–1967 | Manchester United |
| 1965–1966 | Liverpool |
| 1964–1965 | Manchester United |
| 1963–1964 | Liverpool |
| 1962–1963 | Everton |
| 1961–1962 | Ipswich Town |
| 1960–1961 | Tottenham Hotspur |
| 1959–1960 | Burnley |
| 1958–1959 | Wolverhampton Wanderers |
| 1957–1958 | Wolverhampton Wanderers |
| 1956–1957 | Manchester United |
| 1955–1956 | Manchester United |
| 1954–1955 | Chelsea |
| 1953–1954 | Wolverhampton Wanderers |
| 1952–1953 | Arsenal |
| 1951–1952 | Manchester United |
| 1950–1951 | Tottenham Hotspur |
| 1949–1950 | Portsmouth |
| 1948–1949 | Portsmouth |
| 1947–1948 | Arsenal |
| 1946–1947 | Liverpool |
| 1938–1939 | Everton |
| 1937–1938 | Arsenal |
| 1936–1937 | Manchester City |
| 1935–1936 | Sunderland |
| 1934–1935 | Arsenal |
| 1933–1934 | Arsenal |
| 1932–1933 | Arsenal |
| 1931–1932 | Everton |
| 1930–1931 | Arsenal |
| 1929–1930 | Sheffield Wednesday |
| 1928–1929 | Sheffield Wednesday |
| 1927–1928 | Everton |
| 1926–1927 | Newcastle United |
| 1925–1926 | Huddersfield Town |
| 1924–1925 | Huddersfield Town |
| 1923–1924 | Huddersfield Town |
| 1922–1923 | Liverpool |
| 1921–1922 | Liverpool |
| 1920–1921 | Burnley |
| 1919–1920 | West Bromwich Albion |
| 1914–1915 | Everton |
| 1913–1914 | Blackburn Rovers |
| 1912–1913 | Sunderland |
| 1911–1912 | Blackburn Rovers |
| 1910–1911 | Manchester United |
| 1909–1910 | Aston Villa |
| 1908–1909 | Newcastle United |
| 1907–1908 | Manchester United |
| 1906–1907 | Newcastle United |
| 1905–1906 | Liverpool |
| 1904–1905 | Newcastle United |
| 1903–1904 | Sheffield Wednesday |
| 1902–1903 | Sheffield Wednesday |
| 1901–1902 | Sunderland |
| 1900–1901 | Liverpool |
| 1899–1900 | Aston Villa |
| 1898–1899 | Aston Villa |
| 1897–1898 | Sheffield United |
| 1896–1897 | Aston Villa |
| 1895–1896 | Aston Villa |
| 1894–1895 | Sunderland |
| 1893–1894 | Aston Villa |
| 1892–1893 | Sunderland |
| 1891–1892 | Sunderland |
| 1890–1891 | Everton |
| 1889–1890 | Preston North End |
| 1888–1889 | Preston North End |

\* Known as First Division 1888–1992. Not played 1916–1919 due to World War I and 1940–1946 due to World War II.

## ENGLAND: FA CUP*

| | |
|---|---|
| 2008–2009 | Chelsea |
| 2007–2008 | Portsmouth |
| 2006–2007 | Chelsea |
| 2005–2006 | Liverpool |
| 2004–2005 | Arsenal |
| 2003–2004 | Manchester United |
| 2002–2003 | Arsenal |
| 2001–2002 | Arsenal |
| 2000–2001 | Liverpool |
| 1999–2000 | Chelsea |
| 1998–1999 | Manchester United |
| 1997–1998 | Arsenal |
| 1996–1997 | Chelsea |
| 1995–1996 | Manchester United |
| 1994–1995 | Everton |
| 1993–1994 | Manchester United |
| 1992–1993 | Arsenal |
| 1991–1992 | Liverpool |
| 1990–1991 | Tottenham Hotspur |
| 1989–1990 | Manchester United |
| 1988–1989 | Liverpool |
| 1987–1988 | Wimbledon |
| 1986–1987 | Coventry City |
| 1985–1986 | Liverpool |
| 1984–1985 | Manchester United |
| 1983–1984 | Everton |
| 1982–1983 | Manchester United |
| 1981–1982 | Tottenham Hotspur |
| 1980–1981 | Tottenham Hotspur |
| 1979–1980 | West Ham United |
| 1978–1979 | Arsenal |
| 1977–1978 | Ipswich Town |
| 1976–1977 | Manchester United |
| 1975–1976 | Southampton |
| 1974–1975 | West Ham United |
| 1973–1974 | Liverpool |
| 1972–1973 | Sunderland |
| 1971–1972 | Leeds United |
| 1970–1971 | Arsenal |
| 1969–1970 | Chelsea |
| 1969–1960 | Wanderers |
| 1968–1969 | Manchester City |
| 1967–1968 | West Bromwich Albion |
| 1966–1967 | Tottenham Hotspur |
| 1965–1966 | Everton |
| 1964–1965 | Liverpool |
| 1963–1964 | West Ham United |
| 1962–1963 | Manchester United |
| 1961–1962 | Tottenham Hotspur |
| 1960–1961 | Tottenham Hotspur |
| 1958–1959 | Nottingham Forest |
| 1957–1958 | Bolton Wanderers |
| 1956–1957 | Aston Villa |
| 1955–1956 | Manchester City |
| 1954–1955 | Newcastle United |
| 1953–1954 | West Bromwich Albion |
| 1952–1953 | Blackpool |
| 1951–1952 | Newcastle United |
| 1950–1951 | Newcastle United |
| 1949–1950 | Arsenal |
| 1948–1949 | Wolverhampton Wanderers |
| 1947–1948 | Manchester City |
| 1946–1947 | Charlton Athletic |
| 1945–1946 | Derby County |
| 1938–1939 | Portsmouth |
| 1937–1938 | Preston North End |
| 1936–1937 | Sunderland |
| 1935–1936 | Arsenal |
| 1934–1935 | Sheffield Wednesday |
| 1933–1934 | Manchester City |
| 1932–1933 | Everton |
| 1931–1932 | Newcastle United |
| 1930–1931 | West Bromwich Albion |
| 1929–1930 | Arsenal |
| 1928–1929 | Bolton Wanderers |
| 1927–1928 | Blackburn Rovers |
| 1926–1927 | Cardiff City |
| 1925–1926 | Bolton Wanderers |
| 1924–1925 | Sheffield United |
| 1923–1924 | Newcastle United |
| 1922–1923 | Bolton Wanderers |
| 1921–1922 | Huddersfield Town |
| 1920–1921 | Tottenham Hotspur |
| 1919–1920 | Aston Villa |
| 1914–1915 | Sheffield United |
| 1913–1914 | Burnley |
| 1912–1913 | Aston Villa |
| 1911–1912 | Barnsley |
| 1910–1911 | Bradford City |
| 1909–1910 | Newcastle United |
| 1908–1909 | Manchester United |
| 1907–1908 | Wolverhampton Wanderers |
| 1906–1907 | Sheffield Wednesday |
| 1905–1906 | Everton |
| 1904–1905 | Aston Villa |
| 1903–1904 | Manchester City |
| 1902–1903 | Bury |
| 1901–1902 | Sheffield United |
| 1900–1901 | Tottenham Hotspur |
| 1899–1900 | Bury |
| 1898–1899 | Sheffield United |
| 1897–1898 | Nottingham Forest |
| 1896–1897 | Aston Villa |
| 1895–1896 | Sheffield Wednesday |
| 1894–1895 | Aston Villa |
| 1893–1894 | Notts County |
| 1892–1893 | Wolverhampton Wanderers |
| 1891–1892 | West Bromwich Albion |
| 1890–1891 | Blackburn Rovers |
| 1889–1890 | Blackburn Rovers |
| 1888–1889 | Preston North End |
| 1887–1888 | West Bromwich Albion |
| 1886–1887 | Aston Villa |
| 1885–1886 | Blackburn Rovers |
| 1884–1885 | Blackburn Rovers |
| 1883–1884 | Blackburn Rovers |
| 1882–1883 | Blackburn Olympic |
| 1881–1882 | Old Etonians |
| 1880–1881 | Old Carthusians |
| 1879–1880 | Clapham Rovers |
| 1878–1879 | Old Etonians |
| 1877–1878 | Wanderers |
| 1876–1877 | Wanderers |
| 1875–1876 | Wanderers |
| 1874–1875 | Royal Engineers |
| 1873–1874 | Oxford University |
| 1872–1873 | Wanderers |
| 1871–1872 | Wanderers |

\* Not played 1915–1919 due to World War I and 1939–1945 due to World War II.

## ENGLAND: LEAGUE CUP

| | |
|---|---|
| 2008–2009 | Manchester United |
| 2007–2008 | Tottenham Hotspur |
| 2006–2007 | Chelsea |
| 2005–2006 | Manchester United |
| 2004–2005 | Chelsea |
| 2003–2004 | Middlesbrough |
| 2002–2003 | Liverpool |
| 2001–2002 | Blackburn Rovers |
| 2000–2001 | Liverpool |
| 1999–2000 | Leicester City |
| 1998–1999 | Tottenham Hotspur |
| 1997–1998 | Chelsea |
| 1996–1997 | Leicester City |
| 1995–1996 | Aston Villa |
| 1994–1995 | Liverpool |
| 1993–1994 | Aston Villa |
| 1992–1993 | Arsenal |
| 1991–1992 | Manchester United |
| 1990–1991 | Sheffield Wednesday |

| | |
|---|---|
| 1989–1990 | Nottingham Forest |
| 1988–1989 | Nottingham Forest |
| 1987–1988 | Luton Town |
| 1986–1987 | Arsenal |
| 1985–1986 | Oxford United |
| 1984–1985 | Norwich City |
| 1983–1984 | Liverpool |
| 1982–1983 | Liverpool |
| 1981–1982 | Liverpool |
| 1980–1981 | Liverpool |
| 1979–1980 | Wolverhampton Wanderers |
| 1978–1979 | Nottingham Forest |
| 1977–1978 | Nottingham Forest |
| 1976–1977 | Aston Villa |
| 1975–1976 | Manchester City |
| 1974–1975 | Aston Villa |
| 1973–1974 | Wolverhampton Wanderers |
| 1972–1973 | Tottenham Hotspur |
| 1971–1972 | Stoke City |
| 1970–1971 | Tottenham Hotspur |
| 1969–1970 | Manchester City |
| 1968–1969 | Swindon Town |
| 1967–1968 | Leeds United |
| 1966–1967 | Queens Park Rangers |
| 1965–1966 | West Bromwich Albion |
| 1964–1965 | Chelsea |
| 1963–1964 | Leicester City |
| 1962–1963 | Birmingham City |
| 1961–1962 | Norwich City |
| 1960–1961 | Aston Villa |

## ENGLAND: LEAGUE TOP SCORERS*

| | |
|---|---|
| 2008–2009 | Nicolas Anelka (Chelsea) 19 |
| 2007–2008 | Cristiano Ronaldo (Manchester United) 31 |
| 2006–2007 | Didier Drogba (Chelsea) 20 |
| 2005–2006 | Thierry Henry (Arsenal ) 27 |
| 2004–2005 | Thierry Henry (Arsenal) 25 |
| 2003–2004 | Thierry Henry (Arsenal) 30 |
| 2002–2003 | Ruud van Nistelrooy (Manchester United) 25 |
| 2001–2002 | Thierry Henry (Arsenal) 24 |
| 2000–2001 | Jimmy Floyd Hasselbaink (Chelsea) 23 |
| 1999–2000 | Kevin Philips (Sunderland) 30 |
| 1998–1999 | Jimmy Floyd Hasselbaink (Leeds United) 18 |
| | Michael Owen (Liverpool) 18 |
| | Dwight Yorke (Manchester United) 18 |
| 1997–1998 | Chris Sutton (Blackburn Rovers) 18 |
| | Dion Dublin (Coventry City) 18 |
| | Michael Owen (Liverpool) 18 |
| 1996–1997 | Alan Shearer (Newcastle United) 25 |
| 1995–1996 | Alan Shearer (Blackburn Rovers) 31 |

| | |
|---|---|
| 1994–1995 | Alan Shearer (Blackburn Rovers) 34 |
| 1993–1994 | Andy Cole (Newcastle United) 34 |
| 1992–1993 | Teddy Sheringham (Tottenham Hotspur) 22 |
| 1991–1992 | Ian Wright (Crystal Palace and Arsenal) 29 |
| 1990–1991 | Alan Smith (Arsenal) 22 |
| 1989–1990 | Gary Lineker (Tottenham Hotspur) 24 |
| 1988–1989 | Alan Smith (Arsenal) 23 |
| 1987–1988 | John Aldridge Liverpool) 26 |
| 1986–1987 | Clive Allen (Tottenham Hotspur) 33 |
| 1985–1986 | Gary Lineker (Everton) 30 |
| 1984–1985 | Kerry Dixon (Chelsea) 24 |
| | Gary Lineker (Leicester City) 24 |
| 1983–1984 | Ian Rush (Liverpool) 32 |
| 1982–1983 | Luther Blissett (Watford) 27 |
| 1981–1982 | Kevin Keegan (Southampton) 26 |
| 1980–1981 | Peter Withe (Aston Villa) 20 |
| | Steve Archibald (Tottenham Hotspur) 20 |
| 1979–1980 | Phil Boyer (Southampton) 23 |
| 1978–1979 | Frank Worthington (Bolton Wanderers) 24 |
| 1977–1978 | Bob Latchford (Everton) 30 |
| 1976–1977 | Malcolm Macdonald (Arsenal) 25 |
| | Andy Gray (Aston Villa) 25 |
| 1975–1976 | Ted MacDougall (Norwich City) 23 |
| 1974–1975 | Malcolm Macdonald (Newcastle United) 21 |
| 1973–1974 | Mick Channon (Southampton) 21 |
| 1972–1973 | Bryan "Pop" Robson (West Ham United) 28 |
| 1971–1972 | Francis Lee (Manchester City) 33 |
| 1970–1971 | Tony Brown (West Bromwich Albion) 28 |
| 1969–1970 | Jeff Astle (West Bromwich Albion) 25 |
| 1968–1969 | Jimmy Greaves (Tottenham Hotspur) 27 |
| 1967–1968 | George Best (Manchester United) 28 |
| | Ron Davies (Southampton) 28 |
| 1966–1967 | Ron Davies (Southampton) 37 |
| 1965–1966 | Willie Irvine (Burnley) 29 |
| 1964–1965 | Andy McEvoy (Blackburn Rovers) 29 |
| | Jimmy Greaves (Tottenham Hotspur) 29 |
| 1963–1964 | Jimmy Greaves (Tottenham Hotspur) 35 |
| 1962–1963 | Jimmy Greaves (Tottenham Hotspur) 37 |
| 1961–1962 | Ray Crawford (Ipswich Town) 33 |
| | Derek Kevan (West Bromwich Albion) 33 |

| | |
|---|---|
| 1960–1961 | Jimmy Greaves (Chelsea) 41 |
| 1959–1960 | Dennis Viollet (Manchester United) 32 |
| 1958–1959 | Jimmy Greaves (Chelsea) 33 |
| 1957–1958 | Bobby Smith (Tottenham Hotspur) 36 |
| 1956–1957 | John Charles (Leeds United) 38 |
| 1955–1956 | Nat Lofthouse (Bolton Wanderers) 33 |
| 1954–1955 | Ronnie Allen (West Bromwich Albion) 27 |
| 1953–1954 | Jimmy Glazzard (Huddersfield Town) 29 |
| 1952–1953 | Charlie Wayman (Preston North End) 24 |
| 1951–1952 | George Robledo (Newcastle United) 33 |
| 1950–1951 | Stan Mortensen (Blackpool) 30 |
| 1949–1950 | Dickie Davis (Sunderland) 25 |
| 1948–1949 | Willie Moir (Bolton Wanderers) 25 |
| 1947–1948 | Ronnie Rooke (Arsenal) 33 |
| 1946–1947 | Dennis Westcott (Wolverhampton Wanderers) 37 |
| 1938–1939 | Tommy Lawton (Everton) 35 |
| 1937–1938 | Tommy Lawton (Everton) 28 |
| 1936–1937 | Freddie Steel (Stoke City) 33 |
| 1935–1936 | Pat Glover (Grimsby Town) 31 |
| | Raich Carter (Sunderland) 31 |
| | Bobby Gurney (Sunderland) 31 |
| 1934–1935 | Ted Drake (Arsenal) 42 |
| 1933–1934 | Jack Bowers (Derby County) 34 |
| 1932–1933 | Jack Bowers (Derby County) 35 |
| 1931–1932 | Dixie Dean (Everton) 44 |
| 1930–1931 | Tom "Pongo" Waring (Aston Villa) 49 |
| 1929–1930 | Vic Watson (West Ham United) 41 |
| 1928–1929 | Dave Halliday (Sunderland) 43 |
| 1927–1928 | Dixie Dean (Everton) 60 |
| 1926–1927 | Jimmy Trotter (Sheffield Wednesday) 37 |
| 1925–1926 | Ted Harper (Blackburn Rovers) 43 |
| 1924–1925 | Frank Roberts (Manchester City) 31 |
| 1923–1924 | Wilf Chadwick (Everton) 28 |
| 1922–1923 | Charlie Buchan (Sunderland) 30 |
| 1921–1922 | Andy Wilson (Middlesbrough) 31 |
| 1920–1921 | Joe Smith (Bolton Wanderers) 38 |
| 1919–1920 | Fred Morris (West Bromwich Albion) 37 |
| 1914–1915 | Bobby Parker (Everton) 35 |

| | |
|---|---|
| 1913–1914 | George Elliot (Middlesbrough) 32 |
| 1912–1913 | David McLean (Sheffield Wednesday) 30 |
| 1911–1912 | Harry Hampton (Aston Villa) 25 |
| | George Holley (Sunderland) 25 |
| | David McLean (Sheffield Wednesday) 25 |
| 1910–1911 | Albert Shepherd (Newcastle United) 25 |
| 1909–1910 | Jack Parkinson (Liverpool) 30 |
| 1908–1909 | Bert Freeman (Everton) 38 |
| 1907–1908 | Enoch West (Nottingham Forest) 27 |
| 1906–1907 | Alf Young (Everton) 30 |
| 1905–1906 | Albert Shepherd (Bolton Wanderers) 26 |
| 1904–1905 | Arthur Brown (Sheffield United) 22 |
| 1903–1904 | Steve Bloomer (Derby County) 20 |
| 1902–1903 | Sam Raybould (Liverpool) 31 |
| 1901–1902 | Jimmy Settle (Everton) 18 |
| 1900–1901 | Steve Bloomer (Derby County) 23 |
| 1899–1900 | Billy Garraty (Aston Villa) 27 |
| 1898–1899 | Steve Bloomer (Derby County) 23 |
| 1897–1898 | Fred Wheldon (Aston Villa) 21 |
| 1896–1897 | Steve Bloomer (Derby County) 22 |
| 1895–1896 | Johnny Campbell (Aston Villa) 20 |
| | Steve Bloomer (Derby County) 20 |
| 1894–1895 | Johnny Campbell (Sunderland) 22 |
| 1893–1894 | Jack Southworth (Everton) 27 |
| 1892–1893 | Johnny Campbell (Sunderland) 31 |
| 1891–1892 | Johnny Campbell (Sunderland) 32 |
| 1890–1891 | Jack Southworth (Blackburn Rovers) 26 |
| 1889–1890 | Jimmy Ross (Preston North End) 24 |
| 1888–1889 | John Goodall (Preston North End) 21 |

\* Not played 1916–1919 due to World War I and 1940–1946 due to World War II.

# DOMESTIC STATS

**SCOTLAND: LEAGUE CHAMPIONS* ***

| | |
|---|---|
| 2008–2009 | Rangers |
| 2007–2008 | Celtic |
| 2006–2007 | Celtic |
| 2005–2006 | Celtic |
| 2004–2005 | Rangers |
| 2003–2004 | Celtic |
| 2002–2003 | Rangers |
| 2001–2002 | Celtic |
| 2000–2001 | Celtic |
| 1999–2000 | Rangers |
| 1998–1999 | Rangers |
| 1997–1998 | Celtic |
| 1996–1997 | Rangers |
| 1995–1996 | Rangers |
| 1994–1995 | Rangers |
| 1993–1994 | Rangers |
| 1992–1993 | Rangers |
| 1991–1992 | Rangers |
| 1990–1991 | Rangers |
| 1989–1990 | Rangers |
| 1988–1989 | Rangers |
| 1987–1988 | Celtic |
| 1986–1987 | Rangers |
| 1985–1986 | Celtic |
| 1984–1985 | Aberdeen |
| 1983–1984 | Aberdeen |
| 1982–1983 | Dundee United |
| 1981–1982 | Celtic |
| 1980–1981 | Celtic |
| 1979–1980 | Aberdeen |
| 1978–1979 | Celtic |
| 1977–1978 | Rangers |
| 1976–1977 | Celtic |
| 1975–1976 | Rangers |
| 1974–1975 | Rangers |
| 1973–1974 | Celtic |
| 1972–1973 | Celtic |
| 1971–1972 | Celtic |
| 1970–1971 | Celtic |
| 1969–1970 | Celtic |
| 1968–1969 | Celtic |
| 1967–1968 | Celtic |
| 1966–1967 | Celtic |
| 1965–1966 | Celtic |
| 1964–1965 | Kilmarnock |
| 1963–1964 | Rangers |
| 1962–1963 | Rangers |
| 1961–1962 | Dundee |
| 1960–1961 | Rangers |
| 1959–1960 | Heart of Midlothian |
| 1958–1959 | Rangers |
| 1957–1958 | Heart of Midlothian |
| 1956–1957 | Rangers |
| 1955–1956 | Rangers |
| 1954–1955 | Aberdeen |
| 1953–1954 | Celtic |
| 1952–1953 | Rangers |
| 1951–1952 | Hibernian |
| 1950–1951 | Hibernian |
| 1949–1950 | Rangers |
| 1948–1949 | Rangers |
| 1947–1948 | Hibernian |
| 1946–1947 | Rangers |
| 1938–1939 | Rangers |
| 1937–1938 | Celtic |
| 1936–1937 | Rangers |
| 1935–1936 | Celtic |
| 1934–1935 | Rangers |
| 1933–1934 | Rangers |
| 1932–1933 | Rangers |
| 1931–1932 | Motherwell |
| 1930–1931 | Rangers |
| 1929–1930 | Rangers |
| 1928–1929 | Rangers |
| 1927–1928 | Rangers |
| 1926–1927 | Rangers |
| 1925–1926 | Celtic |
| 1924–1925 | Rangers |
| 1923–1924 | Rangers |
| 1922–1923 | Rangers |
| 1921–1922 | Celtic |
| 1920–1921 | Rangers |
| 1919–1920 | Rangers |
| 1918–1919 | Celtic |
| 1917–1918 | Rangers |
| 1916–1917 | Celtic |
| 1915–1916 | Celtic |
| 1914–1915 | Celtic |
| 1913–1914 | Celtic |
| 1912–1913 | Rangers |
| 1911–1912 | Rangers |
| 1910–1911 | Rangers |
| 1909–1910 | Celtic |
| 1908–1909 | Celtic |
| 1907–1908 | Celtic |
| 1906–1907 | Celtic |
| 1905–1906 | Celtic |
| 1904–1905 | Celtic |
| 1903–1904 | Third Lanark |
| 1902–1903 | Hibernian |
| 1901–1902 | Rangers |
| 1900–1901 | Rangers |
| 1899–1900 | Rangers |
| 1898–1899 | Rangers |
| 1897–1898 | Celtic |
| 1896–1897 | Heart of Midlothian |
| 1895–1896 | Celtic |
| 1894–1895 | Heart of Midlothian |
| 1893–1894 | Celtic |
| 1892–1893 | Celtic |
| 1891–1892 | Dumbarton |
| 1890–1891 | Dumbarton/Rangers (shared title) |

\* Top league known as the First Division until 1975.
\*\* Not played 1940–1946 due to World War II.

**SCOTLAND: FA CUP***

| | |
|---|---|
| 2008–2009 | Rangers |
| 2007–2008 | Rangers |
| 2006–2007 | Celtic |
| 2005–2006 | Heart of Midlothian |
| 2004–2005 | Celtic |
| 2003–2004 | Celtic |
| 2002–2003 | Rangers |
| 2001–2002 | Rangers |
| 2000–2001 | Celtic |
| 1999–2000 | Rangers |
| 1998–1999 | Rangers |
| 1997–1998 | Heart of Midlothian |
| 1996–1997 | Kilmarnock |
| 1995–1996 | Rangers |
| 1994–1995 | Celtic |
| 1993–1994 | Dundee United |
| 1992–1993 | Rangers |
| 1991–1992 | Rangers |
| 1990–1991 | Motherwell |
| 1989–1990 | Aberdeen |
| 1988–1989 | Celtic |
| 1987–1988 | Celtic |
| 1986–1987 | St Mirren |
| 1985–1986 | Aberdeen |
| 1984–1985 | Celtic |
| 1983–1984 | Aberdeen |
| 1982–1983 | Aberdeen |
| 1981–1982 | Aberdeen |
| 1980–1981 | Rangers |
| 1979–1980 | Celtic |
| 1978–1979 | Rangers |
| 1977–1978 | Rangers |
| 1976–1977 | Celtic |
| 1975–1976 | Rangers |
| 1974–1975 | Celtic |
| 1973–1974 | Celtic |
| 1972–1973 | Rangers |
| 1971–1972 | Celtic |
| 1970–1971 | Celtic |
| 1969–1970 | Aberdeen |
| 1968–1969 | Celtic |
| 1967–1968 | Dunfermline Athletic |
| 1966–1967 | Celtic |
| 1965–1966 | Rangers |
| 1964–1965 | Celtic |
| 1963–1964 | Rangers |
| 1962–1963 | Rangers |
| 1961–1962 | Rangers |
| 1960–1961 | Dunfermline Athletic |
| 1959–1960 | Rangers |
| 1958–1959 | St Mirren |
| 1957–1958 | Clyde |
| 1956–1957 | Falkirk |
| 1955–1956 | Heart of Midlothian |
| 1954–1955 | Clyde |
| 1953–1954 | Celtic |
| 1952–1953 | Rangers |
| 1951–1952 | Motherwell |
| 1950–1951 | Celtic |
| 1949–1950 | Rangers |
| 1948–1949 | Rangers |
| 1947–1948 | Rangers |
| 1946–1947 | Aberdeen |
| 1938–1939 | Clyde |
| 1937–1938 | East Fife |
| 1936–1937 | Celtic |
| 1935–1936 | Rangers |
| 1934–1935 | Rangers |
| 1933–1934 | Rangers |
| 1932–1933 | Celtic |
| 1931–1932 | Rangers |
| 1930–1931 | Celtic |
| 1929–1930 | Rangers |
| 1928–1929 | Kilmarnock |
| 1927–1928 | Rangers |
| 1926–1927 | Celtic |
| 1925–1926 | St Mirren |
| 1924–1925 | St Mirren |
| 1923–1924 | Airdrieonians |
| 1922–1923 | Celtic |
| 1921–1922 | Morton |
| 1920–1921 | Partick Thistle |
| 1919–1920 | Kilmarnock |
| 1913–1914 | Celtic |
| 1912–1913 | Falkirk |
| 1911–1912 | Celtic |
| 1910–1911 | Celtic |
| 1909–1910 | Dundee |
| 1908–1909 | Trophy withheld after a riot during Celtic vs Rangers |
| 1907–1908 | Celtic |
| 1906–1907 | Celtic |
| 1905–1906 | Heart of Midlothian |
| 1904–1905 | Third Lanark |
| 1903–1904 | Celtic |
| 1902–1903 | Rangers |
| 1901–1902 | Hibernian |
| 1900–1901 | Heart of Midlothian |
| 1899–1900 | Celtic |
| 1898–1899 | Celtic |
| 1897–1898 | Rangers |
| 1896–1897 | Rangers |
| 1895–1896 | Heart of Midlothian |
| 1894–1895 | St Bernard's |
| 1893–1894 | Rangers |
| 1892–1893 | Queen's Park |
| 1891–1892 | Celtic |
| 1890–1891 | Heart of Midlothian |
| 1889–1890 | Queen's Park |
| 1888–1889 | Third Lanark |
| 1887–1888 | Renton |
| 1886–1887 | Hibernian |
| 1885–1886 | Queen's Park |
| 1884–1885 | Renton |
| 1883–1884 | Queen's Park |
| 1882–1883 | Dumbarton |
| 1881–1882 | Queen's Park |
| 1880–1881 | Queen's Park |
| 1879–1880 | Queen's Park |
| 1878–1879 | Vale of Leven |
| 1877–1878 | Vale of Leven |
| 1876–1877 | Vale of Leven |
| 1875–1876 | Queen's Park |
| 1874–1875 | Queen's Park |
| 1873–1874 | Queen's Park |

\* Not played 1914–1919 due to World War I and 1939–1946 due to World War II.

**SCOTTISH LEAGUE CUP***

| | |
|---|---|
| 2008–2009 | Celtic |
| 2007–2008 | Rangers |
| 2006–2007 | Hibernian |
| 2005–2006 | Celtic |
| 2004–2005 | Rangers |
| 2003–2004 | Livingston |
| 2002–2003 | Rangers |
| 2001–2002 | Rangers |
| 2000–2001 | Celtic |
| 1999–2000 | Celtic |
| 1998–1999 | Rangers |
| 1997–1998 | Celtic |
| 1996–1997 | Rangers |
| 1995–1996 | Aberdeen |
| 1994–1995 | Raith Rovers |
| 1993–1994 | Rangers |
| 1992–1993 | Rangers |
| 1991–1992 | Hibernian |
| 1990–1991 | Rangers |
| 1989–1990 | Aberdeen |
| 1988–1989 | Rangers |
| 1987–1988 | Rangers |
| 1986–1987 | Rangers |
| 1985–1986 | Aberdeen |

| | |
|---|---|
| 1984–1985 | Rangers |
| 1983–1984 | Rangers |
| 1982–1983 | Celtic |
| 1981–1982 | Rangers |
| 1980–1981 | Dundee United |
| 1979–1980 | Dundee United |
| 1978–1979 | Rangers |
| 1977–1978 | Rangers |
| 1976–1977 | Aberdeen |
| 1975–1976 | Rangers |
| 1974–1975 | Celtic |
| 1973–1974 | Dundee |
| 1972–1973 | Hibernian |
| 1971–1972 | Partick Thistle |
| 1970–1971 | Rangers |
| 1969–1970 | Celtic |
| 1968–1969 | Celtic |
| 1967–1968 | Celtic |
| 1966–1967 | Celtic |
| 1965–1966 | Celtic |
| 1964–1965 | Rangers |
| 1963–1964 | Rangers |
| 1962–1963 | Heart of Midlothian |
| 1961–1962 | Rangers |
| 1960–1961 | Rangers |
| 1959–1960 | Heart of Midlothian |
| 1958–1959 | Heart of Midlothan |
| 1957–1958 | Celtic |
| 1956–1957 | Celtic |
| 1955–1956 | Aberdeen |
| 1954–1955 | Heart of Midlothian |
| 1953–1954 | East Fife |
| 1952–1953 | Dundee |
| 1951–1952 | Dundee |
| 1950–1951 | Motherwell |
| 1949–1950 | East Fife |
| 1948–1949 | Rangers |
| 1947–1948 | East Fife |
| 1946–1947 | Rangers |

## SCOTLAND: LEAGUE TOP SCORERS

| | |
|---|---|
| 2008–2009 | Kris Boyd (Rangers) 27 |
| 2007–2008 | Scott McDonald (Celtic) 25 |
| 2006–2007 | Kris Boyd (Rangers) 19 |
| 2005–2006 | Kris Boyd (Rangers) 32 |
| 2004–2005 | John Hartson (Celtic) 25 |
| 2003–2004 | Henrik Larsson (Celtic) 30 |
| 2002–2003 | Henrik Larsson (Celtic) 28 |
| 2001–2002 | Henrik Larsson (Celtic) 29 |
| 2000–2001 | Henrik Larsson (Celtic) 35 |
| 1999–2000 | Mark Viduka (Celtic) 25 |
| 1998–1999 | Henrik Larsson (Celtic) 29 |
| 1997–1998 | Marco Negri (Rangers) 32 |
| 1996–1997 | Jorge Cadete (Celtic) 25 |
| 1995–1996 | Pierre van Hooijdonk (Celtic) 26 |
| 1994–1995 | Tommy Coyne (Motherwell) 16 |
| 1993–1994 | Mark Hateley (Rangers) 22 |
| 1992–1993 | Ally McCoist (Rangers) 34 |
| 1991–1992 | Ally McCoist (Rangers) 34 |
| 1990–1991 | Tommy Coyne (Celtic) 18 |
| 1989–1990 | John Robertson (Heart of Midlothian) 17 |
| 1988–1989 | Mark McGhee (Celtic)16 Charlie Nicholas (Aberdeen) 16 |
| 1987–1988 | Tommy Coyne (Dundee) 33 |
| 1986–1987 | Brian McClair (Celtic) 35 |
| 1985–1986 | Ally McCoist (Rangers) 24 |

| | |
|---|---|
| 1984–1985 | Frank McDougall (Aberdeen) 22 |
| 1983–1984 | Brian McClair (Celtic) 23 |
| 1982–1983 | Charlie Nicholas (Celtic) 29 |
| 1981–1982 | George McCluskey (Celtic) 21 |
| 1980–1981 | Frank McGarvey (Celtic) 23 |
| 1979–1980 | Douglas Somner (St Mirren) 25 |
| 1978–1979 | Andy Ritchie (Morton) 22 |
| 1977–1978 | Derek Johnstone (Rangers) 25 |
| 1976–1977 | Willie Pettigrew (Motherwell) 21 |
| 1975–1976 | Kenny Dalglish (Celtic) 24 |
| 1974–1975 | Andy Gray (Motherwell) 20 Willie Pettigrew (Motherwell) 20 |
| 1973–1974 | John "Dixie" Deans (Celtic) 26 |
| 1972–1973 | Alan Gordon (Hibernian) 27 |
| 1971–1972 | Joe Harper (Aberdeen) 33 |
| 1970–1971 | Harry Hood (Celtic) 22 |
| 1969–1970 | Colin Stein (Rangers) 24 |
| 1968–1969 | Kenny Cameron (Dundee United) 26 |
| 1967–1968 | Bobby Lennox (Celtic) 32 |
| 1966–1967 | Stevie Chalmers (Celtic) 21 |
| 1965–1966 | Joe McBride (Celtic) 31 Alex Ferguson (Dunfermline) 31 |
| 1964–1965 | Jim Forrest (Rangers) 30 |
| 1963–1964 | Alan Gilzean (Dundee) 32 |
| 1962–1963 | Jimmy Millar (Rangers) 27 |
| 1961–1962 | Alan Gilzean (Dundee) 24 |
| 1960–1961 | Alex Harley (Third Lanark) 42 |
| 1959–1960 | Joe Baker (Hibernian) 42 |
| 1958–1959 | Joe Baker (Hibernian) 25 |
| 1957–1958 | Jimmy Wardhaugh (Heart of Midlothian) 28 Jimmy Murray (Heart of Midlothian) 28 |
| 1956–1957 | Hugh Baird (Airdrieonians) 33 |
| 1955–1956 | Jimmy Wardhaugh (Heart of Midlothian) 28 |
| 1954–1955 | Willie Bauld (Heart of Midlothian) 21 |
| 1953–1954 | Jimmy Wardhaugh (Heart of Midlothian) 27 |
| 1952–1953 | Lawrie Reilly (Hibernian) 30 Charles Fleming (East Fife) 30 |
| 1951–1952 | Lawrie Reilly (Hibernian) 27 |
| 1950–1951 | Lawrie Reilly (Hibernian) 22 |
| 1949–1950 | Willie Bauld (Hearts) 30 |
| 1948–1949 | Alexander Stott (Dundee) 30 |
| 1947–1948 | Archie Aikman (Falkirk) 20 |
| 1946–1947 | Bobby Mitchell (Third Lanark) 22 |
| 1938–1939 | Alex Venters (Rangers) 35 |
| 1937–1938 | Andy Black (Heart of Midlothian) 40 |
| 1936–1937 | David Wilson (Hamilton Academical) 34 |
| 1935–1936 | Jimmy McGrory (Celtic) 50 |
| 1934–1935 | Dave McCulloch (Heart of Midlothian) 38 |
| 1933–1934 | Jimmy Smith (Rangers) 41 |
| 1932–1933 | Willie McFadden |

| | |
|---|---|
| | (Motherwell) 45 |
| 1931–1932 | Willie McFadden (Motherwell) 52 |
| 1930–1931 | Barney Battles (Heart of Midlothian) 44 |
| 1929–1930 | Benny Yorston (Aberdeen) 38 |
| 1928–1929 | Evelyn Morrison (Falkirk) 43 |
| 1927–1928 | Jimmy McGrory (Celtic) 47 |
| 1926–1927 | Jimmy McGrory (Celtic) 49 |
| 1925–1926 | Willie Devlin (Cowdenbeath) 40 |
| 1924–1925 | Willie Devlin (Cowdenbeath) 33 |
| 1923–1924 | David Halliday (Dundee) 38 |
| 1922–1923 | John White (Heart of Midlothian) 30 |
| 1921–1922 | Duncan Walker (St Mirren) 45 |
| 1920–1921 | Hugh Ferguson (Motherwell) 43 |
| 1919–1920 | Hugh Ferguson (Motherwell) 33 |
| 1918–1919 | David McLean (Rangers) 29 |
| 1917–1918 | Hugh Ferguson (Motherwell) 35 |
| 1916–1917 | Bert Yarnall (Airdrieonians) 39 |
| 1915–1916 | James McColl (Celtic) 34 |
| 1914–1915 | Tom Gracie (Heart of Midlothian) 29 James Richardson (Ayr) 29 |
| 1913–1914 | James Reid (Airdrieonians) 27 |
| 1912–1913 | James Reid (Airdrieonians) 30 |
| 1911–1912 | Willie Reid (Rangers) 33 |
| 1910–1911 | Willie Reid (Rangers) 38 |
| 1909–1910 | Jimmy Quinn (Celtic) 24 John Simpson (Falkirk) 24 |
| 1908–1909 | John Hunter (Dundee) 29 |
| 1907–1908 | John Simpson (Falkirk) 32 |
| 1906–1907 | Jimmy Quinn (Celtic) 29 |
| 1905–1906 | Jimmy Quinn (Celtic) 20 |
| 1904–1905 | Robert C Hamilton (Rangers) 19 Jimmy Quinn (Celtic) 19 |
| 1903–1904 | Robert C Hamilton (Rangers) 28 |
| 1902–1903 | David Reid (Hibernian) 14 |
| 1901–1902 | William Maxwell (Third Lanark) 10 |
| 1900–1901 | Robert C Hamilton (Rangers) 20 |
| 1899–1900 | Robert C Hamilton (Rangers) 15 William Michael (Heart of Midlothian) 15 |
| 1898–1899 | Robert C Hamilton (Rangers) 25 |
| 1897–1898 | Robert C Hamilton (Rangers) 18 |
| 1896–1897 | William Taylor (Heart of Midlothian) 12 |
| 1895–1896 | Allan Martin (Celtic) 19 |
| 1894–1895 | James Miller (Clyde) 12 |
| 1893–1894 | Sandy McMahon (Celtic) 16 |
| 1892–1893 | Sandy McMahon (Celtic) 11 John Campbell (Celtic) 11 |
| 1891–1892 | John Bell (Dumbarton) 23 |
| 1890–1891 | John Bell (Dumbarton) 20 |

\* Not played 1940–1946 due to World War II.

## LEAGUE OF WALES CHAMPIONS

| | |
|---|---|
| 2008–2009 | Rhyl |
| 2007–2008 | Llanelli |
| 2006–2007 | TNS |
| 2005–2006 | TNS |
| 2004–2005 | TNS |
| 2003–2004 | Rhyl |
| 2002–2003 | Barry Town |
| 2001–2002 | Barry Town |
| 2000–2001 | Barry Town |
| 1999–2000 | TNS |
| 1998–1999 | Barry Town |
| 1997–1998 | Barry Town |
| 1996–1997 | Barry Town |
| 1995–1996 | Barry Town |
| 1994–1995 | Bangor City |
| 1993–1994 | Bangor City |
| 1992–1993 | Cwmbran Town |

## WELSH CUP*

| | |
|---|---|
| 2008–2009 | Bangor City |
| 2007–2008 | Bangor City |
| 2006–2007 | Carmarthen Town |
| 2005–2006 | Rhyl |
| 2004–2005 | TNS |
| 2003–2004 | Rhyl |
| 2002–2003 | Barry Town |
| 2001–2002 | Barry Town |
| 2000–2001 | Barry Town |
| 1999–2000 | Bangor City |
| 1998–1999 | Inter Cardiff |
| 1997–1998 | Bangor City |
| 1996–1997 | Barry Town |
| 1995–1996 | Llansantffraid |
| 1994–1995 | Wrexham |
| 1993–1994 | Barry Town |
| 1992–1993 | Cardiff City |
| 1991–1992 | Cardiff City |
| 1990–1991 | Swansea City |
| 1989–1990 | Hereford United |
| 1988–1989 | Swansea City |
| 1987–1988 | Cardiff City |
| 1986–1987 | Merthyr Tydfil |
| 1985–1986 | Kidderminster Harriers |
| 1984–1985 | Shrewsbury Town |
| 1983–1984 | Shrewsbury Town |
| 1982–1983 | Swansea City |
| 1981–1982 | Swansea City |
| 1980–1981 | Swansea City |
| 1979–1980 | Newport County |
| 1978–1979 | Shrewsbury Town |
| 1977–1978 | Wrexham |
| 1976–1977 | Shrewsbury Town |
| 1975–1976 | Cardiff City |
| 1974–1975 | Wrexham |
| 1973–1974 | Cardiff City |
| 1972–1973 | Cardiff City |
| 1971–1972 | Wrexham |
| 1970–1971 | Cardiff City |
| 1969–1970 | Cardiff City |
| 1968–1969 | Cardiff City |
| 1967–1968 | Cardiff City |
| 1966–1967 | Cardiff City |
| 1965–1966 | Swansea Town |
| 1964–1965 | Cardiff City |
| 1963–1964 | Cardiff City |
| 1962–1963 | Borough United |
| 1961–1962 | Bangor City |
| 1960–1961 | Swansea Town |
| 1959–1960 | Wrexham |

| Season | Winner |
|---|---|
| 1958–1959 | Cardiff City |
| 1957–1958 | Wrexham |
| 1956–1957 | Wrexham |
| 1955–1956 | Cardiff City |
| 1954–1955 | Barry Town |
| 1953–1954 | Flint Town United |
| 1952–1953 | Rhyl |
| 1951–1952 | Rhyl |
| 1950–1951 | Merthyr Tydfil |
| 1949–1950 | Swansea Town |
| 1948–1949 | Merthyr Tydfil |
| 1947–1948 | Lovells Athletic |
| 1946–1947 | Chester |
| 1939–1940 | Wellington |
| 1938–1939 | South Liverpool |
| 1937–1938 | Shrewsbury Town |
| 1936–1937 | Crewe Alexandra |
| 1935–1936 | Crewe Alexandra |
| 1934–1935 | Tranmere Rovers |
| 1933–1934 | Bristol City |
| 1932–1933 | Chester |
| 1931–1932 | Swansea Town |
| 1930–1931 | Wrexham |
| 1929–1930 | Cardiff City |
| 1928–1929 | Connah's Quay |
| 1927–1928 | Cardiff City |
| 1926–1927 | Cardiff City |
| 1925–1926 | Ebbw Vale |
| 1924–1925 | Wrexham |
| 1923–1924 | Wrexham |
| 1922–1923 | Cardiff City |
| 1921–1922 | Cardiff City |
| 1920–1921 | Wrexham |
| 1919–1920 | Cardiff City |
| 1914–1915 | Wrexham |
| 1913–1914 | Wrexham |
| 1912–1913 | Swansea Town |
| 1911–1912 | Cardiff City |
| 1910–1911 | Wrexham |
| 1909–1910 | Wrexham |
| 1908–1909 | Wrexham |
| 1907–1908 | Chester |
| 1906–1907 | Oswestry |
| 1905–1906 | Wellington |
| 1904–1905 | Wrexham |
| 1903–1904 | Druids |
| 1902–1903 | Wrexham |
| 1901–1902 | Wellington |
| 1900–1901 | Oswestry |
| 1899–1900 | Aberystwyth |
| 1898–1899 | Druids |
| 1897–1898 | Druids |
| 1896–1897 | Wrexham |
| 1895–1896 | Bangor Town |
| 1894–1895 | Newtown |
| 1893–1894 | Chirk |
| 1892–1893 | Wrexham |
| 1891–1892 | Chirk |
| 1890–1891 | Shrewsbury Town |
| 1889–1890 | Chirk |
| 1888–1889 | Bangor City |
| 1887–1888 | Chirk |
| 1886–1887 | Chirk |
| 1886–1886 | Druids |
| 1884–1885 | Druids |
| 1883–1884 | Oswestry |
| 1882–1883 | Wrexham |
| 1881–1882 | Druids |
| 1880–1881 | Druids |


| Season | Winner |
|---|---|
| 1879–1880 | Druids |
| 1878–1879 | Newtown |
| 1877–1878 | Wrexham |

* Not played 1915–1919 due to World War I and 1940–1946 due to World War II.

### WALES: LEAGUE TOP SCORERS

| Season | Top scorer |
|---|---|
| 2008–2009 | Rhys Griffiths (Llanelli) 31 |
| 2007–2008 | Rhys Griffiths (Llanelli) 40 |
| 2006–2007 | Rhys Griffiths (Llanelli) 30 |
| 2005–2006 | Rhys Griffith (Llanelli) 28 |
| 2004–2005 | Marc Lloyd–Williams (TNS) 34 |
| 2003–2004 | Andy Moran (Rhyl) 27 |
| 2002–2003 | Graham Evans (Caersws) 24 |
| 2001–2002 | Marc Lloyd–Williams (Bangor City) 47 |
| 2000–2001 | Graham Evans (Caersws) 25 |
| 1999–2000 | Chris Summers (Cwmbran Town) 28 |
| 1998–1999 | Eifion Williams (Barry Town) 28 |
| 1997–1998 | Eifion Williams (Barry Town) 40 |
| 1996–1997 | Tony Bird (Barry Town) 42 |
| 1995–1996 | Ken McKenna (Conwy United) 38 |
| 1994–1995 | Frank Mottram (Bangor City) 30 |
| 1993–1994 | David Taylor (Porthmadog) 43 |
| 1992–1993 | Steve Woods (Ebbw Vale) 29 |

### NORTHERN IRELAND: IFA PREMIERSHIP* **

| Season | Winner |
|---|---|
| 2008–2009 | Glentoran |
| 2007–2008 | Linfield |
| 2006–2007 | Linfield |
| 2005–2006 | Linfield |
| 2004–2005 | Glentoran |
| 2003–2004 | Linfield |
| 2002–2003 | Glentoran |
| 2001–2002 | Portadown |
| 2000–2001 | Linfield |
| 1999–2000 | Linfield |
| 1998–1999 | Glentoran |
| 1997–1998 | Cliftonville |
| 1996–1997 | Crusaders |
| 1995–1996 | Portadown |
| 1994–1995 | Crusaders |
| 1993–1994 | Linfield |
| 1992–1993 | Linfield |
| 1991–1992 | Glentoran |
| 1990–1991 | Portadown |
| 1989–1990 | Portadown |
| 1988–1989 | Linfield |
| 1987–1988 | Glentoran |
| 1986–1987 | Linfield |
| 1985–1986 | Linfield |
| 1984–1985 | Linfield |
| 1983–1984 | Linfield |
| 1982–1983 | Linfield |
| 1981–1982 | Linfield |
| 1980–1981 | Glentoran |
| 1979–1980 | Linfield |
| 1978–1979 | Linfield |


| Season | Winner |
|---|---|
| 1977–1978 | Linfield |
| 1976–1977 | Glentoran |
| 1975–1976 | Crusaders |
| 1974–1975 | Linfield |
| 1973–1974 | Coleraine |
| 1972–1973 | Crusaders |
| 1971–1972 | Glentoran |
| 1970–1971 | Linfield |
| 1969–1970 | Glentoran |
| 1968–1969 | Linfield |
| 1967–1968 | Glentoran |
| 1966–1967 | Glentoran |
| 1965–1966 | Linfield |
| 1964–1965 | Derry City |
| 1963–1964 | Glentoran |
| 1962–1963 | Distillery |
| 1961–1962 | Linfield |
| 1960–1961 | Linfield |
| 1959–1960 | Glenavon |
| 1958–1959 | Linfield |
| 1957–1958 | Ards |
| 1956–1957 | Glenavon |
| 1955–1956 | Linfield |
| 1954–1955 | Linfield |
| 1953–1954 | Linfield |
| 1952–1953 | Glentoran |
| 1951–1952 | Glenavon |
| 1950–1951 | Glentoran |
| 1949–1950 | Linfield |
| 1948–1949 | Linfield |
| 1947–1948 | Belfast Celtic |
| 1939–1940 | Belfast Celtic |
| 1938–1939 | Belfast Celtic |
| 1937–1938 | Belfast Celtic |
| 1936–1937 | Belfast Celtic |
| 1935–1936 | Belfast Celtic |
| 1934–1935 | Linfield |
| 1933–1934 | Linfield |
| 1932–1933 | Belfast Celtic |
| 1931–1932 | Linfield |
| 1930–1931 | Glentoran |
| 1929–1930 | Linfield |
| 1928–1929 | Belfast Celtic |
| 1927–1928 | Belfast Celtic |
| 1926–1927 | Belfast Celtic |
| 1925–1926 | Belfast Celtic |
| 1924–1925 | Glentoran |
| 1923–1924 | Queen's Island |
| 1922–1923 | Linfield |
| 1921–1922 | Linfield |
| 1920–1921 | Glentoran |
| 1919–1920 | Belfast Celtic |
| 1914–1915 | Belfast Celtic |
| 1913–1914 | Linfield |
| 1912–1913 | Glentoran |
| 1911–1912 | Glentoran |
| 1910–1911 | Linfield |
| 1909–1910 | Cliftonville |
| 1908–1909 | Linfield |
| 1907–1908 | Linfield |
| 1906–1907 | Linfield |
| 1905–1906 | Cliftonville/Distillery (shared title) |
| 1904–1905 | Glentoran |
| 1903–1904 | Linfield |
| 1902–1903 | Distillery |
| 1901–1902 | Linfield |
| 1900–1901 | Distillery |
| 1899–1900 | Belfast Celtic |


| Season | Winner |
|---|---|
| 1898–1899 | Distillery |
| 1897–1898 | Linfield |
| 1896–1897 | Glentoran |
| 1895–1896 | Distillery |
| 1894–1895 | Linfield |
| 1893–1894 | Glentoran |
| 1892–1893 | Linfield |
| 1891–1892 | Linfield |
| 1890–1891 | Linfield |

* Known as the Irish Football League until 2003 and then the Irish Premier League until 2008.

** Not played 1915–1919 due to World War I and 1941–1947 due to World War II.

### NORTHERN IRELAND: IRISH CUP

| Season | Winner |
|---|---|
| 2008–2009 | Crusaders |
| 2007–2008 | Linfield |
| 2006–2007 | Linfield |
| 2005–2006 | Linfield |
| 2004–2005 | Portadown |
| 2003–2004 | Glentoran |
| 2002–2003 | Coleraine |
| 2001–2002 | Linfield |
| 2000–2001 | Glentoran |
| 1999–2000 | Glentoran |
| 1998–1999 | Portadown awarded cup after Cliftonville's disqualification |
| 1997–1998 | Glentoran |
| 1996–1997 | Glenavon |
| 1995–1996 | Glentoran |
| 1994–1995 | Linfield |
| 1993–1994 | Linfield |
| 1992–1993 | Bangor |
| 1991–1992 | Glenavon |
| 1990–1991 | Portadown |
| 1989–1990 | Glentoran |
| 1988–1989 | Ballymena |
| 1987–1988 | Glentoran |
| 1986–1987 | Glentoran |
| 1985–1986 | Glentoran |
| 1984–1985 | Glentoran |
| 1983–1984 | Ballymena United |
| 1982–1983 | Glentoran |
| 1981–1982 | Linfield |
| 1980–1981 | Ballymena United |
| 1979–1980 | Linfield |
| 1978–1979 | Cliftonville |
| 1977–1978 | Linfield |
| 1976–1977 | Coleraine |
| 1975–1976 | Carrick Rangers |
| 1974–1975 | Coleraine |
| 1973–1974 | Ards |
| 1972–1973 | Glentoran |
| 1971–1972 | Coleraine |
| 1970–1971 | Distillery |
| 1969–1970 | Linfield |
| 1968–1969 | Ards |
| 1967–1968 | Crusaders |
| 1966–1967 | Crusaders |
| 1965–1966 | Glentoran |
| 1964–1965 | Coleraine |
| 1963–1964 | Derry City |
| 1962–1963 | Linfield |
| 1961–1962 | Linfield |
| 1960–1961 | Glenavon |
| 1959–1960 | Linfield |
| 1958–1959 | Glenavon |

| | |
|---|---|
| 1957–1958 | Ballymena United |
| 1956–1957 | Glenavon |
| 1955–1956 | Distillery |
| 1954–1955 | Dundela |
| 1953–1954 | Derry City |
| 1952–1953 | Linfield |
| 1951–1952 | Ards 1 |
| 1950–1951 | Glentoran |
| 1949–1950 | Linfield |
| 1948–1949 | Derry City |
| 1947–1948 | Linfield |
| 1946–1947 | Belfast Celtic |
| 1945–1946 | Linfield |
| 1944–1945 | Linfield |
| 1943–1944 | Belfast Celtic |
| 1942–1943 | Belfast Celtic |
| 1941–1942 | Linfield |
| 1940–1941 | Belfast Celtic |
| 1939–1940 | United |
| 1938–1939 | Linfield |
| 1937–1938 | Belfast Celtic |
| 1936–1937 | Belfast Celtic |
| 1935–1936 | Linfield |
| 1934–1935 | Glentoran |
| 1933–1934 | Linfield |
| 1932–1933 | Glentoran |
| 1931–1932 | Glentoran |
| 1930–1931 | Linfield |
| 1929–1930 | Linfield |
| 1928–1929 | Ballymena United |
| 1927–1928 | Willowfield |
| 1926–1927 | Ards |
| 1925–1926 | Belfast Celtic |
| 1924–1925 | Distillery |
| 1923–1924 | Queen's Island |
| 1922–1923 | Linfield |
| 1921–1922 | Linfield |
| 1920–1921 | Glentoran |
| 1919–1920 | Shelbourne awarded cup after Belfast Celtic and Glentoran were expelled from the competition |
| 1918–1919 | Linfield |
| 1917–1918 | Belfast Celtic |
| 1916–1917 | Glentoran |
| 1915–1916 | Linfield |
| 1914–1915 | Linfield |
| 1913–1914 | Glentoran |
| 1912–1913 | Linfield |
| 1911–1912 | Linfield awarded cup after withdrawal of others |
| 1910–1911 | Shelbourne |
| 1909–1910 | Distillery |
| 1908–1909 | Cliftonville |
| 1907–1908 | Bohemians |
| 1906–1907 | Cliftonville |
| 1905–1906 | Shelbourne |
| 1904–1905 | Distillery |
| 1903–1904 | Linfield |
| 1902–1903 | Distillery |
| 1901–1902 | Linfield |
| 1900–1901 | Cliftonville |
| 1899–1900 | Cliftonville |
| 1898–1899 | Linfield |
| 1897–1898 | Linfield |
| 1896–1897 | Cliftonville |
| 1895–1896 | Distillery |
| 1894–1895 | Linfield |
| 1893–1894 | Distillery |
| 1892–1893 | Linfield |
| 1891–1892 | Linfield |
| 1890–1891 | Linfield |

| | |
|---|---|
| 1889–1890 | Gordon Highlanders |
| 1888–1889 | Distillery |
| 1887–1888 | Cliftonville |
| 1886–1887 | Ulster |
| 1885–1886 | Distillery |
| 1884–1885 | Distillery |
| 1883–1884 | Distillery |
| 1882–1883 | Cliftonville |
| 1881–1882 | Queen's Island |
| 1880–1881 | Moyola Park |

## NORTHERN IRELAND: LEAGUE TOP SCORERS

| | |
|---|---|
| 2008–2009 | Curtis Allen (Lisburn Distillery) 29 |
| 2007–2008 | Peter Thompson (Linfield) 29 |
| 2006–2007 | Gary Hamilton (Glentoran) 27 |
| 2005–2006 | Peter Thompson (Linfield) 25 |
| 2004–2005 | Chris Morgan (Glentoran) 19 |
| 2003–2004 | Glenn Ferguson (Linfield) 25 |
| 2002–2003 | Vinny Arkins (Portadown) 29 |
| 2001–2002 | Vinny Arkins (Portadown) 30 |
| 2000–2001 | Davy Larmour (Linfield) 17 |
| 1999–2000 | Vinny Arkins (Portadown) 29 |
| 1998–1999 | Vinny Arkins (Portadown) 19 |
| 1997–1998 | Vinny Arkins (Portadown) 22 |
| 1996–1997 | Garry Haylock (Portadown) 16 |
| 1995–1996 | Garry Haylock (Portadown) 19 |
| 1994–1995 | Glenn Ferguson (Glenavon) 27 |
| 1993–1994 | Darren Erskine (Ards) 22 / Stephen McBride (Glenavon) 22 |
| 1992–1993 | Stevie Cowan (Portadown) 27 |
| 1991–1992 | Harry McCourt (Omagh Town) 18 / Stephen McBride (Glenavon) 18 |
| 1990–1991 | Stephen McBride (Glenavon) 22 |
| 1989–1990 | Martin McGaughey (Linfield) 19 |
| 1988–1989 | Stephen Baxter (Linfield) 17 |
| 1987–1988 | Martin McGaughey (Linfield) 18 |
| 1986–1987 | Ray McCoy (Coleraine) 14 / Gary McCartney (Glentoran) 14 |
| 1985–1986 | Trevor Anderson (Linfield) 14 |
| 1984–1985 | Martin McGaughey (Linfield) 34 |
| 1983–1984 | Martin McGaughey (Linfield) 15 / Trevor Anderson (Linfield) 15 |
| 1982–1983 | Jim Campbell (Ards) 15 |
| 1981–1982 | Gary Blackledge (Glentoran) 18 |

| | |
|---|---|
| 1980–1981 | Des Dickson (Coleraine) 18 / Paul Malone (Ballymena United) 18 |
| 1979–1980 | Jimmy Martin (Glentoran) 17 |
| 1978–1979 | Tommy Armstrong (Ards) 21 |
| 1977–1978 | Warren Feeney (Glentoran) 17 |
| 1976–1977 | Ronnie McAteer (Crusaders) 20 |
| 1975–1976 | Des Dickson (Coleraine) 23 |
| 1974–1975 | Martin Malone (Portadown) 19 |
| 1973–1974 | Des Dickson (Coleraine) 24 |
| 1972–1973 | Des Dickson (Coleraine) 23 |
| 1971–1972 | Peter Watson (Distillery) 15 / Des Dickson (Coleraine) 15 |
| 1970–1971 | Bryan Hamilton (Linfield) 18 |
| 1969–1970 | Des Dickson (Coleraine) 21 |
| 1968–1969 | Danny Hale (Derry City) 21 |
| 1967–1968 | Sammy Pavis (Linfield) 30 |
| 1966–1967 | Sammy Pavis (Linfield) 25 |
| 1965–1966 | Sammy Pavis (Linfield) 28 |
| 1964–1965 | Kenny Halliday (Coleraine) 19 / Dennis Guy (Glenavon) 19 |
| 1963–1964 | Trevor Thompson (Glentoran) 12 |
| 1962–1963 | Joe Meldrum (Distillery) 27 |
| 1961–1962 | Mick Lynch (Ards) 20 |
| 1960–1961 | Trevor Thompson (Glentoran) 22 |
| 1959–1960 | Jimmy Jones (Glenavon) 29 |
| 1958–1959 | Jackie Milburn (Linfield) 26 |
| 1957–1958 | Jackie Milburn (Linfield) 29 |
| 1956–1957 | Jimmy Jones (Glenavon) 33 |
| 1955–1956 | Jimmy Jones (Glenavon) 26 |
| 1954–1955 | Fay Coyle (Coleraine) 20 |
| 1953–1954 | Jimmy Jones (Glenavon) 32 |
| 1952–1953 | Sammy Hughes (Glentoran) 28 |
| 1951–1952 | Jimmy Jones (Glenavon) 27 |
| 1950–1951 | Sammy Hughes (Glentoran) 23 / Walter Allen (Portadown) 23 |
| 1949–1950 | Sammy Hughes (Glentoran) 23 |
| 1948–1949 | Billy Simpson (Linfield) 19 |
| 1947–1948 | Jimmy Jones (Belfast Celtic) 28 |

## FRANCE LEAGUE 1 CHAMPIONS*

| | |
|---|---|
| 2008–2009 | Bordeaux |
| 2007–2008 | Lyon |
| 2006–2007 | Lyon |
| 2005–2006 | Lyon |
| 2004–2005 | Lyon |
| 2003–2004 | Lyon |
| 2002–2003 | Lyon |
| 2001–2002 | Lyon |
| 2000–2001 | Nantes |

| | |
|---|---|
| 1999–2000 | Monaco |
| 1998–1999 | Bordeaux |
| 1997–1998 | Lens |
| 1996–1997 | Monaco |
| 1995–1996 | Auxerre |
| 1994–1995 | Nantes |
| 1993–1994 | Paris Saint–Germain |
| 1992–1993 | No winner (Marseille stripped of title) |
| 1991–1992 | Marseille |
| 1990–1991 | Marseille |
| 1989–1990 | Marseille |
| 1988–1989 | Marseille |
| 1987–1988 | Monaco |
| 1986–1987 | Bordeaux |
| 1985–1986 | Paris Saint–Germain |
| 1984–1985 | Bordeaux |
| 1983–1984 | Bordeaux |
| 1982–1983 | Nantes |
| 1981–1982 | Monaco |
| 1980–1981 | Saint–Étienne |
| 1979–1980 | Nantes |
| 1978–1979 | Strasbourg |
| 1977–1978 | Monaco |
| 1976–1977 | Nantes |
| 1975–1976 | Saint–Étienne |
| 1974–1975 | Saint–Étienne |
| 1973–1974 | Saint–Étienne |
| 1972–1973 | Nantes |
| 1971–1972 | Marseille |
| 1970–1971 | Marseille |
| 1969–1970 | Saint–Étienne |
| 1968–1969 | Saint–Étienne |
| 1967–1968 | Saint–Étienne |
| 1966–1967 | Saint–Étienne |
| 1965–1966 | Nantes |
| 1964–1965 | Nantes |
| 1963–1964 | Saint–Étienne |
| 1962–1963 | Monaco |
| 1961–1962 | Stade Reims |
| 1960–1961 | Monaco |
| 1959–1960 | Stade Reims |
| 1958–1959 | Nice |
| 1957–1958 | Stade Reims |
| 1956–1957 | Saint–Étienne |
| 1955–1956 | Nice |
| 1954–1955 | Stade Reims |
| 1953–1954 | Lille |
| 1952–1953 | Stade Reims |
| 1951–1952 | Nice |
| 1950–1951 | Nice |
| 1949–1950 | Bordeaux |
| 1948–1949 | Stade Reims |
| 1947–1948 | Marseille |
| 1946–1947 | CO Roubaix–Tourcoing |
| 1945–1946 | Lille |
| 1938–1939 | Sète |
| 1937–1938 | Sochaux |
| 1936–1937 | Marseille |
| 1935–1936 | RCF Paris |
| 1934–1935 | Sochaux |
| 1933–1934 | Sète |
| 1932–1933 | Lille |

* Not played 1939–1945 due to World War II.

## COUPE DE FRANCE (FRENCH CUP)

| | |
|---|---|
| 2009 | Guingamp |
| 2008 | Lyon |
| 2007 | Sochaux |
| 2006 | Paris Saint–Germain |
| 2005 | Auxerre |

2004 Paris Saint–Germain
2003 Auxerre
2002 Lorient
2001 RC Strasbourg
2000 Nantes
1999 Nantes
1998 Paris Saint–Germain
1997 Nice
1996 Auxerre
1995 Paris Saint–Germain
1994 Auxerre
1993 Paris Saint–Germain
1992 Not played due to Furiani Stadium disaster in Bastia
1991 Monaco
1990 Montpellier
1989 Marseille
1988 Metz
1987 Bordeaux
1986 Bordeaux
1985 Monaco
1984 Metz
1983 Paris Saint–Germain
1982 Paris Saint–Germain
1981 Bastia
1980 Monaco
1979 Nantes
1978 AS Nancy
1977 Saint–Étienne
1976 Marseille
1975 Saint–Étienne
1974 Saint–Étienne
1973 Lyon
1972 Marseille
1971 Rennes
1970 Saint–Étienne
1969 Marseille
1968 Saint–Étienne
1967 Lyon
1966 RC Strasbourg
1965 Rennes
1964 Lyon
1963 Monaco
1962 Saint–Étienne
1961 CS Sedan
1960 Monaco
1959 Le Havre
1958 Stade Reims
1957 Toulouse FC (1937)
1956 CS Sedan
1955 Lille
1954 Nice
1953 Lille
1952 Nice
1951 Strasbourg
1950 Stade Reims
1949 RCF Paris
1948 Lille
1947 Lille
1946 Lille
1945 RCF Paris
1944 ÉF Nancy–Lorraine
1943 Marseille
1942 Red Star
1941 Bordeaux
1940 RCF Paris
1939 RCF Paris
1938 Marseille
1937 Sochaux

1936 RCF Paris
1935 Marseille
1934 Sète
1933 Excelsior AC Roubaix
1932 Cannes
1931 Club Français
1930 Sète
1929 Montpellier
1928 Red Star
1927 Marseille
1926 Marseille
1925 CASG Paris
1924 Marseille
1923 Red Star
1922 Red Star
1921 Red Star
1920 CA Paris
1919 CASG Paris
1918 Olympique de Paris

## FRANCE: LEAGUE TOP SCORERS*

2008–2009 André-Pierre Gignac (Toulouse) 24
2007–2008 Karim Benzema (Lyon) 20
2006–2007 Pauleta (Paris Saint–Germain) 15
2005–2006 Pauleta (Paris Saint–Germain) 21
2004–2005 Alexander Frei (Rennes) 20
2003–2004 Djibril Cissé (Auxerre) 26
2002–2003 Shabani Nonda (Monaco) 26
2001–2002 Djibril Cissé (Auxerre) 22 / Pauleta (Bordeaux) 22
2000–2001 Sonny Anderson (Lyon) 22
1999–2000 Sonny Anderson (Lyon) 23
1998–1999 Sylvain Wiltord (Bordeaux) 22
1997–1998 Stéphane Guivarc'h (Auxerre) 21
1996–1997 Stéphane Guivarc'h (Rennes) 22
1995–1996 Sonny Anderson (Monaco) 21
1994–1995 Patrice Loko (Nantes) 22
1993–1994 Youri Djorkaeff (Monaco) 20 / Roger Boli (Lens) 20 / Nicolas Ouédec (Nantes) 20
1992–1993 Alen Boksic (Marseille) 22
1991–1992 Jean–Pierre Papin (Marseille) 27
1990–1991 Jean–Pierre Papin (Marseille) 23
1989–1990 Jean–Pierre Papin (Marseille) 30
1988–1989 Jean–Pierre Papin (Marseille) 22
1987–1988 Jean–Pierre Papin (Marseille) 19
1986–1987 Bernard Zénier (Metz) 18
1985–1986 Jules Bocandé (Metz) 23
1984–1985 Vahid Halilhodzic (Nantes) 28
1983–1984 Patrice Garande (Auxerre) 21 / Delio Onnis (Sporting Toulon Var) 21
1982–1983 Vahid Halilhodzic (Nantes) 27
1981–1982 Delio Onnis (Tours) 29
1980–1981 Delio Onnis (Tours) 24
1979–1980 Delio Onnis (Monaco) 21 / Erwin Kostedde (Stade Laval) 21
1978–1979 Carlos Bianchi (Paris Saint–Germain) 27
1977–1978 Carlos Bianchi (Paris Saint–Germain) 37
1976–1977 Carlos Bianchi (Stade Reims) 28
1975–1976 Carlos Bianchi (Stade Reims) 34
1974–1975 Delio Onnis (Monaco) 30
1973–1974 Carlos Bianchi (Stade Reims) 30
1972–1973 Josip Skoblar (Marseille) 26
1971–1972 Josip Skoblar (Marseille) 30
1970–1971 Josip Skoblar (Marseille) 44
1969–1970 Hervé Revelli (Saint–Étienne) 28
1968–1969 André Guy (Lyon) 25
1967–1968 Étienne Sansonetti (AC Ajaccio) 26
1966–1967 Hervé Revelli (Saint–Étienne) 31
1965–1966 Philippe Gondet (Nantes) 36
1964–1965 Jacques Simon (Nantes) 24
1963–1964 Ahmed Oudjani (Lens) 30
1962–1963 Serge Masnaghetti (Valenciennes) 35
1961–1962 Sékou Touré (Montpellier HSC) 25
1960–1961 Roger Piantoni (Stade Reims) 28
1959–1960 Just Fontaine (Stade Reims) 28
1958–1959 Tadeusz Cisowski (RCF Paris) 30
1957–1958 Just Fontaine (Stade Reims) 34
1956–1957 Tadeusz Cisowski (RCF Paris) 33
1955–1956 Tadeusz Cisowski (RCF Paris) 31
1954–1955 René Bliard (Stade Reims) 30
1953–1954 Édouard Kargulewicz (Bordeaux) 27
1952–1953 Gunnar Andersson (Marseille) 35
1951–1952 Gunnar Andersson (Marseille) 31
1950–1951 Roger Piantoni (FC Nancy) 28
1949–1950 Jean Grumellon (Rennes) 24
1948–1949 Jean Baratte (Lille) 26 / Jozef Humpal (Sochaux) 26
1947–1948 Jean Baratte (Lille) 31
1946–1947 Pierre Sinibaldi (Stade Reims) 33
1945–1946 René Bihel (Lille) 28
1938–1939 Roger Courtois (Sochaux) 27 / Désiré Koranyi (Sète) 27
1937–1938 Jean Nicolas (Rouen) 26
1936–1937 Oskar Rohr (Strasbourg) 30
1935–1936 Roger Courtois (Sochaux) 34
1934–1935 André Abbeglen (Sochaux) 30
1933–1934 István Lukacs (Sète) 28
1932–1933 Robert Mercier (Club Français) 15 / Walter Kaiser (Rennes) 15

* Not played 1939–1945 due to World War II.

## ITALY: SERIE A CHAMPIONS*

2008–2009 Internazionale
2007–2008 Internazionale
2006–2007 Internazionale
2005–2006 Internazionale (Juventus stripped of title)
2004–2005 Not awarded (Juventus stripped of title)
2003–2004 AC Milan
2002–2003 Juventus
2001–2002 Juventus
2000–2001 Roma
1999–2000 Lazio
1998–1999 AC Milan
1997–1998 Juventus
1996–1997 Juventus
1995–1996 AC Milan
1994–1995 Juventus
1993–1994 AC Milan
1992–1993 AC Milan
1991–1992 AC Milan
1990–1991 Sampdoria
1989–1990 Napoli
1988–1989 Internazionale
1987–1988 AC Milan
1986–1987 Napoli
1985–1986 Juventus
1984–1985 Hellas Verona
1983–1984 Juventus
1982–1983 Roma
1981–1982 Juventus
1980–1981 Juventus
1979–1980 Internazionale
1978–1979 AC Milan
1977–1978 Juventus
1976–1977 Juventus
1975–1976 Torino
1974–1975 Juventus
1973–1974 Lazio
1972–1973 Juventus
1971–1972 Juventus
1970–1971 Internazionale
1969–1970 Cagliari
1968–1969 Fiorentina
1967–1968 AC Milan
1966–1967 Juventus
1965–1966 Internazionale
1964–1965 Internazionale
1963–1964 Bologna
1962–1963 Internazionale
1961–1962 AC Milan
1960–1961 Juventus
1959–1960 Juventus
1958–1959 AC Milan
1957–1958 Juventus

| | |
|---|---|
| 1956–1957 | AC Milan |
| 1955–1956 | Fiorentina |
| 1954–1955 | AC Milan |
| 1953–1954 | Internazionale |
| 1952–1953 | Internazionale |
| 1951–1952 | Juventus |
| 1950–1951 | AC Milan |
| 1949–1950 | Juventus |
| 1948–1949 | Torino |
| 1947–1948 | Torino |
| 1946–1947 | Torino |
| 1945–1946 | Torino |
| 1942–1943 | Torino |
| 1941–1942 | Roma |
| 1940–1941 | Bologna |
| 1939–1940 | Ambrosiana–Inter |
| 1938–1939 | Bologna |
| 1937–1938 | Ambrosiana–Inter |
| 1936–1937 | Bologna |
| 1935–1936 | Bologna |
| 1934–1935 | Juventus |
| 1933–1934 | Juventus |
| 1932–1933 | Juventus |
| 1931–1932 | Juventus |
| 1930–1931 | Juventus |
| 1929–1930 | Ambrosiana–Inter |
| 1928–1929 | Bologna |
| 1927–1928 | Torino |
| 1926–1927 | Not awarded (Torino stripped of title) |
| 1925–1926 | Juventus |
| 1924–1925 | Bologna |
| 1923–1924 | Genoa |
| 1922–1923 | Genoa |
| 1921–1922 | Pro Vercelli (awarded by the CCI federation) |
| | US Novese (awarded by the FIGC federation) |
| 1920–1921 | Pro Vercelli |
| 1919–1920 | Internazionale |
| 1914–1915 | Genoa |
| 1913–1914 | AS Casale |
| 1912–1913 | Pro Vercelli |
| 1911–1912 | Pro Vercelli |
| 1910–1911 | Pro Vercelli |
| 1909–1910 | Internazionale |
| 1909 | Pro Vercelli |
| 1908 | Pro Vercelli |
| 1907 | AC Milan |
| 1906 | AC Milan |
| 1905 | Juventus |
| 1904 | Genoa |
| 1903 | Genoa |
| 1902 | Genoa |
| 1901 | AC Milan |
| 1900 | Genoa |
| 1899 | Genoa |
| 1898 | Genoa |

\* Not played 1915–1919 due to World War I and 1943–1945 due to World War II.

## COPPA ITALIA (ITALIAN CUP)

| | |
|---|---|
| 2008–2009 | Lazio |
| 2007–2008 | Roma |
| 2006–2007 | Roma |
| 2005–2006 | Internazionale |
| 2004–2005 | Internazionale |
| 2003–2004 | Lazio |
| 2002–2003 | AC Milan |
| 2001–2002 | Parma |
| 2000–2001 | Fiorentina |

| | |
|---|---|
| 1999–2000 | Lazio |
| 1998–1999 | Parma |
| 1997–1998 | Lazio |
| 1996–1997 | Vicenza |
| 1995–1996 | Fiorentina |
| 1994–1995 | Juventus |
| 1993–1994 | Sampdoria |
| 1992–1993 | Torino |
| 1991–1992 | Parma |
| 1990–1991 | Roma |
| 1989–1990 | Juventus |
| 1988–1989 | Sampdoria |
| 1987–1988 | Sampdoria |
| 1986–1987 | Napoli |
| 1985–1986 | Roma |
| 1984–1985 | Sampdoria |
| 1983–1984 | Roma |
| 1982–1983 | Juventus |
| 1981–1982 | Internazionale |
| 1980–1981 | Roma |
| 1979–1980 | Roma |
| 1978–1979 | Juventus |
| 1977–1978 | Internazionale |
| 1976–1977 | AC Milan |
| 1975–1976 | Napoli |
| 1974–1975 | Fiorentina |
| 1973–1974 | Bologna |
| 1972–1973 | AC Milan |
| 1971–1972 | AC Milan |
| 1970–1971 | Torino |
| 1969–1970 | Bologna |
| 1968–1969 | Roma |
| 1967–1968 | Torino |
| 1966–1967 | AC Milan |
| 1965–1966 | Fiorentina |
| 1964–1965 | Juventus |
| 1963–1964 | Roma |
| 1962–1963 | Atalanta |
| 1961–1962 | Napoli |
| 1960–1961 | Fiorentina |
| 1959–1960 | Juventus |
| 1958–1959 | Juventus |
| 1957–1958 | Lazio |
| 1942–1943 | Torino |
| 1941–1942 | Juventus |
| 1940–1941 | Venezia |
| 1939–1940 | Fiorentina |
| 1938–1939 | Internazionale |
| 1937–1938 | Juventus |
| 1936–1937 | Genoa |
| 1935–1936 | Torino |
| 1923–1935 | Not played |
| 1922 | Vado |

## ITALY: LEAGUE TOP SCORERS\*

| | | |
|---|---|---|
| 2008–2009 | Zlatan Ibrahimovic (Internazionale) | 25 |
| 2007–2008 | Alessandro Del Piero (Juventus) | 21 |
| 2006–2007 | Francesco Totti (Roma) | 26 |
| 2005–2006 | Luca Toni (Fiorentina) | 31 |
| 2004–2005 | Cristiano Lucarelli (Livorno) | 24 |
| | Alberto Gilardino (Parma) | 24 |
| 2003–2004 | Andriy Shevchenko (AC Milan) | 24 |
| 2002–2003 | Christian Vieri (Internazionale) | 24 |
| 2001–2002 | David Trézéguet (Juventus) | 24 |

| | | |
|---|---|---|
| | Dario Hubner (Piacenza) | 24 |
| 2000–2001 | Hernán Crespo (Lazio) | 26 |
| 1999–2000 | Andriy Shevchenko (AC Milan) | 24 |
| 1998–1999 | Márcio Amoroso (Udinese) | 22 |
| 1997–1998 | Oliver Bierhoff (Udinese) | 27 |
| 1996–1997 | Filippo Inzaghi (Atalanta) | 24 |
| 1995–1996 | Giuseppe Signori (Lazio) | 24 |
| | Igor Protti (Bari) | 24 |
| 1994–1995 | Gabriel Batistuta (Fiorentina) | 26 |
| 1993–1994 | Giuseppe Signori (Lazio) | 23 |
| 1992–1993 | Giuseppe Signori (Lazio) | 26 |
| 1991–1992 | Marco van Basten (AC Milan) | 25 |
| 1990–1991 | Gianluca Vialli (Sampdoria) | 17 |
| 1989–1990 | Marco van Basten (AC Milan) | 19 |
| 1988–1989 | Aldo Serena (Internazionale) | 22 |
| 1987–1988 | Diego Maradona (Napoli) | 15 |
| 1986–1987 | Pietro Paolo Virdis (AC Milan) | 17 |
| 1985–1986 | Roberto Pruzzo (Roma) | 19 |
| 1984–1985 | Michel Platini (Juventus) | 18 |
| 1983–1984 | Michel Platini (Juventus) | 20 |
| 1982–1983 | Michel Platini (Juventus) | 16 |
| 1981–1982 | Roberto Pruzzo (Roma) | 15 |
| 1980–1981 | Roberto Pruzzo (Roma) | 18 |
| 1979–1980 | Roberto Bettega (Juventus) | 16 |
| 1978–1979 | Bruno Giordano (Lazio) | 19 |
| 1977–1978 | Paolo Rossi (Vicenza) | 24 |
| 1976–1977 | Francesco Graziani (Torino) | 21 |
| 1975–1976 | Paolino Pulici (Torino) | 21 |
| 1974–1975 | Paolino Pulici (Torino) | 18 |
| 1973–1974 | Giorgio Chinaglia (Lazio) | 24 |
| 1972–1973 | Paolino Pulici (Torino) | 17 |
| | Gianni Rivera (AC Milan) | 17 |
| | Giuseppe Savoldi (Bologna) | 17 |
| 1971–1972 | Roberto Boninsegna (Internazionale) | 22 |
| 1970–1971 | Roberto Boninsegna (Internazionale) | 24 |
| 1969–1970 | Gigi Riva (Cagliari) | 21 |
| 1968–1969 | Gigi Riva (Cagliari) | 20 |
| 1967–1968 | Pierino Prati (AC Milan) | 15 |
| 1966–1967 | Gigi Riva (Cagliari) | 18 |
| 1965–1966 | Luis Vinicio (Vicenza) | 25 |
| 1964–1965 | Sandro Mazzola (Internazionale) | 17 |
| | Alberto Orlando (Fiorentina) | 17 |
| 1963–1964 | Harald Nielsen (Bologna) | 21 |
| 1962–1963 | Pedro Manfredini (Roma) | 19 |
| | Harald Nielsen (Bologna) | 19 |
| 1961–1962 | José Altafini (AC Milan) | 22 |
| | Aurelio Milani (Fiorentina) | 22 |
| 1960–1961 | Sergio Brighenti (Sampdoria) | 27 |
| 1959–1960 | Omar Sivori (Juventus) | 27 |
| 1958–1959 | Antonio Valentin Angelillo (Internazionale) | 33 |
| 1957–1958 | John Charles (Juventus) | 28 |
| 1956–1957 | Dino Da Costa (Roma) | 22 |

| | | |
|---|---|---|
| 1955–1956 | Gino Pivatelli (Bologna) | 29 |
| 1954–1955 | Gunnar Nordahl (AC Milan) | 27 |
| 1953–1954 | Gunnar Nordahl (AC Milan) | 23 |
| 1952–1953 | Gunnar Nordahl (AC Milan) | 26 |
| 1951–1952 | John Hansen (Juventus) | 30 |
| 1950–1951 | Gunnar Nordahl (AC Milan) | 34 |
| 1949–1950 | Gunnar Nordahl (AC Milan) | 35 |
| 1948–1949 | Stefano Nyers (Internazionale) | 26 |
| 1947–1948 | Giampiero Boniperti (Juventus) | 27 |
| 1946–1947 | Valentino Mazzola (Torino) | 29 |
| 1945–1946 | Eusebio Castigliano (Torino) | 13 |
| 1942–1943 | Silvio Piola (Lazio) | 21 |
| 1941–1942 | Aldo Boffi (AC Milan) | 22 |
| 1940–1941 | Ettore Puricelli (Bologna) | 22 |
| 1939–1940 | Aldo Boffi (AC Milan) | 24 |
| 1938–1939 | Aldo Boffi (AC Milan) | 19 |
| | Ettore Puricelli (Bologna) | 19 |
| 1937–1938 | Giuseppe Meazza (Internazionale) | 20 |
| 1936–1937 | Silvio Piola (Lazio) | 21 |
| 1935–1936 | Giuseppe Meazza (Internazionale) | 25 |
| 1934–1935 | Enrico Guaita (Roma) | 28 |
| 1933–1934 | Felice Borel (Juventus) | 31 |
| 1932–1933 | Felice Borel (Juventus) | 29 |
| 1931–1932 | Pedro Petrone (Fiorentina) | 25 |
| | Angelo Schiavio (Bologna) | 25 |
| 1930–1931 | Rodolfo Volk (Roma) | 29 |
| 1929–1930 | Giuseppe Meazza (Internazionale) | 31 |

\* Not played 1943–1945 due to the 2nd World War.

## GERMANY: BUNDESLIGA CHAMPIONS

| | |
|---|---|
| 2008–2009 | VfL Wolfsburg |
| 2007–2008 | Bayern Munich |
| 2006–2007 | VfB Stuttgart |
| 2005–2006 | Bayern Munich |
| 2004–2005 | Bayern Munich |
| 2003–2004 | Werder Bremen |
| 2002–2003 | Bayern Munich |
| 2001–2002 | Borussia Dortmund |
| 2000–2001 | Bayern Munich |
| 1999–2000 | Bayern Munich |
| 1998–1999 | Bayern Munich |
| 1997–1998 | Kaiserslautern |
| 1996–1997 | Bayern Munich |
| 1995–1996 | Borussia Dortmund |
| 1994–1995 | Borussia Dortmund |
| 1993–1994 | Bayern Munich |
| 1992–1993 | Werder Bremen |
| 1991–1992 | VfB Stuttgart |
| 1990–1991 | Kaiserslautern |
| 1989–1990 | Bayern Munich |
| 1988–1989 | Bayern Munich |
| 1987–1988 | Werder Bremen |
| 1986–1987 | Bayern Munich |
| 1985–1986 | Bayern Munich |
| 1984–1985 | Bayern Munich |
| 1983–1984 | VfB Stuttgart |

| | |
|---|---|
| 1982–1983 | Hamburg |
| 1981–1982 | Hamburg |
| 1980–1981 | Bayern Munich |
| 1979–1980 | Bayern Munich |
| 1978–1979 | Hamburg |
| 1977–1978 | Köln |
| 1976–1977 | Borussia Mönchengladbach |
| 1975–1976 | Borussia Mönchengladbach |
| 1974–1975 | Borussia Mönchengladbach |
| 1973–1974 | Bayern Munich |
| 1972–1973 | Bayern Munich |
| 1971–1972 | Bayern Munich |
| 1970–1971 | Borussia Mönchengladbach |
| 1969–1970 | Borussia Mönchengladbach |
| 1968–1969 | Bayern Munich |
| 1967–1968 | Nürnberg |
| 1966–1967 | Eintracht Braunschweig |
| 1965–1966 | 1860 Munich |
| 1964–1965 | Werder Bremen |
| 1963–1964 | Köln |

## GERMANY: DFB–POKAL (GERMAN CUP)

| | |
|---|---|
| 2009 | Werder Bremen |
| 2008 | Bayern Munich |
| 2007 | Nürnberg |
| 2006 | Bayern Munich |
| 2005 | Bayern Munich |
| 2004 | Werder Bremen |
| 2003 | Bayern Munich |
| 2002 | Schalke |
| 2001 | Schalke |
| 2000 | Bayern Munich |
| 1999 | Werder Bremen |
| 1998 | Bayern Munich |
| 1997 | VfB Stuttgart |
| 1996 | Kaiserslautern |
| 1995 | Borussia Mönchengladbach |
| 1994 | Werder Bremen |
| 1993 | Bayer Leverkusen |
| 1992 | Hannover 96 |
| 1991 | Werder Bremen |
| 1990 | Kaiserslautern |
| 1989 | Borussia Dortmund |
| 1988 | Eintracht Frankfurt |
| 1987 | Hamburg |
| 1986 | Bayern Munich |
| 1985 | Bayer Uerdingen |
| 1984 | Bayern Munich |
| 1983 | Köln |
| 1982 | Bayern Munich |
| 1981 | Eintracht Frankfurt |
| 1980 | Fortuna Düsseldorf |
| 1979 | Fortuna Düsseldorf |
| 1978 | Köln |
| 1977 | Köln |
| 1976 | Hamburg |
| 1975 | Eintracht Frankfurt |
| 1974 | Frankfurt |
| 1973 | Borussia Mönchengladbach |
| 1972 | Schalke |
| 1971 | Bayern Munich |
| 1970 | Kickers Offenbach |
| 1969 | Bayern Munich |

| | |
|---|---|
| 1968 | Köln |
| 1967 | Bayern Munich |
| 1966 | Bayern Munich |
| 1965 | Borussia Dortmund |
| 1964 | 1860 Munich |
| 1963 | Hamburg |
| 1962 | Nürnberg |
| 1961 | Werder Bremen |
| 1960 | Borussia Mönchengladbach |
| 1959 | Schwarz–Weiss Essen |
| 1958 | Stuttgart |
| 1957 | Bayern Munich |
| 1956 | Karlsruher |
| 1955 | Karlsruher |
| 1954 | VfB Stuttgart |
| 1953 | Rot–Weiss Essen |
| 1944–1952 | Not played |
| 1943 | First Vienna |
| 1942 | 1860 Munich |
| 1941 | Dresdner SC |
| 1940 | Dresdner SC |
| 1939 | Nürnberg |
| 1938 | Rapid Vienna |
| 1937 | Schalke |
| 1936 | VfB Leipzig |
| 1935 | Nürnberg |

## GERMANY: TOP SCORERS

| | |
|---|---|
| 2008–2009 | Grafite (VfL Wolfsburg) 28 |
| 2007–2008 | Luca Toni (Bayern Munich) 24 |
| 2006–2007 | Theofanis Gekas (VfL Bochum) 20 |
| 2005–2006 | Miroslav Klose (Werder Bremen) 25 |
| 2004–2005 | Marek Mintál (Nürnberg) 24 |
| 2003–2004 | Ailton (Werder Bremen) 28 |
| 2002–2003 | Thomas Christiansen (VfL Bochum) 21 |
| | Giovane Elber (Bayern Munich) 21 |
| 2001–2002 | Márcio Amoroso (Borussia Dortmund) 18 |
| | Martin Max (1860 Munich) 18 |
| 2000–2001 | Sergej Barbarez (Hamburg) 22 |
| | Ebbe Sand (Schalke) 22 |
| 1999–2000 | Martin Max (1860 Munich) 19 |
| 1998–1999 | Michael Preetz (Hertha Berlin) 23 |
| 1997–1998 | Ulf Kirsten (Bayer Leverkusen) 22 |
| 1996–1997 | Ulf Kirsten (Bayer Leverkusen) 22 |
| 1995–1996 | Fredi Bobic (VfB Stuttgart) 17 |
| 1994–1995 | Mario Basler (Werder Bremen) 20 |
| | Heiko Herrlich (Borussia Mönchengladbach) 20 |
| 1993–1994 | Stefan Kuntz (Kaiserslautern) 18 |
| | Tony Yeboah (Eintracht Frankfurt) 18 |
| 1992–1993 | Ulf Kirsten (Bayer Leverkusen) 20 |

| | |
|---|---|
| | Tony Yeboah (Eintracht Frankfurt) 20 |
| 1991–1992 | Fritz Walter (VfB Stuttgart) 22 |
| 1990–1991 | Roland Wohlfarth (Bayern Munich) 21 |
| 1989–1990 | Jørn Andersen (Eintracht Frankfurt) 18 |
| 1988–1989 | Thomas Allofs (Köln) 17 |
| | Roland Wohlfarth (Bayern Munich) 17 |
| 1987–1988 | Jürgen Klinsmann (VfB Stuttgart) 19 |
| 1986–1987 | Uwe Rahn (Borussia Mönchengladbach) 24 |
| 1985–1986 | Stefan Kuntz (VfL Bochum) 22 |
| 1984–1985 | Klaus Allofs (Köln) 26 |
| 1983–1984 | Karl–Heinz Rummenigge (Bayern Munich) 26 |
| 1982–1983 | Rudolf Völler (Werder Bremen) 23 |
| 1981–1982 | Horst Hrubesch (Hamburg) 27 |
| 1980–1981 | Karl–Heinz Rummenigge (Bayern Munich) 29 |
| 1979–1980 | Karl–Heinz Rummenigge (Bayern Munich) 26 |
| 1978–1979 | Klaus Allofs (Fortuna Düsseldorf) 22 |
| 1977–1978 | Dieter Müller (Köln) 24 |
| | Gerd Müller (Bayern Munich) 24 |
| 1976–1977 | Dieter Müller (Köln) 34 |
| 1975–1976 | Klaus Fischer (Schalke) 29 |
| 1974–1975 | Jupp Heynckes (Borussia Mönchengladbach) 27 |
| 1973–1974 | Gerd Müller (Bayern Munich) 30 |
| | Jupp Heynckes (Borussia Mönchengladbach) 30 |
| 1972–1973 | Gerd Müller (Bayern Munich) 36 |
| 1971–1972 | Gerd Müller (Bayern Munich) 40 |
| 1970–1971 | Lothar Kobluhn (Rot–Weiß Oberhausen) 24 |
| 1969–1970 | Gerd Müller (Bayern Munich) 38 |
| 1968–1969 | Gerd Müller (Bayern Munich) 30 |
| 1967–1968 | Johannes Löhr (Köln) 27 |
| 1966–1967 | Lothar Emmerich (Borussia Dortmund) 28 |
| | Gerd Müller (Bayern Munich) 28 |
| 1965–1966 | Lothar Emmerich (Borussia Dortmund) 31 |
| 1964–1965 | Rudolf Brunnenmeier (1860 Munich) 24 |
| 1963–1964 | Uwe Seeler (Hamburg) 30 |

## NETHERLANDS: EREDIVISIE CHAMPIONS

| | |
|---|---|
| 2008–2009 | AZ Alkmaar |
| 2007–2008 | PSV Eindhoven |
| 2006–2007 | PSV Eindhoven |
| 2005–2006 | PSV Eindhoven |
| 2004–2005 | PSV Eindhoven |

| | |
|---|---|
| 2003–2004 | Ajax |
| 2002–2003 | PSV Eindhoven |
| 2001–2002 | Ajax |
| 2000–2001 | PSV Eindhoven |
| 1999–2000 | PSV Eindhoven |
| 1998–1999 | Feyenoord |
| 1997–1998 | Ajax |
| 1996–1997 | PSV Eindhoven |
| 1995–1996 | Ajax |
| 1994–1995 | Ajax |
| 1993–1994 | Ajax |
| 1992–1993 | Feyenoord |
| 1991–1992 | PSV Eindhoven |
| 1990–1991 | PSV Eindhoven |
| 1989–1990 | Ajax |
| 1988–1989 | PSV Eindhoven |
| 1987–1988 | PSV Eindhoven |
| 1986–1987 | PSV Eindhoven |
| 1985–1986 | PSV Eindhoven |
| 1984–1985 | Ajax |
| 1983–1984 | Feyenoord |
| 1982–1983 | Ajax |
| 1981–1982 | Ajax |
| 1980–1981 | AZ Alkmaar |
| 1979–1980 | Ajax |
| 1978–1979 | Ajax |
| 1977–1978 | PSV Eindhoven |
| 1976–1977 | Ajax |
| 1975–1976 | PSV Eindhoven |
| 1974–1975 | PSV Eindhoven |
| 1973–1974 | Feyenoord |
| 1972–1973 | Ajax |
| 1971–1972 | Ajax |
| 1970–1971 | Feyenoord |
| 1969–1970 | Ajax |
| 1968–1969 | Feyenoord |
| 1967–1968 | Ajax |
| 1966–1967 | Ajax |
| 1965–1966 | Ajax |
| 1964–1965 | Feyenoord |
| 1963–1964 | DWS |
| 1962–1963 | PSV Eindhoven |
| 1961–1962 | Feyenoord |
| 1960–1961 | Feyenoord |
| 1959–1960 | Ajax |
| 1958–1959 | Sparta Rotterdam |
| 1957–1958 | DOS |
| 1956–1957 | Ajax |
| 1955–1956 | Rapid JC |
| 1954–1955 | Willem II |
| 1953–1954 | FC Eindhoven |
| 1952–1953 | RCH |
| 1951–1952 | Willem II |
| 1950–1951 | PSV Eindhoven |
| 1949–1950 | Limburgia |
| 1948–1949 | SVV |
| 1947–1948 | BVV |
| 1946–1947 | Ajax |
| 1945–1946 | HFC Haarlem |
| 1943–1944 | Volewijckers |
| 1942–1943 | ADO Den Haag |
| 1941–1942 | ADO Den Haag |
| 1940–1941 | Heracles |
| 1939–1940 | Feyenoord |
| 1938–1939 | Ajax |
| 1937–1938 | Feyenoord |
| 1936–1937 | Ajax |
| 1935–1936 | Feyenoord |
| 1934–1935 | PSV Eindhoven |

| | |
|---|---|
| 1933–1934 | Ajax |
| 1932–1933 | Go Ahead |
| 1931–1932 | Ajax |
| 1930–1931 | Ajax |
| 1929–1930 | Go Ahead |
| 1928–1929 | PSV Eindhoven |
| 1927–1928 | Feyenoord |
| 1926–1927 | Heracles |
| 1925–1926 | Sportclub Enschede |
| 1924–1925 | HBS |
| 1923–1924 | Feyenoord |
| 1922–1923 | RCH |
| 1921–1922 | Go Ahead |
| 1920–1921 | NAC Breda |
| 1919–1920 | Be Quick |
| 1918–1919 | Ajax |
| 1917–1918 | Ajax |
| 1916–1917 | Go Ahead |
| 1915–1916 | Willem II |
| 1914–1915 | Sparta Rotterdam |
| 1913–1914 | Kon HVV |
| 1912–1913 | Sparta Rotterdam |
| 1911–1912 | Sparta Rotterdam |
| 1910–1911 | Sparta Rotterdam |
| 1909–1910 | Kon HVV |
| 1908–1909 | Sparta Rotterdam |
| 1907–1908 | Quick |
| 1906–1907 | Kon HVV |
| 1905–1906 | Kon HBS |
| 1904–1905 | Kon HVV |
| 1903–1904 | HBS |
| 1902–1903 | Kon HVV |
| 1901–1902 | Kon HVV |
| 1900–1901 | Kon HVV |
| 1899–1900 | Kon HVV |
| 1898–1899 | RAP |
| 1897–1898 | RAP |

## KNVB CUP (DUTCH CUP)

| | |
|---|---|
| 2008–2009 | SC Heerenveen |
| 2007–2008 | Feyenoord |
| 2006–2007 | Ajax |
| 2005–2006 | Ajax |
| 2004–2005 | PSV Eindhoven |
| 2003–2004 | Utrecht |
| 2002–2003 | Utrecht |
| 2001–2002 | Ajax |
| 2000–2001 | FC Twente |
| 1999–2000 | Roda JC |
| 1998–1999 | Ajax |
| 1997–1998 | Ajax |
| 1996–1997 | Roda JC |
| 1995–1996 | PSV Eindhoven |
| 1994–1995 | Feyenoord |
| 1993–1994 | Feyenoord |
| 1992–1993 | Ajax |
| 1991–1992 | Feyenoord |
| 1990–1991 | Feyenoord |
| 1989–1990 | PSV Eindhoven |
| 1988–1989 | PSV Eindhoven |
| 1987–1988 | PSV Eindhoven |
| 1986–1987 | Ajax |
| 1985–1986 | Ajax |
| 1984–1985 | Utrecht |
| 1983–1984 | Feyenoord |
| 1982–1983 | Ajax |
| 1981–1982 | AZ Alkmaar |
| 1980–1981 | AZ Alkmaar |
| 1979–1980 | Feyenoord |
| 1978–1979 | Ajax |
| 1977–1978 | AZ Alkmaar |
| 1976–1977 | FC Twente |

| | |
|---|---|
| 1975–1976 | PSV Eindhoven |
| 1974–1975 | FC Den Haag |
| 1973–1974 | PSV Eindhoven |
| 1972–1973 | NAC Breda |
| 1971–1972 | Ajax |
| 1970–1971 | Ajax |
| 1969–1970 | Ajax |
| 1968–1969 | Feyenoord |
| 1967–1968 | ADO Den Haag |
| 1966–1967 | Ajax |
| 1965–1966 | Sparta Rotterdam |
| 1964–1965 | Feyenoord |
| 1963–1964 | Fortuna Sittard |
| 1962–1963 | Willem II |
| 1961–1962 | Sparta Rotterdam |
| 1960–1961 | Ajax |
| 1959–1966 | Not played |
| 1958–1959 | VVV |
| 1957–1958 | Sparta Rotterdam |
| 1956–1957 | Fortuna Sittard |
| 1950–1956 | Not played |
| 1949–1950 | PSV Eindhoven |
| 1948–1949 | Quick |
| 1947–1948 | Wageningen |
| 1944–1947 | Not played |
| 1943–1944 | Willem II |
| 1942–1943 | Ajax |
| 1939–1942 | Not played |
| 1938–1939 | Wageningen |
| 1937–1938 | VSV |
| 1936–1937 | FC Eindhoven |
| 1935–1936 | Roermond |
| 1934–1935 | Feyenoord |
| 1933–1934 | Groningen |
| 1932–1933 | Not played |
| 1931–1932 | DFC |
| 1930–1931 | Not played |
| 1929–1930 | Feyenoord |
| 1928–1929 | Not played |
| 1927–1928 | RCH |
| 1926–1927 | VUC |
| 1925–1926 | LONGA |
| 1924–1925 | ZFC |
| 1923–1924 | Not played |
| 1922–1923 | Not played |
| 1921–1922 | Not played |
| 1920–1921 | Schoten |
| 1919–1920 | CVV |
| 1918–1919 | Not played |
| 1917–1918 | RCH |
| 1916–1917 | Ajax |
| 1915–1916 | Quick |
| 1914–1915 | HFC |
| 1913–1914 | DFC |
| 1912–1913 | HFC |
| 1911–1912 | Haarlem |
| 1910–1911 | Quick |
| 1909–1910 | Quick |
| 1908–1909 | Quick |
| 1907–1908 | HBS |
| 1906–1907 | VOC |
| 1905–1906 | Concordia |
| 1904–1905 | VOC |
| 1903–1904 | HFC |
| 1902–1903 | HVV |
| 1901–1902 | Haarlem |
| 1900–1901 | HBS |
| 1899–1900 | Velocitas Breda |
| 1898–1899 | RAP |

## NETHERLANDS: LEAGUE TOP SCORERS

| | |
|---|---|
| 2008–2009 | Mounir El Hamdaoui (AZ Alkmaar) 23 |
| 2007–2008 | Klaas-Jan Huntelaar (Ajax) 33 |
| 2006–2007 | Afonso Alves (SSC Heerenveen) 34 |
| 2005–2006 | Klaas-Jan Huntelaar (SC Heerenveen and Ajax) 33 |
| 2004–2005 | Dirk Kuyt (Feyenoord) 29 |
| 2003–2004 | Mateja Kežman (PSV Eindhoven) 31 |
| 2002–2003 | Mateja Kežman (PSV Eindhoven) 35 |
| 2001–2002 | Pierre van Hooijdonk (Feyenoord) 24 |
| 2000–2001 | Mateza Kežman (PSV Eindhoven) 24 |
| 1999–2000 | Ruud van Nistelrooy (PSV Eindhoven) 29 |
| 1998–1999 | Ruud van Nistelrooy (PSV Eindhoven) 29 |
| 1997–1998 | Nikos Machlas (Vitesse) 34 |
| 1996–1997 | Luc Nilis (PSV Eindhoven) 21 |
| 1995–1996 | Luc Nilis (PSV Eindhoven) 21 |
| 1994–1995 | Ronaldo (PSV Eindhoven) 30 |
| 1993–1994 | Jari Litmanen (Ajax) 26 |
| 1992–1993 | Dennis Bergkamp (Ajax) 26 |
| 1991–1992 | Dennis Bergkamp (Ajax) 22 |
| 1990–1991 | Romário (PSV Eindhoven) 25 Dennis Bergkamp (Ajax) 25 |
| 1989–1990 | Romário (PSV Eindhoven) 23 |
| 1988–1989 | Romário (PSV Eindhoven) 19 |
| 1987–1988 | Wim Kieft (PSV Eindhoven) 29 |
| 1986–1987 | Marco van Basten (Ajax) 31 |
| 1985–1986 | Marco van Basten (Ajax) 37 |
| 1984–1985 | Marco van Basten (Ajax) 22 |
| 1983–1984 | Marco van Basten (Ajax) 28 |
| 1982–1983 | Peter Houtman (Feyenoord) 30 |
| 1981–1982 | Wim Kieft (Ajax) 32 |
| 1980–1981 | Ruud Geels (Sparta Rotterdam) 22 |
| 1979–1980 | Kees Kist (AZ Almaar) 27 |
| 1978–1979 | Kees Kist (AZ Alkmaar) 34 |
| 1977–1978 | Ruud Geels (Ajax) 30 |
| 1976–1977 | Ruud Geels (Ajax) 34 |
| 1975–1976 | Ruud Geels (Ajax) 29 |
| 1974–1975 | Ruud Geels (Ajax) 30 |
| 1973–1974 | Willy van der Kuijlen (PSV Eindhoven) 27 |
| 1972–1973 | Cas Janssens (NEC) 18 Willy Brokamp (MVV Maastricht) 18 |
| 1971–1972 | Johan Cruyff (Ajax) 25 |
| 1970–1971 | Ove Kindvall (Feyenoord) 24 |
| 1969–1970 | Willy van der Kuijlen (PSV Eindhoven) 26 |
| 1968–1969 | Dick van Dijk (FC Twente) 30 Ove Kindvall (Feyenoord) 30 |
| 1967–1968 | Ove Kindvall (Feyenoord) 28 |
| 1966–1967 | Johan Cruyff (Ajax) 33 |
| 1965–1966 | Willy van Kuijlen (PSV Eindhoven) 23 Piet Kruiver (Feyenoord) 23 |
| 1964–1965 | Frans Geurtsen (DWS) 23 |
| 1963–1964 | Frans Geurtsen (DWS) 28 |
| 1962–1963 | Pierre Kerkhofs (PSV Eindhoven) 22 |
| 1961–1962 | Dick Tol (Volendam) 27 |
| 1960–1961 | Henk Groot (Ajax) 41 |

| | |
|---|---|
| 1959–1960 | Henk Groot (Ajax) 38 |
| 1958–1959 | Leon Canjels (NAC Breda) 34 |
| 1957–1958 | Leo Canjels (NAC Breda) 32 |
| 1956–1957 | Coen Dillon (PSV Eindhoven) 43 |

## SPAIN: LA LIGA CHAMPIONS

| | |
|---|---|
| 2008–2009 | Barcelona |
| 2007–2008 | Real Madrid |
| 2006–2007 | Real Madrid |
| 2005–2006 | Barcelona |
| 2004–2005 | Barcelona |
| 2003–2004 | Valencia |
| 2002–2003 | Real Madrid |
| 2001–2002 | Valencia |
| 2000–2001 | Real Madrid |
| 1999–2000 | Deportivo La Coruña |
| 1998–1999 | Barcelona |
| 1997–1998 | Barcelona |
| 1996–1997 | Real Madrid |
| 1995–1996 | Atlético Madrid |
| 1994–1995 | Real Madrid |
| 1993–1994 | Barcelona |
| 1992–1993 | Barcelona |
| 1991–1992 | Barcelona |
| 1990–1991 | Barcelona |
| 1989–1990 | Real Madrid |
| 1988–1989 | Real Madrid |
| 1987–1988 | Real Madrid |
| 1986–1987 | Real Madrid |
| 1985–1986 | Real Madrid |
| 1984–1985 | Barcelona |
| 1983–1984 | Athletic Bilbao |
| 1982–1983 | Athletic Bilbao |
| 1981–1982 | Real Sociedad |
| 1980–1981 | Real Sociedad |
| 1979–1980 | Real Madrid |
| 1978–1979 | Real Madrid |
| 1977–1978 | Real Madrid |
| 1976–1977 | Atlético Madrid |
| 1975–1976 | Real Madrid |
| 1974–1975 | Real Madrid |
| 1973–1974 | Barcelona |
| 1972–1973 | Atlético Madrid |
| 1971–1972 | Real Madrid |
| 1970–1971 | Valencia |
| 1969–1970 | Atlético Madrid |
| 1968–1969 | Real Madrid |
| 1967–1968 | Real Madrid |
| 1966–1967 | Real Madrid |
| 1965–1966 | Atlético Madrid |
| 1964–1965 | Real Madrid |
| 1963–1964 | Real Madrid |
| 1962–1963 | Real Madrid |
| 1961–1962 | Real Madrid |
| 1960–1961 | Real Madrid |
| 1959–1960 | Barcelona |
| 1958–1959 | Barcelona |
| 1957–1958 | Real Madrid |
| 1956–1957 | Real Madrid |
| 1955–1956 | Athletic Bilbao |
| 1954–1955 | Real Madrid |
| 1953–1954 | Real Madrid |
| 1952–1953 | Barcelona |
| 1951–1952 | Barcelona |
| 1950–1951 | Atlético Madrid |
| 1949–1950 | Atlético Madrid |
| 1948–1949 | Barcelona |
| 1947–1948 | Barcelona |
| 1946–1947 | Valencia |

# DOMESTIC STATS

**1945–1946** Sevilla
**1944–1945** Barcelona
**1943–1944** Valencia
**1942–1943** Athletic Bilbao
**1941–1942** Valencia
**1940–1941** Atlético Madrid
**1939–1940** Atlético Madrid
**1936–1939** Not played due to the Spanish Civil War
**1935–1936** Athletic Bilbao
**1934–1935** Real Betis
**1933–1934** Athletic Bilbao
**1932–1933** Real Madrid
**1931–1932** Real Madrid
**1930–1931** Athletic Bilbao
**1929–1930** Athletic Bilbao
**1928–1929** Barcelona

## SPAIN: COPA DEL REY (SPANISH CUP)

**2009** Barcelona
**2008** Valencia
**2007** Sevilla
**2006** Espanyol
**2005** Real Betis
**2004** Real Zaragoza
**2003** Mallorca
**2002** Deportivo La Coruña
**2001** Real Zaragoza
**2000** Espanyol
**1999** Valencia
**1998** Barcelona
**1997** Barcelona
**1996** Atlético Madrid
**1995** Deportivo La Coruña
**1994** Real Zaragoza
**1993** Real Madrid
**1992** Atlético Madrid
**1991** Atlético Madrid
**1990** Barcelona
**1989** Real Madrid
**1988** Barcelona
**1987** Real Sociedad
**1986** Real Zaragoza
**1985** Atlético Madrid
**1984** Athletic Bilbao
**1983** Barcelona
**1982** Real Madrid
**1981** Barcelona
**1980** Real Madrid
**1979** Valencia
**1978** Barcelona
**1977** Real Betis
**1976** Atlético Madrid
**1975** Real Madrid
**1974** Real Madrid
**1973** Athletic Bilbao
**1972** Atlético Madrid
**1971** Barcelona
**1970** Real Madrid
**1969** Athletic Bilbao
**1968** Barcelona
**1967** Valencia
**1966** Real Zaragoza
**1965** Atlético Madrid
**1964** Real Zaragoza
**1963** Barcelona
**1962** Real Madrid
**1961** Atlético Madrid

**1960** Atlético Madrid
**1959** Barcelona
**1958** Athletic Bilbao
**1957** Barcelona
**1956** Athletic Bilbao
**1955** Athletic Bilbao
**1954** Valencia
**1953** Barcelona
**1952** Barcelona
**1951** Barcelona
**1950** Athletic Bilbao
**1949** Valencia
**1948** Sevilla
**1947** Real Madrid
**1946** Real Madrid
**1945** Athletic Bilbao
**1944** Athletic Bilbao
**1943** Athletic Bilbao
**1942** Barcelona
**1941** Valencia
**1940** Espanyol
**1939** Sevilla
**1938** Not played due to the Spanish Civil War
**1937** Not played due to the Spanish Civil War
**1936** Real Madrid
**1935** Sevilla
**1934** Real Madrid
**1933** Athletic Bilbao
**1932** Athletic Bilbao
**1931** Athletic Bilbao
**1930** Athletic Bilbao
**1929** Espanyol
**1928** Barcelona
**1927** Real Unión
**1926** Barcelona
**1925** Barcelona
**1924** Real Unión
**1923** Athletic Bilbao
**1922** Barcelona
**1921** Athletic Bilbao
**1920** Barcelona
**1919** Arenas de Getxo
**1918** Real Unión
**1917** Real Madrid
**1916** Athletic Bilbao
**1915** Athletic Bilbao
**1914** Athletic Bilbao
**1913** Racing Irún
**1913** Barcelona
**1912** Barcelona
**1911** Athletic Bilbao
**1910** Barcelona
**1910** Athletic Bilbao
**1909** Ciclista (later Real Sociedad)
**1908** Real Madrid
**1907** Real Madrid
**1906** Real Madrid
**1905** Real Madrid
**1904** Not played, Athletic Bilbao awarded the trophy
**1903** Athletic Bilbao
**1902** Club Vizcaya (later Athletic Bilbao)

## SPAIN: LEAGUE TOP SCORERS

**2008–2009** Diego Forlán (Atlético Madrid) 32
**2007–2008** Dani Güiza (Mallorca) 27

**2006–2007** Ruud van Nistelrooy (Real Madrid) 25
**2005–2006** Samuel Eto'o (Barcelona) 26
**2004–2005** Diego Forlán (Villareal) 25
**2003–2004** Ronaldo (Real Madrid) 24
**2002–2003** Roy Makaay (Deportivo La Coruña) 29
**2001–2002** Diego Tristán (Deportivo La Coruña) 21
**2000–2001** Raúl (Real Madrid) 24
**1999–2000** Salva Ballesta (Racing Santander) 27
**1998–1999** Raúl (Real Madrid) 23
**1997–1998** Christian Vieri (Atlético Madrid) 24
**1996–1997** Ronaldo (Barcelona) 34
**1995–1996** Juan Antonio Pizzi (Tenerife) 31
**1994–1995** Iván Zamorano (Real Madrid) 27
**1993–1994** Romário (Barcelona) 30
**1992–1993** Bebeto (Deportivo La Coruña) 29
**1991–1992** Manolo Sánchez (Atlético Madrid) 27
**1990–1991** Emilio Butragueño (Real Madrid) 19
**1989–1990** Hugo Sánchez (Real Madrid) 38
**1988–1989** Baltazar (Atlético Madrid) 35
**1987–1988** Hugo Sánchez (Real Madrid) 29
**1986–1987** Hugo Sánchez (Real Madrid) 34
**1985–1986** Hugo Sánchez (Atlético Madrid) 22
**1984–1985** Hugo Sánchez (Atlético Madrid) 19
**1983–1984** Jorge da Silva (Real Valladolid) 17
Juanito (Real Valladolid) 17
**1982–1983** Poli Rincón (Real Betis) 20
**1981–1982** Quini (Barcelona) 26
**1980–1981** Quini (Barcelona) 20
**1979–1980** Quini (Sporting Gijón) 24
**1978–1979** Hans Krankl (Barcelona) 29
**1977–1978** Mario Kempes (Valencia) 28
**1976–1977** Mario Kempes (Valencia) 24
**1975–1976** Quini (Sporting Gijón) 18
**1974–1975** Carlos (Athletic Bilbao) 19
**1973–1974** Quini (Sporting Gijón) 20
**1972–1973** Marianín (Real Oviedo) 19
**1971–1972** Enrique Porta (Granada) 20
**1970–1971** José Eulogio Gárate (Atlético Madrid) 17
Carles Rexach (Barcelona) 17
**1969–1970** Amancio (Real Madrid) 16
Luis Aragonés (Atlético Madrid) 16
José Eulogio Gárate (Atlético Madrid) 16
**1968–1969** Amancio (Real Madrid) 14
José Eulogio Gárate (Atlético Madrid) 14
**1967–1968** Fidel Uriarte (Athletic Bilbao) 22
**1966–1967** Waldo (Valencia) 24
**1965–1966** Vavá (Elche) 19
**1964–1965** Cayetano Ré (Barcelona) 25

**1963–1964** Ferenc Puskás (Real Madrid) 20
**1962–1963** Ferenc Puskás (Real Madrid) 26
**1961–1962** Juan Seminario (Real Zaragoza) 25
**1960–1961** Ferenc Puskás (Real Madrid) 27
**1959–1960** Ferenc Puskás (Real Madrid) 26
**1958–1959** Alfredo di Stéfano (Real Madrid) 23
**1957–1958** Manuel Badenes (Real Valladolid) 19
Alfredo di Stéfano (Real Madrid) 19
Ricardo (Valencia) 19
**1956–1957** Alfredo di Stéfano (Real Madrid) 31
**1955–1956** Alfredo di Stéfano (Real Madrid) 24
**1954–1955** Juan Arza (Sevilla) 28
**1953–1954** Alfredo di Stéfano (Real Madrid) 27
**1952–1953** Telmo Zarra (Athletic Bilbao) 24
**1951–1952** Pahiño (Real Madrid) 28
**1950–1951** Telmo Zarra (Athletic Bilbao) 38
**1949–1950** Telmo Zarra (Athletic Bilbao) 25
**1948–1949** César (Barcelona) 28
**1947–1948** Pahiño (Celta Vigo) 23
**1946–1947** Telmo Zarra (Athletic Bilbao) 34
**1945–1946** Telmo Zarra (Athletic Bilbao) 24
**1944–1945** Telmo Zarra (Athletic Bilbao) 19
**1943–1944** Mundo (Valencia) 27
**1942–1943** Mariano Martín (Barcelona) 32
**1941–1942** Mundo (Valencia) 27
**1940–1941** Pruden (Atlético Madrid) 30
**1939–1940** Victor Unamuno (Athletic Bilbao) 26
**1936–1939** Not played due to Spanish Civil War
**1935–1936** Isidro Lángara (Real Oviedo) 27
**1934–1935** Isidro Lángara (Real Oviedo) 26
**1933–1934** Isidro Lángara (Real Oviedo) 27
**1932–1933** Manuel Olivares (Real Madrid) 16
**1931–1932** Guillermo Gorostiza (Athletic Bilbao) 12
**1930–1931** Bata (Athletic Bilbao) 27
**1929–1930** Guillermo Gorostiza (Athletic Bilbao) 19
**1928–1929** Paco Bienzobas (Real Sociedad) 14

## BRAZIL: CAMPEONATO BRASILEIRO CHAMPIONS

**2009** Flamengo
**2008** São Paulo
**2007** São Paulo

| Year | Champion |
|------|----------|
| 2005 | Corinthians |
| 2004 | Santos |
| 2003 | Cruzeiro |
| 2002 | Santos |
| 2001 | Atlético Paranaense |
| 2000 | Not played |
| 1999 | Corinthians |
| 1998 | Corinthians |
| 1997 | Vasco da Gama |
| 1996 | Grêmio |
| 1995 | Botafogo |
| 1994 | Palmeiras |
| 1993 | Palmeiras |
| 1992 | Flamengo |
| 1991 | São Paulo |
| 1990 | Corinthians |
| 1989 | Vasco da Gama |
| 1988 | Bahia |
| 1987 | Sport Club Recife |
| 1986 | São Paulo |
| 1985 | Coritiba |
| 1984 | Fluminense |
| 1983 | Flamengo |
| 1982 | Flamengo |
| 1981 | Grêmio |
| 1980 | Flamengo |
| 1979 | Internacional |
| 1978 | Guarani |
| 1977 | São Paulo |
| 1976 | Internacional |
| 1975 | Internacional |
| 1974 | Vasco da Gama |
| 1973 | Palmeiras |
| 1972 | Palmeiras |
| 1971 | Atlético Mineiro |

## BRAZIL: COPA DO BRASIL (BRASILIAN CUP)*

| Year | Champion |
|------|----------|
| 2009 | Corinthians |
| 2008 | Sport-PE |
| 2007 | Fluminense |
| 2006 | Flamengo |
| 2005 | Paulista |
| 2004 | Santo André |
| 2003 | Cruzeiro |
| 2002 | Corinthians |
| 2001 | Grêmio |
| 2000 | Cruzeiro |
| 1999 | Juventude |
| 1998 | Palmeiras |
| 1997 | Grêmio |
| 1996 | Cruzeiro |
| 1995 | Corinthians |
| 1994 | Grêmio |
| 1993 | Cruzeiro |
| 1992 | Internacional |
| 1991 | Criciúma |
| 1990 | Flamengo |
| 1989 | Grêmio |
| 1968 | Botafogo |
| 1967 | Palmeiras |
| 1966 | Cruzeiro |
| 1965 | Santos |
| 1964 | Santos |
| 1963 | Santos |
| 1962 | Santos |
| 1961 | Santos |
| 1960 | Palmeiras |
| 1959 | Bahia |

* Known as Taça Brasil 1959–1968.

## BRAZIL: LEAGUE TOP SCORERS

| Year | Scorer |
|------|--------|
| 2008 | Washington (Fluminense) 21 |
|      | Keirrison (Coritiba) 21 |
|      | Kléber Pereira (Santos) 21 |
| 2007 | Josiel (Paraná) 20 |
| 2006 | Souza (Goiás) 17 |
| 2005 | Romário (Vasco da Gama) 22 |
| 2004 | Washington (Atlético Paranaense) 34 |
| 2003 | Dimba (Goiás) 31 |
| 2002 | Luís Fabiano (São Paulo) 19 |
|      | Rodrigo Fabri (Grêmio) 19 |
| 2001 | Romário (Vasco da Gama) 21 |
| 2000 | Dill (Goiás) 20 |
|      | Magno Alves (Fluminense) 20 |
|      | Romário (Vasco da Gama) 20 |
| 1999 | Guilherme (Atlético Mineiro) 28 |
| 1998 | Viola (Santos) 21 |
| 1997 | Edmundo (Vasco da Gama) 29 |
| 1996 | Paulo Nunes (Grêmio) 16 |
|      | Renaldo (Atlético Mineiro) 16 |
| 1995 | Túlio (Botafogo) 23 |
| 1994 | Márcio Amoroso (Guarani) 19 |
| 1993 | Guga (Santos) 15 |
| 1992 | Bebeto (Vasco da Gama) 18 |
| 1991 | Paulinho McLaren (Santos) 15 |
| 1990 | Charles (Bahia) 11 |
| 1989 | Túlio (Goiás) 11 |
| 1988 | Nilson (Internacional) 15 |
| 1987 | Muller (São Paulo) 10 |
| 1986 | Careca (São Paulo) 25 |
| 1985 | Edmar (Guarani) 20 |
| 1984 | Roberto Dinamite (Vasco da Gama) 16 |
| 1983 | Serginho (Santos) 22 |
| 1982 | Zico (Flamengo) 20 |
| 1981 | Nunes (Flamengo) 16 |
| 1980 | Zico (Flamengo) 21 |
| 1979 | César (América) 13 |
| 1978 | Paulinho (Vasco da Gama) 19 |
| 1977 | Reinaldo (Atlético Mineiro) 28 |
| 1976 | Dario (Internacional) 16 |
| 1975 | Flávio (Internacional) 16 |
| 1974 | Roberto Dinamite (Vasco da Gama) 16 |
| 1973 | Ramón (Santa Cruz) 21 |
|      | Túlio (Botafogo) 19 |
| 1972 | Dario (Atlético Mineiro) 17 |
|      | Pedro Rocha (São Paulo) 17 |
| 1971 | Dario (Atlético Mineiro) 15 |

## ARGENTINA: PRIMERA DIVISION CHAMPIONS*

| Year | Champion |
|------|----------|
| 2009C | Vélez Sársfield |
| 2008A | Boca Juniors |
| 2008C | River Plate |
| 2007A | Lanús |
| 2007C | San Lorenzo |
| 2006A | Estudiantes |
| 2006C | Boca Juniors |
| 2005A | Boca Juniors |
| 2005C | Vélez Sársfield |
| 2004A | Newell's Old Boys |
| 2004C | River Plate |
| 2003A | Boca Juniors |
| 2003C | River Plate |
| 2002A | Independiente |
| 2002C | River Plate |
| 2001A | Racing Club |
| 2001C | San Lorenzo |
| 2000A | Boca Juniors |
| 2000C | River Plate |
| 1999A | River Plate |
| 1999C | Boca Juniors |
| 1998A | Boca Juniors |
| 1998C | Vélez Sársfield |
| 1997A | River Plate |
| 1997C | River Plate |
| 1996A | River Plate |
| 1996C | Vélez Sársfield |
| 1995A | Vélez Sársfield |
| 1995C | San Lorenzo |
| 1994A | River Plate |
| 1994C | Independiente |
| 1993A | River Plate |
| 1993C | Vélez Sársfield |
| 1992A | Boca Juniors |
| 1992C | Newell's Old Boys |
| 1991A | River Plate |
| 1990–1991 | Newell's Old Boys |
| 1989–1990 | River Plate |
| 1988–1989 | Independiente |
| 1987–1988 | Newell's Old Boys |
| 1986–1987 | Rosario Central |
| 1985–1986 | River Plate |
| 1985N | Argentinos Juniors |
| 1984N | Ferro Carril Oeste |
| 1984M | Argentinos Juniors |
| 1983N | Estudiantes |
| 1983M | Independiente |
| 1982N | Ferro Carril Oeste |
| 1982M | Estudiantes |
| 1981M | Boca Juniors |
| 1981N | River Plate |
| 1980M | River Plate |
| 1980N | Rosario Central |
| 1979M | River Plate |
| 1979N | River Plate |
| 1978M | Quilmes |
| 1978N | Independiente |
| 1977M | River Plate |
| 1977N | Independiente |
| 1976M | Boca Juniors |
| 1976N | Boca Juniors |
| 1975M | River Plate |
| 1975N | River Plate |
| 1974M | Newell's Old Boys |
| 1974N | San Lorenzo |
| 1973M | Huracán |
| 1973N | Rosario Central |
| 1972M | San Lorenzo |
| 1972N | San Lorenzo |
| 1971M | Independiente |
| 1971N | Rosario Central |
| 1970M | Independiente |
| 1970N | Boca Juniors |
| 1969M | Chacarita Juniors |
| 1969N | Boca Juniors |
| 1968M | San Lorenzo |
| 1968N | Vélez Sársfield |
| 1967M | Estudiantes |
| 1967N | Independiente |
| 1966 | Racing Club |
| 1965 | Boca Juniors |
| 1964 | Boca Juniors |
| 1963 | Independiente |
| 1962 | Boca Juniors |
| 1961 | Racing Club |
| 1960 | Independiente |
| 1959 | San Lorenzo |
| 1958 | Racing Club |
| 1957 | River Plate |
| 1956 | River Plate |
| 1955 | River Plate |
| 1954 | Boca Juniors |
| 1953 | River Plate |
| 1952 | River Plate |
| 1951 | Racing Club |
| 1950 | Racing Club |
| 1949 | Racing Club |
| 1948 | Independiente |
| 1947 | River Plate |
| 1946 | San Lorenzo |
| 1945 | River Plate |
| 1944 | Boca Juniors |
| 1943 | Boca Juniors |
| 1942 | River Plate |
| 1941 | River Plate |
| 1940 | Boca Juniors |
| 1939 | Independiente |
| 1938 | Independiente |
| 1937 | River Plate |
| 1936 | River Plate |
| 1935 | Boca Juniors |
| 1934 | Boca Juniors |
| 1933 | San Lorenzo |
| 1932 | River Plate |
| 1931 | Boca Juniors |

* In 1999 the championship was split into two tournaments: Apertuna (August to December) and Clausura (February to June).

Championship was previously split into two tournaments in 1967–1986: Metropolitano (open only to teams affilated to the national association) and Nacional (open to teams from the provinces).

## ARGENTINA: LEAGUE TOP SCORERS

| Year | Scorer |
|------|--------|
| 2009C | José Sand (Lanús) 13 |
| 2008A | José Sand (Lanús) 15 |
| 2008C | Darío Cvitanich (Banfield) 13 |
| 2007A | German Denis (Independiente) 18 |
| 2007C | Martín Palermo (Boca Juniors) 11 |
| 2006A | Mauro Zárate (Vélez Sársfield) 12 |
|       | Rodrigo Palacio (Boca Juniors) 12 |
| 2006C | Gonzalo Vargas (Gimnasia) 12 |
| 2005A | Javier Cámpora (Tiro Federal) 13 |
| 2005C | Mariano Pavone (Estudiantes) 16 |
| 2004A | Lisandro López (Racing Club) 12 |
| 2004C | Rolando Zárate (Vélez Sársfield) 13 |
| 2003A | Ernesto Farías (Estudiantes) 12 |
| 2003C | Luciano Figueroa (Rosario Central) 17 |
| 2002A | Néstor Silvera (Independiente) 16 |
| 2002C | Fernando Cavenaghi (River Plate) 15 |
| 2001A | Martín Cardetti (River Plate) 17 |
| 2001C | Bernardo Romeo (San Lorenzo) 15 |
| 2000A | Juan Pablo Ángel (River Plate) 13 |

| Year | Player |
|------|--------|
| 2000C | Esteban Fuertes (Colón) 17 |
| 1999A | Javier Saviola (River Plate) 15 |
| 1999C | José Luis Calderon (Independiente) 17 |
| 1998A | Martín Palermo (Boca Juniors) 20 |
| 1998C | Roberto Sosa (Gimnasia) 17 |
| 1997A | Rubén Da Silva (Rosario Central) 15 |
| 1997C | Sergio Martínez (Boca Juniors) 15 |
| 1996A | Gustavo Reggi (Ferro Carril Oeste) 11 |
| 1996C | Ariel López (Lanús) 12 |
| 1995A | José Luis Calderon (Estudiantes) 13 |
| 1995C | José Oscar Flores (Vélez Sársfield) 14 |
| 1994A | Enzo Francescoli (River Plate) 12 |
| 1994C | Hernán Crespo (River Plate) 11 |
| | Marcelo Espina (Platense) 11 |
| 1993A | Sergio Martínez (Boca Juniors) 12 |
| 1993C | Rubén Da Silva (River Plate) 13 |
| 1992A | Alberto Acosta (San Lorenzo) 12 |
| 1992C | Diego Latorre (Boca Juniors) 9 |
| 1991A | Ramón Angel Díaz (River Plate) 14 |
| 1990–1991 | Esteban González (Vélez Sársfield) 18 |
| 1989–1990 | Ariel Cozzoni (Newell's Old Boys) 23 |
| 1988–1989 | Oscar Dertycia (Argentinos Juniors) 20 |
| | Néstor Raúl Gorosito (San Lorenzo) 20 |
| 1987–1988 | José Luis Rodriguez (Deportivo Español) 18 |
| 1986–1987 | Omar Palma (Rosario Central) 20 |
| 1985–1986 | Enzo Francescoli (River Plate) 25 |
| 1985N | Jorge Comas (Vélez Sársfield) 12 |
| 1984N | Pedro Pablo Pasculli (Argentinos Juniors) 9 |
| 1984M | Enzo Francescoli (River Plate) 24 |
| 1983N | Armando Husillos (Loma Negra) 11 |
| 1983M | Víctor Ramos (Newell's Old Boys) 30 |
| 1982N | Miguel Juárez (Ferro Carril Oeste) 22 |
| 1982M | Carlos Manuel Morete (Independiente) 20 |
| 1981M | Raúl Chaparro (Instituto) 20 |
| 1981N | Carlos Bianchi (Vélez Sársfield) 15 |
| 1980M | Diego Maradona (Argentinos Juniors) 25 |
| 1980N | Diego Maradona (Argentinos Juniors) 17 |
| 1979M | Diego Maradona (Argentinos Juniors) 14 |
| | Sergio Fortunato (Estudiantes) 14 |
| 1979N | Diego Maradona (Argentinos Juniors) 12 |
| 1978M | Diego Maradona (Argentinos Juniors) 22 |
| | Luis Andreucci (Quilmes) 22 |
| 1978N | José Omar Reinaldi (Talleres) 18 |
| 1977M | Carlos Álvarez (Argentinos Juniors) 27 |
| 1977N | Alfredo Letanu (Estudiantes) 13 |
| 1976M | Mario Kempes (Rosario Central) 21 |
| 1976N | Norberto Eresuma (San Lorenzo de Mar del Plata) 12 |
| | Luis Ludueña (Talleres) 12 |
| | Víctor Marchetti (Atlético Unión) 12 |
| 1975M | Héctor Scotta (San Lorenzo) 32 |
| 1975N | Héctor Scotta (San Lorenzo) 28 |
| 1974M | Carlos Manuel Morete (River Plate) 18 |
| 1974N | Mario Kempes (Rosario Central) 25 |
| 1973M | Oscar Más (River Plate) 17 |
| | Hugo Curioni (Boca Juniors) 17 |
| | Ignacio Peña (Estudiantes) 17 |
| 1973N | Juan Gómez Voglino (Atlanta) 18 |
| 1972M | Miguel Ángel Brindisi (Huracán) 21 |
| 1972N | Carlos Manuel Morete (River Plate) 14 |
| 1971M | Carlos Bianchi (Vélez Sársfield) 36 |
| 1971N | Alfredo Obberti (Newell's Old Boys) 10 |
| | José Luñis (Juventud Antoniana) 10 |
| 1970M | Oscar Más (River Plate) 16 |
| 1970N | Carlos Bianchi (Vélez Sársfield) 18 |
| 1969M | Walter Machado (Racing Club) 14 |
| 1969N | Rodolfo Fischer (San Lorenzo) 14 |
| | Carlos Bulla (Platense) 14 |
| 1968M | Alfredo Obberti (Los Andes) 13 |
| 1968N | Omar Wehbe (Vélez Sársfield) 13 |
| 1967M | Bernardo Acosta (Lanús) 18 |
| 1967N | Luis Artime (Independiente) 11 |
| 1966 | Luis Artime (Independiente) 23 |
| 1965 | Juan Carlos Carone (Vélez Sársfield) 19 |
| 1964 | Héctor Rodolfo Viera (San Lorenzo) 17 |
| 1963 | Luis Artime (River Plate) 25 |
| 1962 | Luis Artime (River Plate) 25 |
| 1961 | José Sanfilippo (San Lorenzo) 26 |
| 1960 | José Sanfilippo (San Lorenzo) 34 |
| 1959 | José Sanfilippo (San Lorenzo) 31 |
| 1958 | José Sanfilippo (San Lorenzo) 28 |
| 1957 | Roberto Zarate (River Plate) 22 |
| 1956 | Juan Alberto Castro (Rosario Central) 17 |
| | Ernesto Grillo (Independiente) 17 |
| 1955 | Oscar Massei (Rosario Central) 21 |
| 1954 | Ángel Berni (San Lorenzo) 19 |
| | Norberto Conde (Vélez Sársfield) 19 |
| | José Borello (Boca Juniors) 19 |
| 1953 | Juan José Pizzuti (Racing Club) 22 |
| | Juan Benavidez (San Lorenzo) 22 |
| 1952 | Eduardo Ricagni (Huracán) 28 |
| 1951 | Santagio Vernazza (River Plate) 22 |
| 1950 | Mario Papa (San Lorenzo) 24 |
| 1949 | Llamil Simes (Racing Club) 26 |
| | Juan José Pizzuti (Banfield) 26 |
| 1948 | Benjamín Santos (Rosario Central) 21 |
| 1947 | Alfredo di Stéfano (River Plate) 27 |
| 1946 | Mario Boye (Boca Juniors) 24 |
| 1945 | Ángel Labruna (River Plate) 25 |
| 1944 | Atilio Mellone (Huracán) 26 |
| 1943 | Luis Arrieta (Lanús) 23 |
| | Ángel Labruna (River Plate) 23 |
| | Raúl Frutos (Platense) 23 |
| 1942 | Rinaldo Martino (San Lorenzo) 25 |
| 1941 | José Canteli (Newell's Old Boys) 30 |
| 1940 | Delfín Benitez (Racing Club) 33 |
| | Isidro Langara (San Lorenzo) 33 |
| 1939 | Arsenio Erico (Independiente) 40 |
| 1938 | Arsenio Erico (Independiente) 43 |
| 1937 | Arsenio Erico (Independiente) 47 |
| 1936 | Evaristo Barrera (Racing Club) 32 |
| 1935 | Agustín Cosso (Vélez Sársfield) 33 |
| 1934 | Evaristo Barrera (Racing Club) 34 |
| 1933 | Francisco Varallo (Boca Juniors) 34 |
| 1932 | Bernabé Ferreyra (River Plate) 43 |
| 1931 | Alberto Zozaya (Estudiantes) 33 |

## USA: NORTH AMERICAN SOCCER LEAGUE CHAMPIONS

| Year | Champion |
|------|----------|
| 1984 | Chicago Sting |
| 1983 | Tulsa Roughnecks |
| 1982 | New York Cosmos |
| 1981 | Chicago Sting |
| 1980 | New York Cosmos |
| 1979 | Vancouver Whitecaps |
| 1978 | New York Cosmos |
| 1977 | New York Cosmos |
| 1976 | Toronto Metros–Croatia |
| 1975 | Tampa Bay Rowdies |
| 1974 | Los Angeles Aztecs |
| 1973 | Philadelphia Atoms |
| 1972 | New York Cosmos |
| 1971 | Dallas Tornado |
| 1970 | Rochester Lancers |
| 1969 | Kansas City Spurs |
| 1968 | Atlanta Chiefs |

## NORTH AMERICAN SOCCER LEAGUE TOP SCORERS

| Year | Player |
|------|--------|
| 1984 | Steve Zungul (Golden Bay Earthquakes) 20 |
| 1983 | Roberto Cabanas (New York Cosmos) 25 |
| 1982 | Ricardo Alonso (Jacksonville Tea Men) 21 |
| 1981 | Giorgio Chinaglia (New York Cosmos) 29 |
| 1980 | Giorgio Chinaglia (New York Cosmos) 32 |
| 1979 | Giorgio Chinaglia (New York Cosmos) 26 |
| 1978 | Giorgio Chinaglia (New York Cosmos) 34 |
| 1977 | Steve David (Los Angeles Aztecs) 26 |
| 1976 | Derek Smethurst (Tampa Bay Rowdies) 20 |
| 1975 | Steve David (Miami Toros) 23 |
| 1974 | Paul Child (San Jose Earthquakes) 15 |
| 1973 | Warren Archibald (Miami Toros) 12 |
| | Ilija Mitic (Dallas Tornado) 12 |
| 1972 | Randy Horton (New York Cosmos) 9 |
| 1971 | Carlos Metidieri (Rochester Lancers) 19 |
| 1970 | Kirk Apostolidis (Dallas Tornado) 16 |
| 1969 | Kaiser Motaung (Atlanta Apollos) 16 |
| 1968 | John Kowalik (Chicago Mustangs) 30 |
| | Cirilo Fernandez (San Diego Toros) 30 |

## USA: MAJOR LEAGUE SOCCER CHAMPIONS – MLS CUP

| Year | Champion |
|------|----------|
| 2008 | Columbus Crew |

| 2007 | Houston Dynamo |
|------|----------------|
| 2006 | Houston Dynamo |
| 2005 | Los Angeles Galaxy |
| 2004 | DC United |
| 2003 | San Jose Earthquakes |
| 2002 | Los Angeles Galaxy |
| 2001 | San Jose Earthquakes |
| 2000 | Kansas City Wizards |
| 1999 | DC United |
| 1998 | Chicago Fire |
| 1997 | DC United |
| 1996 | DC United |

## MLS TOP SCORERS

| 2008 | Landon Donovan (Los Angeles Galaxy) 20 |
|------|----------------|
| 2007 | Luciano Emilio (DC United) 20 |
| 2006 | Jeff Cunningham (Real Salt Lake) 16 |
| 2005 | Taylor Twellman (New England Revolution) 17 |
| 2004 | Brian Ching (San Jose Earthquakes) 12 |
| 2003 | Carlos Ruiz (Los Angeles Galaxy) 15 |
| 2002 | Carlos Ruiz (Los Angeles Galaxy) 24 |
| 2001 | Alex Pineda Chacón (Miami Fusion) 19 |
| 2000 | Mamadou Diallo (Tampa Bay Mutiny) 26 |
| 1999 | Jason Kreis (Dallas Burn) 18 |
| 1998 | Stern John (Columbus Crew) 26 |
| 1997 | Jaime Moreno (DC United) 16 |
| 1996 | Roy Lassiter (Tampa Bay Mutiny) 27 |

## JAPAN: J.LEAGUE CHAMPIONSHIP

| 2008 | Kashima Antlers |
|------|----------------|
| 2007 | Kashima Antlers |
| 2006 | Urawa Red Diamonds |
| 2005 | Gamba Osaka |
| 2004 | Yokohama F. Marinos |
| 2003 | Yokohama F. Marinos |
| 2002 | Júbilo Iwata |
| 2001 | Kashima Antlers |
| 2000 | Kashima Antlers |
| 1999 | Júbilo Iwata |
| 1998 | Kashima Antlers |
| 1997 | Júbilo Iwata |
| 1996 | Kashima Antlers |
| 1995 | Yokohama Marinos |
| 1994 | Verdy Kawasaki |
| 1993 | Verdy Kawasaki |

## JAPAN: ALL-JAPAN FOOTBALL CHAMPIONSHIP*

| 1991–1992 | Yomiuri |
|------|----------------|
| 1990–1991 | Yomiuri |
| 1989–1990 | Nissan |
| 1988–1989 | Nissan |
| 1987–1988 | Yamaha Motors |
| 1986–1987 | Yomiuri |
| 1985–1986 | East Furukawa |
| 1984 | Yomiuri |
| 1983 | Yomiuri |
| 1982 | Mitsubishi Motors |
| 1981 | Fujita |
| 1980 | Yanmar Diesel |
| 1979 | Fujita |
| 1978 | Mitsubishi Motors |
| 1977 | Fujita |

| 1976 | East Furukawa |
|------|----------------|
| 1975 | Yanmar Diesel |
| 1974 | Yanmar Diesel |
| 1973 | Mitsubishi Motors |
| 1972 | Hitachi |
| 1971 | Yanmar Diesel |
| 1970 | Toyo Kogyo |
| 1969 | Mitsubishi Motors |
| 1968 | Toyo Kogyo |
| 1967 | Toyo Kogyo |
| 1966 | Toyo Kogyo |
| 1965 | Toyo Kogyo |

* Amateur tournament played until the formation of the J.League. Amateur league was highest level of the sport in Japan until 1992.

## JAPAN: EMPEROR'S CUP*

| 2008 | Gamba Osaka |
|------|----------------|
| 2007 | Kashima Antlers |
| 2006 | Urawa Reds |
| 2005 | Urawa Reds |
| 2004 | Tokyo Verdy 1969 |
| 2003 | Júbilo Iwata |
| 2002 | Kyoto Purple Sanga |
| 2001 | Shimizu S–Pulse |
| 2000 | Kashima Antlers |
| 1999 | Nagoya Grampus Eight |
| 1998 | Yokohama Flügels |
| 1997 | Kashima Antlers |
| 1996 | Verdy Kawasaki |
| 1995 | Nagoya Grampus Eight |
| 1994 | Bellmare Hiratsuka |
| 1993 | Yokohama Flügels |
| 1992 | Yokohama Marinos |
| 1991 | Nissan |
| 1990 | Matsushita |
| 1989 | Nissan |
| 1988 | Nissan |
| 1987 | Yomiuri |
| 1986 | Yomiuri |
| 1985 | Nissan |
| 1984 | Yomiuri Club |
| 1983 | Nissan |
| 1982 | Yamaha |
| 1981 | NKK |
| 1980 | Mitsubishi Heavy Industries |
| 1979 | Fujita Industries |
| 1978 | Mitsubishi Heavy Industries |
| 1977 | Fujita Industries |
| 1976 | Furukawa Electric |
| 1975 | Hitachi |
| 1974 | Yanmar Diesel |
| 1973 | Mitsubishi Heavy Industries |
| 1972 | Hitachi |
| 1971 | Mitsubishi Heavy Industries |
| 1970 | Yanmar Diesel |
| 1969 | Toyo Industries |
| 1968 | Yanmar Diesel |
| 1967 | Toyo Industries |
| 1966 | Waseda University |
| 1965 | Toyo Industries |
| 1964 | Title shared between Yawata Steel and Furukawa Electric |
| 1963 | Waseda University |
| 1962 | Chuo University |
| 1961 | Furukawa Electric |
| 1960 | Furukawa Electric |
| 1959 | Kwangaku |
| 1958 | Kwangaku |
| 1957 | Chuo University |
| 1956 | Keio BRB |

| 1955 | All Kwangaku |
|------|----------------|
| 1954 | Keio BRB |
| 1953 | Kwangaku |
| 1952 | All Keio University |
| 1951 | Keio BRB |
| 1950 | All Kwangaku |
| 1949 | Tokyo University LB |
| 1946 | Tokyo University |
| 1940 | Keio BRB |
| 1939 | Keio BRB |
| 1938 | Waseda University |
| 1937 | Keio University |
| 1936 | Keio BRB |
| 1935 | Seoul Shukyu–dan |
| 1933 | Tokyo Old Boys 4 |
| 1932 | Keio |
| 1931 | Tokyo University |
| 1930 | Kwangaku |
| 1929 | Kwangaku |
| 1928 | Waseda University WMW |
| 1927 | Kobe–Ichi Junior High School |
| 1925 | Rijo Shukyu–dan |
| 1924 | Rijo |
| 1923 | Astra |
| 1922 | Nagoya Shukyu–dan |
| 1921 | Tokyo Shukyu–dan |

* Not played 1926 due to Emperor Taisho's death; not played 1934 due to East Asian Games; not played 1941–1945 due to World War II; not played 1947–1948 due to post World War II disorder.

## JAPAN LEAGUE TOP SCORERS

| 2008 | Marquinhos (Kashima Antlers) 21 |
|------|----------------|
| 2007 | Juninho (Kawasaki Frontale) 22 |
| 2006 | Washington (Urawa Red Diamonds) 26 |
|      | Magno Alves (Gamba Osaka) 26 |
| 2005 | Araújo (Gamba Osaka) 33 |
| 2004 | Emerson (Urawa Reds) 27 |
| 2003 | Ueslei (Nagoya Grampus Eight) 22 |
| 2002 | Naohiro Takahara (Júbilo Iwata) 26 |
| 2001 | Will (Consadole Sapporo) 24 |
| 2000 | Masashi Nakayama (Júbilo Iwata) 20 |
| 1999 | Hwang Sun–Hong (Cerezo Osaka) 24 |
| 1998 | Masashi Nakayama (Júbilo Iwata) 36 |
| 1997 | Patrick Mboma (Gamba Osaka) 25 |
| 1996 | Kazuyoshi Miura (Verdy Kawasaki) 23 |
| 1995 | Masahiro Fukuda (Urawa Reds) 32 |
| 1994 | Frank Ordenewitz (JEF United Ichihara) 30 |
| 1993 | Ramón Diaz (Yokohama Marinos) 28 |

## AUSTRALIA: A–LEAGUE*

| 2007–2008 | Newcastle Jets |
|------|----------------|
| 2006–2007 | Melbourne Victory |
| 2005–2006 | Sydney FC |
| 2004–2005 | Not played |
| 2003–2004 | Perth Glory |
| 2002–2003 | Perth Glory |
| 2001–2002 | Olympic Sharks |
| 2000–2001 | Wollongong City Wolves |
| 1999–2000 | Wollongong City Wolves |
| 1998–1999 | South Melbourne |
| 1997–1998 | South Melbourne |
| 1996–1997 | Brisbane Strikers |
| 1995–1996 | Melbourne Knights |

| 1994–1995 | Melbourne Knights |
|------|----------------|
| 1993–1994 | Adelaide City |
| 1992–1993 | Marconi Fairfield |
| 1991–1992 | Adelaide City |
| 1990–1991 | South Melbourne Hellas |
| 1989–1990 | Olympic UTS |
| 1989 | Marconi Fairfield |
| 1988 | Marconi Fairfield |
| 1987 | Apia Leichhardt |
| 1986 | Adelaide City |
| 1985 | Brunswick Juventus |
| 1984 | South Melbourne Hellas |
| 1983 | Budapest St. George |
| 1982 | Sydney City Hakoah |
| 1981 | Sydney City Hakoah |
| 1980 | Sydney City Hakoah |
| 1979 | Marconi Fairfield |
| 1978 | West Adelaide Hellas |
| 1977 | Sydney City Hakoah |

* Known as Australian National Soccer League and played under a different format until 2004.

## AUSTRALIA A–LEAGUE TOP SCORERS

| 2007–2008 | Joel Griffiths (Newcastle Jets) 12 |
|------|----------------|
| 2006–2007 | Daniel Allsopp (Melbourne Victory) 11 |
| 2005–2006 | Alex Brosque (Queensland Roar) 8 |
|      | Bobby Despotovski (Perth Glory) 8 |
|      | Archie Thompson (Melbourne Victory) 8 |
|      | Stewart Petrie (Central Coast Mariners) 8 |

# GLOSSARY

**AGGREGATE**
When a fixture is played over two legs, the aggregate is the scores of both games added together.

**ASSISTANT REFEREES**
The flag-carrying officials positioned on either touchline who help the referee.

**AWAY GOALS**
In games played over two legs, goals scored in the away game count extra if the aggregate score is tied.

**BENCH**
A bench at the side of the field to seat players who are waiting their chance to play or who have been removed from play due to injury or other reasons. A substitute is often referred to as being "on the bench."

**BRACE**
Two goals by one player in a single game are sometimes known as a "brace."

**CAP**
An appearance for an international team. The term originated in England, where players were once presented with a white silk cap every time they played for their country.

**CENTER SPOT**
The point in the center of the field where the game starts and restarts after a goal.

**CHIP**
A pass or shot in which the bottom of the ball is struck with a short stabbing motion with no follow through.

**CORNER FLAG**
A flag marking the corner arc.

**CORNER KICK**
An attacking dead ball situation arising when the defending team puts the ball over its own goal line, between the corner flag and the goal post.

**CROSS**
To kick or pass the ball across the field, usually into the penalty area to create a goal-scoring opportunity.

**CRUYFF TURN**
A deceptive turn named after the world-famous Dutch player of the 1970s, Johan Cruyff, who perfected it.

**DEAD BALL**
A break in play, often due to a free kick or throw in.

**DERBY GAME**
A game between two local rival teams.

**DISTRIBUTION**
Passing the ball to teammates. Good distribution is making the right type of pass at the best moment.

**DIVE**
An attempt by a player to convince the referee (falsely) that a foul has been committed against him or her by diving to the ground. This is against the Laws of the Game.

**DRAG-BACK**
When a player drags the ball behind him and executes a quick turn and change of direction.

**DRAW**
When scores are level at the end of a game.

**DUMMY**
To deceive an opponent by pretending to pass or shoot in one direction and then moving the opposite way.

**EIGHTEEN-YARD BOX**
The larger marked area around the goal, in which a penalty may be given.

**EXTRA TIME, OR OVERTIME**
Additional period of time played at the end of a game that has resulted in a draw to try to decide the winner. Extra time (overtime) is usually only played in a knockout competition where a winner must be decided.

**FAR POST**
The goal post farthest away from the point of attack.

**FIELD**
The field of play.

**FIELD OF PLAY**
The soccer field; the surface on which the game is played and its markings.

**FOURTH OFFICIAL**
A game official who assists the referee in a number of different tasks. The fourth official may also be called on to replace any other official who cannot continue in a game.

**FOUL**
An infringement of the laws of soccer, such as when a player trips, kicks, or pushes an opponent (accidentally or deliberately).

**FREE KICK**
When play is stopped by the referee and a kick awarded to the opposing side, usually due to a foul or infringement.

**FREE TRANSFER**
When a player transfers from one team to another after their contract has expired, so that no transfer fee is paid. It is also known as the Bosman ruling.

**FRIENDLY GAME**
A game where there is no trophy, prize, or ranking dependent on the result. This is sometimes called an exhibition game.

**GEAR**
The clothing worn by a player during a game, including shorts, shirt, socks, cleats, and shin pads.

**GOAL**
1. The nets supported by two posts and a crossbar at each end of the field, where the goalkeepers stand.
2. When the ball crosses the line into the goal area and a team scores.

**GOAL KICK**
A kick awarded to the defending team when the ball has crossed the goal line last touched by an attacking player, but no goal has been scored.

**GOAL LINE**
The line linking the corner flags with the goal posts.

**GOLDEN BOOT**
Award given to the top scoring player in a particular soccer competition.

**GOLDEN GOAL**
A way of deciding the winner when a game in a knock-out contest ends in a draw. The first goal scored in extra time, known as a "golden goal", wins the match instantly. If there is no Golden Goal in 30 minutes of extra time, a penalty shootout decides the game.

**HALFWAY LINE**
The marked-out line that separates one half of the field from the other.

**HANDBALL**
A type of foul. It is illegal for an outfield player to touch the ball with his or her hand in open play.

**HAT TRICK**
Three goals scored by the same player in one game.

**INFRINGEMENT**
To break one of the laws of soccer.

**INJURY TIME**
Time added at the end of a match to allow for time lost due to injuries, substitutions or other stoppages. The fourth official notifies the teams how much time has been added.

**INTERCEPT**
To steal possession of or get in the way of an opponent's pass.

**KICKOFF**
The way of starting each half of a soccer game. The kickoff is the first kick of the half which sets the ball in play. It is taken from the center spot. The kick which restarts play after a goal is scored is also known as a kickoff.

**LEG**
One game of a game between two teams that is played over two individual games. The winner is the team with the better aggregate score.

**MAN OF THE MATCH**
Award given to the player judged to be the most outstanding in a particular

game.

**MARK**
To position yourself close to an opponent so that it is difficult for him to receive or pass the ball.

**MATCH**
A competitive game, usually comprising two halves of 45 minutes.

**NEAR POST**
The goal post nearest to the point of attack.

**NUTMEG**
To kick the ball through an opponent's legs and then collect it on the other side. The word is thought to originate from the Victorian term "to nutmeg," meaning "to trick."

**OFFSIDE**
When an attacker has moved beyond the second last defender as the ball is played forward.

**ONE-TWO**
A quick back-and-forth pass between two players, also known as a wall pass.

**OWN GOAL**
A goal scored accidentally by a player into his own net.

**PASS**
When a player passes the ball to another member of his team during a game.

**PENALTY**
A specific kind of free kick awarded when an attacker is fouled in the penalty area.

**PENALTY SHOOTOUT**
A way of deciding the winner in a knockout competition where the game ends in a draw. The teams take turn to shoot at goal from the penalty spot. Usually the best of five wins, however if the teams are level after five penalties they play until one team misses.

**PENALTY SPOT**
The place from where the penalty is taken.

**PHYSIO**
Short for a physical therapist, a health worker who treats injuries during a game and helps players to recover from long-term injuries.

**PLAYMAKER**
A player who creates attacking moves and opportunities for his team to score.

**PLAYOFF**
A game or group of matches contested for a single prize, such as third place in the World Cup, the MLS Cup or a place in an higher soccer league.

**POSSESSION**
To have the ball.

**QUARTERFINALS**
In a knock-out competition, the four games that decide which four of the eight remaining teams will play in the semifinals.

**READING THE GAME**
Playing the game intelligently e.g. using tactical knowledge to improve positioning, passing, tackling, and intercepting.

**RED CARD**
A player is shown this after an extremely serious foul or infringement, or after receiving two yellow cards in a game. They usually receive a suspension.

**REFEREE**
The official in charge of the game, who checks that the laws of soccer are not broken.

**REPLAY**
A game played between two teams for a second time at a later date, because the first game resulted in a draw.

**ROUND ROBIN**
A competition where all teams play each other in turn and the team with the highest points score is the winner. In some other competitions, the first round has the teams split into groups who then play round robins to decide which will through to later rounds. The rest of the tournament is played as knockout rounds.

**RUNNER-UP**
The team that finishes in second place in a competition.

**SCORE**
To get a goal.

**SEMIFINALS**
In a knock-out competition, the two matches that decide which two of the four remaining teams will play in the final.

**SENT OFF**
When a player receives a red card and is sent from the field of play.

**SHIN PADS**
Protective shields for the shins and ankles, usually worn underneath the socks.

**SHOOT**
To aim a kick or pass at the goal.

**SHUTOUT**
When a team do not concede any goals during a match, it is known as a 'keeping a clean sheet'. The phrase may also refer specifically to goalkeepers.

**SILVER GOAL**
A way of deciding the winner when a match in a knock-out contest ends in a draw. The team leading after a fifteen-minute period of extra time win the match, with the goal that gives them the lead known as a "silver goal". If the score is level, another fifteen-minute period is played. If the score is still level, the game is decided by a penalty shootout.

**SIX-YARD BOX**
The small marked-out area around the goal.

**SKIPPER**
Another word for "team captain".

**STOP TURN**
A way of changing direction quickly by stopping the ball at speed.

**SUBSTITUTE**
A player who replaces another player during a match, either for tactical reasons or because the first player is injured or not playing well. Up to three substitutes are allowed in most matches.

**SWERVE**
To kick or strike across the back of the ball so that it bends in the opposite direction.

**TACKLE**
To fairly challenge a player for the ball. A tackle can be block or sliding.

**THROW-IN**
A throw from the touchline awarded by the referee when the opposition have kicked the ball out of play.

**TOUCHLINES**
The two lines running down the length of the field.

**TRANSFER**
The movement of a player under contract from one team to another team.

**TRANSFER FEE**
When a player transfers from one team to another, the team he is joining pay a sum of money, known as a transer fee, to the team he is leaving.

**VOLLEY**
To kick the ball before it touches the ground, usually as a shot on goal.

**WALL**
A line of two or more players defending their goal against a free kick.

**WARM-DOWN**
Period of gradual decrease in physical activity after a match or training session. Warming down allows the body to transition smoothly to a resting state.

**WARM-UP**
Preparation for a game or training session by gradual increase in physical activity. Warming up properly reduces the risk of injury and improves performance.

**YELLOW CARD**
This is shown by the referee for a serious offense or persistent offending.

# INDEX

# PICTURE CREDITS

**THE PUBLISHER WOULD LIKE TO THANK THE FOLLOWING FOR THEIR KIND PERMISSION TO REPRODUCE THEIR PHOTOGRAPHS:**

(Key: a-above; b-below/bottom; c-centre; f-far; l-left; r-right; t-top)

Action Images: 11fbl, 46r, 48bl, 171cl, 172fbr, 173tl, 181br; Andrew Budd Digital 172br; Roy Beardsworth 11cl; Ryan Browne 17tc; The FA / Matthew Childs 38-39; GN / CRB Reuters 179cla; Jean Marie Hervio / Flash Press 143c; Robin Hume / Sporting Pictures 171cr; Alex Morton 125tl, 177fcr; MSI 44bl; Tony O'Brien 14bc, 140cl, 179cl; Carl Recine 130-131; Michael Regan 77ca; Michael Regan / Livepic 21tc; Reuters / Brendan McDermid Picture 123b; Reuters / Claro Cortes IV WC / LA Reuters 173cr; Reuters / Enrique Marcarian 172ftl; Reuters / Gil Cohen Magen 146cl; Reuters / Henry Romero 135c; Reuters / Marcos Brindicci 175tr; Reuters / Nacho Doce Picture 153tr; Reuters / Pilar Olivares / MB Reuters 121c; Reuters / Thomas Bohlen 170br; Reuters / Toby Melville (Britain) 39c; Aris Salonique / UEFA / Sporting Pictures (UK) Ltd 142bl; John Sibley 24crb, 174fbl, 181fcr; Lee Smith 36crb; Sporting Pictures 43br, 46c, 170ftl; Sporting Pictures / Nick Kidd 44crb; Paul Thomas / Livepic 21b. Alamy Images: Aerial Archives 180ftl; Associated Sports Photography 27tr, 51c; Enrique Diamantini 180br; F1online digitale Bildagentur GmbH 181ftl; Interfoto 174bl; Camille Moirenc / Hemis 181ftr; Stefano Paterna 181tl; RIA Novosti 50cra. Corbis: Jose L. Argueta / isiphotos.com 16bc; Matthew Ashton / AMA 39clb, 181cl; Armando Babani / EPA 65cra; Matteo Bazzi / EPA 145cl; Bettmann 175cl; Sandor Bojar / EPA 59br; Russell Boyce / Reuters 63fcr; Joao Luiz Bulcao 6-7; Katia Christodoulou / EPA 61crb; Tim Clayton 99ca; Daniel Dal Zennaro / EPA 42-43; Marcos Delgado / EPA 121b; Dominic Favre 26crb; Helmut Fohringer / Epa 56tc; Andrew Fox 110-111; Tom Fox / Dallas Morning News 128cr; Marc Francotte / TempSport 52bl, 173tr; Eric Gaillard / Reuters 143br; Maurizio Gambarini / EPA 112-113; Ali Haider / EPA 127cl; Mast Irham / EPA 127b; Catherine Ivill / AMA 50c; Michael Janosz / isiphotos.com 11br; Carmen Jaspersen / EPA 64tr; Andres Kudacki 2-3, 79ca, 172fcl; Kim Kyung-Hoon / Reuters 171br; C. Liewig / Corbis Sygma 41br; Christian Liewig 85l, 92br, 125r, 132br; Christian Liewig / Liewig Media Sports 91tl, 171fbl, 181cr; Christian Liewig / Tempsport 92tr; Jo Lillini 181fcl; Neil Marchand / Liewig Media Sports 82, 92cb, 93tl; Vesa-Matti Väärä / EPA 15tr; Stefan Matzke / Sampics 55c; Tannen Maury / EPA 76crb, 122bl; Markku Ojala / Finland Out / EPA / UEFA 129cla; Kerim Okten / EPA 134bl; Claudio Onorati / EPA 144clb; Gerry Penny / EPA 151bl; Jerome Prevost / TempSport 58fcr, 118bl, 143clb; Ben Radford 27tl, 28crb; Stephane Reix / For Picture 32l, 53c, 53crb, 59cb, 64crb; Eric Renard / For Picture 142r; Reuters 74bl; Reuters / Juan Carlos Ulate 121fcr; Reuters / Kim Kyung-Hoon 22tr; Reuters / Lee Jae-Won 97br; Reuters / Marcelo Del Pozo 134ca; S. Ruet / Corbis Sygma 60br; Jean-Yves Ruszniewski / TempSport 34bl, 72-73; Sampics 181fbl; Lee Sanders / EPA 26l; Darren Staples / Reuters 11tr, 20tl; John Todd / internationalsportsimages.com 173ftl; Underwood & Underwood 10bl; Bob Van Den Cruijsem / Icon SMI 27tc; Vincent Van Doornick / Photo & Co. 148cl; Horacio Villalobos 71tc; Jens Wolf / EPA 41c; Wu Xiaoling / Xinhua Press 16clb; Tadayuki Yoshikawa / EPA 101clb. Getty Images: 43tl; AFP Photo 40b, 50bl, 62br, 113tl, 117tl, 118tl, 120cr, 170tr, 172ftr, 174br, 174cr, 174tr, 175ftl, 175ftr; AFP Photo / Adek Berry 106bl; AFP Photo / Adrian Dennis 33tr, 106cla; AFP Photo / Alberto Pizzoli 63bl; AFP Photo / Alejandro Pagni 157br; AFP Photo / Alfredo Estrella 135bl, 162br; AFP Photo / Amin Chami 166tl; AFP Photo / ANP / Ed Oudenaarden 149b; AFP Photo / Antonio Scorza 13tr, 120cb, 136bl; AFP Photo / Arni Torfason 63cl; AFP Photo / Choi Won-Suk 126fcrb; AFP Photo / Christine Vanzella 81bl; AFP Photo / Daniel Garcia 59fcla; AFP Photo / Daniel Mihailescu 66fcr, 153bl; AFP Photo / DDP / Juergen Schwarz 85fcrb; AFP Photo / Denis Charlet 91br; AFP Photo / Evaristo SA 15crb; AFP Photo / Fabrice Coffrini 61tr, 65ftr, 132tl; AFP Photo / Fethi Belaid 24l; AFP Photo / Franck Fife 124bc, 173fbl; AFP Photo / Fred Tanneau 95tl; AFP Photo / Frederic J. Brown 104cr, 127tc, 181bl; AFP Photo / Gaspard Lenoir 91fcr; AFP Photo / Gerard Burkhart 135fcl; AFP Photo / Gianluigi Guercia 49l; AFP Photo / Glyn Kirk 32br; AFP Photo / Graham Stuart 56crb; AFP Photo / Hoang Dinh Nam 129tr; AFP Photo / Hrvoje Polan 64fcrb; AFP Photo / Ilmars Znotins 57cra; AFP Photo / Issouf Sanogo 11bl, 92ca, 92fcr, 138cl, 177cr; AFP Photo / Jack Guez 66br; AFP Photo / Jacques Demarthon 171tr; AFP Photo / Javier Soriano 177crb, 177fcrb; AFP Photo / Jefferson Bernardes 159br; AFP Photo / Jewel Samad 106fcra, 107bc; AFP Photo / Jiji Press / STR 167tc; AFP Photo / John Gurzinski 135clb; AFP Photo / John Macdougall 146br; AFP Photo / John Thys 60cla; AFP Photo / Jose Jordan 150cl; AFP Photo / Juan Barreto 120tl; AFP Photo / Juan Mabromata 156bl; AFP Photo / Jung Yeon-Je 139cl; AFP Photo / Kambou Sia 165br; AFP Photo / Karim Jaafar 103tl, 105cra, 105tl, 167bl; AFP Photo / Khaled Desouki 138cr; AFP Photo / Luis Acosta 135br; AFP Photo / Mauricio Lima 158cl; AFP Photo / Michael Urban 55clb; AFP Photo / Michel Gangne 12-13; AFP Photo / Miguel Avarez 80bl; AFP Photo / Miguel Rojo 175fcl; AFP Photo / Mladen Antonov 57br; AFP Photo / Nader Del Rio 171ftl; AFP Photo / Natalia Kolesnikova 152ca; AFP Photo / Nicholas Kamm 80tl; AFP Photo / Niklas Larsson 25clb; AFP Photo / Norberto Duarte 159tl; AFP Photo / Oliver Lang 48crb; AFP Photo / Omar Torres 117cr; AFP Photo / Pablo Porciuncula 158bl; AFP Photo / Pascal Pavani 117br; AFP Photo / Patrick Hertzog 40cr; AFP Photo / Peter Muhly 49tl, 61cl; AFP Photo / Petras Malukas 64bl; AFP Photo / Pius Utomi Ekpei 89fbr, 165tl; AFP Photo / Roberto Schmidt 49br, 181fbr; AFP Photo / Ronaldo Schemidt 162cl; AFP Photo / Saeed Khan 104bl, 105bl, 126tr; AFP Photo / Sergei Supinsky 66bl; AFP Photo / Simon Amaina 94tl; AFP Photo / Ted Aljibe 95cr; AFP Photo / Thomas Coex 116cb; AFP Photo / Timothy A. Clary 123tc; AFP Photo / Torsten Blackwood 98bl, 99b; AFP Photo / Toshifumi Kitamura 107br; AFP Photo / Vadim Denisov 65cla; AFP Photo / Vanderlei Almeida 136br; AFP Photo / Vano Shlamov 25crb, 65tl; AFP Photo / Vladimir Kmet 66tl; AFP Photo / Wils Yanick Maniengui 91cb; AFP Photo DDP / Lennart Preiss 45tc; AFP Photo DDP / Nigel Treblin 23br; Allsport 67clb; Allsport / Hulton Archive 115bl, 115cr; Allsport UK 1c, 62tc, 65br, 94cra, 116tc, 122cl; Phil Cole / Allsport 66tr; Lars Baron / Bongarts 45l, 60tr, 73clb; Greg Bartram / MLS 160bl; Sandra Behne / Bongarts 54cl, 61fcla; Giuseppe Bellini 145br; Gunnar Berning / Bongarts 56fcla; Bongarts 170fcl; Lutz Bongarts / Bongarts 103cra; Shaun Botterill 41tl, 47bc, 52br, 52cra, 100crb, 103fcl, 133clb, 175fbl; Shaun Botterill / Allsport 164tr; Shaun Botterill / Allsport UK 119tl, 120bl; Clive Brunskill 39br, 67tr; Clive Brunskill / Pepsi 25c; Simon Bruty / Allsport 56fclb, 117cl, 134cr; David Cannon / Allsport 38cb, 40fcl, 44br, 141tl, 175fcr, 176crb; Gareth Cattermole 25t; Central Press / Hulton Archive 10br, 48cla, 53cla, 103cb, 174fcl; China Photos 45c, 102tr; Robert Cianflone 98r, 109cl; Rodrigo Coca / Fotoarena / LatinContent 154cl, 154r; Chris Cole 176fcrb; Phil Cole 178cl; Mark Dadswell 106cr; Felipe Dana / FotoArena / LatinContent 155tl; Jonathan Daniel 76-77, 77br, 94bl; Victor Decolongon 161cra, 169r; DigitalGlobe 180bl; Kevork Djansezian 29cl; Denis Doyle 180cl; Duif du Toit / Gallo Images 164br; Alvinho Duarte / FotoArena / LatinContent 180-181 (background); Stephen Dunn 122cr; Stephen Dunn / Allsport 77tl; Darren England / Allsport 109cr; Evening Standard / Stringer / Hulton Archive 10bc, 83, 101fbr; Stu Forster 47tc, 56tr, 67br, 79bc, 174ftr; Stu Forster / Allsport 18tl, 84cr, 179ftr; Fox Photos / Stringer / Hulton Archive 14cl, 140cb; Stuart Franklin / Bongarts 147l; Paul Gilham 43bc, 88c; David Goddard 180fbl; Laurence Griffiths 57clb, 62bl, 119bl, 119cr, 133br; Alexandre Guzanshe / Fotoarena / LatinContent 137b; Anthony Harris / LatinContent 81fbr; Alexander Hassenstein / Bongarts 57cla, 85bc, 148cr; Noriko Hayakusa 88crb, 89clb, 100bl; Haynes Archive / Popperfoto 64ca, 115tr; Richard Heathcote 62cra; Marcelo Hernandez / LatinContent 158br; Mike Hewit 70c; Mike Hewitt 133cla; Tobias Heyer / Bongarts 67cla; Harry How 169tl; Hulton Archive 56clb, 78cl, 137tl, 175br, 176fbl; Isifa / Stringer / Filip Singer 153crb; Jed Jacobsohn 150r; Jasper Juinen 20bc, 22-23, 33clb, 33tl, 151cr; Koichi Kamoshida 163tl; Paul Kane 166bl, 166c; Allen Kee / Major League Soccer / MLS 20br; Keystone / Hulton Archive 1, 4-5, 57cb, 67cb, 114cb, 115tl, 156crb; Keystone / Stringer / Hulton Archive 40clb, 48fcra, 113fcr; Junko Kimura 155br; Ross Kinnaird 169clb, 178br; Ross Kinnaird / Allsport 51cla; Christof Koepsel / Bongarts 26cr, 31r, 52c; Dima Korotayev / Epsilon 152bl; Michael Kunkel / Bongarts 65clb; David Leah / Allsport 41bl, 121tl; David Leah / Allsport / Mexsport 136tl; Bryn Lennon 51br, 59cra; Feng Li 12bl; Alex Livesey 54br, 140fcrb; Melissa Majchrzak / MLS 160-161 (background); Ronald Martinez 172tl; Clive Mason 55cl, 58fbl, 66c; Jamie McDonald 53clb, 71fbr, 77clb, 86cr, 173ftr; Jim McIsaac 80fcra; Jeff J. Mitchell 12cb; Don Morley 171fcl; NF / AFP Photo / Jens Kr. Vang / Scanpix 2005 63br; Guang Niu 102cb; Mark Nolan 98cl; Keith Nordstrom / MLS 160crb; Ralph Orlowski 69tr; Doug Pensinger / Allsport 81tl; John Peters / Manchester United 180fbr; Photographer's Choice RF / Peter Hince 20clb; Ryan Pierse 47br, 60cb; Joern Pollex / Bongarts 28tr; Popperfoto 8b, 61tc, 65bl, 90bl, 90br, 94ftr, 114c, 120cl, 172fbl, 173bl, 174fbr, 175cr, 176cla, 176clb, 176ftl, 177c, 177cl, 177fcl, 177ftr, 178clb, 179clb, 179fclb; Popperfoto / John Mcdermott / Bob Thomas 58fcl; Andrew Powell / Liverpool FC 30cr; Steve Powell / Allsport 42cl; Gary M. Prior / Allsport 87bc, 180tr; Dean Purcell 108l; Ben Radford 58cra, 93br, 170ftr; Ben Radford / Allsport 103cr; Andreas Rentz / Bongarts 54clb, 102cr, 170bl, 181tr; Santiago Rios / LatinContent 156-157, 157tc; David Rogers 58tl; Rolls Press / Popperfoto 114tc, 115br, 176tl, 178tr; Martin Rose / Bongarts 173fbr; Vladimir Rys / Bongarts 20c, 71l, 168cl; Lefty Shivambu / Gallo Images 86br, 89c; Cameron Spencer 172tr; Michael Steele 43ca, 59tc, 60bl; STR / AFP 180fcr; Chung Sung-Jun 34c, 99tl, 107fcra; Henri Szwarc / Bongarts 88fclb; T-Mobile 64tl; Bob Thomas / Bob Thomas Sports Photography 13cr, 50crb, 51clb, 54ca, 55cla, 58br, 58clb, 62fcla, 63cla, 91cl, 91cr,104tl, 116c, 117bl, 117tr, 174cl, 175bl, 175fbr,175tl, 176ftr, 176tr, 177bl,178tl, 179crb, 179fcrb, 179tr; Bob Thomas / Popperfoto 115cl, 174ftl; Mark Thompson / Allsport 61bc, 84cl, 124cr; Mirek Towski / Time Life Pictures 180ftr; William G. Vanderson 177tr; Claudio Villa / Allsport 23tr, 179cr; Friedemann Vogel / Bongarts 153cl, 168crb; Friedemann Vogel / Bongarts / DFB 13br; Darren Walsh / Chelsea FC 24clb; Ian Walton 15tl, 174fcr, 174tl; Lee Warren / Gallo Images 125clb; Koji Watanabe 15fclb, 101c, 103br, 139b; World Sport Group 100c; Rick Yeatts / MLS 161bc. Mary Evans Picture Library: 9bl, 9r, 9t, 10cr, 10tl; Illustrated London News Ltd 177tl. The National Soccer Hall of Fame, Oneonta, NY: 10fcr, 76bl. Panapress: MAXPPP 90ca, 129bc. Press Association Images: 38bl, 38cr; Abaca Abaca Press 171tl; Africa Visuals 84bl, 85tc; AP Photo / Anja Niedringhaus 128l; AP Photo / Ariel Schalit 124clb, 124tl; AP Photo / Bernat Armangue 31clb; AP Photo / Carlo Fumagalli 72bl; AP Photo / Gregorio Borgia 33br; AP Photo / Hans Punz 79br; AP Photo / Jae C. Hong 129br; AP Photo / Jasper Juinen 28bl; AP Photo / Massimo Pinca 144bl; AP Photo / Michael Sohn 29c; AP Photo / Nasser Nasser 86c; AP Photo / Peter Morrison 63cra; AP Photo / Petros Giannakouris 118cl; AP Photo / Roberto Candia 78r; AP Photo / Vincent Thian 126cl; Matthew Ashton / Empics Sport 15ca, 38br, 88bl, 101fcl, 112cla, 122tr, 126cr, 173br; Bruno Press 149tl; Jon Buckle / Empics Sport 14bl, 74tr; Buzzi / Empics 42cra, 145tl; Cordon Press 151tl; David Davies / PA Archive 112tr; Adam Davy / Empics Sport 14r, 84br, 103c; Deutsche Press-Agentur / DPA / Empics 42bl, 44cl, 45br, 170tl, 172cr, 204-205, 206-207; Mike Egerton / Empics Sport 16-17, 27br, 30bl, 34clb, 71cb, 79cb, 101bl; Empics Sport 26fbr, 70bl, 74c, 87bl; Nigel French / Empics Sport 87fcrb; Gouhier-Hahn-Orban / Cameleon / abacapress.com 30tl; Ross Kinnaird / Empics Sport 171fcr; Christian Liewig 91tr; Chritian Liewig / Cameleon / abacapress.com 73c; Sydney Mahlangu / Sports Inc. 138br; Tony Marshall / Empics Sport 27c, 36clb, 67cra, 73bc, 73tl, 75br, 75tr, 87cl, 89crb, 102cl, 144cr, 147br, 172cl; Ricardo Mazalan / AP 47c; Steve Morton / Empics Sport 75ca; Daniel Motz 113tr; PA Archive / Empics 46bl, 113cr, 171bl; PA Wire 180tl; Photocome 126bl; Nick Potts / Empics Sport 133tc; Presse Sports 70fbr, 118cr; Rangers FC 132ca; Peter Robinson / Empics Sport 42br, 44fcr, 46br, 63ftr, 72c, 72crb, 100cr, 113cl, 119cla, 170fbl, 170fcr, 172fcr; S&G And Barratts / Empics Sport 108br, 112cra, 171ftr, 172bl, 173fcl; Neal Simpson / Empics Sport 134br, 143tl, 171fbr, 173cl; SMG 75bl, 132clb, 136cr; Topham Picturepoint 70crb, 170fbr; John Walton / Empics Sport 27cl. Reuters: Amr Dalsh 164bl, 165r; Edgard Garrido 163br; Phil Noble 141b; Robin van Lonkhuijsen 15fbl. Wikipedia, The Free Encyclopedia: 8cla, 173fcr.

Front Endpapers. Varley Picture Agency. Back Endpapers: Varley Picture Agency.

Jacket images: Back: Getty Images: Alex Livesey.

All other images © Dorling Kindersley
For further information see: www.dkimages.com